EVOLVING NATIONALISM

EVOLVING NATIONALISM

Homeland, Identity, and Religion in Israel, 1925–2005

NADAV G. SHELEF

Cornell University Press
Ithaca and London

First published 2010 by Cornell University Press
Printed in the United States of America

Library of Congress Cataloging-in-Publication Data

Shelef, Nadav G. (Nadav Gershon), 1974–
   Evolving nationalism : homeland, identity, and religion in Israel, 1925–2005 / Nadav G. Shelef.
      p. cm.
   Includes bibliographical references and index.
   ISBN 978-0-8014-4870-6 (cloth : alk. paper)
   ISBN 978-0-8014-7675-4 (pbk. : alk. paper)
   1. Nationalism—Israel.   2. Jews—Israel—Identity.   3. National characteristics, Israeli.   4. Judaism and state—Israel.
   5. Cartography—Israel.   6. Israel—Boundaries.   I. Title.

   DS113.3.S57   2010
   320.5409569409'04—dc22   2010005561

Cornell University Press strives to use environmentally responsible suppliers and materials to the fullest extent possible in the publishing of its books. Such materials include vegetable-based, low-VOC inks and acid-free papers that are recycled, totally chlorine-free, or partly composed of nonwood fibers. For further information, visit our website at www.cornellpress.cornell.edu.

Cloth printing   10 9 8 7 6 5 4 3 2 1
Paperback printing   10 9 8 7 6 5 4 3 2 1

Contents

Preface

This is a book about how nationalism changes. How do responses to the basic questions about the political community—what is the extent of the homeland, who is part of it, and what principles should guide it—change over time? Even true believers modify their answers to these questions. For observers of Israel, Benjamin Netanyahu's dramatic declaration that he accepted the principle of partition and a two-state solution—made as this book was in production—was another reminder that hard-line nationalists can change their cherished beliefs. This possibility was more widely evident in the context of Israel's "disengagement" from the Gaza Strip in the summer of 2005. During the disengagement, demonstrators burned Israeli flags, hurled rocks at Israeli soldiers, and compared Ariel Sharon to Adolf Hitler and the atrocities of the state of Israel to those of the Nazi regime. These protestors were not Palestinian. They were religious nationalists who once sanctified the state of Israel as the harbinger of the Messiah and the dawn of redemption. How was it that this particular group now delegitimized the state to the degree that it was acceptable to compare it with, of all things, Nazi Germany? Nationalists, especially religiously motivated ultranationalists, are not supposed to change their minds. Yet they do, and not just in Israel.

Nationalism evolves. Literally. Changes in the basic understandings of the nation are the unguided by-products of attempts to solve mundane, local, political problems. Strategic reactions to new realities and the changing incentives of nationalist leaders play important supporting roles, but they rarely cause change. I base this claim on a head-to-head comparison of the ability of these alternative explanations to account for the pattern of changes in Zionisms and Israeli nationalisms over the last eighty years. Which nationalist movement changed? When? What was the substantive content of the transformation? What leaders, if any, enacted the change? How consistent were they? The systematic reconstruction of the pattern of change shows that, more often than not, Israeli nationalisms evolved. The argument that nationalism evolves does not negate its power. In fact, the very real potency of nationalism may be one reason intentional explanations of change fare so poorly in accounting for its transformation.

Many consider the Israeli case special, but it is not unique. In its construction, internal variation, contestation, experience of historical shocks, and cast of characters, Israel has a lot in common with other deeply divided societies. Even more broadly, conflicts over territory, religion and state, and citizenship rage in many places that we no longer think of as "deeply divided." The lesson that the basic aspects of the political community evolve can be used to understand the contours of these broader conflicts as well as the prospects for their resolution.

• • •

I would not have been able to complete this project, or even to begin it, without the help of many people over the years. While I am surely leaving someone out, I am grateful to all.

I am especially grateful to the faculty at the University of California, Berkeley, as well as at the other stops I made along this journey, who provided invaluable intellectual and professional guidance. Out of my conversations with Bob Price grew the insight that ideological contention must also be grounded in daily politics, and that the two were probably linked. Ruth Collier's focus on drawing out the causal links, and her ability to see where I was going before I got there, helped me translate my often inchoate thoughts into political science. Claude Fischer's guidance on de-jargoning my prose proved especially prophetic. My debt to Ian Lustick is especially profound. He directed a young undergraduate to the study of politics and has served as a mentor and sounding board ever since. His careful reading and sharp comments on the manuscript that became this book shaped the project in innumerable ways. David Collier was extremely generous with his time and advice. Hanna Pitkin taught me to read in an entirely new way. Finally, the core of this book germinated under the guidance of Ernie Haas. Ernie's untimely death while I was conducting the research for this book left us all poorer. I hope the book lives up to his expectations.

I am also indebted to the many friends and colleagues who commented on portions of the manuscript throughout the years: Mike Aronoff, Scott Gehlbach, Yoi Herrera, Tamir Moustafa, Ilan Peleg, Jon Pevehouse, Michael Schatzberg, Bernard Shapiro, Noam Shelef, Orie Shelef, and Scott Straus. David Leheney, Joel Migdal, Howard Schweber, Crawford Young, Ron Zweig, and an anonymous reviewer commented on the entire manuscript. The junior faculty "book club"—Mark Copelovitch, Helen Kinsella, Jimmy Klausen, and Nils Ringe—helped whip the book into shape and get over those last hurdles. Generosity has also come in the form of comments, criticism, and encouragement in less formal ways. Robert Adcock, Barry Burden, David Canon, Christina Ewig, Ed Friedman, Ken Goldstein, Ron Hassner, Paul Hutchcroft, Ira Katznelson, Andy Kydd, Mara Loveman, Leigh Payne, Sally Roever, Gay Seidman, Aseema Sinha, Aili Tripp, Mark Vail, and Sara Watson all contributed in their own ways. I wish I could have taken all of their advice. All errors of omission and commission are mine alone.

The research and writing of the book would have been impossible without the support of the Berkeley Department of Political Science, which funded the fieldwork. Ron Zweig and the Taub Center for Israel Studies at New York University provided a year of much needed reflection. Bud Meyerhoff's generosity in endowing my position at Wisconsin enabled me to have time (and space) to complete the project.

The archival research on which this book is based depended on the help of devoted archivists who often went beyond the call of duty. I am grateful to Amira Stern and the staff at the Jabotinsky Institute in Israel (JI), Dr. Michael Polishchuk and the staff at the Moshe Sharett Israel Labor Party Archives (Berl Katznelson Foundation) (LPA), and the staffs at the Institute for the Study of Religious Zionism at Bat-Ilan University (RZA), the Religious Zionism archive at Mosad Harav Kook, and the Central Zionist Archives (CZA). I also wish to thank the Jabotinsky Institute in Israel, the Moshe Sharett Israel Labor Party Archives, the World Bnei Akiva Archives, the Pinchas Lavon Institute for Labour Movement Research, and the National Religious Party for permission to reproduce some of their materials. Daniel Huffman of the UW-Madison Cartographic Laboratory drew the maps that accompany the book. Matan Field and Dan Miodownik provided last-minute research assistance.

The book also includes some materials that previously appeared in two articles: "From 'Both Banks of the Jordan' to the 'Whole Land of Israel': Ideological Change in Revisionist Zionism," *Israel Studies* 9, no. 1 (2004): 125–48; and "Testing the Logic of Unilateral Withdrawal: Lessons from the History of the Labor Zionist Movement," *Middle East Journal* 61, no. 3

(2007): 460–75. I thank Indiana University Press and the Middle East Institute for permission to use those materials. Roger Haydon, Susan Specter, Priscilla Hurdle, and Marion Rogers at Cornell University Press worked tirelessly to make this a better book.

My family has had to put up with this project for as long as I have. My mother, Loni Shelef, and my late father, Eliezer Shelef, provided unending encouragement. My son, Aharon, was born as the book was taking final form. His arrival put the project in perspective and his presence provided a much needed spur to finish the manuscript. Finally, this project would have remained one more unfulfilled idea without my wife, Miriam. Her love, wisdom, forbearance, and encouragement allowed me to surmount all the obstacles that stood in the way. This book is for her.

EVOLVING NATIONALISM

Nationalism, Change, and Evolution

Almost a century ago, David Ben-Gurion, Israel's first prime minister and founding father, believed that the conflict between Jews and Arabs in Palestine was irresolvable. "There's a national question here," he argued. "We want the country to be ours. The Arabs want the country to be theirs."[1] Ninety years later, Edward Said, the scholar and Palestinian advocate, said much the same thing: "The conflict appears intractable because it is a contest over the same land by two people who always believed that they had valid title to it and who hoped that the other side would in time give up or go away. One side won the war, the other lost, but the contest is as alive as ever."[2]

Both men were half-right. The Israeli-Palestinian conflict is a poignant reminder of the power of nationalism. The core nationalist story—that a group of people is a nation and, as such, deserves control of their political destiny—mobilizes masses to kill and be killed in its name. It also motivates acts of untold heroism. Nationalism is powerful because it provides the most salient answers to basic, or foundational, questions for countless people around the world. These responses to "Who are we?" "What should our society look like?" and "Where is our homeland?" set the bounds within which normal daily politics take place. They constitute the "assumed givens" of modern political societies.

Ben-Gurion and Said were also half-wrong. Both based their prognosis on a false assumption: namely, that the answers to these questions (in this case, the answer to "Where is the homeland?") do not and can not change.

[handwritten margin note: nationalism is not a fixed concept]

Yet for all of their power these answers do change. In recent years, a tremendous amount of scholarship has demonstrated transformations in the building blocks of nations in a variety of historical, political, and geographical contexts.[3] This book shows that Israeli nationalisms—whose territory and membership appear to be written in stone, the first biblically defined and the second ethnically circumscribed—experienced analogous transformations.

If there is widespread acceptance of the idea that the answers to the fundamental questions offered by any nationalism can change, the story of *how* they do so is less clear. The scholarship on nationalism has not ignored the question of change. It assumed, however, that the "how" is obvious.[4] As I will discuss shortly, most studies of nationalism (and of ideology more generally) take it for granted that either rational adaptation to new realities or elite manipulation drives change. Unfortunately, to the extent that these assumptions are built into the analysis, they are not subjected to empirical scrutiny. As a result, we do not actually know when rational adaptation or elite imposition drives change...or even *if* either does. Using the context provided by Israeli nationalisms since 1925, I test the ability of alternative explanations to account for changes in the answers these nationalisms provided to foundational questions. The analysis shows that most of these changes came about in an unguided manner akin to evolution. In this process, the complex interactions among competing nationalist movements and outside pressures led first to tactical adjustments to the specific claims articulated by political leaders and eventually to critical changes in their core beliefs. Israeli nationalisms, in other words, literally evolved over time.

The Transformations of Israeli Nationalisms

Zionism was born in the nineteenth century as a response to anti-Semitism. The first Zionist ideologues concluded that the three other main ways Jews responded to the modern era—assimilation, insulation, and religious reformation—could not prevent the recurrent persecution of Jews. Not only did assimilation come at the cost of eliminating Jews as a people, but, the Zionists argued, it was destined to fail. The Dreyfus trial, in which an assimilated French military officer was falsely convicted of treason, convinced them that Jews would never be allowed to integrate fully even into the most emancipated societies. The Zionists also found the traditional Jewish response of insulation in their own communities and awaiting salvation by divine intervention to be insufficient. They sought to make Jews subjects of history, not merely its passive objects. The early Zionists were also largely secular. As such, they doubted that prayer had the power to prevent the next pogrom. From the Zionist perspective, the third response, the religious

reform movement of the nineteenth century, which attempted to modern-
ize Judaism and render Jews Germans, French, or Britons "of the Mosaic
faith," also missed the point. The problem with Jews did not lie in the realm
of religion at all; nor did the Zionists believe that their integration into the
German, French, or British people was possible. Zionism identified the root
cause of anti-Semitism as the fact that "Jews were everywhere a minority,
nowhere a majority." Given this diagnosis, the cure for anti-Semitism was to
"ingather the Jewish exiles" and create a Jewish national home.

[handwritten margin note: had to make Jews the majority]

While all Zionists shared this ideological imperative, they had sometimes
radically different visions of what this home ought to look like. As the nov-
elist Amos Oz noted,

> Some people expected Israel to be a moral light unto the nations. Others ex-
> pected it to be a nonstop macho show—Entebbe every week. Others wanted it
> to be an incarnation of the Jewish shtetl from Eastern Europe....There were
> people who came here to humbly wait for the messiah. There were others,
> more ambitious, who intended to make the messiah come immediately. Others
> wanted to BE the messiah, or to reconstruct the ancient kingdoms of David
> and Solomon with all their glory, or to build a Marxist paradise....There were
> Europeans who hoped to rebuild Vienna or Prague in the heart of the Middle
> East, with good manners and tea and European decorum, music....Next door
> were people who wanted this place to become a fifty-second state of the U.S. or a
> Scandinavian social democracy. The founders of my own kibbutz, Hulda, semi-
> religious social anarchists, maintained that it was time for the Jewish people
> to come back to Israel to create a loose federation of rural communities where
> the Jews would undergo a deep religious renewal, not in a synagogue, but by
> being in touch with the elements of nature, by hard physical work and sharing
> everything with each other. There was, in short, a rainbow of fantasies.[5]

The early Jewish nationalists even disagreed about where, exactly, the
Jewish national home ought to be located. Jewish nationalists were initially
split between "territorialists"—whose main goal was the achievement of
a Jewish state, regardless of its location—and "Zionists"—who saw Zion
(whatever its perceived borders) as the appropriate location for the Jewish
state. The territorialists finally lost this battle when the proposal to establish a Jewish state in Uganda failed in 1905, though some still occasionally
called for the establishment of the Jewish state in Argentina, Birobidjan
(USSR), or the Sinai Peninsula in the early twentieth century.[6] Even once
they settled on Zion, Israeli nationalist movements added or subtracted the
East Bank of the Jordan, Southern Lebanon, the West Bank, Gaza Strip,
Golan Heights, and the Sinai Peninsula from their image of the appropriate
borders of their nation-state.

Even the membership of the Jewish national home was not straightforward. From the beginning, the Zionists faced two key difficulties. First, a large non-Jewish population inhabited the putative homeland. Second, most of the Jewish population lived outside this homeland. The various definitions of the appropriate membership in the nation and in its state reflected the different ways in which the Zionist movements struggled with these problems. On one end of the spectrum, some, such as the Canaanite movement, articulated territorial (civic) notions of membership, which included Arabs but excluded Diaspora Jews. On the other end were those who put forth strongly ethnic notions of membership, which included Diaspora Jews but excluded Arabs. Others stood in between.

Table 1 provides a snapshot of the ways in which the three most important Israeli nationalist movements answered these basic questions at the beginning and end of the period covered by this book. Labor Zionism, Religious Zionism, and Revisionist Zionism do not exhaust the variety of Jewish nationalist movements, or even of Zionist movements. They were (and are), however, the main contenders for power. The vast majority of the population of the Jewish community in Palestine and later in the state of Israel identified with one of them. As a result, they play the most significant role in shaping the answers Israelis provide to foundational questions.

Labor Zionism was the largest and most important movement within the Zionist panoply. The central stream of Labor Zionism (institutionalized in Mapai—Mifleget Poalei Eretz Israel, the Land of Israel Worker's Party—and later in the Israel Labor Party) dominated the political scene in the Jewish community in Palestine/Israel from 1933 until 1977. Labor Zionism initially sought to eradicate the Jewish Diaspora by gathering all Jews in a secular socialist society that would be a "light unto the nations." Their goals have changed. Their socialism disappeared. They replaced the drive to create a new, secular Jew with an acceptance of religion and its role in shaping the public realm. They even replaced the cardinal Zionist goal of eradicating the Jewish Diaspora with a commitment to saving Jews *in* the dispersion. The Labor Zionist definition of the appropriate borders of the Jewish state also changed. Their initial vision of the homeland included present-day Israel, the West Bank, Gaza Strip, Golan Heights, Southern Lebanon up to the Litani River, and the East Bank of the Jordan River up to the Hejaz Railway. Today, their image of the appropriate borders of the Jewish state corresponds (more or less) to the 1949 armistice borders.[7]

Importantly for our purposes, Labor Zionist leaders disdained ideological constraints. They preferred concrete results to abstract dreams even if the former fell short of their aspirations.[8] This pragmatism creates the expectation that the Labor Zionist movement would be especially sensitive to exogenous shocks and nimbly adapt to them. Nonetheless, despite this

TABLE 1
Changes in the Claims of Zionist/Israeli Nationalist Movements

	Where is the homeland?		Who are we?		What are we to do?	
	1925	2005	1925	2005	1925	2005
Labor Zionist movement	"The sea to the desert"—including present day-Israel, the West Bank, Gaza Strip, Jordan, and Southern Lebanon (see map A)	The 1949 armistice boundaries (see map B)	Entire Jewish nation	Resident Jews	Build a socialist utopia Create a new secular nation Eradicate the diaspora	Build a state Allow a role for religion in the public realm Save Jews in the dispersion
Revisionist Zionist movement	"Both banks of the Jordan"—including present-day Israel, the West Bank, Gaza Strip, Jordan, and Southern Lebanon (see map C)	"Whole land of Israel"—including present-day Israel, the West Bank, Gaza Strip, and Golan Heights (see map D)	Entire Jewish nation	Entire Jewish nation	Pursue a nationalism undiluted by other principles	Allow a role for religion in the public realm
Religious Zionist movement	"The River of Egypt to...the River Euphrates"—including present-day Israel, the West Bank, Gaza Strip, Jordan, Lebanon, Syria, and parts of Iraq and Turkey (see map E)	"Whole land of Israel"—including present-day Israel, the West Bank, Gaza Strip, and Golan Heights (see map D)	Entire Jewish nation	Entire Jewish nation	Sanctify the state above other considerations	Entrench Israeli control over the territories

(handwritten margin note: change in nationalist goals over time)

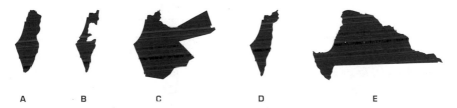

A   B   C   D   E

Maps A–E. Representations of the ideological delineation of territory described in table 1. Please note that these maps are not drawn to scale and are not all proportionate to one another.

"most likely scenario," rational adaptation accounts for only one of the transformations in this movement's nationalist claims.

For most of the history of Israeli nationalism, the ultranationalist Revisionist Zionist movement constituted the main opposition to Labor Zionism. The Revisionist movement sought to "revise" the Zionists' reluctance to openly spell out their goals in the late 1920s. They argued that the Zionists should clearly declare their demand for a Jewish majority state on both banks of the Jordan River for all to hear. As table 1 shows, the strident rhetoric of their movement notwithstanding, the Revisionist Zionists also reformulated their answers to foundational questions. The redefinition of the extent of the homeland is the most dramatic of these changes. Their original claim of the appropriate homeland encompassed "both banks of the Jordan," including present-day Israel, the territories, and Jordan. Today, their vision of the "whole land of Israel" does not extend beyond the Jordan River. Less visibly, but as importantly, they also changed their idea of the national mission. Revisionist Zionism originally focused on "monism"—a nationalism "undiluted" by commitments to any other ideology, including religion or socialism. As a result, Revisionists envisioned a society in which the individual was king and where religion was a private affair.[9] Since then, however, they have come to accept, indeed promote, a significant role for religious law in shaping the Israeli public realm.

From its foundation in 1925 by Vladimir (Ze'ev) Jabotinsky until Menachem Begin's withdrawal from public life in 1983, the leaders of the Revisionist Zionist movement exercised tremendous personal control over the movement's politics, policies, and ideology. Jabotinsky's writings were elevated to near biblical heights.[10] Begin's power "emanated from his being perceived as the symbol and the embodiment of myths with which party members and voters identified."[11] The national conventions of their political party (Herut, meaning "Liberty") took "on the appearance of a mass revival rally where the faithful renew their loyalty by the unquestioning reaffirmation of faith," with "near religious" incantations of devotion to Begin. As one sympathetic observer noted, this meant "disagreement was seen as personal treason."[12] The dominance of this movement by charismatic leadership increases the likelihood that elite imposition would account for any ideological change—if only because no one would be able to stand up to the ideological decisions of the charismatic leader. Yet none of the ideological changes summarized in table 1 were intentionally imposed from the top down.

The third movement included in this book emerged in 1902 to protect the interests of the religious segment of the Zionist movement. Whereas the vast majority of traditional Orthodox Jewry rejected Zionism as dangerous and blasphemous, Merkaz Ruhani (The Spiritual Center), whose acronym, Mizrachi, was the name by which the Religious Zionist movement became known, engaged nationalism from within. In the late 1920s, Mizrachi and Hapoel Hamizrachi (The Mizrachi Worker), an outgrowth of the original group influenced by the socialist ideals of the Labor movement, began to formally coordinate their activities, and in 1956, they formally merged into the National Religious Party (NRP). After the Yom Kippur War in 1973, the ideological (and increasingly political) leadership of the Religious Zionist movement was taken by Gush Emunim (Bloc of the Faithful) and the Young Guard of the NRP.

Since it is a religiously inspired nationalist movement, the bar for changing its definition of nationalism is very high. With regard to the territorial dimension, for example, this movement based its claim to the homeland on the divine promise of the land from "the River of Egypt to ... the Euphrates" (Genesis 15:18). Since these are God-given borders, mere mortals have no right to modify them. Nonetheless, contemporary Religious Zionism restricts its claim of the homeland to the area covered by Israel, the West Bank, the Gaza Strip, and the Golan Heights. The Religious Zionists also shifted their sense of national mission. Whereas they once sanctified the state, placing it above other considerations, the commitment to maintaining Israeli control of the (redefined) land of Israel now supersedes the sanctity of the state.

Alternative Explanations of Change

This book explains how these changes came about. To do so, I compare the ability of three potential explanations to account for the actual process of ideological transformation: rational adaptation, elite imposition, and an evolutionary dynamic. The first two mechanisms of change are extrapolated from the literature on nationalism. Both rational adaptation and elite imposition offer reasonable explanations of how change in the meaning of nationalism takes place. Both, however, are also constrained by the assumptions required to make them logically coherent. After drawing out the logic of these two explanations, I suggest that an evolutionary dynamic can provide a more powerful explanation of change in the foundational aspects of nationalism.

Rational Adaptation

Rational adaptation starts from the observation that nationalism is "sticky." It takes nationalism's persistence and demonstrated power to mean that while scholars should recognize the constructed character of any particular nationalism, they should still treat nationalism "as if" it was primordial. Once nations emerge, in Anthony Smith's words, they become "social facts."[13] While this perspective focuses on accounting for nationalism's stability, it contains a sensible implication about how change takes place. Ideologies cannot be totally disconnected from the reality in which their adherents live. Disjunctures between the expectations bred by an ideology and the experience of its adherents are likely to produce pressure for change. In this theory, exogenous shocks act as a "cognitive punch" that shifts the otherwise durable nationalist ideology off its track by offering an incentive to change and punishing intransigence.[14] Frequently hidden behind this rationale is an implicit comparison to the pressures on a firm to adjust to changing market conditions. Politicians and pundits also rely on this logic when they claim that the passage of time will lead to change, as people "get used to" a new reality. People, in other words, will recognize that they live in a world in which their previous beliefs are no longer appropriate, and modify them accordingly.

In the case of Israeli nationalisms, the convergence on a territorially more constrained vision of the appropriate extent of the homeland (see table 1) suggests that something like rational adaptation might have been taking place. Given the similar end point (at least regarding the exclusion of the East Bank of the Jordan River), Israeli nationalist movements could have moved toward this position in response to the same external strictures. The historical story, however, is more complicated. Israeli nationalist movements did not begin to abandon the claim to the land east of the Jordan River at the same time or even in the same decade. As a result, it is impossible to link these changes to a particular exogenous shock or to a new reality to which they were all adapting. Nor was the direction of change unambiguously rational. If it was irrational to continue claiming Transjordan once Britain separated it from the Palestine Mandate in 1922, it ought to have been equally irrational to continue claiming East Jerusalem, the West Bank, and the Gaza Strip after these were no longer accessible. Yet all the Zionist movements continued to do so.

These empirical complications reflect a deeper conceptual problem. There is no rubric for distinguishing between new realities that will lead to change and those that will not. Individual scholars tend to emphasize the influence of a particular force or constellation of forces, usually choosing among globalization, war, natural catastrophe, demographic shifts, superpower diktat, and economic upheaval, among others.[15] In the absence of a good theoretical reason to expect only a single one of these to act as a cognitive punch, this vast array of potential exogenous shocks suggests that change in nationalist ideologies would actually be quite common. The implication of frequent change, however, conflicts with the starting premise that change is rare and difficult. To overcome this tension, rational adaptation explanations of change therefore assume that the environmental shock to which ideologies adapt is so traumatic that it obliterates the possibility of alternatives to survive. In other words, big ideological changes must be brought about by big causes.

Elite Imposition

If rational adaptation privileges stability, elite imposition emphasizes nationalism's fluidity. By this explanation, change in the meaning of nationalism is not a product of big exogenous shocks but originates from individual actors. According to Eric Hobsbawm, "Nationalism, the nation-state, national symbols, histories and the rest…rest on exercises in social engineering which are often deliberate and always innovative."[16] Expansive versions of this argument all but ignore the role of structural and institutional constraints, asserting, for example, that peoplehood is a construct "which, in each particular instance, has constantly changing boundaries."[17] Accordingly, "the form, content and meaning of [nations and national identities] remain open to individual interpretation and negotiation."[18] National identities are "constructed according to audience, setting, topic, and substantive content. National identities are therefore malleable, fragile and, frequently, ambivalent and diffuse."[19] Michael Banton summarized the basic claim of this account in his assertion that "when [groups] change, it is because individual motivations have changed."[20]

Unfortunately, the expectation of constant (or even frequent) change, paradoxically, removes ideological transformation as a phenomenon requiring explanation in the first place.[21] Perhaps as a result, while this literature frequently notes the existence of change, it rarely specifies the mechanisms that drive it.[22] As a result, we don't know why people choose one identity over the available alternatives or how frequently such switches take place.

The expectation of constant change is also often too strongly stated. It ignores the very power and stability of nationalism so ably captured by the "as if" primordial approaches. As Michael Billig sardonically noted, "One can eat Chinese tomorrow and Turkish the day after; one can even dress in Chinese or Turkish styles. But *being* Chinese or Turkish are not commercially available options."[23] Far from being ethereal ideals, nationalist ideologies concretely delimit the people from whom sovereignty derives and to whom rights are granted, and the territory over which this sovereignty ought to extend.[24] The vision of the ideal nation-state also crucially informs the positions taken by political leaders and their followers on issues ranging from territorial disputes and citizenship to the appropriate role of religion in the state. Given their epistemic quality, if the answers to such fundamental questions really did constantly change, the resulting social dislocation would make coherent political life virtually impossible.

When analyses that privilege the fluidity of nationalism deal with mechanisms of change, they tend to do so in two basic ways. The first, clustered in works that focus on the microfoundations of nationalism and the rational decisions made by the individuals who imagine the nation, offers a version of rational adaptation. According to this view, the identities chosen by actors depend on the incentives they face. As a result, change in the character of the identities depends on a modification of these incentives. Since these approaches are usually based in a materialist paradigm, shifts in nationalism are most commonly explained by changes in the institutions or structures that created the tangible incentives to choose those identities in the first place.[25] Such institutional or structural change functions much like the exogenous shocks in rational adaptation, with similarly deterministic expectations.

A second strand focuses on the role of nationalist elites. After all, elites are the ones that actually lead the movements that create, take over, and legitimate states. They also write the history textbooks, plays, poetry, novels, and propaganda through which everyone else imagines the nation. Individuals may still select from among the identities available to them, but others defined the content of those identities—in this case, the meanings of nationalism—that they select among.[26] As a result, when shifts in the meaning of nationalism take place, they are understood to be the product of conscious elite manipulation of national symbols and identities in the pursuit of power, economic advantage, or both.[27]

This too is a plausible explanation of change. Nationalist leaders exercise disproportionate influence in shaping the answers to foundational questions. Ideological change therefore very well might be the result of self-conscious and overt manipulation by opportunistic leaders, even if it is not actually "constant." As a trigger of change, however, elite imposition tends to exaggerate the ability of elites to manipulate the masses and fails to explain why so many people are prepared to die for such machinations. In so doing, it usually assumes an unsustainable difference between the devious, craven, and ideologically opportunistic elites and the innocent, naive masses that they dupe into following them.[28] Confronted with the power and persistence of nationalist ideologies, this theory tends to require the corollary that the content of nationalist ideology is not important. Elites will choose to construct whatever identity they benefit from. Nationalist claims are seen as invidious ways of getting people to act in ways they might not otherwise. They are thus little more than a convenient way for elites to manipulate mass sentiment in the pursuit of power.

Such an account of change, however, just shifts the burden of explanation to the beliefs of the nationalist leaders. While the assumption that the elites who consciously modify their ideological claims are not "true believers" is sometimes warranted, the relative inaccessibility of the thoughts and innermost beliefs of nationalist leaders makes this difficult to verify empirically. Nationalist leaders also frequently cling to particular claims even when these run counter to their visible interests. In the Israeli case, the Revisionist

Zionist movement maintained the claim to the land east of the Jordan River long after suffering widespread ridicule for doing so. Similarly, Religious Zionist leaders continue to desire a religious public realm despite the fact that the majority of Israeli Jews are not religiously observant. Surely, they could expand their electoral appeal if they abandoned this stance. At the very least, elite imposition provides no convincing way to account for such counterintuitive persistence.

[handwritten margin note: f public do not support why would certain elites still try and convince]

The Evolutionary Dynamic

The evolutionary dynamic offers a third account of how change takes place. Evolution holds that whenever and wherever we find variation among units, meaningful competition among these units (or their vehicles), and the retention of their traits over time, the proportion of those variants that succeed at this competition at higher rates will increase at the expense of other varieties.[29] Applied to nationalism, the evolutionary dynamic expects change to take place when a new rhetorical variant of a nationalist ideology is so successful that it is promoted at the expense of the old ideological formulation until, under the right conditions, the new version displaces the old one.

The application of an evolutionary logic to nationalism starts from the premise that nations are not unitary. They often contain two or more visions of the appropriate borders, boundaries, and collective mission of the nation. This possibility builds on the central constructivist insights that nations are first and foremost "a state of mind, an act of consciousness," and that people are likely to differ in their knowledge of "everyday life."[30] As a result, there is little reason to assume that everyone in a particular society imagines the borders, destiny, and identity of the nation in the same way. To be sure, the nationalist idea loudly proclaims the homogeneity of the nation. Actual uniformity in the way in which people understand the nation's defining features is also certainly possible. However, such a situation is less likely to be the natural condition of a nation than the product of the (more or less temporary) victory of one nationalist movement—which promotes itself as the sole true embodiment of the nation, and its respective vision as representing the true national identity—over its alternatives.[31] This means that whether the nationalism of any particular case is contested or not is a variable condition and not a natural state.

Recognizing the possibility of such variation within groups conventionally seen as unitary nations is particularly important for an exploration of how change takes place. The conceptualization of the nation as a unitary entity (e.g., of French, German, Russian, or Israeli nationalism), whatever its merit in other contexts, underestimates the possibility of internally driven change because it deemphasizes domestic differences on foundational questions.

Just because we recognize that there is no single, empirical, objective criterion that links the members of a nation together does not tell us, however, where to find the most meaningful variations. The most common response uses the "type" of nationalism as the relevant level of analysis. Some categorize nationalisms according to people's location in the social or political structure or by their relationship to the state—distinguishing between state or official nationalism and its counterpart among the masses.[32] Others emphasize class and distinguish between elite and popular nationalisms.[33] Still others reduce visions of national identity to a dichotomy of conceptions of national membership, usually "civic" or "ethnic."[34]

While an improvement over unitary conceptions of the nation, focusing on the type of nationalism remains problematic for an explanation of how change in the meaning of nationalism takes place. Because such analyses tend to rely on a single criterion to distinguish among types of nationalism, the extent of the variation is a priori limited to the two sides of whatever criterion they choose. Unfortunately, the resulting dichotomization of nationalism may not accurately reflect the extent of the relevant variation. For example, South African nationalisms included transethnic, racial, civic, and Africanist definitions of national membership. American nationalism has its cosmopolitan, liberal, nativist, and multicultural versions. Prior to World War II, Japanese membership in the nation was contested between those who believed that Japanese national identity should rest on a statist (elite) basis and those who believed it should be ethnically grounded. The definition of membership in the Japanese nation also varied based on whether or not one believed that Koreans and Taiwanese were Japanese. Indian history has been marked by a conflict between secular nationalism, Hindu nationalism, and at least two versions of separatist nationalism, one in Kashmir and the other in Punjab. The spectrum of Turkish nationalisms includes Kemalist, Islamist, and Pan-Turanist visions of the nation and its land. And even Russian nationalism can be thought of as containing Western, Orthodox, and Pan-Slavic varieties.[35] The list, of course, could go on. The point is that much of the time, especially in deeply divided societies, more than two alternatives coexist.

The dichotomization of nationalism is also problematic because it leads to an overemphasis on the competition between the two visions of the nation. Reduced to a two-player game, the battle between them becomes a zero-sum contest. Since players in a zero-sum game, by definition, have no common interests and thus no reason to cooperate, the impact of any cooperation is obscured even if it exists.[36] Intranationalist politics can be zero-sum, as when alternative movements disagree on every foundational question; but they do not have to be. The multidimensionality of nationalism means that even if movements disagree, for example, on the extent of the homeland and the national mission, their shared idea of the nation's membership criteria makes cooperation possible.

Finally, dichotomous conceptualizations of nations limit how we think of change to a "swing" from one alternative to another. Because the common pendulum metaphor essentializes the ends of the swing as opposite poles, it artificially fixes their position. By placing the ideologies and their adherents outside the influence of politics, history, and social change, this metaphor limits our ability to ask how substantive transformations in the content of nationalist claims take place. At the very least, it privileges the wholesale replacement of the dominant ideology over explorations of partial, incremental, transformations in the content of these ideologies.

Noting the flattening effect of dichotomizations, Rogers Smith advises us "to eschew categorizing existing political communities as fundamentally 'civic' or 'ethnic,' 'liberal' or 'republican' or 'democratic'" and "instead [to] adopt alternative frameworks that can provide a place for all the dimensions of peoplehood that we can expect to find empirically."[37] This is sage advice. It can, however, be taken to excess. This most commonly happens when the analysis focuses on the individual members of the nation. According to this framing of nationalism, because individuals imagine and articulate nationalism, there are likely to be as many different definitions of the nation as there are individuals doing the imagining. Indeed, in its extreme guise, such analysis leads to the claims that nations "do not just [exist], they are made real to the individual by the individual in the course of her/his deliberations and interactions."[38]

Unfortunately, in the context of an explanation of how change in nationalist ideologies takes place, this logic is paralyzing. Breaking nationalism down to the level of the individual eliminates it as a useful analytical construct distinct from personal identity. This deconstruction of nationalism may be warranted, but as long as nations remain the primary (or even an important) organizing principle of societies around the globe, it does more to limit our understanding of nations than to promote it. Despite the role of each individual, national identity remains a social, collective, and relational phenomenon. Imaginations about the nation held by individuals have to overlap at least enough for them to be mutually intelligible. Moreover, nationalism is a *political* ideology—aimed at shaping the world according to its vision. Unless individuals publicly engage one another in meaningful ways to bring this about, the individual variations remain analytically irrelevant.

Rather than framing the exploration of how change takes place either at the "national" level, at the level of the "type" of nationalism, or at the individual level, this book situates the analysis at the level of the nationalist movement. Nationalist movements aggregate and articulate a particular vision of the appropriate borders, boundaries, and mission of the nation that shapes (and is shaped by) the individual imagination of adherents of the movement. Nationalist movements also act in the political world to actualize their goals. Focusing on the level of the nationalist movement accepts the constructivist logic that there may be (at least theoretically) many ways in which "the nation" is understood, but limits the range of meaningful alternatives to those variants that are large and motivated enough to publicly organize as such. There may still be one, two, or many nationalist movements, each of which articulates its own understanding of the nation and corresponding nationalism, but the actual number of alternatives in a particular case varies as an empirical matter. Moreover, from the perspective of the evolutionary dynamic, since the most meaningful competition among variants of nationalist ideology takes place within and between the movements that articulate them, this level of analysis is best suited to exploring how nationalism changes. Finally, analysis at the level of nationalist movements (in this case the different Zionist/Israeli nationalist movements rather than "Zionism" per se) is particularly constructive because it accommodates the full range of their interactions.

These interactions spur the variation that, according to the evolutionary dynamic, can lead to ideological transformation. Where no single movement can gain power on its own, the pursuit of mundane political projects may lead nationalist leaders to hold their collective noses and cooperate with rival movements despite deep disagreements over foundational issues. While not infrequent (after all, the history of nationalism is filled with unholy alliances of one kind or another), such cooperation is not easy. It demands more than do alliances that take place where foundational questions are not disputed or that merely aggregate different interest groups (though it does that as well). At the same time, cooperation despite these basic differences does not necessitate the sudden conversion of one of the movements. Nor does it demand that the movements like each other very much.

The creation of such alliances does require bridging the gaps between the divergent understandings of those foundational aspects of the nation for which nationalists are notoriously ready to give their lives. Nationalist politicians often do so by engaging in a rhetorical fudging of those ideological claims that would otherwise make cooperation impossible. If the new alliance (or its leaders) fails to achieve the mundane goals for which such adjustments were deployed, the new rhetoric is likely to dissipate. If, on the other hand, these adjustments prove politically successful, the new rhetoric may become increasingly difficult to abandon. After all, political success carries rewards that even ideologically driven politicians find alluring. As a result, the adjusted version of the ideological claim is likely to become more prominent within the movement, perhaps even eventually displacing the traditional position, and thereby becoming the new ideological orthodoxy. In this way, a relatively small change (the initially tactical adjustment of a deeply held claim for an ideologically neutral short-term goal) may bring about a significant transformation in the substantive ideology articulated by the nationalist movement.

This process is not automatic. The often unpredictable political struggles within nationalist movements, and the contests among them, help determine the success or failure of new ideological variants. Within the movement, ideological hard-liners ("truth tellers") will predictably cast the new rhetoric as an abandonment of their cherished ideals and as a betrayal of the nation. Advocates of adjusting the ideological claim ("consensus builders"), in turn, are likely to respond that the tactical modulation is just that—a temporary ploy that not only does not represent a deviation from the ideal, but is actually the best way to achieve their unchanged goals.[39] In the Zionist/Israeli context, the consensus builders explicitly understood the rhetorical adjustments they advocated as ways of *preserving* their ideology in imperfect conditions. If the truth tellers win this intramovement struggle, no change in the fundamental nationalist claims of the movement is likely to take place. If, however, the advocates of the tactical modulation carry the day, and the adjusted claim proves politically successful, the increasing returns to this success may lead to the institutionalization of the adjusted claim as the new orthodoxy.[40] Importantly, the overtly ideological debate is not necessarily the most important factor in deciding these outcomes. Personality clashes, petty politics, organizational ability, policy competence, and mundane, even arbitrary events are as—if not more—likely to shape the political fortunes of both truth-telling and consensus-building politicians.

Unlike either rational adaptation or elite imposition, the evolutionary dynamic does not predetermine the frequency of ideological transformation. While rational adaptation assumes that change is rare, and elite imposition assumes that it is common, the evolutionary dynamic pegs the frequency of change to the cadence of the domestic political struggle among nationalist movements. When and where this battle is particularly heated, the evolutionary dynamic expects change to be relatively frequent—perhaps accounting for the instances marshaled to support the fluidity of nationalism.[41] Conversely, when and where the foundational issues confronting the polity are (at least temporarily) resolved, the frequency of change is likely to be relatively low—perhaps matching the expectations of those who treat nations as largely stable. Thus, rather than assume that nations should be treated "as if" primordial, or presume that nationalism is fluid, the evolutionary dynamic anchors nationalism in the politics of the people whose identity is at stake.

While explanations based on rational adaptation are frequently called "Darwinian," rational adaptation and the evolutionary dynamic are actually quite distinct. Unlike the strategic calculation assumed by rational adapta-tion, evolution is myopic. It is not guided by any plan, foresight, or grand design. Nor, it is worth mentioning, does it imply any normative progress.[42] The units subject to it cannot look into the future, decide that they are outmoded, and calculate how to change; they cannot be, in other words, literally strategic. At most, evolution predicts that those variations that by dumb luck are better suited to thrive in the new environment would survive at greater rates than those that are not. If this evolutionary "landscape" is stable for long enough, the lucky variant may come to entirely displace the unlucky ones in the population. However, the evolutionary algorithm can-not a priori distinguish lucky variants from unlucky ones. While the eventual outcome may look "preordained" or "rational" with hindsight, its success is actually the contingent result of unpredictable lower-level interactions. The eventual outcome is thus only one of the many possible outcomes. As a result, where evolution guides change, a counterfactual replaying of history is incredibly unlikely to yield exactly the same result every time. Evolution, in other words, is inherently probabilistic rather than deterministic.[43]

In addition, evolution tells a story about the relative rates of survival of variants within a population. Evolution does not explain individual de-velopment. As a result, the evolutionary dynamic and rational adaptation posit the opposite chronological order between variation and environmental changes. In rational adaptation, new ideological versions emerge after a sys-temic shock (otherwise, there is nothing new to adapt to). In the evolution-ary dynamic, variation comes first. Challenges posed by the environment shape the selection pressures experienced by these preexisting variants and thus influence their relative chances of success or failure. Nevertheless, the variation exists before the environmental change.

By allowing us to avoid making any assumption about the sincerity, in-tegrity, or mental state of nationalist leaders, the evolutionary dynamic also resolves one of the problems with the elite imposition hypothesis. According to the evolutionary dynamic, substantive ideological change can take place regardless of the intentions of movement leaders. Tactical adjustments may be little more than the machinations of conniving elites or they may reflect sincere attempts by well-meaning "consensus builders" to maintain their core beliefs in difficult circumstances. In either case, these adjustments in-troduce a new ideological variant that, if politically successful, can become difficult to abandon.

The limited role of individual intentions has led to arguments against the application of an evolutionary logic to social and political phenomena. Since people can decide to change their minds in ways that individual genes cannot change the code that makes them up after their formation, goes the argument, translating evolutionary theory to the social sphere is misguided.[44] While applying an evolutionary logic to nationalist transformation does complicate the link between intentions and outcomes, it does not eliminate agency. Intentional actions by autonomous political actors are a primary source of the ideological adjustments that are then available to be selected at the population-wide (i.e., nationalist movement) level. The agency of political entrepreneurs thus remains a key part of the story, though the evolutionary dynamic contextualizes it as part of a broader process.

don't neglect political agencies

Assessing Alternative Explanations

This book's main argument is that changes in nationalism do not have to be intentional. Yet they clearly can be. Nationalists do respond strategically to new realities, and nationalist elites do manipulate ideologies for their own gain. How can we tell if an evolutionary dynamic or one of the intentional mechanisms caused a particular instance of change? While each explanation has its advantages and disadvantages, all of them are plausible. As a result, there is no purely conceptual or normative way to adjudicate among them. We can decide the question of whether a particular transformation was the product of an evolutionary dynamic, rational adaptation, or elite imposition only on empirical grounds.

has to be posed or empirical evidence

Identifying the mechanisms of change empirically is actually somewhat easier in the context of nationalism than in other nonexperimental settings. As Daniel Dennett noted, natural selection (at least in biology) cannot prove "exactly how (pre)history was, [it only has] the power to prove how it could have been, given what we know about how things are." Moreover, Dennett argues, it would be impossible, "in the absence of insider information on the actual history that created the organism," to tell natural selection apart from any alternative hypothesis.[45] Richard Burian similarly warns that the application of an evolutionary dynamic is particularly difficult because its use "requires comparative evidence and difficult reconstructive inference regarding the process of design."[46] As students of nationalism, however, we do (sometimes) have "insider information" in the form of detailed historical data about the "process of design" that can be used to judge the relative plausibility of the alternative explanations of change.

The rubric for disentangling the relative plausibility of the evolutionary dynamic, rational adaptation, and elite imposition takes advantage of the different expectations of each about the when, where, and who of change. Table 2 summarizes these expectations. To the extent that the fit between

TABLE 2
Expectations of Alternative Explanations of How Nationalism Changes

	When?	Where?	Who?
Evolutionary dynamic	After tactical adjustment of foundational claims	The partners in the alliance move toward each other	Movements that made tactical adjustments to foundational claims
Rational adaptation	After the reality-shaping shock	Toward alignment with new reality	Everyone exposed to the new reality
Elite imposition	When elites see potential for benefit	Toward maximizing leaders' utility	Movements whose leaders choose change

the expectations of an explanation and the historical record is better in any particular case, we can be more confident of its role in accounting for the change that took place.[47]

Each explanation links the timing of change to a different factor. If that link is empirically tenuous, then so is the explanation. Where the evolutionary dynamic drives an ideological transformation, the onset of change is tied to the deployment of an adjusted claim in the pursuit of a solution to a local, short-term political problem. Rational adaptation expects ideological transformations to occur in the aftermath of a traumatic exogenous shock that makes the prior answers to foundational questions meaningless or irrational. Elite imposition predicts that changes would begin in response to new elite incentives.

Both rational adaptation and elite imposition expect an ideological change, once it begins, to proceed quickly and smoothly throughout the movement. After all, if it were irrational or costly to continue articulating the old ideology, there would be little reason for those adapting to prevaricate. The evolutionary dynamic, however, does not require such consistency. It links the spread of the new rhetoric to the result of the contingent intra-movement struggles between the truth tellers and the consensus builders, the degree of the success of the new variant in achieving its short-term goals, and the meaningfulness of the political benefits that accrue from this success. In these cases, the turning point of change is reached when the new framing of the ideological claim is more common than the old orthodoxy.

Each mechanism of change also contains different expectations for the substantive direction of ideological change and the ideological dimension on which it takes place (the "where"). Elite imposition is the most permissive of the three explanations in this regard. This explanation expects change to proceed in almost any direction as long as it serves the interests of the movement's leaders. Rational adaptation is considerably more deterministic. Because it assumes that a movement's ideology has to become congruent with the new reality, the exogenous shock dictates the substance and direction of any ideological change. The evolutionary dynamic, in contrast, links the direction and substance of change to the details of the tactical adjustment and the particular character of the alliance forged among nationalist movements. It expects change to occur only with regard to those fundamental issues that are rearticulated in order to enable cooperation between rival nationalist movements. In terms of the direction of change, the evolutionary dynamic predicts that the ideology of members of the newly enabled alliance will shift toward that of their partners.

Each explanation also has different expectations about who actually undergoes the ideological transformation. Rational adaptation's ultimate reliance on "big" shocks predicts that change, or at least the pressure to change, would affect the entire population, in this case all nationalist (and, actually, nonnationalist) movements. Leaving little room for the influence of the people living through and interpreting these changes, rational adaptation is thus limited in its ability to account for variation in who experiences transformation, its timing, and its direction. After all, everyone's ideology is expected to fall into alignment with the new reality if it is to survive. The evolutionary dynamic, in contrast, expects ideological change only on the part of those nationalist movements that adjust their rhetoric in an attempt to solve mundane political problems *and* that achieve these short-term political goals. Elite imposition limits the object of change to those movements whose leaders decide to execute such a transformation.

A record of the when, where, and who of transformations in nationalist ideologies is available not just in the actual account of discussions where movement policy and ideology are formulated, but in the broader explicit and banal articulations of nationalist tenets over time. The use of the discourse about the nation by nationalists as the relevant record for such an investigation has a distinguished history in the study of nationalism.[48] It is particularly compelling in the Israeli case as Israeli politicians made tremendous efforts to control the terminology used and the images put forth precisely because they believed that these had an impact.

It is admittedly difficult to answer conclusively the question of when an initially tactical, even insincere, adjustment of an ideological claim becomes reinterpreted as the orthodox position. It is always possible that the "real" position remains hidden away, nursed in the privacy of inner sanctums, and invisible to the researcher. Nonetheless, in order to increase the confidence that changes in the pattern of articulation were real phenomena, I balanced discourse meant for "external consumption"—such as speeches at public meetings, publications, media interviews, and electoral propaganda—with ideological articulations in settings in which political leaders could be reasonably expected to be less dissembling. These included closed leadership meetings, at which nationalist leaders frequently discussed questions of tactical rhetoric openly and explicitly (and which should therefore make it possible to detect instances of elite imposition), and, more significantly, the pedagogical materials of the youth movements associated with each nationalist movement. Assuming that the leaders of nationalist movements want their children to believe in the same vision of the nation and the same ideology as they do, it is unlikely that purely tactical considerations would influence the ideological claims promoted in these settings. Substantive transformation also differs from merely tactical changes in that it is long lasting and reflected in concrete actions. As a result, sustained changes in the overall pattern of articulation by the movement's leadership are more significant than any particular instance of a new variant.

The Israeli context is an especially productive one in which to test the ability of alternative explanations to account for changes in the meaning of nationalism. Because of the highly mobilized character of Jewish Israeli nationalisms, its ideologues expended a great deal of energy distinguishing themselves not only from Palestinian Arabs, but also from nonnationalist Jewish groups and rival nationalist movements. These ongoing struggles took place in a relatively open society with a highly literate and politically energized population. As a result, the historical record needed to reconstruct the process of change, which, in turn, allows us to judge the relative plausibility of alternative explanations, is readily accessible. The scope of the historical record is particularly rich because each Zionist/Israeli nationalist movement acted not only "as a travel agency for prospective immigrants but...also established its own agricultural settlements, investment firm, urban housing scheme, bank, trade union, labor exchange, kindergarten and schools, publishing house, newspaper, and sick fund. At one time or another several...even maintained private underground armies."[49] This large array of activities means that we can check the pattern of ideological articulation of foundational questions in a range of arenas, audiences, and topics.

While the Israeli case places disputes over foundational questions in sharp relief, it is not unique. The range of competing nationalist movements and the variation in visions of the homeland's borders, the nation's membership boundaries, and national mission that characterize Israel mirrors those found in deeply divided societies more generally. The Israeli case poses, however, a "harder" test of the ability of alternative mechanisms to account for change because it is one where transformation is least expected. The encompassing character of Zionist/Israeli nationalist movements meant, in Abba Eban's words, that these movements were "considered to be the 'homes' of all members, creating the background and context of their worlds of ideas, [and] defining the social proprieties in which they moved."[50] The combination of the fervent adherence to different versions of national identity and the (internally and externally) contested nature of Israeli nationalist claims leads us to expect that these nationalist movements would "circle the wagons" rather than open themselves to ideological compromise. The ability of the evolutionary dynamic to explain change that takes place under such adverse conditions makes us more confident that it can be applied to other contexts as well.

Plan of the Book

The chapters that follow test the expectations of each alternative explanation of change against the empirical record of the actual transformations in Israeli nationalisms between 1925 and 2005. Part 1 focuses on the changes in the vision of the appropriate homeland articulated by each movement. Chapters 1–3 show that (with the partial exception of the Labor Zionist movement's acceptance of the 1949 armistice borders) the character of the transformation of the area Israeli nationalists considered the homeland does not correspond to the expectations that follow from theories of rational adaptation to exogenous shocks (including Israel's wars, superpower diktat, the Holocaust, or the establishment of the state). Nor does it fit the expectations that follow from theories of elite imposition. Rather, the changes in the borders of the appropriate homeland articulated by the Zionist movements were the product of an evolutionary dynamic in which rhetorical adjustments to the map image of the homeland, initially intended to solve mundane political problems, were institutionalized as the new ideological orthodoxy.

Part 2 turns our attention to the transformations of two additional dimensions of Israeli nationalism. Mirroring the explication of change in part 1, chapter 4 also tests the ability of alternative explanations to account for the empirical benchmarks of change. This time, however, the focus is placed on transformations in the Zionist notions of national mission. This chapter shows that the Revisionist Zionist movement replaced its understanding of a religiously neutral state (where religion was considered a matter of individual preference) with an endorsement of religion as shaping the public character of the Jewish state. Among Labor Zionists, a commitment to saving the Jews in exile from assimilation and an acceptance of a significant and prominent role for religion in the public realm replaced the goal of "normalizing" the Jews through the eradication of the Diaspora and the creation of a new secular Jewish society. Labor Zionists also, importantly, abandoned the goal of a socialist society that once animated them so strongly. The nationalist mission even changed among the Religious Zionists. Whereas they once considered the state of Israel to be God's "pedestal on earth" and the "Dawn of the Redemption," today the imperative to entrench Israeli control in the land of Israel trumps the value of the state of Israel. While the evolutionary dynamic explains most of these changes in the definition of the national mission, elite imposition accounted for the transformation in the Religious Zionists' conceptualization of their national mission.

Chapter 5 turns our attention to the question of membership in the nation. All three of the movements examined initially articulated an ethnic definition of membership that included all Jews around the world and excluded Palestinian Arabs. The Labor movement, however, came to accept American Jews as partners meant to help the Zionist project from the outside rather than as actual members of the national community. The continuous exclusion of resident (and later citizen) Palestinian Arabs from the national community despite the formal granting of citizenship, the ideological opening provided by the liberalism of the Revisionists and the socialism of the Labor movement, the intense international pressure for integration, and clear political incentives for doing so provide an additional check on the evolutionary dynamic. This examination of the "dog that didn't bark" shows that tactical variations that are not part of an alliance between rival nationalist movements are less likely to be subject to increasing returns, and therefore less likely to become institutionalized as the new ideological status quo.

Despite the attention paid to the "origin of species," evolution describes a process rather than an origin or an ending point. In this vein chapter 6 analyzes some of the ongoing, but not completed, transformations in Israeli nationalism, including the apparent acceptance within Revisionist Zionism of the principle of partition of the land between the Jordan River and the sea, the desacralization of the state within Religious Zionism, and Religious Zionists' related reexamination of their relationship with secular Israelis.

The conclusion extends the lessons of the evolutionary dynamic in three ways. First, it points out that the usefulness of the evolutionary dynamic in accounting for change in the meaning of nationalism in the Israeli case suggests that it may satisfactorily resolve the debate over the frequency of change in nationalist ideologies more broadly. Second, it demonstrates the ability of the evolutionary dynamic to shed light on other cases by briefly discussing some of the significant changes in Palestinian and Turkish nationalisms. Finally, the conclusion lays out the implications of the evolutionary dynamic for how democracies might confront religious fundamentalism and for conflict resolution.

I

WHERE IS THE LAND OF ISRAEL?

1

Labor Zionist Mapping of the Homeland

All nationalisms delineate the appropriate territorial borders of the homeland. While abstract nations are not necessarily tied to any *particular* geographical location, the crux of nationalist ideology is the belief that a nation ought to be in control of its own destiny. Such authority usually entails a demand for a measure of control over some territory. Contrary to nationalist claims, however, the extent of the homeland is not self-evident. Nationalists are often consumed with drawing maps precisely because the inclusion or exclusion of particular tracts in the homeland is contested. Thus the images of the appropriate homeland that nationalists produce are important because, as Benedict Anderson suggested, they are attempts to order reality. Maps are not "something which already [exist] objectively 'there.'" They anticipate "social spatial reality, not vice versa. In other words, a map [is] a model for, rather than a model of, what it purport[s] to represent....It [becomes] a real instrument to concretize projections on the earth's surface." The map images of the homeland created by nationalist movements generate an "instantly recognizable, everywhere visible" logo that penetrates the popular imagination and forms a powerful emblem for the nationalist movement.[1] These map images, both explicit and banal, identify the extent of the homeland as envisioned by nationalist movements at particular historical junctures. Tracing their development over time allows us to track, therefore, the nationalist movement's changing vision of the homeland.

The exploration of the changes in the ways in which Zionisms defined the homeland begins with the Labor Zionist movement. In its contemporary

[handwritten margin notes: "Maps = ordering reality" and "always rooted in historical context"]

form, this movement is associated with policies of territorial compromise and an acceptance of partition. The Labor movement was party to the Oslo Accords in 1993, (theoretically) agreed to return the Golan Heights to Syria in the context of a peace agreement, and withdrew Israeli troops from Lebanon in 2000. All of these moves reflect the movement's underlying acceptance of the 1949 armistice lines (see fig. 3) as the basis for the final and appropriate borders of the state of Israel.

This was not always the case. Originally, the Labor Zionists' conception of the appropriate extent of the homeland corresponded to the much more expansive borders outlined in the 1919 Zionist Memorandum to the Paris Peace Conference. This memorandum set the desired boundaries of the homeland as the Litani River in the north, the international border with Egypt in the south, and the "desert" in the east (see fig. 1).[2] A 1918 book by David Ben-Gurion and Yitzhak Ben-Zvi (who was later to become Israel's second president) articulated the same claim. They placed the eastern border of the Land of Israel in the "Syrian Desert" (somewhere in present-day Jordan) and declined to be more precise, because "as more desert land will be prepared for development, the eastern border of Eretz Israel [the Land of Israel] will be adjusted eastward and Eretz Israel will grow."[3] Ben-Gurion also included Transjordan as part of the Land of Israel in a 1918 essay and the Hauran (the southern region of present-day Syria) in a 1921 memorandum to the British Labour Party. He also articulated this larger vision of the Land of Israel in Mapai's founding congress in 1929.[4]

The first transformation of the Labor Zionists' map image of the homeland involved the removal of the East Bank of the Jordan River and the area between the international border and the Litani River from their conception of the appropriate territory (reflecting a shift from claiming the area in fig. 1 to claiming the lightly shaded area in fig. 2). Rather than a reaction to a new reality or to the whims of movement leaders, the empirical benchmarks of this change are more consistent with the expectations of the evolutionary dynamic.

The second transformation in the Labor Zionists' map image of the appropriate territory (from claiming the lightly shaded area in fig. 2 to claiming the lightly shaded area in fig. 3) reflected the growing acceptance of the 1949 armistice borders as the (more or less) appropriate boundaries for the nation-state. For the most part, the characteristics of this change correspond to the expectations of rational adaptation to the establishment of the state of Israel. The nearly forty-year gap between the onset of the new reality and its spread within the movement suggests, however, that even if rational adaptation triggered this transformation, its actual progression depended on the same political selection process that plays such a crucial role in the evolutionary dynamic.

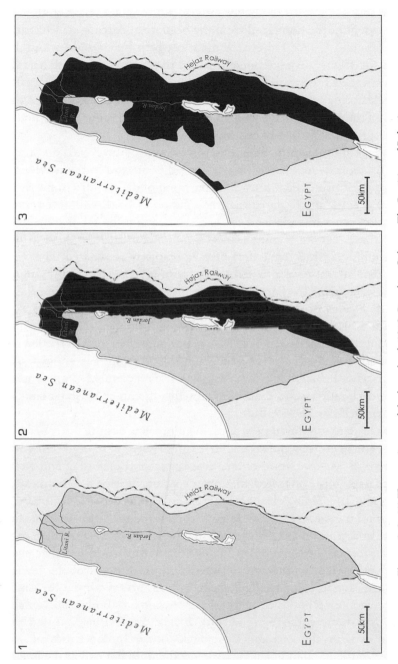

Figures 1–3. (1) The map image of the homeland, 1919. Based on Galnoor, *The Partition of Palestine* (1995). (2) The first revision to Labor Zionism's map image of the appropriate homeland. (3) The second revision to Labor Zionism's map image of the appropriate homeland.

The Elision of the East Bank and Southern Lebanon

Significant shocks buffeted the Labor movement's original vision of the appropriate extent of the homeland from the beginning. Already in 1920 and 1922, Britain and France redrew the area in which they would allow the pursuit of the Jewish national home. As part of the division of the Middle East between their spheres of influence, and in order to meet other imperial commitments, they excluded Southern Lebanon and the East Bank of the Jordan from the area originally available to the Jewish national home under the terms of the League of Nations Mandate.

The Zionist movement, including Labor Zionism, however, did not automatically adapt its map image of the desired homeland to the newly imposed borders. It protested against "the partition of the country to pieces in its north and east" and declared that the "nation of Israel will never agree to the tearing of its historic land to shreds."[5] Despite the relative inaccessibility of these regions, Zionist leaders continued to include them in the definitions of Eretz Israel (the Land of Israel) that they articulated. The textbooks in Zionist schools continued to lay claim to Transjordan by, among other things, including the East Bank of the Jordan as part of the "homeland geography" lessons of the time. As part of this effort, the Jewish Agency published a 1933 children's book that elaborated the Jewish claim to the East Bank of the Jordan River. In 1937 a newly published map of the Jewish National Fund, titled "This Is the Land That Shall Be Your Patrimony," still included parts of Lebanon and Syria as part of "Eretz Israel."[6] Not content with mere declarations, the Zionists repeatedly attempted to settle land in Transjordan well into the 1930s.[7]

Mapai's leaders supported these settlement projects despite the economic drain they entailed. They did so for the express purpose of countering the development of an "awareness of an abyss between Transjordan and western Eretz Israel." They wanted to stop the emergence of a "complex of alienation and frightening strangeness ... as if [Transjordan] was really a different state in which we have no part or patrimony."[8] Ben-Gurion, the ideological and political powerhouse within the Labor movement, also continued to articulate the claim to both banks of the Jordan. In 1934, he even declared, with regard to the appropriate territorial borders of the Jewish state, that he was in complete agreement with his archrival, the Revisionist leader Vladimir Jabotinsky, who famously claimed "both banks of the Jordan."[9] In a representative argument, Yitzhak Ben-Zvi insisted that the distinction between the East and West banks of the Jordan was artificial. The border of the Land of Israel, he contended, "does not end at the line at which the Jordan passes, or [at] the Rafiah-Han Yunis line, neither was it ended by the Hula [marsh] when E[retz] I[srael] was divided between France and England. Even today such a Chinese Wall does not exist. It exists only in the sick Jewish psychology. For the Arabs there is no difference between this part of E[retz] I[srael] and between the second part, and so neither is there any in the healthy Jewish brain."[10]

Even those who opposed immediate settlement in Transjordan on practical grounds spoke of the East Bank as appropriately part of their future nation-state. Yitzhak Vilkansky affirmed that "not a single one of us sees the land of Transjordan as outside the borders of Eretz Israel. This land is as much our homeland as the west of the country. And if we are not crying in a great voice 'on both sides of the Jordan' [the slogan of the opposing Revisionist Zionist movement (see chapter 3)]—the desire to establish hold of it is [still] sealed in our hearts."[11]

In 1937, Great Britain dispatched a Royal Commission led by Lord Robert Peel to investigate the causes of the 1936 Arab revolt in Palestine. The Peel Commission ultimately recommended the partition of the British Mandate for Palestine into two states. The Jewish state was to cover most of the coastal plain and the Galilee, while the rest was to become an Arab state, with Jerusalem and a corridor leading from it to Jaffa remaining under British control. While the Labor movement eventually endorsed the principle of partition, the significant segment within it that rejected the Peel partition plan did so, in part, because of the exclusion of Transjordan from the proposed Jewish state. Rachel Yanait, when asked if she did not give up on Transjordan, replied: "Certainly not! We will never give up on Transjordan, just as we never gave up on Eretz Israel during all the years of our exile." She also took the opportunity to reiterate her belief that Eretz Israel extended "much further north" than the current border.[12]

The persistence of the East Bank of the Jordan River as part of the map image of the appropriate nation-state is best illustrated, however, by the fact that those who *accepted* the principle of partition still claimed it as part of the homeland. The most significant of these was Ben-Gurion, whose tactical acceptance of partition was nestled in a theory of stages and a well-noted preference for proceeding "one acre" at a time.[13] He emphasized that the tactical acceptance of partition "does not obligate us to sign that we are giving up on Transjordan, that is not how these things are done, no one is demanding that anyone abandon a vision. And we will receive a state in the borders that will be determined now, but *the borders of the aspiration* of Zionism—that is a matter for the Jewish nation, these will not be reduced by any outside force."[14] Ben-Gurion contended that if the choice was "between a Jewish state in all of Western Eretz Israel in return for our abandoning our historic right to all of Eretz Israel—I would reject the state."[15]

Invoking the Land of Israel *"in its entirety*, with Transjordan," Ben-Gurion insisted on the distinction "between *Eretz Israel* and the Jewish state in

Eretz Israel.... *Eretz Israel* extends between the Red Sea in the south and the Lebanon and the Hermon in the north, and between the Mediterranean Sea in the west and the desert or Syria in the east. And I believe today *no less* than I believed thirty or thirty-five years ago, *that this country will be ours.*"[16] He argued: "Not only am I not willing to give up on western E[retz] I[srael]...I am not giving up on Transjordan, not just that which is Abdullah's, but also that which is under the French Mandate. I am not even giving up on the north of E[retz] I[srael] that is beyond the border of the Mandate—the area which is now part of Lebanon, south of the Litani River, and I believe with perfect faith that we will settle in all these places sooner or later."[17]

By the late 1930s, there was some evidence that the claim to the land east of the Jordan River was weakening within the movement. Some came to see the claim for Transjordan as irrelevant (unlike the claim to Jerusalem and the rest of the land west of the Jordan) or even dangerous.[18] Moshe Shertok (Sharett), a relatively dovish member of Mapai's leadership, explicitly included Arabs from Transjordan in his calculation of the number of "labor infiltrators," that is, *non-Palestinian* Arab labor, in his testimony to the Peel Commission. Indeed, another Labor leader, Yitzhak Tabenkin, criticized the testimony for not placing a clear enough emphasis on the demand for Transjordan.[19] Also suggesting that its view of the land east of the Jordan was changing, Mapai's 1938–39 intelligence assessments labeled events in Palestine as "internal" but categorized events in Transjordan as taking place "outside" the country.[20]

By the early 1940s, this changed vision of the appropriate extent of the homeland was increasingly visible. The timing is important because it shows that the transformation was underway before Labor Zionist leaders learned of the full extent of the Holocaust.[21] As a result, neither elite imposition in the wake of the Holocaust nor rational adaptation to the post-Holocaust reality can account for the introduction of the version of the homeland that excluded the East Bank.

One of the first public signals of the elision of the East Bank and Southern Lebanon from the area of the appropriate homeland was a 1941 memorandum by Ben-Gurion on Zionist policy. Prepared for an American audience, this memorandum not only equated "Palestine" and "western Palestine" but also argued that the rejection of partition meant a demand for the "western Land of Israel" rather than a claim to the East Bank.[22] Similarly reflecting the position that Transjordan was a distinct entity, Pinchas Lavon argued: "Already in 1922 the partition of Israel to a half-independent state, which is purely Arab [i.e., Transjordan], and to a Mandate State in the western part of the country was fulfilled. This possibility also exists today: *to divide Eretz Israel in two*, into an Arab part that will be joined to Transjordan and into a Mandatory part in which there will be certain rights for the Jews."[23]

This recasting of the meaning of partition, from referring to the split between Transjordan and Palestine to indicating a division *within* Palestine, also characterized the more dovish wing of the movement. In his reply to King Abdullah's 1945 inquiry about Zionist intentions, Sharett defined "partition" as the annexation of the non-Jewish part of Palestine to Transjordan. Sharett also listed Transjordan as a country outside of the Land of Israel in a letter to the British government protesting the findings of the Anglo-American Commission in 1946.[24] By the mid-1940s, the leaders of the Labor movement saw what had been the western half of the homeland as a single political entity, complete in its own right. In this spirit, Ben-Gurion even presented a plan for the establishment of two independent states that explicitly gave up on the claim to Transjordan.[25]

The reformulation of the appropriate map image also included abandoning the claim to the Litani River. In 1943, Ben-Gurion argued that the Zionist movement should base their relationship with Lebanon, in part, on the fact that Lebanon controlled Israel's water sources—indicating some acceptance of the exclusion of the Litani from the nation-state. By 1948, Ben-Gurion reported to the Provisional Government (even if not completely sincerely) that despite having the ability to do so, Israel did not want to conquer Lebanon. To be sure, Israeli troops did take control of the Litani River during the war. However, not only was this conquest never authorized by Israel's political leadership, but even the military rationale behind the operation was based on an awareness that any captured territory would be used as a bargaining chip in the peace talks with Lebanon—a logic that would not be applied to areas considered appropriately part of the homeland. By 1949, Mapai claimed that the *natural border* between Israel and Lebanon and Syria corresponded to the (clearly arbitrary!) borders between the British Mandate and these neighboring states.[26]

Labor Zionist propaganda from the period illustrates the new map image of the "Land of Israel." A 1944 May Day poster by the Labor-dominated Histadrut (the General Federation of Hebrew Workers in the Land of Israel) depicted the "Land of Israel" ripping through the "White Paper" that limited Jewish immigration to Palestine (fig. 4). Two elements of this poster are particularly significant. First, the contours of the "Land of Israel" in the 1944 poster do not match those of the map image articulated by Labor Zionism in 1919 (compare figs. 1 and 4). Specifically, the 1944 poster excludes most of the area east of the Jordan River and the area of Southern Lebanon up to the Litani River that Labor Zionists once claimed. Second, by 1944, the leadership of the Labor movement was clearly comfortable enough with the new image to publicize it. By 1949, this map image of the homeland graced the poster announcing the annual conference of the Mapai Youth (fig. 5). This poster, whose caption reads "The Young Generation in

Figure 4. Histadrut May Day poster showing the "Land of Israel" splitting the "White Paper," 1944. Courtesy of the Pinhas Lavon Institute for Labour Movement Research.

Israel: Destiny and Roles" calls for the young generation to put down their roots in the country—a country whose eastern border is clearly set along the Jordan River. The presentation of this map image to the Mapai Youth movement as the goal to which they ought to aspire suggests that, by this time, it was accepted within the Labor movement as the appropriate extent of the homeland.

Other indicators point to the same conclusion. By the time the United Nations Special Commission on Palestine (UNSCOP) began its deliberations over what to do with Palestine in 1947, the Labor movement did not even list the inclusion of the East Bank as part of the Jewish state in a discussion of the best possible scenarios that could have emerged from Lake Success.[27] Moshe Sharett started his testimony before UNSCOP by recounting that the area allocated to the Jews was already reduced in 1922. He clarified, however, that, "when we speak of Eretz Israel in a political discussion, we mean the country that lies between the Mediterranean Sea and the Jordan, and which is bound within the existing political borders from north and south."[28] In November 1947 the United Nations General Assembly

Figure 5. Poster announcing the annual conference of the Mapai Youth, 1949. The caption reads "The Young Generation in Israel: Destiny and Roles." Courtesy of the Moshe Sharett Israel Labor Party Archives (Berl Katznelson Foundation).

approved the majority UNSCOP proposal to partition Palestine. Unlike in 1937, whatever mixed feelings existed within the Labor Zionist movement about this partition plan stemmed from the exclusion of the Galilee and Jerusalem from the area of the proposed Jewish state, not from the exclusion of Transjordan. Speaking only days after the announcement that a Jewish state would be created, Ben-Gurion noted that they did not get everything they wanted, but did not include Transjordan in the list of the areas of the homeland that were left out. In fact, he was so enthusiastic about the UN's decision to include the Negev within the Jewish state that he suggested that the common biblical delineation of the extent of the Land of Israel "should be revised: not 'from Dan to Beersheva' but 'from Dan to Eilat.'"[29]

The map image of the homeland reflected in the discussions among Mapai leaders in the period between the UNSCOP decision and the establishment of the state in May 1948 reinforces the notion that they no longer considered the East Bank appropriately part of the Land of Israel. They consistently situated Transjordan outside "the country" and perceived the Jordanian Legion as invading the Land of Israel from the "outside."[30]

Similarly, Ben-Gurion classified the area under the British Mandate in 1947 as "Eretz Israel" and spoke of the British leaving "all of the country," despite the fact that they remained in Transjordan.[31] Ben-Gurion even divided "Eretz Israel" into four regions (the Center, the Galilee, the Negev, and Jerusalem), none of which included the darkly shaded areas in figure 2.[32] Golda Meirson (Meir) spoke of the "Arabs of Eretz Israel," referring to those Arabs in the land of Israel *not* under King Abdullah's rule.[33] A similar distinction characterized Ben-Gurion's division of the Arabs west of the Jordan River (who had no state or army) and those east of the river (who did), in terms of "the Arabs of Eretz Israel, [and]...the armies of the Arab states."[34] Evidently, the leaders of the Labor movement no longer considered the population of Transjordan to be living in the Land of Israel. By 1949, Ben-Gurion used the legitimacy of the self-determination of the Arabs in Transjordan to justify the Jews' right to a state of their own.[35] When the claim to Transjordan was made, as it still occasionally was, it tended to be raised as a purely historical reference and in the context of an argument that "we already compromised."[36]

Even the evidence for the *nonacceptance* within Mapai of the 1949 armistice borders demonstrates that this nationalist movement no longer considered Transjordan part of the Land of Israel. Expressions that Israel "missed an opportunity" to expand its borders during the war referred to its failure to conquer the West Bank and Jerusalem, not Jordan.[37] Even Ben-Gurion, whose pragmatism never reflected a lack of territorial ambition, took this stance toward Transjordan. Judging by the orders he gave to Israel's nascent military, and his proposals to the government, his vision of the desired borders included all of Palestine, but excluded Transjordan.[38] In fact, in the context of the negotiations over the armistice agreement with Jordan, Ben-Gurion framed the debate as being between "the entire Eretz Israel" (thus excluding the East Bank) and "a Jewish state in part of Eretz Israel."[39]

Reinforcing the notion that the leaders of the Labor Zionist movement no longer claimed Transjordan, Sharett's report about Arab refugees from "Eretz Israel" listed Transjordan as one of the countries *outside* the Land of Israel to which a portion of the refugees went, while "the majority...remained within the area of Eretz Israel."[40] In internal reports to Mapai's leadership, Sharett remarked that the proportion of the land under Israeli control had increased through the various partition plans. He noted that UNSCOP proposed a division of 62 percent to Israel and 38 percent to the Arab state, that the UN decision on November 29, 1947, divided the land 55 percent and 45 percent, and that, after the war, Israel held approximately 79 percent.[41] These calculations, importantly, assume that 100 percent would not include Transjordan or Southern Lebanon up to the Litani River. Nor do Transjordan and Southern Lebanon make the grade as enemy-held territory in accounts of the progress of the war.[42] Ben-Gurion and Sharett even began speaking of the Jordan River as "the most natural border." In fact, this was Mapai's official position at the Lausanne talks at the end of the war.[43] Yigal Allon, despite being one of the most hawkish proponents of changing the armistice borders, also contended that "a stronger border than *the line of the Jordan to the length of the state* cannot be described."[44] In terms of military strength, this statement is difficult to support. The Jordan River, after all, runs along the valley floor between two mountain ridges. From a tactical military perspective, the high ground on these ridges is surely preferable to the valley.

[margin note: Mapai discuss River Jordan as the border]

After the war, Mapai's leadership had reservations about the negotiations with Jordan because they implicitly recognized Jordan's annexation of the West Bank, and not, as was the case for Menachem Begin and the Revisionist movement, because they recognized Jordan itself.[45] Even the perception of the potential for territorial expansion created by King Abdullah's assassination in 1951 was limited to the area west of the Jordan. While Ben-Gurion asked about the readiness of the Israeli army to take advantage of the situation, his questions were limited to an inquiry into its ability to capture the territory up to the Jordan.[46] Similarly, during the negotiations with the French leading up to the 1956 Suez War, Ben-Gurion proposed that the area east of the Jordan River should be given to Iraq, while the area west of the river should become an autonomous province in Israel.[47]

Even the territorial maximalists within the Labor Zionist movement articulated a map image of the Land of Israel that ended at the Jordan. The Movement for the Whole Land of Israel, which was established after the 1967 war by prominent members of the Labor movement, provides a striking example. Both the movement's name and its overt declaration that the "whole of Eretz Israel is now in the hands of the Jewish people" imply that the "whole land of Israel" excludes the East Bank of the Jordan and the Litani River, since these areas were clearly not "in the hands of the Jewish people."[48] In this vein, the nationalist poet Natan Alterman explicitly equated the borders of the Land of Israel with the extent of the post-1967 state of Israel:

The issue with this victory [in 1967] is not just that it returned to the Jews the ancient and most sublime holies of the nation, those carved in its memory and in the depths of its history more than anything. *The issue with this victory is that it erased the difference between the state of Israel and the Land of Israel. This is the first time since the destruction of the second Temple that Eretz Israel is in our hands. The state and the country are henceforth a single entity.*[49]

Less poetically, but as significantly, the view that the entire land of Israel ended at the Jordan was also articulated by members of Ahdut Haavoda (Labor Unity, the hawkish wing of the Labor movement) in their opposition to proposals of territorial compromise after 1967. For example, Benny Marshek objected to the terminology "policy in the territories," arguing: "In my eyes it is the policy in Eretz Israel. I don't have to add the word 'entire.'"[50] More generally, Ahdut Haavoda's denial of the existence of a Palestinian nation assumed the legitimate existence of a Jordanian nation, undermining the claim to Transjordan.[51]

As in the late 1940s, when Labor movement leaders made the occasional reference to the East Bank of the Jordan, they used it as a way to enable territorial compromise rather than as an actual claim to Jordan as appropriately part of the Land of Israel.[52] As Amos Yadlin put it, "We never ceded our rights over Eretz Israel and we always ceded the actualization of this right in all its scope."[53] Most prominently, Yigal Allon and Abba Eban used the claim to both banks of the Jordan to argue that both banks contained a single Palestinian nation, and to claim that the appropriate extent of *the Palestinian state* included Jordan and most of the West Bank.[54] Rather than establish the claim to the East Bank, such declarations demonstrated an acceptance of its exclusion from the land appropriately part of the nation-state.

Evolution at Work: Explaining the Elision of the East Bank of the Jordan and Southern Lebanon

The timing, direction, and process of this transformation in the vision of the appropriate homeland match the expectations of the evolutionary dynamic better than the predictions of either elite imposition or rational adaptation to an exogenous shock. This shift was an unintended by-product of Labor Zionism's grand political project at the time. In the early 1940s, the Labor Zionist movement was already at the head of the nationalist alliance that was the Zionist movement. The leaders of the Labor movement foresaw that the turbulence of World War II would reshape the world and redraw its borders. As a result, they sought to put themselves in a position from which they could take advantage of this decisive historical moment (for both themselves and their nationalist cause). They took two related steps to do so. First, they sought to cement their status at the helm of the Zionist movement. This required deepening their alliance with the Religious Zionists, who were wavering between throwing in their lot with the Labor movement or the Revisionists; ensuring the continued backing of the middle-class General Zionists; and soliciting the support of American Jews, including the majority non-Zionists among them.

Second, they sought to have all these different groups singing the same tune. They wanted to make sure that they could present a united Jewish front vis-à-vis the outside world. Orchestrating this was not easy. In addition to all of their other differences, some of the potential members of this grand nationalist alliance articulated different answers to "Where is the homeland?" (See chapter 2 for a discussion of the Religious Zionist view of the homeland.) Bridging these radically different views of the homeland posed a serious political dilemma. On the one hand, if Mapai openly declared its support for partition it risked losing the support of the Religious Zionists and alienating the territorial maximalists within its own ranks. The divisive debate over the 1937 partition plan was also still fresh in the minds of Mapai members. Their endorsement of the principle of partition in 1937 almost led to a schism in the movement and endangered Mapai's dominance. They were not going to repeat this again. Indeed, this was a main reason behind Ben-Gurion's unwillingness to reiterate openly his support of partition in the early 1940s.[55] On the other hand, if they insisted on a state in the entire area they believed was appropriately theirs, they risked alienating American Jewry and the world powers on which they knew the achievement of statehood depended.

The attempt to navigate between these pressures led to the development of a slogan that advocated the establishment of a Jewish state but pointedly avoided demarcating its borders. Known as the Biltmore Programme, for the New York hotel in which it was adopted in 1942, the territorially ambiguous formula "A Jewish Commonwealth in the Land of Israel" was vague enough to be accepted by the other groups Mapai was attempting to co-opt. The formula succeeded, in part, because it was presented as the lowest common denominator on which they could all agree. Contending that the formula was a purely tactical maneuver, Ben-Gurion explained to the Zionist Executive:

> This decision is not a formulation of the end-goal. We did not intend to formulate the end-goal, nor do we think that this is within our authority or that there is a need for this now. Neither is it a formulation of an ideological program, but simply a formulation of the direction of our policy in this period: what we shall say to the world...what we will say to the Arabs, what we will say to the Jewish nation, those that are as yet outside the Zionist movement and those that are in it.[56]

Again, in a Histadrut Council meeting in March 1944, Ben-Gurion reiterated his stance on the Biltmore Programme:

> [It is] not a formulation of a final goal, and not a formulation of Zionist ideology. There is no need to formulate a final goal, neither...is there the ability to do so....The Zionist movement was unable to find the common language for the foundation of a *final* goal."[57]

Not everyone, however, went along with this tactic. Mapai's "Faction B," led by Yitzhak Tabenkin, staked out a truth-telling position. They continued to claim the entire Land of Israel, including the East Bank of the Jordan. Together with Mapam (a party to Mapai's left), they derided the Biltmore Programme as "missing...an unrelenting demand for the entire land of Israel, unpartitioned, entirely open to immigration and settlement, to concentration of the Jewish people, and to full political independence."[58] The consensus builders could not easily dismiss this criticism because it came from leaders with impeccable Labor Zionist credentials. These leading lights accused Mapai's leadership of betraying their beliefs and endangering their ultimate goals by deviating from the true path of Zionism.

In the process of defending their position, Mapai's leaders shifted the terms with which they claimed the land west of the Jordan River. Instead of arguing that the new claim reflected the best tactical position given what was possible, they recast the new delineation of the homeland as the just, right, and natural one. Responding to the attacks on the territorial formula of the Biltmore Programme, Ben-Gurion, in addition to presenting it as a temporary tactical maneuver, added the justification that, in any case, it was nothing new. The Biltmore Programme was, he argued, merely a restatement of what had always been the Zionist aim—a Jewish state, whatever its character.[59] In later years, he would engage in more overt historical revisionism, even deleting the claim to the East Bank (which he made in a famous letter to his son dated October 5, 1937) from a 1968 edited collection of his letters.[60] In order to minimize the change that had taken place, Ben-Gurion also dismissed the notion that the historic or religious borders were relevant. When Menachem Ussishkin pressed him on this issue, Ben-Gurion (contradicting his claims from the 1920s) replied that the phrase "the historic borders" did not refer to a particular map, and that now, in the midst of World War II, their demand was for all of western Eretz Israel.[61] In a similar revision of earlier claims, by September 1948, Sharett would argue that the demand articulated in the Biltmore Programme for "the entire Western Land of Israel as a Jewish state" was a just claim of what they deserved, although they would settle for less.[62] Sharett's formulation is particularly revealing because the Biltmore Programme itself called for a state in a "land of Israel" unmodified by any adjectives, not in the "western land of Israel." The equation of the map images delineated by these two geographically distinct terms and the depiction of the latter as the appropriate area for the nation-state both promoted and masked the change in the area the Labor Zionists considered appropriately theirs.

Two concurrent processes reinforced the transformation of the new map image from a tactical rhetorical adjustment to the new ideological orthodoxy. Most importantly, the transformation worked. The short-term goals in whose name the new variant was promoted—cementing Mapai's position at the helm of the Zionist movement and forging a more united Jewish front vis-à-vis the outside world—were achieved. As a result, it became increasingly costly to deviate from the territorial ambiguity involved in the Biltmore Programme, because doing so might have jeopardized this bloc and the gains associated with it. (As part of this grand project the Labor movement also had to yield on other foundational questions. The consequences of these concessions are discussed in chapters 4 and 5.)

Of course, not everyone agreed that this trade-off was worthwhile. The ideological truth tellers within the Labor movement opposed the rhetorical modulations it required precisely because they feared the slippery slope to ideological change. Organized in Faction B, the truth tellers lost the intramovement political battle. Their eventual decision to form a separate party in 1944, Hatneuah Le'Ahdut Haavoda (the Movement for Labor Unity), left no organized faction within Mapai that could effectively contest the articulation of the new map image. The political benefits of adhering to this new formulation meant that the original orthodoxy was articulated less and less often. As a result, over a relatively short period, Mapai changed the way it delimited the desired borders of the homeland, even though this was not necessarily the original intention behind the formulation of the Biltmore Programme.

While both rational adaptation and elite imposition appear to offer plausible explanations of this shift, a closer examination reveals that they cannot account for the timing, direction, and process of change. According to the logic of rational adaptation, Mapai's leaders would have recognized that their original map image of the homeland no longer made sense. In response, they would have consciously adapted their vision of the desired homeland to the new realm of the possible at that point. Objectively, however, this should have happened in the 1920s, when the imperial powers actually split the East Bank and Southern Lebanon from Palestine, and not in the early 1940s. Rational adaptation cannot account for this fifteen- or twenty-year lag. Moreover, because rational adaptation expects everyone subjected to the new environment to experience pressure to change, its plausibility is also undermined by the even longer gaps that exist between the imperial redrawing of borders and the transformation in the vision of the homeland articulated by the other nationalist movements (see chapters 2 and 3).

Certainly, there is some indirect evidence that some rational adaptation may have been taking place. Labor leaders, including Ben-Gurion, lamented at the time that they sometimes heard the notion that Transjordan was not part of Eretz Israel "even among Zionists."[63] Chaim Arlozorov also contended that they themselves unwittingly contributed to the "psychosis of the separation of Transjordan." He rationalized the apparently imprudent investment in Transjordan with the logic that "ties must be tied, relations established, so that the psychological wall between the east of the Jordan and its west that has rooted even among us to the point that we see Transjordan as one sees a second state—as a distinct political unit whose border may not be crossed—must be destroyed."[64]

This diagnosis suggests that at least some within the Labor movement adapted to the 1922 partition by excluding Transjordan from their map image of the desired state. Despite the explicit intention of the majority of Mapai's leaders to maintain the vision of the eastern and western banks of the Jordan as a single unit, some Labor Zionist leaders nonetheless combined the claim to the East Bank of the Jordan with a willingness to sacrifice it in the pursuit of other goals. While Arlozorov affirmed that they "never came to terms with the administrative division between the parts...of the Mandate," he admitted that it was not important enough to wage "actual political war" over. He emphasized that they had to change their policy and invest in Transjordan mainly as a way of fortifying their position in the "western part of the country." They saw settlement on the East Bank as a way of improving security and reducing land prices in the *western* Land of Israel, slowing down the flow of Arab immigrants from Transjordan, and providing a land reserve to resettle Arabs "cleared" by Zionist settlement.[65]

The interpretation of the apparently ambivalent stance toward the eastern part of the homeland as evidence of rational adaptation overlooks, however, the fact that it was anchored in a metahistorical analysis that assumed that the division between Palestine and Transjordan was artificial and necessarily temporary. Labor Zionist leaders believed that since Palestine needed a market for its goods and Transjordan needed an outlet to the sea, the requisite economic cooperation between these areas would inevitably lead to political unity.[66] The ambivalence toward the inclusion of Transjordan in the homeland also reflected the pragmatic character of the Labor Zionist leadership and their belief that the Zionist movement ought first to ensure its status in the western part of the land. This order of priorities was reinforced by a lack of resources, the desire to avoid a confrontation with the British, and the assumption that Transjordan's poverty meant that its inhabitants were incapable of developing the area on their own and that, as a result, the Zionists would be able to incorporate it later.[67] There is no doubt that this order of priorities set the stage for the subsequent elision of the East Bank by making it an area over which they could negotiate, and therefore, a lesser part of the homeland. At this juncture, however, even the apparently early adapters still considered the "eastern part of the country" to be just that—a part of the country, even if it was temporarily inaccessible.

Moreover, the mainstream of the movement, including its most significant leaders, continued to articulate the original vision of the homeland through the 1930s. Those who adapted their vision of the map image of the appropriate borders to fit the new reality remained a minority that was too weak to set the ideological tone for the movement as a whole. As a result, the overall pattern of articulation about the appropriate borders within and by the movement continued to reflect the original claims despite the new reality.

The emergence of the new variant of the definition of the homeland in the late 1930s and early 1940s raises the possibility that the change was a rational adaptation to the Peel partition plan. However, if the timing matches the potential impact of this historical event, the actual direction of change does not. Rational adaptation to the Peel partition plan, or even to the recognition that Palestine would ultimately be divided, would have drawn a line somewhere within "western Palestine," not at its edge. Abba Eban's claim that they saw the Biltmore Programme as only the starting point for negotiations is disingenuous. It begs the question of why the Labor Zionists set the starting point here and not in the "Syrian Desert" in 1942. Indeed, this was Ben-Gurion's explicit strategy during the discussions over the Peel partition, and there he did not hesitate to claim Transjordan.[68]

The Holocaust and the achievement of Transjordanian independence in 1946 are also sometimes cited as exogenous shocks that forced Mapai's leaders to change their ideology.[69] Those significant events reinforced the plausibility and political fortunes of the more limited claim to the "western land of Israel" at the expense of the more expansive vision of the homeland. The onset of the transformation before these events, however, means that they could not have triggered the ideological change. While the destruction of European Jewry certainly contributed to Mapai's willingness to accept the principle of partition, it does not account for the change in the maximum of what they claimed as appropriately theirs. While it may be sensible to shift one's minimum demand given the perception of the possible, by definition such pragmatism does not affect the ideal. Indeed, pragmatism can be defined only in reference to the maintenance of the ideal maximum demands.

An appeal to Mapai's pragmatism in the 1940s as an explanation of this change is problematic for other reasons as well. First, it cannot account for the actual direction of the transformation. The Labor movement continued to claim the West Bank, Gaza Strip, and Jerusalem as appropriately part of the Jewish state. It is not clear, however, that in 1947 this claim was any more practical than the claim to the East Bank and Litani River. Both were unattainable. Second, Mapai's leaders were just as pragmatic in 1937 as in 1947, but they claimed Transjordan at the earlier date and excluded it from the homeland at the later despite its clear inaccessibility in both 1937 and 1947. Finally, as the next two chapters will show, the Holocaust did not trigger changes in the definition of the extent of the appropriate borders of the state in the other movements either. The variation in the timing of change in the definitions of the homeland among all three movements undermines the appeal to any single exogenous shock as the trigger of change.

It is possible that the introduction of a map image of the homeland that excluded the East Bank of the Jordan and the Litani River was part of a concerted effort by perhaps dovish movement leaders to modify the movement's ideology. Moshe Sharett's testimony to the Peel Commission (see above) provides the strongest support for this possibility. However, the expectation that individuals would continue to consistently articulate a changed position under these circumstances was not met. Even Sharett, only a year after his testimony to the Peel Commission, argued that they could not flatly reject a proposal for the creation of a state in Palestine that would limit the proportion of Jews in it to 49 percent—a Zionist anathema—because it held open the possibility of the unification of the land east and west of the Jordan River.[70] Of course, Sharett was also an ambitious politician. He certainly could have modified the map image of the homeland to suit the incentives of the moment. However, the particular audiences to which he made his case suggest otherwise. Speaking to the Zionist leadership, it must have been politically costly for Sharett to publicly consider a limitation on Jewish immigration to Palestine, especially so because when this debate was taking place in 1938, unfettered Jewish immigration was a higher priority for Mapai than independent statehood. Conversely, we might have expected Sharett's carefully crafted testimony before the Peel Commission to claim as much as possible for the Jewish nationalist movement, if only as part of the negotiating strategy set out by Ben-Gurion. That Sharett undertook the costly position at each of these opportunities reduces our confidence that elite imposition drove the introduction of this variant.

While Mapai's leaders played an undeniable role in the tactical rhetorical adjustments they made, the way in which this adjusted version became the new ideological status quo does not match the expectations of either elite imposition or rational adaptation. If it had been a conscious and directed modification of Labor Zionist ideology, we would have expected the pattern of articulation about the appropriate borders to be more consistent than it actually was. Rather than executing the uniform replacement of one ideological formulation by another, Labor Zionist leaders continued to articulate the claim to the old map image even as the transformation to the new one was taking place. Not only did the truth tellers within the movement continue to articulate the original claims, but even the consensus builders who advocated the (tactical) articulation of the more limited territorial claims occasionally still claimed Transjordan and Southern Lebanon as appropriately part of the homeland. While this was especially true of Ben-Gurion, he was not alone in doing so.[71]

The Politics of Rational Adaptation:
The Acceptance of the 1949 Armistice Lines

Today the Labor movement not only excludes the East Bank of the Jordan from the area it claims as the homeland, but it advocates the establishment of a Palestinian state in the West Bank and Gaza Strip. The Labor Zionist image of the appropriate homeland shifted from claiming the lightly shaded area in figure 2 to claiming the lightly shaded area in figure 3. There is little other than the reality created by the 1949 armistice agreements to justify the growing legitimacy of these particular borders of the state of Israel. The establishment of the state certainly reshuffled the territorial deck. At the very least, the physical delineation of the state's borders, with its fences, minefields, and barbed wire, made the difference between "here" and "there" difficult to ignore.[72]

The assumption that the borders were more or less fixed opened the door for their institutionalization as the new ideological status quo. Supporting the logic of rational adaptation, following independence, Mapai turned its attention to the myriad problems of the new state and virtually eliminated the once all-consuming question of borders from its political agenda. In fact, Mapai's Political Committee did not hold a single meeting dealing with border issues between 1949 and 1952.[73] The shift in Mapai's priorities suggests that many within it were willing to settle for the armistice borders as those of the state. Some even argued that they already accomplished the territorial mission of the Zionist movement, and that only the Zionist mission of in-gathering the exiles remained outstanding.[74] Haim Ben-Asher, for example, went so far as to declare that, after the war of independence, "the whole of the country is now open before us."[75]

The emphasis on the institutionalization of the state (including its borders) was also consistent with Ben-Gurion's policy of statism (*mamlachtiyut*), which emphasized the state above all other considerations, even if he did not (yet) accept this implication.[76] Even some of Mapai's educational materials began to exclude the West Bank and Gaza Strip from a list of the country's regions.[77] The increasing feeling of safety and prosperity in Israel, especially after 1956, also facilitated the routinization of Israel's borders as the appropriate ones. Perhaps as a result, the map images used in Mapai propaganda in the 1950s proudly depicted the borders of the armistice agreements (see figs. 6 and 7). By 1957, Sharett could note an Israeli

Figure 6. Labor movement campaign poster, "Our power building the country," no. 7713/T-576, 1960. Courtesy of the Moshe Sharett Israel Labor Party Archives (Berl Katznelson Foundation).

Figure 7. Labor movement Independence Day poster: "The growth of the settlement," 1951. Courtesy of the Pinhas Lavon Institute for Labour Movement Research.

consensus about the "territorial wholeness of the state of Israel."[78] Reflecting on that period, Abba Eban described the routinization of these borders: "As water flows into a canal, so did Israeli life grow and develop within the [1949] armistice lines until their quaint contours were to become the familiar shape of Israel."[79]

There is even some evidence that this adaptation was spreading to the more territorially maximalist wing of the movement. One of its members recounted in 1969 that "when we introduced the unity [of the territories and Israel] to the instructors seminar [in 1959]... it was impossible to convince our son, not to mention some of the teachers, who thought that it was crazy; it was impossible to convince [them] that borders might change in the Middle East."[80]

While this "impossibility" illustrates the routinization of the 1949 borders, it also shows that it would be a mistake to press the acceptance of the 1949 borders too far during this period. After all, the leaders of the movement still attempted to counter the growing acceptance of the borders by educating their youth that the West Bank, Gaza Strip, and east Jerusalem were part of the Land of Israel. Indeed, as we saw earlier in this chapter, the fact that most Labor Zionist leaders continued to claim the "whole land of Israel" well after the establishment of the state complicates the adaptationist story. After all, they held the Jordan River, not the armistice lines, to be "the natural border." As in the case of the reaction to the exogenous shock of the new borders in 1922, even if some adapted to the exogenously imposed new definition of the possible, they were still a minority within the movement and did not dictate the map image articulated by the movement as a whole. The uneven response among its leaders and the time lag between the imposition of the new reality in 1949 and the turning point of the modification in Mapai's pattern of articulation in the mid-1970s muddle the conventional story of a pragmatic movement adapting to reality.

Even those who advocated coming to terms with the 1949 armistice lines as the borders of the state did so because they were expedient, not because these borders were appropriate. Pinchas Lavon's representative justification of the borders illustrates this rationale:

If someone tries to ask: if you give up on Shchem—what is your right to sit in Tel Aviv? I answer them with a question: who gave you the right to give up on the East Bank? If it is a sacred principle, then whoever gives up on the East Bank it is as if he gave up on the entire land. And who gave you the right to give up on Damascus which is also included in the divine promise? But in any case you give up from practical, political, and geopolitical reasons. So the matter of Shchem needs to be answered with realistic reasons, tied to a political reality, and for this reason I return to the assumption that the commandment of maintaining the Jewish character of the state of Israel supersedes any other commandment that is formulated as a commandment of the liberation of the whole land.[81]

The Labor Zionist leadership saw one overarching benefit to the 1949 borders: the existence of a Jewish majority within them. Indeed, Ben-Gurion explicitly told a meeting gathered to formulate Israel's strategy for the 1949 armistice negotiations that increasing the Jewish population of the state was much more important than the particular borders that they might negotiate.[82]

In 1967, Israel conquered the West Bank, Gaza Strip, Golan Heights, and Sinai Peninsula as part of a short war with its neighbors. For the Labor movement, the result of the 1967 war disrupted whatever process of routinization and adaptation to the 1949 borders might have been taking place. Labor Zionists now came face to face with the trade-off between maintaining control of the entire land of Israel that they aspired to and the cherished Zionist goal of a Jewish majority state. The ideal outcome for most within the movement was control of the land without integrating the Arabs there into the Israeli population. As Golda Meir put it, "Every one of us" wants "the dowry without the bride."[83] The new geographic and political context forced Labor Zionist leaders to choose between their adherence to a desire for a democratic but largely uninational state, and the map image of the appropriate borders that many of them continued to believe in. In terms of the foundational questions nationalists answer, they faced a choice between their definition of membership and mission and their vision of the homeland.

The 1968 formation of the Israel Labor Party (ILP) delayed the resolution of this dilemma. This consolidation of the various factions of the Labor movement reunited Mapai with the two factions that had splintered off it: Ahdut Haavoda, which as we saw above, split in 1944, and Rafi, which split in 1965. The main goal of this unification was to form a bloc capable of countering the united forces of the Liberal and Revisionist movements on the (economic) right side of the political spectrum. The formation of the ILP, however, involved uniting movements with different territorial agendas. With some notable exceptions (such as Ben-Gurion, who was now heading Rafi, and Yigal Allon and Pinchas Lavon of Ahdut Haavoda) Mapai members were generally grudgingly willing to cede the territories in return for peace with the Arab states, while Ahdut Haavoda and Rafi still adhered to the vision of the appropriate borders as encompassing the "whole land of Israel."

The institutional reorganization that brought these different views into the same organization meant that those who accepted the 1949 armistice lines as the appropriate border could not set the ideological tone for the movement. Indeed, no one could.[84] Until the mid-1970s, the Labor Party's position reflected the lowest common denominator of a theoretical willingness to make some unspecified territorial concessions, but only in the context of (seemingly out of reach) peace agreements. According to this formula, the eventual borders would be "defensible, recognized, and agreed-upon." Their position was anchored in the "Oral Torah," which called for establishing the Jordan River as Israel's eastern security border (not necessarily the border of the state's sovereignty), Israeli control of the Golan Heights and the Gaza Strip, and a territorial link between the Straits of Tiran and Israel.[85]

Only in the mid-1970s did the Labor movement begin to explicitly articulate an acceptance of partition. By then, the territorial maximalists in the movement grew dissatisfied with the party's unwillingness to annex the territories and its continued (tactical) endorsement of some partition as the ultimately desirable outcome. As a result, they formed the Movement for the Whole Land of Israel (see above). Many of them ultimately left the Labor Party to join forces with the territorially hawkish Likud after 1973. Once the territorial maximalists left the movement, those who had adapted to the post-1949 reality could decisively set the movement's agenda. The turning point in the Labor movement's view of the appropriate extent of the homeland took place only once few were left within it to resist the institutionalization of the once-tactical modulations as the new status quo. Thus by 1977 the debate in the Preparatory Committee for the ILP convention centered on how to phrase their willingness to agree to partition, and not on whether or not they should agree to it at all.[86]

The need to defend this position in the post-1967 context reinforced the institutionalization of the new map image as the ideological status quo. Advocates within the Labor movement of the new vision of the appropriate borders increasingly found themselves on the defensive, especially after the rise of the Likud and the ideological momentum of Gush Emunim (Bloc of the Faithful), who vocally claimed the "entire Land of Israel" up to the Jordan. As a result, what had been a grudging acceptance of the 1949 armistice borders was transformed into a marker of devout Zionism. Deviation from these borders was increasingly portrayed as a betrayal of fundamental nationalist principles. There were four basic variants of this argument. Deviation from the 1949 borders was seen as (1) undermining the ability of the state—the pinnacle of the Zionist enterprise—to survive by making peace with its neighbors impossible; (2) emptying the "Jewish" part of the Jewish state of its content by either reducing Jews to a minority or weakening Jewish control of the state (this was the reason for labeling those who wanted to annex the territories as advocates of a binational state); (3) reversing the Labor Zionist social mission of upending the traditional social pyramid of the Jews; or (4) diverting scarce resources needed to absorb

Jewish immigration.[87] As the terms the Labor movement used to defend its positions changed, its leaders increasingly portrayed the 1949 borders as appropriate, not just expedient.

The transition from tactical to principled arguments was also marked by the addition of claims that Israel's historic right to the territories was outweighed by the moral *injustice* that would be caused by Israel's rule over the territories and their population. In an argument that would become commonplace within the movement, Yigal Allon, comparing the potential of Israel's continued rule over the West Bank and the Gaza Strip without giving political and civic rights to their inhabitants to South Africa, contended that continuing in this vein was patently immoral:

> The choice is simple and cruel, at least for me. If we fulfill the commandment of the whole land of Israel, and I would be happy if we could fulfill this commandment, and would grant the Arab population full civic rights, and I cannot imagine the annexation of populated territories under conditions other than with the granting of full civic rights, the state of Israel would automatically become a binational state with a bad balance of forces which would increasingly become worse....If, on the other hand, we fulfill the commandment of the whole land of Israel—and we deny civic rights to the Arabs of Israel, we shall cease to be a democratic state. I want the state of Israel to be both Jewish and democratic.[88]

Shimon Peres even claimed that because the territories were heavily populated by Arabs, they (meaning the territories) "were not really Israeli."[89] In 1984, the platform of the Labor-led Alignment even stated that the heavily populated Palestinian areas in the West Bank "*are not meant* to be under Israeli sovereignty."[90] By 1992, the notion that annexing the territories was fundamentally anti-Zionist starred in Labor's election campaign. They overtly presented investment in the territories as undermining the Zionist task par excellence of "ingathering the exiles." They portrayed the choice as being "between absorbing a million immigrants from Russia or a million Gazans."[91] The 1993 Oslo Accords, which were widely understood as leading to a Palestinian state in the West Bank and Gaza Strip, were enabled by this halting and inconsistent process of change. The acceptance of the 1949 armistice lines (more or less) as the appropriate borders means that today few Labor leaders claim that Israel ought to control the West Bank and Gaza Strip.[92]

• • •

This nationalist movement changed its answer to the foundational question "Where is the homeland?" twice over the last century. The sustained beginnings of the first shift, the elision of the East Bank of the Jordan from the Labor Zionists' image of the appropriate homeland, took place in the late 1930s. By 1946, this transformation was largely completed. Taken together, the timing, direction, and process of the elision of the East Bank of the Jordan and Southern Lebanon from the area of the homeland correspond more closely to the expectations of the evolutionary dynamic than to either elite imposition or rational adaptation. The onset of the second change, the acceptance of the 1949 borders (more or less) as appropriate, however, is best explained in terms of a rational adaptation to the new reality created by the establishment of the state of Israel.

On some level, this is not surprising. The pragmatism of the Labor movement leads us to expect that it would be quick to adapt rationally to new circumstances. It is surprising, however, that it did not rationally adapt in both instances. Even in the second shift, the long gap between the onset of the new reality and the actual transformation of Labor's vision of the homeland suggests that the adaptation to a conscious shock hypothesis is often too strongly stated. While the creation of a new reality triggered the transformation, the movement did not adapt to it uniformly or automatically. Rather, only a small minority of the movement can be categorized as "early adapters." It was not until these early adapters won the intramovement struggle in the 1970s (itself waged over a combination of ideological, personal, and mundane political factors), and those who continued to adhere to the old map image actually left the movement, that the pattern of articulation regarding the appropriate borders reached a turning point. The particular political contingencies that brought this about were far from inevitable. This suggests that rational adaptation, rather than leading to change on its own, should be seen as one of the processes that contribute to variation in ideological articulation. The actual success or failure of the variants created by rational adapters depends more on the evolutionary dynamic than on the objective reality itself.

2

Religious Zionist Mapping of the Homeland

For the religious nationalists in the Zionist movement, the answer to the question "Where is the Land of Israel?" was obvious. The land belonging to the people of Israel is that promised to them by God. The divine designation of a particular parcel of land as the nation's would seem to make it more difficult for any change in its borders to take place. Indeed, Religious Zionists commonly argue that mere mortals have no right to modify the divinely delimited borders of the Land of Israel.[1] The territorial claims of this nationalist movement lie, in other words, outside the reach of history, much less that of politics.[2]

This artfully constructed impression is a mirage. The map image of the appropriate homeland articulated by the Religious Zionist movement actually changed over time. Mirroring the transformation that took place in the ideology of the Labor Zionists, Religious Zionism ceased claiming the East Bank of the Jordan and Southern Lebanon as appropriately part of the Jewish state.

The presence of ideological change does not require us to question the piety of the Religious Zionists. Even a sincere religious outlook allows for transformation of the prescribed borders, because the particular territorial delineation of the biblical Land of Israel is not clear-cut. The Bible and Jewish history contain several different map images of the Land of Israel. For example, the "borders of the promise" (Gen. 15:18; Exod. 3:8, 23:31; Josh. 1:4) are wider than the "borders of the exodus" from Egypt—that is, the borders of the biblical settlement in the country (Num. 34:1–13; Deut.

2:1–23, 3:8; Josh. 12:1, 13:3–6), and these are wider than the borders described in the vision of the prophet Ezekiel (Ezek. 47:15–21), but narrower than the actual extent of the kingdoms of David and Solomon (1 Chron. 13:5, 15:8–18; 2 Chron. 9:26).[3] As figures 8 and 9 show, even the same verse can be cartographically rendered in significantly different ways. In fact, a prominent leader of the Religious Zionist movement argued that if generals can disagree over what borders constitute secure boundaries, rabbis could disagree about their biblical designation.[4] Transformation in the territorial claims of Religious Zionists was also theologically possible because while they considered the entire land sacred, they imbued different areas with different degrees of holiness.[5] While we might expect the most expansive interpretation to be used whenever possible, the availability of alternatives allows claims to different areas to be equally "religious."

This chapter first shows that the Religious Zionists' vision of the homeland actually changed. Then the historical record is compared with the expectations of elite imposition, rational adaptation, and the evolutionary dynamic regarding the timing, direction, and process of change. This analysis shows that the evolutionary dynamic offers a more plausible account than the alternatives. The final part of the chapter takes advantage of a natural experiment created by the rise of Gush Emunim (Bloc of the Faithful) to ideological and political dominance within Religious Zionism. Despite their remarkable success in imposing their vision of the appropriate national mission on Religious Zionism (discussed in chapter 4), Gush Emunim failed to have a similar impact on the territorial dimension of Religious Zionism's vision. The evolutionary dynamic clarifies the reasons for this failure.

The Shift from "the River of Egypt to . . . the River Euphrates" to the "Whole Land of Israel"

Initially, the Religious Zionist movement invoked the definition of the land as promised to Abraham in Genesis 15:18: "From the River of Egypt to . . . the great river, the River Euphrates." Both the hawkish and the dovish wings of the movement shared this map image. It was articulated, for example, by Rabbi Binyamin (Yehoshua Radler-Feldmann), who was affiliated with Brit Shalom (Covenant of Peace, a short-lived movement that supported Jewish and Arab coexistence in a binational state), and by Heschel Farberstein, who spearheaded the 1933 land-leasing episode in Transjordan and who was an ally of the Revisionist movement.[6] Guided by this map image, the chief rabbis of Palestine demanded "all of Eretz Israel [the Land of Israel] on both sides of the Jordan" in their testimony before the Peel Commission. The Religious Zionist movement cited this delineation of the appropriate

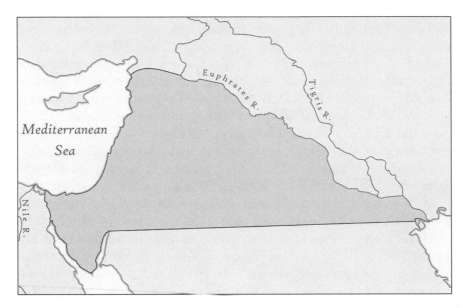

Figure 8. Borders of the divine promise. Based on Ariel, *Atlas of the Land of Israel* (1988).

borders (including the claim to both the East Bank of the Jordan and Southern Lebanon) when they rejected the Peel partition plan.[7] Like the rest of the Zionist movement at the time, Religious Zionist leaders located the eastern border of the Land of Israel with Iraq, not with Transjordan. For example, Rabbi Judah Leib Fishman commented that if Arabs were to be transferred out of the area assigned to the Jewish state, they should be moved to Iraq rather than to Transjordan so as not to concede the Jewish claim to the East Bank.[8]

The redefinition of the extent of the homeland is evident in the shift from the slogan explicitly claiming the area from "the River of Egypt to ... the River Euphrates" to the geographically more ambiguous mantra of the "whole land of Israel." A comparison of figures 8 and 9 with figures 8a and 9a, respectively, illustrates the direction (and magnitude) of this transformation. In both pairs of figures, the darkly shaded area indicates the new definition of the extent of the homeland.

Early articulations within Religious Zionism of a map image that implicitly excluded the East Bank of the Jordan and Southern Lebanon emerged during the controversy over the Peel Commission recommendations. In this context, Daniel Sirkis argued that while they maintained their maximum desires, they ought to demand "the establishment of the entire western Eretz Israel, at the very least, as a Jewish state."[9] A 1939 Hapoel Hamizrachi (the Mizrachi Worker, the dominant political faction within Religious Zionism

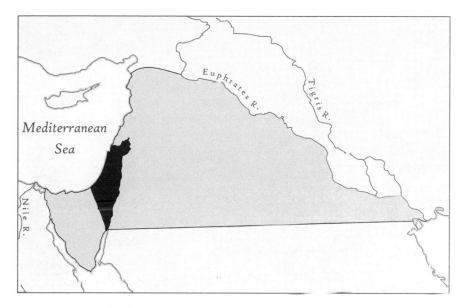

Figure 8a. "Whole Land of Israel" compared to the divine promise. Based on Ariel (1988).

at the time) news digest also implicitly excluded Transjordan from the land of Israel. Under the subheading "Transjordan" it described the Bedouin tribes engaged in clashes there as "aided by the Eretz Israeli refugees who live *near the border of Eretz Israel*."[10] Religious Zionism's endorsement of the Biltmore Programme as a demand for the entire Land of Israel, despite the fact that it (purposefully) did not mention any particular borders and was widely perceived as opening the door to partition, also points to the existence of this variant of the homeland within the movement.[11]

Such instances, however, remained marginal examples until the mid-1940s. Still on February 27, 1946, the "minimized" Executive Committee of Mizrachi declared that Religious "Judaism has not relinquished the wholeness of the Eretz Israel in its historic borders that were determined in the eternal Torah and will never agree to the tearing of the East Bank of the Jordan—the patrimony of the sons of Reuven, Gad, and half the tribe of Menashe."[12] On the eve of the arrival of the Anglo-American Commission, Rabbi Fishman still demanded a Jewish state on both banks of the Jordan.[13] Similarly, a conference of Mizrachi in April of 1946 protested "against the amputation of Transjordan from the borders of the country . . . and declare[d] that the Hebrew nation [would] never agree to give up a single step of land from the land of its native land."[14]

By 1947, however, prominent leaders were already excising Transjordan from the area they claimed as appropriately part of the state.[15]

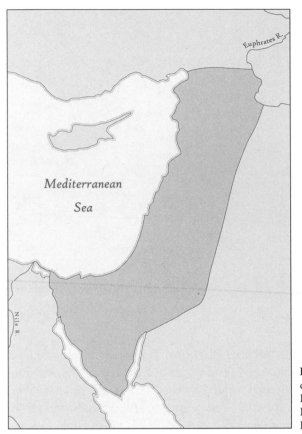

Figure 9. Borders of the divine promise. Based on Elitzur, "The Borders of the Land in the Tradition of Israel" (1977).

Even S. Zalman Shraggai, a territorially hawkish Religious Zionist leader, criticized the UN proposals, not because they excluded the East Bank, or even most of the West Bank, from the area of the proposed Jewish state, but because they excluded Jerusalem and the western Galilee.[16] In 1950, even a prominent territorially expansionist editorial in one of the movement's magazines no longer included the East Bank in its tacit understanding of the borders of the homeland. This editorial listed three reasons for Religious Zionism's opposition to Transjordan's 1950 annexation of "areas of western Eretz Israel" (i.e., the West Bank). First, it noted that the divine promise means that "we see ourselves as the potential owners of the entire land" even if it is currently inaccessible. Second, the annexation would mean the return of the British to the country. Finally, "our relations with Transjordan today are relations of an armistice in the midst of war. The war was fought over the very question of the ownership of the various areas of the country. As long as there is no peace treaty between us and Transjordan, we could

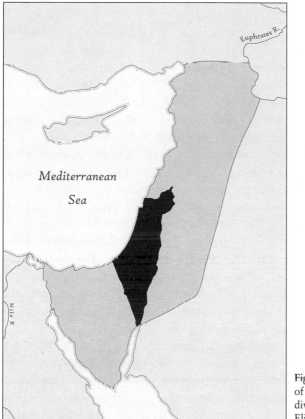

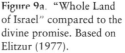

Figure 9a. "Whole Land of Israel" compared to the divine promise. Based on Elitzur (1977).

not agree to any political arrangement that will determine the status of the disputed area, since we see the presence of the [Jordanian] Legion in western Eretz Israel as the presence of an invader."[17]

On one hand, the continued use of the label "western land of Israel" suggests a continued, if tacit, claim to the "eastern" land of Israel, on the other side of the Jordan River. However, if the East Bank was truly part of the area Religious Zionists considered appropriately theirs (given the reasoning in the first objection), they should have found the very existence of the state of Jordan problematic (as the Revisionists did; see chapter 3), and not just its annexation of the West Bank. However, not only did they conceive of a peace treaty with Jordan as possible, but they also limited the scope of the contested land to the West Bank. They did not dispute the appropriate ownership of the East Bank of the Jordan at all. The deputy chair of the Mizrachi movement even limited the drawbacks of a potential peace treaty with Jordan to the institutionalization of the partition of Jerusalem, thus ignoring the implied recognition of a foreign occupation of (what was once considered) part of the homeland.[18] In fact, over the years the Religious Zionists consistently endorsed a peace treaty with Jordan. Any opposition to such an agreement, if it existed, was justified in political or security terms, not because Jordan extended over areas that were appropriately part of the Land of Israel.[19] This continued even in the 1980s, long after the political rise of the more hawkish Young Guard and Gush Emunim to the ideological leadership of Religious Zionism. They maintained the National Religious Party's (NRP) call for negotiations with Jordan on the basis of the Camp David Accords. Even those who argued *against* such negotiations often showed that they no longer considered the East Bank part of the Land of Israel. For example, in the mid-1980s, Beni Katzover and Yossi Vilian argued against negotiating with Jordan, not because it was part of the homeland, but only because it might herald a future withdrawal from the territories.[20]

Strongly reinforcing the notion that the Religious Zionist view of the homeland had shifted, the East Bank of the Jordan virtually disappeared from the materials intended to educate the children in Bnei Akiva (Sons of Akiva, the Religious Zionist youth movement) during this period. For example, figures 10 and 11 show youth group materials whose depictions of the Land of Israel clearly do not extend east of the Jordan (though they are, to be sure, much more ambiguous about the location of the northern border). As figure 10 illustrates, allusions to the appropriate extent of the land of Israel now tended to refer to the area "from Dan to Beersheva" (2 Sam. 3:10, among others) rather than to that "from the River of Egypt to ... the River Euphrates." A comparison of figures 8 and 10 shows that this decision effectively replaced a territorially expansive biblical verse with a significantly more modest one.

There were still some images of the East Bank in the youth movement's materials, but they were relatively rare. In the case of a 1966 instructional booklet about the "people and the land" that contained one such image, the authors even omitted the biblical verse identifying the Land of Israel as extending from the river of Egypt to the Euphrates from a list of passages used to legitimate the claim to the Land of Israel! Instead, those geographically specific verses that were mobilized to this end referred only to the land "from Dan to Beersheva" and to Jerusalem.[21]

Even the hope for future expansion beyond the area outlined in the "Dan to Beersheva" map image tended to be limited to a change in a north-south direction into the land "from the Hermon to Eilat," rather than in an eastward direction.[22] While this specific wish has little resonance in religious tradition, it does recall both the reality of the state's borders and Ben-Gurion's sacrilegious exclamation that the verse "from Dan to Beersheva" should be edited to read "from Dan to Eilat." Bnei Akiva's instructional materials

Figure 10. Bnei Akiva instructor's handbook, 1948. The extent of the Land of Israel is from Dan [in the north] to Beersheva [in the south]. Courtesy of the World Bnei Akiva Archives.

actually carried this out. An earlier edition of the educational unit whose title is depicted in figure 11 and now reads "from Dan to Eilat" used to display the more traditional title "from Dan to Beersheva."[23]

The common judgment that, after the 1967 war, Israel controlled the "entire land of Israel" also demonstrates the waning of the claim to Transjordan and Southern Lebanon, since it excludes these areas from this "entirety." The idiom Eretz Israel Hashlema (the entire Land of Israel) was a consistent, taken-for-granted component of the rhetoric in *Hatzofe* (the movement's newspaper), Bnei Akiva, and other movement forums. In a typical example, Chief Rabbi Isser Unterman declared that the Six-Day War "brought us nearer to our full redemption.... [From the motto of the land

Figure 11. Title of a Bnei Akiva educational unit, 1961: "From Dan to Eilat." Courtesy of the World Bnei Akiva Archives.

of Israel to the people of Israel according to the Torah of Israel] two thirds have already been fulfilled: 'Eretz Israel' is now in our hands and is called in its proper name, the country is in the possession of the nation of Israel."[24] At a celebratory dinner held by the World Center of Mizrachi and Hapoel Hamizrachi in 1968, A. L. Gelman congratulated "our sons who fought for the *wholeness of the land* and the wholeness of Jerusalem."[25] Some within the movement even called for a change in the order of their motto, making "the nation of Israel prior to the land of Israel... [since] the wide Eretz Israel is in our possession, and the hand of Israel rules in it."[26]

The redefinition of the appropriate extent of the homeland also characterized the discourse of the political leadership of the National Religious Party. For example, all of the participants in the 1974 annual *Hatzofe* symposium excluded the East Bank from their conception of the area of the Land of Israel.[27] A few years earlier, Yitzhak Rephael went so far as to argue that Israel's "natural security border" was the Jordan River.[28] Leaving the East Bank and Southern Lebanon not just out of the Land of Israel but even out of the divine promise, Zerach Warhaftig argued: "The main problem... is, what is Eretz Israel?... If Eretz Israel is one country then it is in its borders as a country promised to us. In that same country we have today two-thirds Jews and a third non-Jews.... *Today, when Eretz Israel is in our hands,* when we have a majority in this country, many [Israelis] hesitate as to whether we are allowed to hold it."[29]

Indeed, in 1984, Warhaftig implied that the land of Israel was "mostly" in their hands because the world did not recognize their possession of it, not because there were significant portions of the homeland that remained to be liberated.[30] The notion that the entire land of Israel was already liberated, and thus that the East Bank of the Jordan or the shores of the Litani were not appropriately part of it, was already present in the declarations of the 21st Convention of Mizrachi and Hapoel Mizrachi in 1968. At this meeting, they declared: "The Land of Israel is liberated and all of Jerusalem will be built and made ready, including the mount of our Temple, the Western Wall, and *all the places that are holy to us, [all of these] are in the hands of Israel.*" They mourned the fact that "*while Eretz Israel in its entirety is liberated,* the nation has yet to awaken to return to Zion." Their call for greater immigration "in this period, when our state extends on the *entire Land of Israel* [Eretz Israel Hashlema]" explicitly repeated this notion.[31] Even Rabbi Avraham Shapira, chief rabbi of Israel and one of the spiritual leaders who would later provide religious sanction for mutiny against orders to evacuate settlements, reminded the members of the Jewish Underground. "We must not forget that we rule *the entire country.*"[32]

The constant calls of Religious Zionists to settle the *entire land* also relied on the mantra of the "wholeness of the land," with its implication that none of it was missing.[33] Their argument that they should emphasize their principled right to every inch of land in Eretz Israel did much the same thing. Religious Zionist representatives repeatedly contended that any rejection of the right to the West Bank involved a concession of their rights to the area within the 1949 borders as well.[34] By their own standard, then, the lack of an explicitly articulated claim to the East Bank suggests that they no longer considered it part of the homeland.

Their belief that, after 1967, Israel controlled all of the territory that appropriately belonged to the nation was also evident in the use of the past tense to refer to the task of liberating the Land of Israel. In 1969, the 3rd NRP convention sent "its blessings to the soldiers and commanders of the IDF, who with the help of God *liberated* E[retz] I[srael] and who continue to stand guard over the country." The same year, the World Meeting of the Youth Faction of the NRP sent "its greetings to the soldiers and commanders of [the IDF] who, with the help of God, *liberated* Eretz Israel." Even the chief editor of *Hatzofe,* the official newspaper of the NRP, spoke of the "liberation of Eretz Israel Hashlema" [liberation of the whole land of Israel] in the past tense, implying that it was already done.[35]

Of course, many (though not all) of the spokespersons whose arguments I have used to illustrate the existence and direction of the transformation in the map image articulated by the Religious Zionists have been relative political moderates. The adoption and use of the idiom of the wholeness of the post-1967 Land of Israel by the more militant Young Guard and Gush Emunim would provide a stronger indication of both the elision of Transjordan and Southern Lebanon from the homeland and the spread of this map image within the movement.

Indeed, despite their militancy, the Young Guard of the Religious Zionist movement also commonly used the "whole land of Israel" to refer to the area under Israeli control after 1967. In a representative statement, one of the original leaders of the Young Guard, Zvulun Hammer, spoke of the Land of Israel as already being in their possession in 1975. Shaul Yahalom similarly noted that they "felt the rising need to educate for an awareness of the wholeness of the land." Avner Shaki, briefly the leader of the NRP, argued that "it is our duty to say, and in the clearest language, that *the fact of our return to the land in its historic borders,* serves as a supreme religious-moral response to all the attempts to destroy our nation."[36] The frequent statements by the NRP after the Young Guard took over its reins that "not a single part of Eretz Israel will be given to foreign rule" also suggest that the East Bank of the Jordan was not part of their map image.[37]

The elision of the East Bank from the NRP's conception of the Land of Israel was evident in its election propaganda even after the more hawkish Young Guard began playing a significant role in setting the NRP's rhetoric and policy. Thus in a 1969 advertisement the NRP took credit for "settlers laying phylacteries *in all areas of the entire Eretz Israel.*" Its propaganda routinely framed the political battle as "over the wholeness of the land, its spiritual shape and the substance of its rule and society."[38] Another advertisement featuring Zvulun Hammer promised to stay within the borders of "the whole land of Israel" and to "*guard the wholeness of the promised land.*"[39] In 1992, Rabbi Yitzhak Levy, an NRP member of the Knesset, proclaimed that the NRP "could not be a partner in a government that will not promise the continued settlement of Judea and Samaria, the continued Israeli rule over *all parts of Eretz Israel.*"[40] Speakers for the NRP repeatedly called on voters to support them so that they could defend "Jerusalem and *all of Eretz Israel.*"[41] The party's slogan in the 1992 elections—"The NRP is to your right"—signaled the rejection of any possible coalition with a government that might make territorial concessions. NRP propaganda clearly showed that the area of the homeland to which it applied this territorially hawkish stance was that of the "whole land of Israel" rather than that outlined by the divine promise.[42]

Other campaign images over the years, invariably embedded in territorially hawkish contexts, nonetheless illustrate the exclusion of the land east of the Jordan River and Southern Lebanon from the image of the "entire" land of Israel that they had in mind (see figs. 12–13). Figure 12 is a campaign advertisement from the 1973 elections depicting the iconic religious Zionist

Figure 12. NRP election advertisement, 1973: "We are guarding and protecting our patrimony." Courtesy of the National Religious Party.

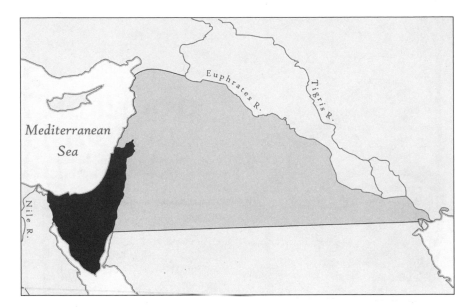

Figure 12a. The new patrimony superimposed on the original claim.

symbol, the religious soldier. Its caption reads: "We are guarding and protecting our patrimony." The term "patrimony," as opposed to "state" or "Israel," invokes the religious link to the land. The particular map of the patrimony displayed by this ad, however, limits it to the area under Israeli control after 1967. The East Bank of the Jordan and Southern Lebanon are missing, though the Sinai Peninsula is included. (The inclusion of the Sinai is a short-lived artifact of the rise of Gush Emunim within the movement, as I will argue in the final section of this chapter.) Figure 13 reproduces pages from a 1988 NRP pamphlet calling for a stronger military response to the first Palestinian intifada. The images of the land of Israel that appear in it clearly correspond to the new vision of the "whole land of Israel." There is no hint of the claim to the East Bank or to Southern Lebanon. When superimposed on the original claim (as in figs. 12a and 13a) it becomes clear that the notion of what should be included in "all the parts" has changed.

That Bnei Akiva also routinely excluded the East Bank and Southern Lebanon from its discussions of the Land of Israel after 1967 (as was the case before the war) suggests that these images were not merely the product of electioneering campaigns.[43] Bnei Akiva mirrored the demand for the establishment of settlements in "the entire land" and similarly framed the discourse over the territories in terms of "the entire land." Even the map images it printed in its educational materials after 1967 portrayed the Land of Israel as extending only to the Jordan (see figs. 14–16).[44] Perhaps most explicitly, Avraham Lipschitz, the general secretary of Bnei Akiva and its chief educator,

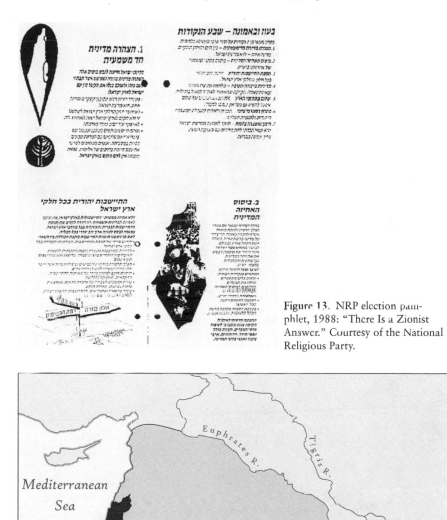

Figure 13. NRP election pamphlet, 1988: "There Is a Zionist Answer." Courtesy of the National Religious Party.

Figure 13a. The "Whole Land of Israel" superimposed on the biblical land of Israel.

wrote in the preface to a 1992 instructional booklet for children that the Six-Day War led to the return "to *our patrimony in the entire Eretz Israel*." On the facing page was a drawing (fig. 16) reinforcing the notion that the entire land of Israel excludes the East Bank and Southern Lebanon.[45]

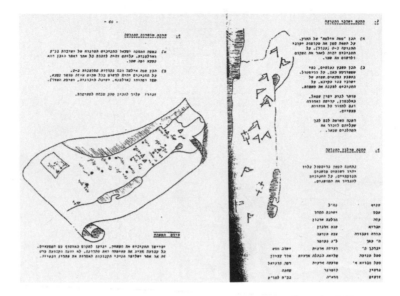

Figure 14. Depictions of the Land of Israel from Bnei Akiva, "Our Essence," post-1967. Courtesy of the World Bnei Akiva Archives.

Figure 15. Montage of images from a Bnei Akiva instructional unit entitled "Eretz Israel," 1986. Courtesy of the World Bnei Akiva Archives.

Even the name of the Religious Zionist youth movement implies an acceptance of the new borders of the "whole" land of Israel. Emphasizing the distinction between the extent of the state of Israel and the scope of the Land of Israel, in 1958, Bnei Akiva changed its name from the Organization

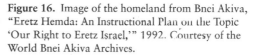

Figure 16. Image of the homeland from Bnei Akiva, "Eretz Hemda: An Instructional Plan on the Topic 'Our Right to Eretz Israel,'" 1992. Courtesy of the World Bnei Akiva Archives.

of Bnei Akiva in Eretz Israel to the Organization of Bnei Akiva in *Israel*. In 1970, its (adult) leaders argued that since the state of Israel now covered the entire land of Israel, it should change its name back to Bnei Akiva in *Eretz Israel*. Justifying the change, Warhaftig commented that the task of the youth movement was to convince others that "this is the land of our fathers, and the land of our fathers is not divided; all of Eretz Israel is the land of our fathers, and if there is a commandment for the conquest of Eretz Israel it applies to all the territory of Eretz Israel, not more; we never wanted to go beyond the borders of Eretz Israel, but *here are the borders; this is our Eretz Israel.*"[46]

In 1995 this symbolic gesture was replayed in the NRP when the party added "in Eretz Israel" to its official name. In recommending this change, the Party Secretariat noted that it "emphasizes the uniqueness of the NRP's struggle for the wholeness of the land."[47]

The change in the Religious Zionists' vision of the appropriate borders of the Jewish state was even evident in the borders desired by Gush Emunim. Gush Emunim was a social movement that originated within Religious Zionism and quickly became its ideological avant-garde. Gush Emunim saw itself as the reinvigorator of a Zionist spirit that had been lost as a result of fatigue and the partial implementation of Zionism's goals. Against the background of the national depression following the 1973 war and the first territorial concessions in the Sinai Peninsula (as part of the disengagement agreement with Egypt), Gush Emunim's founders mobilized to stop further territorial concessions and to address the social anomie they detected.[48]

As Ian Lustick noted, many of Gush Emunim's activists had trouble "modulating their actions and the expression of their beliefs, and especially accepting and implementing a consensus-building strategy toward the wider Israeli public. Actions are liable to be taken and positions articulated that, though tactically unwise, cannot be fully renounced."[49] As a result, Gush Emunin's eventual articulation of the new map image reinforces the conclusion that the change in the definition of the homeland in the Religious nationalist movement was both sincere and widespread.

To be sure, the idiom Eretz Israel Hashlema (the whole land of Israel) was initially less prominent within Gush Emunim. Since the mid-1970s, however, it has become a common feature of the rhetoric in books, speeches, and journals of members of Gush Emunim. Despite Rabbi Zvi Yehuda Kook's reservations (see below), it was not uncommon to hear Gush Emunim ideologues and activists claim that, after 1967, Israel controlled the "entire land of Israel."[50] Mirroring the rest of the Religious Zionist movement, their diction also suggested that they considered the entire land of Israel to be in their hands. Thus they commonly placed the liberation of the "entire land" and of all the Jewish holy places in the past tense,[51] equated the "western land of Israel" and the "Land of Israel,"[52] warned against the division of the, presumably whole, Land of Israel,[53] framed their goal as "guarding" or "protecting" a wholeness of the land (that, by implication, is already in Israeli hands),[54] and called for settlement of "the entire land."[55] An editorial in Nekuda, the monthly of the Yesha Council and the unofficial mouthpiece of Gush Emunim, that protested against the Oslo Accords even argued that a majority in Israel "wants all parts of the land of Israel to remain eternally in the control of the state of Israel."[56] The map images of the Land of Israel that were printed in Nekuda reinforced the notion that they held the post-1967 land of Israel to be whole.[57]

Similarly, Gush Emunim activists frequently framed the political struggle over the future of the territories as a battle for the wholeness of the land— implying, and occasionally openly stating, that if Israel annexed the territories, the territorial battle would be over.[58] Going further, some in Gush Emunim even used the term the "eastern land of Israel" to refer not to Jordan, but to the West Bank![59] Since the mid-1980s the map image articulated in Nekuda, more often than not, held the post-1967 borders of Israel to encompass the entire Land of Israel. Between December 1983 and May 1995, the magazine contained 200 references that implied or stated that the Land of Israel is whole, and only 75 references that implied otherwise. Of these, 36 explicitly laid claim to the East Bank.

In the late 1980s and early 1990s, Gush Emunim members even joined the Likud in arguing that "Jordan is the Palestinian state." Between December 1983 and May 1995, fully 13 of the 36 articles that laid claim to the East Bank in the pages of *Nekuda* did so in the context of making this argument. This even included statements by the Yesha Council itself.[60] As when used elsewhere, this argument involved a "trade" of the land east of the Jordan River for the land to its west.[61] That this may not be an entirely polemical stance (at least for some of its advocates) is suggested by Gush Emunim's clear resistance to engaging in analogous tactical games with respect to other parts of the homeland.[62] Even if the expressed willingness to come to terms with the removal of the East Bank from the area appropriately part of Israel is only a polemical stance, its spread still signals that Gush Emunim members are much less reluctant to use rhetoric that they once saw as the first step down a slippery slope to the renunciation of the homeland. As Elyakim Haetzni, a frequent, though secular, contributor to *Nekuda,* argued, "With the Homeland, one does not play games or tricks of deception."[63]

The exclusion of the East Bank of the Jordan from the Religious Zionist conception of the appropriate territory of the nation-state reached its logical conclusion in 1994 when Zvulun Hammer argued that the NRP supported the peace treaty with Jordan *in principle.*[64] While there were concerns within the party (and the movement) about the treaty, they were largely limited to the manner of negotiations, not the end result. Even when the NRP lamented the territorial concessions made in the context of these negotiations, it referred to the Arava Desert or Jerusalem, not to the East Bank.[65] In fact, once their concerns about Jerusalem were allayed, the NRP Knesset faction unanimously supported the "Washington agreement" normalizing relations between Israel and Jordan. MK Yigal Bibi summarized their position as follows: "If the matter of Jerusalem is taken care of, we have no problem with Jordan."[66] Warhaftig called the peace treaty with Jordan a "dream come true" because it was achieved "without concessions over parts of the Land of Israel."[67] Reflecting the underlying acceptance of the principle of peace with Jordan, *Hatzofe*'s editorials about the peace talks never represented the East Bank of the Jordan as appropriately Israel's or even as a lost part of the homeland. The newspaper of the mainstream of the Religious Zionist movement literally blessed the progress in the negotiations and declared that the signing of the agreement marked a "historic day."[68]

While the reactions to the treaty with Jordan in more radical Religious Zionist circles were, to be sure, less enthusiastic, these members of the movement also accepted the peace treaty rather quietly. Of all the messianic and territorially maximalist groups in Israel, including Hai Vekayam and the Yesha Council, only Neemanei Har Habayit (the Temple Mount Loyalists) explicitly raised the claim to the land east of the Jordan in the context of their response to the peace treaty.[69] Indeed, Gush Emunim's monthly completely avoided the issue. *Nekuda* did not devote a single editorial, positive or negative, to the signing of the second peace treaty between the state of Israel and its neighbors, a treaty that relinquished the formal claim to what had once been, and occasionally still was, claimed as part of the Promised Land. Among the political and ideological leadership associated with Gush Emunim, few publicly raised the claim that the treaty was problematic because it represented a formal ceding of the claim to part of the patrimony.[70] When such claims were raised, they were often dismissed with the argument that "our right to the Land of Israel applies to all areas of the Land of Israel, and no political arrangement has the power to undermine this."[71] The few who expressed reservations on this basis presented their agreement to the treaty as a pragmatic recognition of the need for peace, as a way to prevent bloodshed, and not as a principled concession of their right to the Land of Israel under Hussein's rule.[72] Others rationalized their support for the peace treaty by postponing the actualization of their claim to the East Bank to the days of the Messiah.[73]

However, few within the NRP's leadership let whatever qualms they had affect their support for the treaty. Only Yitzhak Levy chose to absent himself from the procedure, and only Hanan Porat actually abstained during the vote. Others also argued that this was the best course of action, maintaining that while they could not oppose the treaty because it brought peace, neither could they sign a document that formally awarded sovereignty over parts of the Land of Israel to another entity.[74] Not only were these futile gestures in the context of a vote that was not close, but, more importantly for our purposes, they embody the lack of response among those close to Gush Emunim to the ceding of the East Bank. We can only contrast this relative silence with the anguish and pathos that greeted Begin's withdrawal from Sinai or Ariel Sharon's 2005 decision to disengage from the Gaza Strip.[75] In summary, even the territorially maximalist wings of Religious Zionism now tended to exclude the East Bank of the Jordan from their conception of the "whole land of Israel."

Evolution at Work: Explaining the Move to the "Whole Land of Israel"

The Religious Zionist view of the homeland evolved. The transition from claiming the area from "the River of Egypt to....the River Euphrates" to the "whole land of Israel" was a by-product of the tactical steps the Religious Zionists took to remain part of the governing nationalist alliance crafted by the Labor movement in the 1940s.

The dominance of the Labor movement posed a number of practical problems for the Religious Zionists. They feared that the secular, even anticlerical, Labor movement would privatize religion or, at the very least, undercut it by refusing to fund religious schools. The alliance between Labor and the Religious Zionists enabled the latter to protect the religious public from the "godless socialists" who were threatening to eliminate religion, and allowed them to impose a fair degree of religious control over the public realm. (See chapter 4 for an explanation of Labor's acquiescence in this despite its secularism.) Cooperating with the Labor movement did not necessarily require that the Religious Zionists abandon their original vision of the homeland. They did, however, have to avoid contradicting the Labor movement, at least too overtly, on the big political questions of the day. As we saw in chapter 1, this was the Labor movement's minimum goal. Within the Religious Zionist movement, the proponents of self-restraint saw it as a temporary modulation that was both crucial for achieving the movement's other nationalist and political goals and minimal, since it could not affect the Religious Zionist ideal in any case.

The alliance between the Religious Zionists and the Labor movement succeeded. Observers even called it a "historic alliance" (in much the same way that contemporary observers link the religious and the secular right in Israel). While it catapulted the Labor movement to power, it also proved beneficial to the Religious Zionists. They gained a seat at the decision-making table along with access to power and resources. They used these not just to fund their schools and to make sure that religious services were provided by the state, but to impose a religious cast on the public realm in Israel. The success of the "historic alliance" promoted the ambiguity about the territorial claims of Religious Zionism that enabled the alliance to emerge. This ambiguity, in turn, created space for a variant of the image of the homeland that excluded the East Bank and Southern Lebanon. This variant was not conjured from thin air. The Religious Zionists started to articulate the map image of the homeland that Labor Zionism was articulating at the time. The convergence of the members of this "historic alliance" regarding the territorial definition of the homeland is consistent with the predictions of the evolutionary dynamic.

The timing of this shift also corresponds more closely to the expectations of the evolutionary dynamic than to those of either of the alternatives. The new variant emerged in the context of the political debate over the Peel partition proposal. This debate placed the Religious Zionists in a bind. On the one hand, they vehemently rejected the principle of partition on religious grounds. On the other hand, they refused to join forces with the Revisionists despite their common opposition to the principle of partition. They feared that doing so would undermine the access to power afforded by their budding alliance with the Labor movement. The Religious Zionists navigated through these waters by both openly opposing the Peel partition plan and hinting that they would accept it if they had no choice.[76] The ambiguity this

introduced into their statements about the appropriate extent of the homeland created space for a vision of the Land of Israel that differed from the
original one.

While this variant appeared in Religious Zionist discourse in the late
1930s, it did not begin to spread within the movement until the end of 1946.
The renewed debate over partition that took place at the time once again
placed the Religious Zionists in a difficult position. A significant portion
of the movement and its leaders continued to reject any partition, including that of the East Bank, and argued that they should explicitly demand
the entire biblical land of Israel.[77] As a result, an open endorsement of the
principle of partition would have wrecked the movement from within. An
open acceptance of partition would also have left the movement vulnerable
to being outflanked on the right by the Revisionist movement. On the other
side, the consensus builders within the movement argued that openly agi-
tating for their full vision of the homeland would jeopardize their alliance
with the Labor movement. Led by Haim Moshe Shapira, they argued that
losing the support of the Labor movement would impinge on their ability
to implement their equally important views on the other foundational questions they faced. They warned that their nationalist missions of shaping the
religious character of the public realm (see chapter 4) and maintaining, not
to say forging, the "unity of the people" regardless of ideology (see chapter
6) would be lost if they emphasized their more expansive notion of the appropriate territory.

The success of the consensus builders raises the possibility that the change
in the definition of the homeland was the result of their imposition of a new
image on the rest of the movement. To be sure, they personally benefited
from the eventual adoption of their stance because it solidified their place at
the helm of the Religious Zionist movement. The short time it took the Religious Zionists to abandon the open claim to the East Bank of the Jordan is
also consistent with a story of elites smoothly and consistently imposing their
views on the movement. The surprising rapidity of this change is evident in
the comparison of the treatment of the East Bank in Hapoel Hamizrachi's
1946 and 1949 conventions. In 1946 they still "sharply protest[ed] Britain's
illegal declaration of the independence of Transjordan and declare[d] that
the Jewish nation has not ceded and will not cede any part of its land in its
historic borders." By 1949, they dropped this statement.[78]

Nonetheless, the extent and direction of the change undermine the plausibility of this story and bolster the evolutionary explanation. To begin with,
there is no evidence that even the consensus builders intentionally set out to
change the Religious Zionist answer to the foundational question "Where is
the homeland?" Their initial decision to mute their claim to the original map
image was not intended to change their foundational beliefs. They wanted

to preserve their alliance with the Labor movement despite their continued disagreement on the territorial question. In other words, the adjustment of their rhetoric about the extent of the homeland was meant to maintain their ideology, not to transform it, as elite imposition would lead us to expect. The consensus builders did not argue that the map image of the "whole land of Israel" was the right and true one, as we might expect them to have done if they now really believed something new (and as they would later come to argue once the new variant had been institutionalized). Instead, they argued that a measure of ambiguity—because it would minimize friction with the Labor movement—was more useful than shouting their (yet unchanged!) stance from the rooftops. Like the territorial maximalists, the consensus builders still desired and claimed the entire biblical Land of Israel. Unlike the truth tellers, however, they were willing to modulate their rhetoric in the interests of party unity and of achieving their goals on other, equally important dimensions of nationalism.[79]

The quest for ambiguity rather than outright change was evident in the fact that the consensus builders did not openly support any partition (at least not yet) even after the decision to modulate their public position. Instead, they sought to prevent the question of partition from being explicitly decided at all.[80] Their response to the UN vote establishing the state of Israel also displayed the ambiguity they encouraged. Hapoel Hamizrachi's leadership noted that their happiness was muted because "the establishment of the Hebrew state involves the amputation of our land to shreds and most of its territory was taken out of it, including the holy city Jerusalem, the Galilee and many other large and important parts"; exactly which parts they had in mind were not specified.[81] The adoption of this purposefully ambiguous stance enabled the alliance with the Labor Zionist movement to proceed despite the differences in their respective visions of the appropriate extent of the homeland.

This rhetorical ambiguity, however, came at a cost. As we saw above, the ambiguity about the appropriate extent of the homeland was so pervasive that the Religious Zionists almost completely ceased to articulate the explicit claim to the East Bank of the Jordan and Southern Lebanon. They did not deal with the borders issue in their internal discussions. These territorial claims were also missing from their youth movement materials. In fact, after the adoption of the UN partition plan and independence, the Religious Zionist movement turned its focus to shaping the religious character of the state and dropped all claims for a modification of the territorial status quo (with the exception of the continued claim to Jerusalem). Even the movement's Youth Faction, which after the 1967 war took a hawkish stance regarding the occupied territories, did not list the imperfect borders as one of its mobilizing issues between 1961 (when it emerged) and 1967.[82] This neglect was not inconsequential. The failure to articulate the original map image allowed expressions that defined the Land of Israel as excluding the East Bank and Southern Lebanon to become increasingly common.

After the 1967 war, the lack of ideological discourse about the extent of the homeland caught the movement's leadership by surprise. Yitzhak Meltzer, for example, recalled that before 1967 "the only movement that spoke of the wholeness of the land was Herut [i.e., the Revisionists]. In Bnei Akiva they only spoke of the Nahal and the Kibbutz. The Six-Day war changed the reality. All of Eretz Israel was before us.... We were not ready for this question in Bnei Akiva and in the [religious] schools."[83] Note that even this lament excludes the East Bank of the Jordan from the bounds of Eretz Israel. Some even argued that they "did not know how to digest Judea and Samaria."[84] While this overstates the digestive discomfort regarding the West Bank and Gaza Strip, these reactions betray the lack of awareness of the ideological transformation that had taken place within the movement. The surprise at the extent of the territorial ambiguity undermines the notion that the shift in the conceptualization of the extent of the homeland regarding the East Bank was the result of conscious manipulation. These reactions also weaken an explanation of this shift as the result of rational adaptation, because they suggest that no strategic calculation to change the definition of the homeland took place.

It is also difficult to use rational adaptation to account for the timing of this shift. Its onset in the late 1930s challenges a story that relies on rational adaptation to the administrative borders of Mandatory Palestine, because, as in the case of the Labor movement, there is at least a fifteen-year gap between the imposition of these borders and the onset of change. Ruling out this exogenous shock means that there is no other event in the historical record that could plausibly trigger an adaptation that would result in the particular map image of the "whole land of Israel" between 1949 and 1967. The establishment of the state was certainly significant, but rational adaptation is unable to account for the continued claim to East Jerusalem, the West Bank, and Gaza Strip despite the exclusion of these areas from the state after 1949. Rational adaptation would require the assumption that the leaders of Religious Zionism were simultaneously rational (regarding the East Bank) and irrational (regarding the West Bank). In any case, as illustrated earlier in this chapter, the ideological transformation was largely completed before the end of the 1949 war and the tangible delineation of the borders of the state of Israel.

The transformation's turning point in 1946 is, however, consistent with a consideration of the Holocaust as an exogenous shock to which leaders of the Religious Zionist movement might have adapted. The leaders of the Religious Zionist movement certainly felt a responsibility to save what was left of the Jewish people, particularly the Orthodox Jewish public, after the Holocaust. Thus they were more willing to accede to partition than they had been before. Rabbi Fishman expressed the general sense within the movement in the summer of 1946: "I love the Land of Israel and the People of Israel, but the love for the People of Israel comes first, and if, heaven forbid, the People of Israel will be destroyed, we have no hope of living under any government.... But if now we establish a state on part of Eretz Israel, I hope that the People of Israel will survive and someday have all of Eretz Israel." Partition was acceptable, he argued, as a temporary measure to address the immediate need for control over immigration (i.e., a state), even if only in part of the Promised Land.[85] Even Rabbi Meir Berlin, who in 1937 rejected the notion that Jewish suffering was an appropriate reason to agree to partition, modified his position after the Holocaust. While he still rejected any partition, he now justified his rejection on tactical grounds, "because it was not practical" or would not be implemented, not because it was inherently wrong. At the very least, he argued that savvy negotiating required that they avoid making any concessions in advance and keep demanding "a Jewish state in the borders of E[retz] I[srael]."[86]

Nonetheless, while the impact of the Holocaust is consistent with the timing of the turning point in the pattern of articulation, it cannot account for the direction of the ideological change. As with the transformation of the Labor movement's map image, the Holocaust can explain a greater willingness to settle for less, but not a change in the maximum claimed. The variation within the movement despite the horror and scope of the Holocaust also undermines the argument for rational adaptation. No one was unaffected by the Holocaust. Yet nearly half of the leadership of the Religious Zionist movement still opposed even the tactical modulation of their vision of the territorial extent of the homeland. Indeed, the contingency of their decision to mute their territorial claims is highlighted by the fact that the consensus builders' 1946 proposal was accepted by a vote of 23 to 18.[87] It could easily have gone the other way.

Even the strongest factor that might be used to support rational adaptation—the territorial moderation displayed by the Religious Zionists between 1949 and 1973—actually undermines its plausibility. First, as noted earlier, rational adaptation to the borders of the state of Israel during this period cannot account for the continued claim to the West Bank, Gaza Strip, and Jerusalem. The reaction of the Religious Zionist leadership to the 1956 war represents a second, and more problematic, inconsistency between the expectations of rational adaptation and the historical record.

In the course of this short war in 1956, Israel, collaborating with France and Great Britain, conquered the Gaza Strip and the Sinai Peninsula for the first time. An irate Eisenhower forced Israel to withdraw rather quickly,

but in the interim the political leaders of Religious Zionism held a series of
meetings in which they considered how to react to the conquest of these territories. In these discussions, the NRP leaders repeatedly distinguished between the Gaza Strip, which they saw as unambiguously part of the Land of
Israel, and the Sinai Peninsula, whose inclusion in the appropriate homeland
was open to debate.[88] I will return to the particular question of the Sinai in
the next section. At this point, I want to highlight the contrast between the
unanimity regarding the status of the Gaza Strip as unambiguously part of
the homeland and the vacillation about, if not outright exclusion of, the
Sinai Peninsula. Both parcels of land were clearly not part of the state of
Israel after 1949. If anything, including the relatively resource-rich and demographically vacant Sinai Peninsula should have been more palatable to
Religious Zionist leaders than the annexation of the impoverished Gaza
Strip with its teeming Palestinian population. The size of the Sinai Peninsula
also makes it more attractive from a strategic military perspective. Rational
adaptation cannot account for the fact that even the moderate, territorially
conciliatory, old-guard leadership of the NRP still unquestioningly included
the troublesome Gaza Strip in their vision of the appropriate borders of the
homeland after the 1956 war but excluded the Sinai Peninsula.

The unevenness and inconsistency of the transformation in the Religious
Zionists' pattern of articulation more generally also militate against intentional mechanisms of change, because these expect a more consistent break
with the discarded ideologies. However, Religious Zionist publications occasionally included both the traditional map image and the new variant, creating a tension between the implication that the appropriate borders of the
homeland are those promised by God and the assumption that the land under
Israeli control is the totality of the appropriate land of Israel.[89] In 1947, after
the change had begun, Meir Berlin even republished a booklet he prepared in
the context of the 1937 debate over the Peel partition that explicitly articulated the claim to the East Bank and provided a reference for the theological
reasons behind the rejection of territorial compromise.[90] Perhaps the most
striking reminder of the old map image was the emblem of the United Religious Front (1949–1950), which depicted both sides of the Jordan.[91] Other
leaders (including some of the consensus builders advocating the rhetorical
adjustment) also invoked the claim to the East Bank throughout the 1960s
and 1970s.[92] Religious Zionists also admitted the continued sanctity of the
land east of the Jordan when asked directly. This was even true of the consistently dovish members of the Religious Zionist leadership.[93]

While the instructional materials of Bnei Akiva usually reflected the assumption that the area controlled by Israel after 1967 was "whole," there
were still occasional references to the existence of parts of the Land of Israel that were not currently under Israeli control. For example, while the

1992 instructional booklet cited above portrays the appropriate borders as the "whole land of Israel," it also includes a short morality tale by Naomi Shemer (herself not a Religious Zionist) that tells a different story. In it, Shemer compares the 1947 UN declaration to reading Genesis. After the war of independence, "we had in our hands the five books of Moses.... In the Six-Day War the IDF conquered a few more books (say, until the end of Prophets I)." This implies that there are yet other "books" to be conquered.[94] While such instances stand out partly because they were unusual, they also reflect the reality that the old map image continued to have some currency within the movement. Intentional mechanisms of change cannot explain this duality.

A Test of Elite Imposition

In May of 1967, Rabbi Zvi Yehuda Kook made a particularly famous appeal to the old map image. He recalled that, in the hours after the UN decision calling for the establishment of the state, "I could not come to terms with what was done, with those terrible tidings, that it actually happened, 'and my country they divided'! Yes, where is our Hebron—are we forgetting it?! And where is our Shchem, and our Jericho, where are they—are they forgotten?! And all of Transjordan—it is ours, each and every clod of earth, [all of it], every region and length of land that belong to the land of God—is it up to us to give up even a single millimeter of it?"[95]

Kook's students formed the kernel of Gush Emunim and the Young Guard within the Religious Zionist movement. Their emergence and rise to prominence within Religious Zionism heralded a rejection of the consensus builders' victory a generation earlier.[96] Among other elements, this included an overt rejection of the basic premise of the "historic alliance" with the Labor movement. Gush Emunim and the Young Guard of Religious Zionism refused to give up decision-making power on the most critical political matters, including the scope of the nation-state, in return for the ability to protect the needs of the religious community. They wanted to do both. In the words of Rabbi Yoel Ben-Nun,

> We ceased being the keepers of kashrut in the restaurant on the Mapai train.... because I have something to say about the caboose and about the direction in which it goes. On this matter I have no feelings of inferiority before any other Israeli. I grew up in the country, I served in the IDF with friends who are called "not religious," and I have a difference of opinion with [them] as an equal. I do not exclude them from the group and they do not exclude me. If Gush Emunim achieved this, it is more important than the settlements it established.[97]

Part of this speaking out included a rejection of the muting of Religious Zionism's claim to the entire biblical land of Israel. Kook's students interpreted his lament as a prophetic call to change the territorial status quo. Inspired by Rabbi Kook they sought to reinstall the old map image as the dominant vision of the appropriate homeland. In this vein, some of their ideologues openly criticized the discourse of the whole land of Israel "because the land of Israel west of the Jordan is not the whole land of Israel."[98] In 1983, Hanan Porat explained: "For the time being, Judea and Samaria are all we can handle; but we believe that one day the Jews will have the entire land [that is, also the East Bank of the Jordan River], just as the Temple will be built."[99] The loyalty to this map image prevented Rabbi Zvi Yehuda Kook from signing the manifesto of the Movement for the Whole Land of Israel. He argued that, at the very least, the *whole* land of Israel would also include the area covered by Jordan. Following his lead, throughout the 1970s and early 1980s, some Gush Emunim ideologues argued that the area appropriately belonging to the Jewish state also included, at the very least, the East Bank of the Jordan, Southern Lebanon, and the Sinai Peninsula.[100] Rabbi Eliezer Waldman, standing over the newly dug grave of a student of his who was killed in the market in central Hebron in 1980, said that "the command that the dead Yehoshua [i.e., the student] left behind was the divine command to settle in every place, from the wilderness to this Lebanon even unto the great river, the River Euphrates, the whole land of the Hittites and 'unto the great sea toward the going down of the sun shall be your border.'"[101] In a statement representative of the messianic fervor that Gush Emunim attached to the war in Lebanon, Hanan Porat argued that they must prepare themselves "in terms of our consciousness and by establishing new settlement nuclei, to settle those portions of the Land of Israel that today are still not in our hands...nuclei for the Litani area, Gilead, Transjordan, and Sinai."[102] Gush Emunim's initial calls for the establishment of Jewish sovereignty in "the regions of the land of Israel *that are in our possession*," rather than in an unmodified "Land of Israel" as called for by the mainstream Religious Zionists, reflected the belief that Israel did not control all parts of the appropriate homeland. Indeed, Gush Emunim leaders argued that Jews should stop distinguishing between the degrees of sanctity of different parts of Eretz Israel since it was all equally sacred.[103]

Gush Emunim's ability to appeal credibly to the old map image of the homeland as extending from "the River of Egypt to...the River Euphrates," despite its decline among the rest of the Religious Zionist movement, is a function of the fact that evolution is a story of shifts in frequency distributions. Total extinction is relatively rare. Most of the time, the variants whose frequency of articulation is declining do not disappear from the political scene; rather, they remain part of the repertoire of ideological positions available to be used and, if conditions are right, reselected for success. The stage was set for this to take place with the political and ideological ascendance of Gush Emunim. Indeed, for a brief period it appeared as though Gush Emunim might succeed in reimposing the old map image on the rest of the movement. This possibility was most evident in the (short-lived) inclusion of the Sinai Peninsula within the conception of the "Land of Israel" by even mainstream religious Zionism (as we saw in fig. 12).

Mainstream Religious Zionism had traditionally excluded the Sinai Peninsula from the definition of the homeland. Indicating that it was not part of their map image of the homeland in 1957, a number of movement leaders even suggested resettling the Palestinian refugees in Sinai, or using it as a bargaining chip in peace negotiations with Egypt. Those who believed the Sinai was appropriately part of the nation-state were a distinct minority. S. Z. Kahana even had to task a rabbinic scholar with the mission of finding something with which they could substantiate their claim to Sinai, (He did so.)[104] The disagreement over the status of the Sinai Peninsula was such that the chief rabbis of Israel felt obligated to clarify the situation by issuing a declaration in which they defined the Sinai as "part of our country" and its conquest as part of the "fulfillment of God's promise." Nonetheless, throughout the meetings held by the NRP's leadership in the aftermath of the 1956 war, there was only a single, largely ignored voice (Rabbi Oshpiai) that objected to Israel's withdrawal from Sinai because it was a withdrawal from the Land of Israel.[105]

The notion that the Sinai was probably not part of the homeland did not change in the immediate aftermath of the 1967 war. Led by largely the same leaders as in 1956, the NRP supported the government's secret June 19, 1967, decision to return the Sinai and Golan Heights to Egypt and Syria in exchange for peace treaties. Zerach Warhaftig even claimed that in these areas "there are only security problems and not problems of sanctity."[106] Similarly, Yitzhak Rephael contrasted the adherence to Judea and Samaria with the claim to Sinai, "which is not a matter of principle, but rather a political military one." Even Zvulun Hammer was willing to compromise on Sinai in the 1970s. While noting that most of the movement opposed the 1975 Interim Agreements with Egypt, Hammer admitted: "I have no religious, historic, emotional tie to the Sinai."[107] The exclusion of the Sinai from the definition of the homeland was also visible in the acceptance by most of the NRP's leadership (excluding those closely affiliated with Gush Emunim) of the Camp David Accords, despite their reservations about creating a precedent for evacuating settlements, and a return to the June 4 borders.[108]

Gush Emunim, however, considered the Sinai Peninsula unambiguously part of the Land of Israel.[109] In fact, at the end of the standoff in Yamit (one of the settlements evacuated as part of the peace agreement with Egypt), Gush Emunim activists vowed to return, and to remind everyone that "this region is part of Eretz Israel that is stated in the Torah."[110] Following up on this promise, and reflecting Gush Emunim's influence, Bnei Akiva included the Sinai within the map image of the Land of Israel that it articulated for at least a year after the Sinai evacuation.[111]

Yet any success Gush Emunim had in influencing the Religious Zionist map image in this direction was short-lived. Not only did it ultimately fail to impose its view on the rest of the Religious Zionist movement, its own definition of the homeland was transformed. As we saw earlier in this chapter, the map image of the "whole land of Israel" ending at the Jordan became dominant even within Gush Emunim. The failure to impose the map image of "the River of Egypt to ... the River Euphrates" despite Gush Emunim's successful ascendance to the ideological leadership of the Religious Zionist movement runs against the expectations of elite imposition. After all, Gush Emunim was strong enough both to take over the movement and to impose a radically new theology and definition of national mission (see chapter 4). Why was it unable to impose its views of the appropriate extent of the homeland as well? Why, instead, did this theologically rigid and territorially hawkish group experience a change in what it saw as the entirety of the homeland?

The answers lie in the impact of the evolutionary dynamic. Gush Emunim's engagement in politics, specifically its desire to ensure Israel's hold over the territories through a political alliance with the Likud (the heir of Revisionist Zionism), unintentionally led to the institutionalization of the truncated map image of the homeland even within Gush Emunim's own ranks! The alliance between the Likud and Gush Emunim brought together movements with radically different answers to foundational questions, including the appropriate extent of the homeland. While hawkish and certainly committed to Israeli control of the West Bank and Gaza Strip, by this point the Revisionist Zionists articulated a notion of the "whole land of Israel" that placed the western border of Israel at the Jordan River and that excluded the Sinai Peninsula (see chapter 3). In order to cooperate with the Revisionists, Gush Emunim muted its different conception of what the "whole land of Israel" meant. This alliance was not, at least not initially, based on a shared conception of their maximum goals. It was based instead on the lowest common denominator: agreement that Israel should control the territories. Not everyone within the Religious Zionist movement approved of this step. Some even warned that the tactical cooperation with the Likud might yield an unwanted ideological identification with the Likud's goals.[112]

They were right. The mutually beneficial alliance between the Likud and Gush Emunim succeeded in achieving many of its short-term goals. It helped catapult the Revisionists into power. Once there, they reciprocated by aiding the spread of Gush Emunim and deepened its settlement project in the territories. After the Likud's victory in 1977, Menachem Begin rewarded Gush Emunim activists with unprecedented access to the state bureaucracy—meaning both jobs and influence. Abandoning the tactical muting of its full claims that led to this windfall would have jeopardized Gush Emunim's newfound power. As the rewards for adopting the "wholeness" of the land as the frame for the debate over the territories grew, the incentives to deviate from it and articulate the old territorial claims correspondingly declined. Gush Emunim's daily awareness of the limits of its reach to the area under Israeli control also reinforced the equation between this area and the Land of Israel. The shift did not happen all at once. Yet, over time, as the alliance with the Revisionists proved successful, the map image of the "whole land of Israel" sidelined the old map image even within Gush Emunim.

[margin note: incentive to deviate declined]

In addition to the evidence provided earlier in this chapter, the relative silence that greeted the exuberance some Gush Emunim leaders exhibited at the invasion of Lebanon reinforces the notion that Gush Emunim's public increasingly accepted the "whole land of Israel" map image. The notion that this was an opportunity to conquer more of the Land of Israel did not appear in what was perhaps the most likely place for such an argument—a compilation of reactions to the war by the religious soldiers who participated in it, titled "My Land: A Collection of Essays, Thoughts, and Studies for the Clarification of the Living Link between the Nation of Israel and Its Land in Our Generation."[113]

The debate within Gush Emunim about the withdrawal from most of Lebanon in 1985 forced the increasing acceptance of the "whole land of Israel" map image into the open. Perhaps as a result of the high casualty rate suffered by graduates of their seminaries during the war, Israel's 1985 withdrawal from "the lands of Asher, Dan, and Naftali" was not dramatized by the leaders of the NRP, Techiya, Morasha, or Gush Emunim—a stance for which they were criticized by more radical truth tellers within the movement.[114] In response, Gush Emunim's leaders again portrayed their relative silence as a temporary and tactical concession to reality (both political and military) and not as an ideological change.[115] Yoel Ben-Nun argued that already during the Litani operation (1978), Zvi Yehuda Kook's position was that Israel had no territorial claims on Lebanon, but he interpreted it as merely a temporary postponement of Israel's claim.[116] He argued that "in the current historical epoch, the land of Israel is divided in two, on the Jordan, whether or not we want it. We will not forget "our Transjordan," but we will also know that the nation of Israel in its present condition cannot inherit more than the western land of Israel which is in our hands. (Neither can we [inherit] the patrimony of Asher and Naftali that are in

Lebanon!). This is difficult to understand and to digest, but 'this (too) [*sic*] is from God.'"[117]

Yehuda Amital also argued that "it is possible that Lebanon was included in the promise," but because of historical circumstances, they should not deal with the issues of its conquest. Similarly, Avraham Shapira did not agree to the claim of Lebanon as part of the Land of Israel for practical reasons—a "bowing to reality" that he specifically applied only to Lebanon and Transjordan, not to the West Bank, Gaza Strip, or Golan Heights.[118] A strong strand within the movement also claimed the East Bank of the Jordan as part of the homeland but argued that until the entire Jewish nation could agree on its right to the West Bank, it was premature to discuss the East Bank.[119] Even Rabbi Levinger, who claimed Southern Lebanon as part of the Land of Israel, argued that because the nation was not ready to see it as part of the Land of Israel, it was useless to discuss the subject.[120] Despite Religious Zionist claims to the contrary, this reflected a *post-hoc* recognition of the shift that had taken place within the movement regarding the area considered appropriately part of the Jewish state.

The prevalence within Gush Emunim of the "whole land of Israel" map image since the mid-1980s suggests that these consensus builders won the intramovement contest. Eventually, the "whole land of Israel" framing of the homeland displaced the alternative map image even within Gush Emunim. This was not, it should be emphasized, the intention of the consensus builders, some of whom continue to articulate the claim to the East Bank of the Jordan to this day.

While the change progressed widely among Gush Emunim's constituency, it is not yet finished, nor is it irreversible. The old map image is still available in the repertoire of Religious Zionism. This leaves an opening for a new attempt to successfully reenergize the old map image where Gush Emunim failed. Indeed, the Hardal wing of the movement (see chapter 6) has revived the claim to the land from "the River of Egypt to...the River Euphrates" as part of its bid for the leadership of Religious Zionism.[121] To the extent that it succeeds, the claim to the biblical map image as the appropriate extent of the state of Israel will become more prominent within the movement once again.

3

Revisionist Zionist Mapping
of the Homeland

Until the withdrawal from the Gaza Strip in 2005, the Revisionist movement vocally and consistently advocated Israeli control of the "whole land of Israel." The volume with which they asserted their territorially maximalist claims hid, however, a shift in their answer to the question "Where is the homeland?" When it first emerged, this nationalist movement virtually tattooed itself with a vision of the homeland that corresponded to the 1919 British Mandate. In contrast, the "whole land of Israel" that the Revisionist movement came to claim with equal fervor excluded the area east of the Jordan River. This shift was the unintended by-product of short-term rhetorical modulations made to rescue the Revisionists from political irrelevance. As this movement succeeded in reintegrating into the legitimate political spectrum, eventually winning the premiership, the once tactical variation became entrenched as the new ideological orthodoxy.

This chapter explores how this transformation in the ideology of an ultranationalist movement took place. The first part of the chapter establishes the original map image held by the Revisionists and shows that, despite their protestations of unyielding ideological fidelity, the map image did in fact change. The second half of the chapter demonstrates that the fit between the historical record and the expectations of the evolutionary dynamic is more convincing than the congruence between the empirical benchmarks of change and the predictions of either elite imposition or rational adaptation. I return to the issue of changes in the territorial claims made by the Revisionist Zionist movement in chapter 6, where I discuss its apparent acceptance of the principle of partition of the land west of the Jordan River.

The Shift from "Both Banks of the Jordan" to the "Whole Land of Israel"

Of the three nationalist movements examined in this book, the Revisionist Zionists articulated their vision of the homeland most explicitly. From 1925 to the mid-1950s, the virtually exclusive map image of the appropriate territory they articulated encompassed "both banks of the Jordan." A minority within the movement, including the poet Uri Zvi Greenberg, based its claim on the biblical promise and desired the land all the way to the Euphrates.[1] Generally speaking, however, the Revisionist invocation of "both banks of the Jordan" referred to the inescapably secular borders of the 1919 British Mandate for Palestine rather than to any biblical demarcation of the homeland (see figs. 17 and 18). The most evocative rendition of this map image, and the source of the refrain "both banks of the Jordan," was Vladimir Jabotinsky's 1930 hymn "The Left of the Jordan":

> As a bridge is held up by a pillar
> As man is kept erect by his spine,
> So the Jordan, the holy Jordan,
> Is the backbone of my Israel.
>
> Chorus: There are two Banks to the Jordan—
> This one is ours, and that [one]—as well.
>
> Tho' my country may be poor and small
> It is mine from head to foot.
> Stretching from the sea to the desert,
> And the Jordan, the Jordan in the middle.
>
> [Chorus]
>
> From the wealth in our land there shall prosper,
> The Arab, the Christian, and the Jew.
> For our flag is a pure and just one
> Both banks will be lit by you.
>
> [Chorus]

> My two hands I have dedicated to you,
> Both my hands to the shield and the sword.
> If I forget the left bank of the Jordan,
> May my right hand be withered by the Lord.[2]

Jabotinsky's belief that the state of the Jews should encompass both Palestine and Transjordan was a founding principle of the Zionist Revisionist Organization (and, after its formal split from the World Zionist Organization in 1935, of the New Zionist Organization [NZO]).[3] Among Revisionists, the inclusion of Transjordan as part of Eretz Israel (the Land of Israel) was the very standard of obviousness. For example, Benjamin Lubotsky wanted the idea that their paramilitary youth movement should provide the backbone of a future Hebrew army "to become a principle that is taken for granted by all (like 'a Hebrew state on both sides of the Jordan')."[4] Rather than adapt to the imposition of new borders by the imperial powers, Jabotinsky argued that the exclusion of Transjordan from the area of the future Jewish state was "both a historical and a practical injustice," and explained: "Historically, the East Jordan Land was always part of Jewish Palestine: the Jews settled there even before the conquest of Western Palestine.... In view of the great Jewish misery in Eastern Europe it is wrong... to withhold from Jewish colonization this best part of Palestine."[5]

Transjordan also featured prominently in the Revisionist arguments against partition in 1937.[6] Jabotinsky opened his impressive testimony before the Peel Commission by leaving no doubt as to what territory he had in mind: "The term 'Palestine,' when I employ it, will mean the area on both sides of the Jordan, the area mentioned in the original Palestine Mandate."[7] Jabotinsky objected to the Peel partition plan partly because he feared that it would institutionalize the split between Palestine and Transjordan. It would, he argued, provide the desolate East Bank of the Jordan with "the human and financial capital" of the Arabs of the West Bank and turn it into a viable separate state.[8]

Jabotinsky's rejection of the Peel Commission's report used a combination of evocative and instrumental arguments to claim Transjordan. However, even the rationale Jabotinsky used in his instrumental arguments highlights his belief that the 1919 Mandate borders were the *appropriate* ones. For example, he rejected Ben-Gurion's theory of stages (see chapter 1) because he believed that while objective political and military forces would prevent the Jewish state from expanding after its formation, it would be "impossible to prevent this dream ... [because] no Jew ... could really and truly give up Jerusalem, Hebron, and the Land of Gilead east of the Jordan River."[9]

The prominent place reserved for the claim to the East Bank of the Jordan in Betar's (the Revisionist Zionist youth movement) materials also militates against the argument that this claim was anything but sincere. Responding to the Peel partition plan, Betar vowed to fight "*a merciless war against the dismemberment of the body and soul of Zionism*" "for an eternity." Territorially this translated, according to their pronouncement, to a fight "*for the holy city Jerusalem and Eretz Israel from Dan to Beersheva and from the Gilead to the sea.*"[10] Transjordan remained a central and frequently discussed component of the area Betar considered appropriately part of the Jewish state throughout the 1940s. A cartoon in a 1944 Betar camp journal provides a telling example. The cartoon depicted a Betar member with a hoe who complains: "Commander, I have no more strength to work." The "Commander" replies: "Do you want Transjordan? Then work!"[11] Betar even published a 1946 booklet dedicated to the "Jewish Left of the Jordan." Mixing past and present, it implied that the "amputation" of Transjordan took place in 1946 (when Transjordan gained its independence) rather than in 1922:

> In the midst of the days of our mourning—when six million of our slaughtered-dead are still cast before us, and the gates of the homeland are locked before the remnant—in the midst of these terrible days the Mandate government has added a new wound to the wounded soul of the orphaned nation. The Left of the Jordan—that is the land conquered by the master of prophets, Moses, and in which...he died, the land of Reuven, Gad, and half the tribe of Menashe, the birthplace of Elijah the Tishbi and of Yiftah of the Gilead, has been torn from our homeland like a limb from a living body and given as a gift to Abdullah.... We will defend our lives and our rights. We will defend them with the same stubbornness and zealotry that distinguished our ancestors during their fight over the purity of their religion....Dew and rain [may fall] upon you, cities and villages in Transjordan, it does not matter—you were ours, and ours you shall be.[12]

This pathos faithfully reflected the ideology of the Revisionist movement, which continued to demand a Jewish state on both banks of the Jordan throughout the UN debate over Palestine's future. The movement's military wing, the Irgun Zvai Leumi (the National Military Organization, known by its Hebrew acronym, Etzel) asked the UN to consider that "Eretz-Israel (Palestine), in its indivisible area east and west of the Jordan River, is the territory of our people according to all accepted criteria—historical, moral, cultural and ethnic." It declared that Britain, in order to "consolidate her occupation[,]...installed an alien Prince, of the Hashemite family, as a puppet ruler in that part of our national territory known as Transjordan (Transjordan, Eastern Palestine, means the eastern side of the Jordan, just as, according to historical record, the alternate name for the Western side of the Jordan is Western Palestine)."[13]

In a secret meeting with an UNSCOP representative, Menachem Begin, who, following a short transition period, had become the leader of the Revisionist movement after Jabotinsky's unexpected death, "pointed out that none of the Irgun members will not [sic] accept any carving up of the territory which they consider to be the property of the Jewish state of Palestine" and will fight against it.[14] The military wing of the Revisionist movement repeatedly threatened to continue fighting for the "liberation of the whole of Palestine on both sides of the Jordan" even after the state was established.[15] Begin, in "a message to the American People," declared that "we are in revolt in order to reunite our land, West and East of the Jordan,...and we swear that no sacrifice shall be too great, that we will not lay down our arms nor cease fighting until the whole of Palestine is a free and independent state."[16] In a rebuke of Labor's pragmatism, Begin concluded: "As a matter of principle...a country...is a thing no one is entitled to trade."[17]

Begin's autobiography clearly shows that he considered Transjordan appropriately part of the homeland. Describing his journey from Eastern Europe to Palestine in the summer of 1942, he recalled entering "Transjordan. Our heritage....The eastern bank of the Jordan-Eretz Israel. The military convoy stopped. We rested. I left the automobile, waded a little way into the grass, and drank in the odor of the fields of my Homeland."[18]

Despite its unrelenting demand for a Jewish state, the Revisionist movement actually opposed the UN decision that called for the creation of the state partly because it implied giving up the claim to Transjordan.[19] On November 30, 1947, the day after the UN vote calling the Jewish state into existence, while most of Jewish Palestine celebrated the imminent achievement of the national dream, the front page of *Hamashkif* (one of their daily newspapers) featured three obituary boxes containing the following quotations: "If I forget you, Jerusalem, I will forget my right hand"; "To your seed I gave that land from the River of Egypt to the Euphrates"; "Two banks the Jordan has, this one is ours, that one as well."

On the eve of the declaration of the state of Israel, Begin declared:

> It is an iron rule of life: That which comes between the people's state and the people's homeland must disappear. The state will cover the homeland. The homeland will be the state....It is not just *the city* [i.e., Jerusalem] that was stolen from us. We have in mind five-sixths of the territory of our homeland....We shall therefore proudly bear the vision of full salvation, the dream of the liberation under the Hebrew flag, the flag of freedom, the flag of peace and progress. The soldiers of Israel will yet hoist our banner on the Tower of David, and our ploughs will yet plough the fields of the Gilead.[20]

Both the overt reference to the Gilead and the calculation that "five-sixths of the homeland" remained outside the area of the state of Israel convey the inclusion of Transjordan in the Revisionist vision of the appropriate homeland. Moreover, as Arye Naor noted, ideologically and rhetorically, Begin's argument assigned the East Bank of the Jordan the same importance as the sacred city of Jerusalem.[21]

Even the internal opposition to Begin, those Revisionists who emphasized the more liberal and secular aspects of Jabotinsky's legacy, claimed both sides of the Jordan.[22] There were a few voices within the Revisionist movement expressing support for tactical (some even for sincere) acceptance of the UN partition plan, but such pragmatic assessments of political reality were soundly rejected by Begin and the movement's mainstream.[23] This suggests, once again, that even if some members of a nationalist movement appear to rationally adapt to a new reality, their subsequent political success or failure within the movement is as important as the new reality in determining whether such rational adaptation actually leads to substantive ideological change by the movement.

Indeed, neither the Holocaust nor the founding of the state affected the Revisionist movement's continuing adherence to the "both banks of the Jordan" map image. The adoption of the Irgun's logo as the official emblem of Herut—the political party that emerged from it—graphically illustrates this vision's persistence despite these significant shocks. The only change that took place involved replacing the caption "Only Thus" with "Homeland and Freedom" (see figs. 17 and 18). Even the few proposals that called for a modification of the emblem sought only to remove the bayoneted rifle. No one envisioned amending the map on which it was mounted.[24] Begin believed that the map image should be maintained despite the movement's reincarnation as a legitimate political party, because "'the state of Israel' is not *the Land of Israel,* and is not Israel's *homeland;* and the goal is *the homeland* and not [merely] a single strip of its territory—every person in Israel has to be reminded of this day and night until the eternal aspiration becomes a living reality."[25] In this spirit, those who joined Herut signed a membership card affirming the principle that the "Hebrew Homeland" extends "on both sides of the Jordan...[as] a historic and geographic whole."[26]

Even after the birth of the state, Begin and the Revisionist movement consistently included the East Bank among the parts of Eretz Israel that "have not yet been liberated" and were still occupied by the British.[27] Begin tirelessly declared that Britain was the enemy because it "is the one who is blocking our path to the liberation of the homeland, because Britain is the one who created and sustains, at the expense of our nation, within the borders of our land on the two banks of our Jordan, the 'kingdom of Amman.'"[28] Just in case there was any doubt, the Revisionists would often

Figure 17. The emblem of the Irgun from a recruiting pamphlet, 1947. On either side of the emblem is the slogan "Only Thus." Courtesy of the Jabotinsky Institute in Israel.

enumerate what they meant by "Eretz Israel": "You know our viewpoint. The whole of Eretz Israel is our homeland. Our Homeland is the whole of Eretz Israel, yes on both banks of the Jordan; Amman and Shchem, and the Gilead no less than Shomron, the Bashan no less than the Sharon—all are parts of our homeland."[29]

In fact, Herut presented its own theory of stages—the end of which was a Jewish state on both banks of the Jordan.[30] It repeatedly declared that the task of the current generation was to return those parts of the homeland that had been torn from it—explicitly including Transjordan—to Hebrew sovereignty. Indeed, this was the stated goal of Betar as late as 1953.[31] Begin openly called for the conquest of Transjordan and averred that the war of liberation was not yet over, because the entire homeland, on both banks of the Jordan, was not yet liberated. "Despite all of our victories, victory is far away from us.... The Wall of the Old City is not the border of Jerusalem; the Jordan is not the border of our country, and the sea is not the border of our nation. There is a uniform tie between the new Jerusalem and the ancient, between the Gilead and Samaria, between the dispersed [nation of] Israel and the state of Israel."[32] He declared: "We have two maps before our eyes—the

Figure 18. Menachem Begin (standing) with Herut's emblem. The caption reads "Homeland and Freedom." Courtesy of the Jabotinsky Institute in Israel.

strange "zigzag" [of the state] and the historic patrimony of Israel. We will not rest and we will not cease until both these maps shall be one, and the nation will reside securely in its country."[33] In a Knesset speech on May 30, 1951, Begin identified himself and his colleagues as those "who believe with perfect faith—and this belief will be fulfilled—that Hebron and Bethlehem, Shchem and Amman are inseparable parts of the Hebrew homeland."[34]

The ideology of both banks of the Jordan was more than a sacred myth. It provided the basis for an alternative policy to that offered by Labor Zionism, a policy based on the desire to take advantage of perceived opportunities (such as the murder of King Abdullah) to undertake "fulfillment actions" to liberate the entire land of Israel.[35] Consistent with this stance, Begin rejected the holding of armistice negotiations after the 1948 war with King Abdullah of Jordan, since that would leave the latter with "4/5 of our historic patrimony." Rather than make peace, he maintained, the goal of Israeli policy should be "to remove this 'kingdom' from the world."[36] Begin framed their policy options as either having King Abdullah as

our neighbor a few tens of kilometers from Ramat-Gan, or [having] the Hebrew soldiers, eventually and with the help of God...stand in our Amman....[Transjordan] stands abandoned and awaits the plough of the...Hebrew farmer and the conquering Hebrew soldier...is this [Abdullah's] land and his nation? Eretz Israel has historically been divided into the two sides of the Jordan, the East and West Banks of the Jordan, but both are two parts of our whole country.[37]

Herut's second (1951) and third (1954) national conventions ratified this rejection because "Jordan," in the words of Herut's 1951 decision, "extends on territory of our homeland."[38] Begin explicitly refused to recognize the legitimacy of Jordan, because doing so would imply "the legal and explicit recognition of our nation to the tearing of Transjordan" from the homeland.[39] The movement's written material—for both internal and external consumption—consistently spoke of the "so-called kingdom of Jordan" and enclosed Jordan in quotation marks to indicate its illegitimacy. Begin even went to the effort of inserting this delegitimizing punctuation by hand in the official Knesset transcript of his speeches. He also repeatedly called attention to what he termed Mapai's insidious efforts to get people to forget "the Eastern part of our nation." The education of the youth, he argued, should focus on their right to both banks of the Jordan.[40]

The heartfelt claim to the land on both banks of the Jordan notwithstanding, today the Revisionist Zionist movement no longer includes the East Bank of the Jordan in its definition of the appropriate extent of the homeland. Indeed, reminders that Revisionist Zionists once claimed the East Bank are more likely to elicit mild embarrassment than fervent affirmation.[41] As in the case of the Religious Zionists, their everyday speech and banal flagging of the homeland's extent expose the existence and extent of this transformation. Their common use of the past tense to speak of the unification of Eretz Israel assumes that there are no more areas of the homeland that need to be joined to the state of Israel. For example, by the 1970s, Begin argued that "we liberated Eretz Israel" and that the Land of Israel "*was divided* in a war of aggression, and *was united* in a war of self-defense."[42] While Yitzhak Shamir was not entirely consistent, he framed the claim to the East Bank of the Jordan—the few times he articulated it—solely as a historical claim with little or no contemporary practical relevance.[43] Benjamin Netanyahu's ideological treatise also places the claim to the East Bank firmly in the past: "At Versailles the Jewish nation was promised that it would be allowed to establish a state in 'Palestine': the national home included both sides of the Jordan *in those days*. This region, today called 'Mandatory Eretz-Israel,' included the areas of the present-day states of Israel and Jordan."[44] Not only does Netanyahu's use of the past tense suggest that he no longer considers this area part of Israel, but the maps he provides use the label "Mandatory Eretz-Israel" to designate only the area west of the Jordan! Without fanfare he effectively abandons the area Jabotinsky called "the best part of Palestine."

More generally, the Revisionists' strident opposition to territorial compromise over the West Bank surreptitiously removed the East Bank from the land to which they proclaimed their loyalty. Thus, in the 1970s, Begin and his colleagues in the Revisionist movement began to speak consistently of the need to "guard" and "maintain" the wholeness of the Land of Israel.[45] This task makes little sense under the map image of "both banks of the Jordan," since it is impossible to maintain what one does not possess. Similarly, the frequent post-1967 statements that "it cannot be imagined that a single handful of the land of Eretz Israel will again be given to foreign rule"[46] ignored the fact that, at least according to the original vision of the homeland, there were parts of the Land of Israel that were still under "foreign rule."

Also betraying a changed notion of the homeland, Revisionist politicians routinely framed the debate over the occupied territories as a choice between "Eretz Israel in its entirety or its division anew"—a formulation that implies that Eretz Israel (i.e., the land up to the Jordan) is currently whole.[47] An analogous message was conveyed by the ubiquitous calls within and by the Revisionist movement to "open *all the areas of Eretz Israel* for settlement,"[48] to extend Israeli law to "all of Eretz Israel," and to economically integrate "all the areas of Eretz Israel."[49] A 1988 election advertisement targeted at religious Jews warned: "For two thousand years our forefathers prayed to reach Hebron, Shchem, Beth-El, and Bethlehem. And we, who have been privileged to reach and to see the rise of the Jewish state in *all the places* that are holy to our nation, may, God forbid, lose all this."[50] Yosef Paz explicitly articulated the now common meaning of the "whole land of Israel": "There is a demographic problem in the complete Land of Israel, as well as in the incomplete Land of Israel, *meaning without Judea, Samaria, and the Gaza Strip*."[51] The East Bank of the Jordan, once a staple of such enumerations, is gone. This was also true of the definition of the "eternal patrimony of our ancestors." Diverging from his earlier depictions (cited above), Begin's closing address to the 1968 Herut convention defined the Jewish patrimony as "Jerusalem, Hebron, Bethlehem, Judea, [and] Shchem"—thereby dropping the East Bank of the Jordan from the ancestral homeland.[52]

The subtle equation of "western Eretz Israel" with (an unmodified) "Eretz Israel" also promoted the transformation of the map image of the Revisionist movement. The equalization of these two terms contradicts the "both banks of the Jordan" ideology, which saw the first as comprising only half of the second. The shrinking of the Land of Israel through the equation of these two terms was exemplified by the following declaration by Begin: "Western Eretz Israel is not subject to partition. When in the US, I used the expression 'The Land of Israel is unpartitionable.' Eretz Israel is unpartitionable."[53] Begin's assertion was not an isolated example of the equation of the terms. He and other leading lights of the Revisionist movement began to consistently—though not uniformly—use "western Eretz Israel" and "Eretz Israel" interchangeably.[54]

The treatment of the Palestinian refugee problem in the Revisionist Zionist platforms reflected this rhetorical shift. In 1977, the movement affirmed its willingness to rehabilitate the refugees who lived in the "land of Israel"— not in the "state of Israel" or the "western land of Israel."[55] The "land of Israel" now ended at the Jordan. A similar sleight of hand was involved in the claim that the Movement for the Whole Land of Israel had adopted the Revisionists' once "unique" insistence on the wholeness of the homeland.[56] As we saw above, the "wholeness" claimed by the Movement for the Whole Land of Israel did not include the East Bank of the Jordan. Thus, while seeming to enforce a notion of ideological continuity, this claim actually transformed the referent of the "wholeness of the homeland" from "both banks of the Jordan" to "the land west of the Jordan."

This bait and switch was evident elsewhere as well. In his speech to the 1968 Herut convention, Begin equated "Eretz Israel" with "the state of Israel" and even referred to the new status quo as the "full redemption."[57] The significance of this change is underscored by the fact that, twenty years earlier, his vow to equate the borders of the state of Israel and the Land of Israel explicitly included Transjordan (see above). By 1973 some within the movement even claimed that their slogan "Af Sha'al" (Not a Single Step) "always referred to Judea and Samaria" and not to other territories.[58]

The Revisionists also failed to apply the logic they used to claim the West Bank and Gaza Strip to the East Bank. They repeatedly warned against the use of the term "Palestine" and emphasized the terms "Judea and Samaria" rather than "West Bank" because they believed that the war of words was part of the nationalist conflict over the land. They believed that using the "Palestinian" terminology would undermine their claim to this land.[59] Rarely, however, did they apply this logic to the East Bank or to the increasing equalization of "western Eretz Israel" and "Eretz Israel" once the transformation began. Their belief that the act of articulating the right was important on its own, even if it could not be actualized, makes the elimination of Transjordan from their pattern of rhetorical articulation especially striking. By their own reasoning, the elision of the East Bank implied that they relinquished their claim to this (former) part of the homeland.

This point is reinforced by the fact that, given the opportunity to articulate the claim to both banks of the Jordan in a presumably ideologically safe 1973 Herut Central Committee meeting, Begin demurred. When he was pointedly asked "What is the wholeness of the land over which there is a general agreement in the Likud?" rather than articulate the claim to both banks of the Jordan, Begin replied: "The answer is that we are affirming our belief."[60] The redrawing of the vision of the homeland was plainly evident in the new map images that emerged to take the place of the old ones (see figs. 19 and 20).

Reflecting this transformation, the discussion in a Gahal Knesset Faction meeting in November 1968 revolved around what conditions to impose on peace negotiations with Jordan—not, as was the case a decade earlier, whether or not Jordan was a legitimate partner.[61] By the early 1970s, Begin and the Revisionist movement also began to recognize Jordan in their written communications, no longer dismissing it with quotation marks.[62] Tellingly, unlike his condemnations of Ben-Gurion for signing the armistice agreement with the Kingdom of Transjordan in 1950, Begin's criticism of the Allon plan did not include a similar condemnation of its recognition of foreign rule over the East Bank of the Jordan.[63] In contrast to his consistent refusal to recognize Jordan's right to exist in the 1950s, in his response to King Hussein's announcement of a Jordanian federation in 1972, Begin challenged only Jordan's right to the West Bank, not its existence.[64] Even the debate within Herut focused solely on the implications for the West Bank. No one mentioned Jordan's illegitimacy or that it too was part of the Land of Israel.[65] Again, in 1978, Begin criticized the idea that Hussein had a right to Jerusalem, Judea, or Samaria, but not Jordan's right to exist or its right to the East Bank of the Jordan River. At this meeting Dov Shilanski even stated: "[When] I speak of Eretz Israel I mean and include in it Judea, Samaria, and the Gaza Strip."[66]

Begin also attempted retroactively to rewrite the borders component of Revisionist ideology to include only the land west of the Jordan. Unlike the Hebrew versions of his autobiography, a 1972 English edition no longer included those parts of his speeches in which he declared the eternal claim to the East Bank.[67] In 1973, he recalled Revisionist thinking (or what he

Figure 19. Letterhead from Likud's Northern Branch, 1976. Courtesy of the Jabotinsky Institute in Israel.

Figure 19a. The black area indicates areas of the old map image that are now excluded. The striped area indicates temporary additions to the conception of the homeland.

now claimed was their thinking) in 1948: "We said, there is no choice but to win, and, perhaps, the source of all our problems is that *we did not liberate all of Eretz Israel as we could have*...but it is a fact that following this war *the British left Eretz Israel,* and the state of Israel was formed....We could have taken *the entire land,* but there is no denying that in this war the nation of Israel achieved a great deal."[68] This retelling excludes the East Bank of the Jordan (as well as Sinai and Southern Lebanon) from the area of the "whole land" in two ways. First, while Transjordan was nominally independent, the British did not actually leave it in the 1950s—a fact that drew loud complaints from Begin himself (see above). Second, while many believed that Israel could conquer all the land up to the Jordan, virtually no one thought that it was within Israel's power to cross the river. Retroactively including the Revisionists as part of this consensus erases their prior inclusion of the East Bank from their definition of the entirety of the homeland.

The value of Transjordan as part of the homeland decreased so much that, in contrast to Begin's insistence in 1947 that the homeland was not

Figure 20. Likud campaign advertisement, 1981: "We are on the map! This map cannot be reversed (returned)." Courtesy of the Jabotinsky Institute in Israel.

something to be traded (see above), Herut Central Committee members began suggesting that Israel claim Transjordan *as a stratagem* in negotiating with the neighboring states.[69] At its most expansionist, this argument implies that Transjordan was appropriately part of the Land of Israel, but that the Jews, perhaps temporarily, decided to give that part to the Arabs.[70] Another version of this argument (sometimes articulated by the same people) simply states that "Jordan is the Palestinian state"—simultaneously claiming the West Bank and relinquishing the claim to the East Bank.[71] In 1986, Elihu Ben-Elissar, who disagreed with this argument, nonetheless noted that the majority of Herut members adhered to it.[72] Since then, it has become a mainstay of their articulations.[73]

The debate within Herut over the Camp David Accords reaffirmed the notion that the East Bank was no longer part of what they considered the "whole land of Israel." For one, Begin now openly called for a formal peace with Jordan, abandoning his earlier position that such an agreement was impossible and undesirable because Jordan occupied part of the homeland.[74] David Levi, in presenting the Likud-led government's position on the Camp David Accords to the Herut Central Committee, argued that the

Figure 20a. Shaded area indicates areas of the old map image that are now excluded.

[handwritten margin note: Revisionist Ideology now: we still want the whole homeland, it just doesn't include Jordan]

Likud-led government remained loyal to the movement's ideal of the entire land of Israel. In the process, however, he implied that the whole land of Israel stops at the Jordan: "Our position, the position of the Herut movement, does not need somebody's declaration or the preaching of someone from outside this movement, and no one ... will teach us what is Eretz Israel for this movement, what is loyalty to Judea and Samaria." Nor did Levi include Transjordan in outlining what he considered the best possible borders of Israel: "We would all want, and without a doubt every citizen in Israel would want, true peace with all our neighbors and *Sinai, Judea, Samaria, the Gaza Strip and the Golan in our control.*"[75] Even many of the opponents of the Camp David Accords implied that the land of Israel was whole without the East Bank. While there were a few exceptions, they were easily rebuffed.[76]

Begin's rationale for rejecting a potential coalition with the Labor party in 1981 also revealed the exclusion of the East Bank from his map image of the homeland. Begin argued that Rabin's rejection of the policy of the whole land of Israel meant "that the principle that there will be no foreign rule or sovereignty *west of the Jordan* would not be mentioned in the government's basic guidelines."[77] The whole land of Israel and the area "west of the Jordan" were self-evidently seen as one and the same. Begin even went so far as to call the logic of partition "stupid" because the wholeness of the post-1967 land was obvious; it was "as natural as a growing oak, as the breaking dawn, as sand on the seashore, as the stars of the sky."[78] Notably, both Yitzhak Shamir and Benjamin Netanyahu joined Begin in declaring that the Jordan River was the "natural boundary" of "Eretz Israel." In fact, Shamir went so far as to claim that "there is no other natural border."[79] Shamir invoked Jabotinsky to make this claim but minimized the fact that Jabotinsky located this "natural border" in the "desert to the east," not along the Jordan!

By 1982, even Betar, the Revisionist Zionist youth movement, had reformulated its mission according to the new definition of the homeland. In contrast to earlier calls for the conquest and settlement of Transjordan, Yoram Aridor, the general secretary of the Herut movement, now called on Betar members to settle "from the Negev to the Golan, from the Sea to the Jordan." Betar reconfigured its goal as the achievement of "a whole homeland, the concentration of our nation in our land, political sovereignty, a regime of liberty and justice, national culture, and education as loyal citizens to our nation at home and abroad."[80] Gone was the conventional accompanying clause that called for a Hebrew state on both banks of the Jordan. While many of the Web pages of Betar branches still refer in some way to both banks of the Jordan, such references are missing from overt articulations of their ideology. The only mention of both banks in a segment described as "a recent articulation of Betar ideology" is an oblique quote from Jabotinsky's poem "The Left of the Jordan," which Betar uses, not to make a territorial claim, but to argue that Arabs, Jews, and Christians should have equal rights. In fact, Betar assigns Jabotinsky's dream, which he explicitly applied to both banks, only to the area under Israeli control—that is, to the West Bank of the river.[81]

In 1988, the Likud published a pamphlet that included a section titled "Where Is 'Israel?'" Unbelievably in the context of the Revisionist movement, it contained no hint that Transjordan was appropriately part of Eretz Israel, historically or otherwise.[82] In 1991, even Benjamin Begin (Menachem Begin's son, and someone widely recognized for both his personal integrity and his ideological rigidity) implied that the claim to the East Bank of the Jordan was all but gone from the Revisionist movement.[83] This shift within the Revisionist movement culminated in the Likud's "unconditional" endorsement of the 1994 peace treaty with Jordan.[84] No one from the Likud objected to this treaty because it ceded land that appropriately belonged to Israel to a foreign entity.[85] Netanyahu and Shamir even argued that there was no principled reason to oppose the peace agreement with Jordan.[86]

Evolution at Work: Explaining the Move
to the "Whole Land of Israel"

The empirical features of this shift, especially the particular combination of its timing and direction, are more consistent with the expectations of the evolutionary dynamic than with those of either rational adaptation or elite imposition. As in the other cases of evolutionary change, here too an adjustment initially made for short-term political gain became unintentionally institutionalized as the new ideological status quo.

The dawning realization among the Revisionists that they had lost their bid to define Israeli nationalism for the entire nation provided the spur to adjust their rhetorical claims. Until the mid-1950s, the Revisionists persisted in their belief that they had the support of the silent majority of Jews around the world. They continued to argue that they were the only real nationalist movement, that they were primarily responsible for the creation of the state, and that their values and symbols reflected the true spirit of the nation. The leaders of the Revisionist movement attributed their electoral weakness to Labor movement trickery, fraud, or idiosyncratic organizational difficulties.[87]

The reality was different. Stigmatized as fanatic extremists on the one hand, and rendered cartoonish on the other, the Revisionists were marginalized nearly to the point of irrelevance in the early years of the state. Ben-Gurion explicitly excluded them from the realm of legitimate politics in his famous declaration that he would form a coalition with anyone other than Herut and Maki (the, largely Arab, Israeli Communist Party). Herut's consistently poor electoral performances in the 1950s reflected its status on the political fringe. It managed to garner only 12 percent of the vote in 1949, 7 percent in 1951, 13 percent in 1955, and 14 percent in 1959 and 1961. Most political analysts at the time believed that these results reflected the extent of Herut's potential voter pool.[88]

Other political parties shared this view of Herut. Mapai, which historically devoted its energies to fighting the Revisionists, began to consider the General Zionists and Mapam as its main competition.[89] Even the Religious Zionists believed that Herut, while "once an important party in the Zionist movement...has completely disappeared from the public stage."[90] Herut's marginality became even more obvious following the nonmaterialization of the protest against the withdrawal from Sinai in 1957, and the realization that public sentiment was against its bellicose stance.[91] In the past, when the Revisionist movement found itself in the minority on fundamental issues, it split from the Zionist Organization. This "exit" option, however, was unavailable in the postindependence reality. Since the Revisionists could not establish a parallel political system, they faced a choice between fading into complete irrelevance and trying to reenter the political game.

According to Mordechai Olmert (a Herut MK and head of its settlement department), Menachem Begin developed a three-pronged program for re-entry into the political spectrum. He tacked toward the religious position on religion-state issues (see chapter 4), sought a merger with the General Zion-ists in order to appeal to the middle class, and established a faction within the Labor Federation to enlist the support of new immigrants who disdained the Labor movement but still wanted the Histadrut's services.[92]

There is no direct evidence that the softening of Revisionist territorial claims was part of this program. No record exists of a similarly overt deci-sion to change their foundational vision of the homeland. The anecdotal evidence that the old emblem of Herut just "melted away" also implies that there was no actual decision to stop using it.[93] This comparative silence on such a foundational question would be surprising if the movement's leader-ship consciously decided to impose the "whole land of Israel" map image on the rest of the movement.

Nonetheless, the Revisionist movement needed to shed its extremist image. As part of this project, a new variant of the extent of its territorial claims entered its discourse. The unacknowledged softening of its claim to both banks of the Jordan crucially enabled its attempt to reenter the legitimate political spectrum. The projection of an image of (relative) pragmatism to the outside allowed the Revisionists to embark on tactical electoral pacts that would otherwise have been impossible. That this variant was identical to the one then current within the dominant Labor movement was not an accident. As the Revisionists succeeded in relegitimating their movement, this initially tacit new variant became entrenched as the new ideological orthodoxy.

The softening of the Revisionist claim to the East Bank was first evident in its elision from rhetorical depictions of the Land of Israel in the mid-1950s. One of the first instances of this elision is Begin's claim in a 1954 Herut Central Committee meeting that "*five years have passed since Eretz Israel was divided,*" implying that Eretz Israel was divided in 1949, not 1922, and therefore that Transjordan was not a part of the Land of Israel. The state of Israel, he concluded, "*needs to be brought up to the Jordan.*"[94] From this point on, Begin's public statements increasingly dropped Transjordan from the list of areas of the Land of Israel that the government failed to liberate. Whereas in the not-too-distant past he had accused Mapai of forgetting that "the whole of Eretz Israel, yes on both banks of the Jordan; Amman and Shchem, the Gilead no less than Shomron, the Bashan no less than the Sharon—all are parts of our homeland," now, in otherwise nearly identical stump speeches, he accused them only of giving up the claim "to Gaza, to Jerusalem, to Shchem, and to Hebron."[95]

Herut's election propaganda also reflected the deemphasis of the original map-image. While, in 1949 and 1951, Herut's emblem (figs. 17 and 18) appeared on nearly everything it produced, the outline of the 1919 Palestine Mandate was much less in evidence in their election propaganda for the 3rd Knesset (1955). As in the case of the Religious Zionists, the relative muting of the claim to Transjordan introduced a measure of ambiguity to Herut's otherwise strident and militant ideology that opened the door to its replacement, even if that was not its original purpose.

Herut's 1959 election campaign was the first in which it did not put forth a plan for the conquest of the Land of Israel.[96] In fact, in stark contrast to its 1949 rejection of even the idea of negotiating with Transjordan, Herut's 1959 platform called for formal relations and peace treaties between Israel and its neighbors—presumably including Jordan. During this election campaign, the map image of "both banks of the Jordan" on a propaganda publication appeared only in an internal page of a pamphlet describing Herut's program. By the next elections, in 1961, it had dropped even this lonely map from an otherwise nearly identical pamphlet![97] A publication intended for first-time voters in this election also reflected the minimization of the traditional conception of the appropriate borders. For the first time, such a publication said absolutely nothing about the borders of the Land of Israel or even about the wholeness of the homeland.[98]

Betar, too, reflected the deemphasis of "both banks of the Jordan." While the picture on the cover of the report to its 7th World Congress (1957) still portrayed the borders of the 1919 Mandate, its content differed strikingly from that of earlier reports. As we saw above, territorial issues, including the claim to both banks of the Jordan, had been a consistent feature of Betar's conventions, educational materials, and self-image. This report, however, contained only one reference to borders in any form: an announcement of the movement's "absolute opposition to the continuation of the retreat from the Gaza Strip and Mifratz Shlomo [Sharm el-Sheikh]." This statement is shockingly modest when compared with previous incantations emphasizing the wholeness of the land on both banks of the Jordan. For the first time, moreover, none of Betar's resolutions referred to the issue of borders—much less to the concept of the wholeness of the homeland.[99] In 1962, Betar's 9th World Congress appeared to correct this oversight when it "reaffirm[ed] and emphasize[d] that the reunification of Eretz Israel in its entirety as a Hebrew state is the primary mission of the nation in this generation."[100] This formulation corresponded to their parents' decision at Herut's 1961 national convention to replace, for the first time, the explicit demand for both banks of the Jordan with a general statement affirming the right of the nation of Israel to "its entire homeland."[101] This apparent return to ideological normalcy, however, was deceptive. The ambiguousness of the phrase "the entire homeland," especially when compared with the more geographically specific "both banks of the Jordan," allowed new content to be poured into the old

Revisionists had no incentive to maintain old ideology

rhetorical vessel of the "wholeness of the homeland." As the rewards for reintegration into the legitimate political spectrum grew, the willingness of Herut leaders to invoke the "both banks of the Jordan" map image correspondingly declined, and the new vision displaced the old one.

Rational adaptation cannot account for the timing of this change, because there was no observable exogenous shock at the time that can also plausibly account for the particular direction of the shift. The direction is consistent with adaptation to the imposition of new imperial borders in 1922 or to the reality of Jordanian independence in 1946, but the lag between these events and the onset of change in the mid-1950s cannot be explained by rational adaptation. An argument based on rational adaptation would also have to explain why the Religious and Labor Zionist movements engaged in analogous transformations a decade and a decade and a half earlier, respectively.

RA doesn't work b/c Revisionists accepted Labor party's def of territory, no one else's

While the timing of the change is reasonably consistent with an adaptation to the establishment of the state of Israel, the particular borders of the new map image do not match the expectations of rational adaptation to the poststate reality.[102] There is no Archimedean rationality to the choice of the "whole land of Israel" as the new map image. If the Revisionists were adapting to the postindependence reality, why didn't they simply adopt the borders of the state as the appropriate ones? The direction of change is accounted for, however, by the fact that, as we saw in chapter 1, by the mid-1950s this was the dominant map image articulated by the most important player in Israeli politics and the gatekeeper of political legitimacy. What better way to shed the image of extremism than to claim the same territory as the mainstream Labor movement?

Some have argued that Begin's recognition that Israel no longer needed both banks to absorb the masses of European Jewry after the Holocaust caused this shift. Indeed, Begin himself used this justification in 1982.[103] This reasoning, however, fails to explain the forty-year lag between the Holocaust and Begin's open recognition of its implications. This justification also overlooks the way in which members of the Revisionist movement interpreted the Holocaust at the time. Generally speaking, they saw it as evidence that they needed to implement their ideology, rather than as an imperative to change.[104]

The 1967 war, on the other hand, while frequently invoked in an attempt to explain the ideological shift of the Revisionists, occurred too late to account for its onset.[105] While it did influence the Revisionist Zionist conceptualization of the land appropriately belonging to the Jewish nation-state, its impact is not the one that is usually ascribed to it. Rather than "awakening dormant expansionist dreams," the results of the war accelerated a process of *contraction* of the area claimed by Revisionist leaders! The expansion of the territory under Israeli control allowed Revisionist leaders to more effectively shift the meaning of "the whole land of Israel" from "both banks of the Jordan" to "western Eretz Israel" by masking the change with the claim that the object of their heart's desire had been achieved.

Even with regard to the Sinai Peninsula, the preponderance of evidence suggests that the Revisionists did not adapt their map image in response to the new reality created by the war's consequences. Even after it was in their control, and despite appearing in their propaganda between 1967 and 1982 (see fig. 19), the dominant position in the Revisionist movement distinguished between the Sinai (as merely a "security zone") and the homeland (over which there can be no debate).[106] The widespread confusion and disbelief that greeted a 1968 proposal to change Herut's symbol to include Sinai as part of the eternal homeland also reflected this distinction. This proposal was considered so outlandish that it was withdrawn without ever being put to a vote.[107] In 1975, Menachem Begin told a gathering of leaders of the Whole Land of Israel movement that the "Sinai is not Eretz Israel." Perhaps for this reason, his critique of the Rogers initiatives did not address the question of Sinai's future.[108] Even Yitzhak Shamir, despite his opposition to the Camp David Accords, excluded the Sinai Peninsula from the scope of the Land of Israel in his claim that the accords "did not deal with territories in Eretz Israel."[109]

While the empirical benchmarks of the transformation of the map image of Revisionist Zionism do not correspond to the expectations of rational adaptation, the story told so far is still largely consistent with the expectations of elite imposition. The dominance of this movement by charismatic leadership increases the likelihood that any change would be the result of elite imposition—if only because few would have the ability to stand up to the ideological decisions of the charismatic leader. Indeed, some scholars have explained the change in the Revisionists' pattern of articulation by pointing to changes in Begin's political calculations in the early 1960s, arguing that he realized no one else was willing to fight for the East Bank of the Jordan while part of the government between 1967 and 1970, and contending that he consciously decided to highlight consensual issues after 1977.[110] However, the identification of these varying incentives and political calculations as the trigger of ideological transformation is problematic. Not only do these accounts disagree on the timing of the change; they consistently date its onset too late.[111] Rather than trigger the change, it is more plausible that political calculations reinforced the institutionalization of the variant of the homeland that was introduced for other reasons.

Nor can elite imposition explain why the Revisionist conception of the appropriate borders began to change only in the mid-1950s, after members of the movement had endured years of ridicule, ostracism, and even physical attacks for their beliefs. If elite imposition governed change, we ought to have seen their savvy and opportunistic political leaders respond to their marginalization with greater alacrity.

There is also no evidence that Begin actually wanted to change the Revisionist ideology. Yehiel Kadishai, Begin's driver, personal secretary, and confidant, still contends that Begin never changed his belief that the East Bank of the Jordan was appropriately part of the Jewish homeland.[112] Nor do the notions of ideological nimbleness that underlie this perspective match most accounts of Menachem Begin's perspective or personality. Indeed, whatever intent existed appears to have been directed toward preserving Revisionist ideology rather than modifying the map image. As others have noted, "the wish to rescue and realize his ideology" consistently animated Begin. Like the elision of the East Bank beginning in the mid-1950s and the equation of "western Eretz Israel" and an unmodified "Eretz Israel" after 1967, the introduction of ambiguity about Revisionist territorial aspirations allowed Begin to overcome the contradiction between what he saw as his consistent ideological approach (which had called for both sides of the Jordan) and the unwillingness to implement it.[113] The rhetorical modulation, in other words, was intended to allow Herut to prosper *despite* maintaining its ideals, not to change them.

An explicit assessment of the ability of each mechanism to account for the empirical benchmarks of change also shows that even the historical episode that comes closest to supporting an elite imposition mechanism—the 1965 merger between Herut and the Liberal Party—ultimately fails to do so. Herut's institutional alterations and the formation of Gahal in preparations for the 1965 elections can certainly be plausibly understood as intended "to reserve the ideology for party stalwarts while adopting an electorally effective style of communication for the public; in other words to bring about the correspondence of the two distinct aims of maximizing electoral width and of preserving ideological depth."[114] This account certainly explains a lot about Herut's development. However, this alliance took place *after* the onset of change in the territorial dimension of Herut's ideology and therefore cannot be responsible for initiating it. The formation of Gahal marks not the start of a transformation, but how far it proceeded!

We can see this if we compare the attempts to form such an alliance in 1954 and in 1965. In 1954, Begin rejected the formation of this same alliance because the Liberals refused to accept Herut's symbol—that is, because they refused to adhere to the "both banks of the Jordan" ideology.[115] Begin even chastised one of the leaders of the Liberal Party that a generally hawkish position was not identical to Herut's principled claim to both banks of the Jordan.[116] To be sure, Begin had other reasons for resisting the alliance at this time, including the fear that he would lose his leadership position, and Herut's relative weakness vis-à-vis the Liberal Party.[117] Nonetheless, the

differences in the map images of the homeland articulated by both movements were still considered significant enough to torpedo an alliance widely
expected to be politically advantageous.

In 1965, by contrast, Begin admitted that the Liberals' much narrower
conception of the appropriate territory was not important enough to delay
the merger of the parties. Instead, he was satisfied with the rather paltry
substitute, in which each party within Gahal would maintain its separate
stance on the issue. His declarations that this formulation represented a
concession by the Liberals provided the illusion of continuity and ideological steadfastness against internal opposition to Gahal, some of which (e.g.,
that of Yochanan Bader) was partly based on detection of this change.[118]
By 1965, in other words, the old map image was still relevant, but in contrast to a decade earlier, it was no longer important enough to undermine
this alliance. Thus the fact that Herut's 1965 election propaganda did not
reflect the "both banks of the Jordan" ideology should be understood as a
continuation of the trend begun in 1955 rather than as a departure from
previous practice. Gahal's success and the contribution it made to the political rehabilitation of the Revisionists accelerated the minimization of the
original map image in favor of a more general articulation of the right to the
Land of Israel in its "historic borders" by increasing the political payoffs of
using the latter.

The plausibility of intentional mechanisms, including both elite imposition and rational adaptation, is further weakened because the change in the
Revisionist identification of the desired borders was not smooth, consistent,
or uniform across the movement. The very people who, according to the
elite imposition mechanism, had the incentive to change or who, according
to the expectations of rational adaptation, were responding to inexorable
realities simultaneously appealed to both the new ideological variant and the
old map image. This was as true of Begin as of the rest of the movement.[119]

Begin could, on the same day, speak of the division of "western Eretz
Israel" while simultaneously excluding the logically present eastern Eretz
Israel from the patrimony with the claim that it had been liberated.[120] On
the one hand, he listed the institution of the Israeli currency in "all of Eretz
Israel" as one of Gahal's main accomplishments, thereby excluding areas
not in Israel's control from the Land of Israel.[121] On the other hand, he repeatedly noted that Israel's army "liberated all of western Eretz Israel," and
still referred to the "so-called 'kingdom of Jordan.'"[122] A Herut pamphlet
from 1968 mirrored this ambivalence even as it illustrated the ideological
change that was taking place. The pamphlet, written by Yoram Aridor, en-
closes "Jordan" in quotation marks (by comparison, "Syria" is not enclosed
in quotation marks) and simultaneously excludes it from "Eretz Israel" by
calling for the "extension of Israeli law to all of Eretz Israel and the Golan

Heights."[123] Similarly, while the proposed decisions of the Herut's 1968 national convention imply that there are still parts of the homeland that are not under Israeli control, the convention tellingly proposed that citizenship be awarded to the "Arab residents of Eretz Israel" and not to the Arab residents of "western Eretz Israel."[124]

The East Bank continued to be occasionally recalled (though with a noticeably decreased frequency) in the late 1970s and 1980s.[125] To a certain extent, Begin attempted during this period to avoid giving the impression that he gave up the fundamental claim to the East Bank by formulating the area the Revisionist movement referred to in its platforms and in the basic lines of the government as "the land of Israel west of the Jordan."[126] Some prominent figures within the movement, including Geula Cohen, refused to sign the manifesto of the Movement for the Whole Land of Israel because they did not believe it was whole yet. Responding to Zvi Shiloach's criticism that politics is not a contest of absolutes and that the movement needed to concentrate on the fight for Judea and Samaria, Cohen sarcastically retorted: "And if we ever reach Transjordan...what will we say? That now we have in our hands the entire and a half land of Israel?"[127]

Claims that the East Bank appropriately belonged to Israel were still occasionally voiced in the early and mid-1980s and later by members of the Revisionist movement.[128] Betar's Web site continues to contain a banner with the "both banks of the Jordan" map image. A 1982 Herut Youth proclamation emphasized "the right of the Jewish nation to Eretz Israel east and west of the Jordan River."[129] The most famous of these late articulations of the old map image was Begin's 1982 comment that while he still believed the East Bank was part of Eretz Israel, Israel would not invade Jordan.[130] Begin's personal secretary testified that Begin continued to believe and to hope that Jews would someday have "rights" in the East Bank, although he hoped that they would get these through peaceful means and through a confederative agreement with Jordan.[131] Nonetheless, Yehiel Kadishai himself, whose Revisionist credentials are as unquestionable as his loyalty to Begin, stated that "Eretz Israel [after 1967] was entirely in our hands."[132] The very existence of these certainly increasingly dissonant articulations of the old map image militates against the assumption that the movement's leadership consciously imposed the change on its followers.

As we saw in the first part of the chapter, these increasingly isolated claims to the East Bank were drowned out by the articulations of the map image that excluded the East Bank from the homeland. In any case, the simultaneous articulation of both map images of the homeland in the same movement and by the same people is more congruent with a growing ambivalence toward the original claim of the homeland than with a decisive break with it. This ambivalence was already reflected in the near-even split of the delegates to Herut's 1968 national convention, in which nine speakers who raised the issue considered only "part" of the homeland liberated, while eight considered the entire homeland liberated. By 1977, the balance clearly tilted toward the latter. At this convention, twelve of the speakers clearly implied that Eretz Israel was already whole, while only five referred to Transjordan as appropriately part of the Jewish state.[133]

Throughout this period of inconsistency, some of those who continued to raise the claim did so in the context of complaining about the ideological change that was taking place.[134] One of the delegates to Herut's 1958 convention even found it necessary to argue against the trend of "refraining from declaring our full territorial aspirations" and to note with great regret that "some in the upper echelons of the movement" are speaking of the "stabilization of our borders up to the Jordan." He even pointed out that a map of the entire Land of Israel was not to be found in the offices of the movement or in its clubs around the country.[135] In 1972 Dov Shilanski reported that he had heard "in several cases" members of the movement dismissing and speaking contemptuously of the concept of "two banks to the Jordan." He argued that they should continue to claim both banks of the Jordan even in the face of losing votes and members. This call for ideological constancy did not have a large following. Most of those present reacted like Yitzhak Shmueli, who responded: "With all our loyalty to the idea [of both banks of the Jordan] we still have much to do on this bank."[136]

Finally, neither rational adaptation nor elite imposition can account for the length of time it took the new map image to become dominant. Given Begin's personal charisma and stature within the movement, the change progressed too slowly to be consistent with a story of elite imposition. The cadence of change is consistent, however, with rational adaptation through generational replacement. It is reasonable to expect that the new generation of Revisionists, growing up after the partition of the land, would have a reduced attachment to the East Bank of the Jordan. The reduced salience of the East Bank could plausibly have undermined the taken-for-granted assumption that this land ought to be theirs. This argument is strengthened if we take Jordan's achievement of formal independence in 1946, rather than the redrawing of administrative borders in 1922, as the marker closing the door on the fulfillment of this nationalist dream.

While reasonable, this variant of rational adaptation still fails to account for the fact that those who started, articulated, and drove the articulation of the new map image through the movement were the old-timers. While Menachem Begin was the most prominent of these, he was not alone. For example, Esther Raziel-Naor, another of the founders of the Herut movement, hailed the Camp David Accords as "a treaty that gives us a chance for peace *without dividing Eretz Israel*," despite the fact that the accords explicitly recognize the legitimate existence of Jordan as a separate entity. An indication that her position was shared by the mainstream of the movement can be seen in an election poster for the 10th Knesset elections, which repeated her statement that "the Peace Treaty [with Egypt] was obtained without detracting from our rights over Eretz Israel."[137]

The evolutionary dynamic, in contrast, can account for the cadence of change because it pegs it to the pace of the achievement of the short-term goals in whose name the modulation was first articulated. By 1977 not only were the Revisionists a legitimate part of Israeli politics; they even ascended to the state's highest office. The access to power and resources that their political success allowed made it very difficult to return to the original map image. Since none of their gains would have been possible had they continued to articulate the claim to the East Bank, and out of a desire to maintain these benefits, they have not returned to it.

• • •

The operation of the evolutionary dynamic in the particular context of the Revisionist movement illustrates an important variant of the evolutionary process. In this case, the movement engaged in a rhetorical modulation in order to remain part of the legitimate political spectrum rather than as the price of cooperation with a specific rival nationalist movement. This serves as a reminder that the battle for hegemony among nationalist movements has real political consequences and is not simply metaphorical. Simply put, it matters who wins and who loses. The losers (except for those rare cases in which they are physically exterminated) are likely to face a choice of fading into irrelevance or attempting to reenter the legitimate political spectrum. If they attempt to remain part of the political game, they may have to pay an ante in the form of at least a tactical modification of their ideological claims. To the extent that they succeed, the new variant can become institutionalized as the new ideological status quo.

II

DESTINY AND IDENTITY

4

Transformations of the Collective Mission

Nations do not live by territory alone. Nationalism also imbues polities with meaning. As Ernest Renan observed, the answer to the foundational question "What are we to do?"—nationalists' vision of the glorious future and of the society they wish to create or sustain—is as important as any other component of nationalism.[1] Israeli nationalisms are no different. Despite a common desire for a Jewish state, Labor, Religious, and Revisionist Zionisms had sometimes radically opposed visions of what the character of the public realm in their society ought to look like. Their goals varied from normalizing the Jewish people to preserving the spiritual uniqueness of the nation; from building a worker's paradise to bringing the Messiah from heaven to earth; from saving the physical existence of Jews to renewing their culture.

For all of their mobilizing power, these visions of the future have also changed. The main Israeli nationalist movements experienced at least five significant transformations in the nationalist mission they articulated. Labor Zionism abandoned its goal of establishing a socialist society and its attempt to create a new secular Jew. The Religious Zionists subordinated the once-sanctified state of Israel to the Land of Israel. The Revisionist Zionist movement, for its part, abandoned its conception of a liberal public realm that privatized religion in favor of a public realm heavily influenced by traditional religion. A fifth transformation in nationalist mission, in which Labor Zionism shifted from a goal of eradicating the Jewish exile by gathering all the Jews in Israel to saving the exile, will be discussed in chapter 5 because it was so closely interlinked with the Labor movement's change in the definition of the appropriate membership in the nation's state.

These changes provide another context in which we can probe the relative plausibility of alternative explanations of change. Beyond the intrinsic interest in these issues in the Israeli context, this extension is useful for four more general reasons. First, the plausibility of the evolutionary dynamic depends on the inclusion of more than one ideological dimension in the analysis. I argued in chapter 2, for example, that the Religious Zionist adoption of the Labor Zionist map image of the appropriate homeland was facilitated by a tacit bargain in which the Labor Zionists made concessions on religious issues in return. Showing that this took place increases our confidence that the evolutionary dynamic accounts for both changes. This demonstration also highlights the ability of the evolutionary dynamic to account for simultaneous change by different nationalist movements along different ideological dimensions. The ability to account for such variation helps distinguish its impact from that of rational adaptation. Rational adaptation expects simultaneous changes but assumes that, as responses to the same reality, they take place in the same substantive dimension.

Second, the exploration of the transformations that took place with regard to the mission dimension reveals at least two instances where change began as the evolutionary dynamic expects, but ultimately failed to take root. A closer look reveals, however, that the (endogenous) political selection forces that are at the heart of the application of the evolutionary dynamic to nationalism explain the absence of change in these cases. The ability of the evolutionary dynamic to account for both the presence and the absence of ideological transformation bolsters its claim to a place in our explanatory toolkit.

Third, the exploration of the mission dimension increases the number of observations of change. While the sample remains too small for reliable statistical tests, the increased observations provide additional grounding on which to base our intuitions about the distribution of mechanisms of change in nationalism more broadly. Finally, by specifically dealing with the intersection between religion and nationalism, the exploration of this ideological dimension sheds light on the contemporary debates about the possibility of change in the missions of religiously motivated movements in other contexts as well.

This chapter begins with an exploration of the decline of the Labor movement's class mission. The chapter goes on to explain how both the Labor and the Revisionist movements abandoned their vision of a secular society in favor of a public realm heavily influenced by religion. Next, the chapter considers the rise of a new mission within Religious Zionism in which extending Israeli control over the Land of Israel became more important than the state of Israel. The chapter concludes with an exploration of two dogs that didn't bark: the first attempt to link Revisionism and religion and the brief retreat by the Religious Zionists from the idea of a theocracy as an operational goal.

The Eclipse of Socialism in Labor Zionist Ideology

Moving from Class to Nation

The very name of the Labor Zionist movement highlights the original centrality of its class mission. Putting a socialist twist on the Zionist diagnosis of the Jewish problem, Labor Zionists argued that the Jewish class structure in the Diaspora contributed decisively to the existence of anti-Semitism. According to their view, Jews were persecuted not only because they did not have a state of their own, but also because millennia of exile perverted their class structure. While in "normal" nations, the productive classes (i.e., workers and peasants) constitute the bulk of the nation's population, among the Jews, they were a small minority. Labor Zionism proposed to fix these problems through massive Jewish immigration to Palestine, where a new secular Jew would be crafted through manual, especially agricultural, labor. They believed that this would normalize the Jewish people.

To be sure, the various parties grouped under the rubric of the Labor movement differed on some key points of Marxist doctrine, including the degree of their adherence to the principle of class warfare, the inevitable progress of materialist forces, and the desired balance between socialist goals, with their implied universalism, and particularistic nationalist aims. Nonetheless, until the 1930s all the groups within the movement envisioned a socialist society as the desired goal. Even the least doctrinaire segment of the Labor movement maintained the conviction that the national interest and the class interest of the workers were identical. Indeed, a famous 1929 speech by Ben-Gurion identified their mission as the transformation "from working class to working nation."

Today, few vestiges of Labor Zionism's working-class orientation remain. Ehud Barak's short-lived attempt to sever even the nominal connection to "labor" by rebranding the Labor Party as One Israel in 1999 clearly displays the change in the movement's orientation. While this seems like the Israeli vision of Bill Clinton's centrist Democrats or Tony Blair's New Labour, the shift from a focus on the interests of the working class to a concern with the nation as a whole took place much earlier. Already in the 1930s, rather than equating class interest with the national interest as they had initially, the achievement of Labor's socialist goals became *dependent on* the prior achievement of their nationalist goals. Eventually, they discarded the class perspective altogether. By 1933, this shift was well underway. No longer primarily concerned about the working class or the working nation, a collection of Ben-Gurion's speeches, including the one cited above, was titled "From Class to Nation." The workers had disappeared.[2]

By the end of the 1930s, Ben-Gurion's entire frame of reference had changed. "His priority was now the 'ordinary Zionist' and not socialist synthesis. A decade earlier his frame of reference was workers in a class democracy in the Histadrut [the Zionist General Federation of Labor]...now it was 'ordinary' Zionists within the nation. The Marxist-tinged identity of class and nation, so prominent in his earlier statements and arguments, had been replaced by a [class] neutral notion of nation."[3] The reduction of the centrality of the agricultural pioneers—the socialist avant-garde—was also demonstrated in Ben-Gurion's consistent recategorization of the "pioneer." Once the exclusive bearer of national goals, in the 1930s and 1940s, they became only one facet of a broader working class. The working class itself also became one component of the nation rather than its embodiment.[4] On the ground, Mapai's increasingly positive attitude toward private capital mirrored these rhetorical shifts among the leadership.[5]

By the 1950s, the ideal of a socialist state was relegated to the margins of the movement. Indeed, by then, Ben-Gurion even decried the mixture of socialism and statism as "shaatnez." *Shaatnez* refers to the biblical prohibition of mixing linen and wool in the same garment. The term entered Zionist discourse in Jabotinsky's argument that nationalism should not be mixed with any other ideology. Ben-Gurion's use of this particular term is therefore striking because he had strongly defended the concept in the 1930s against Jabotinsky's accusations that the Labor movement's (already diluted) socialism undermined its nationalist struggle.[6] By this point, Ben-Gurion clearly and openly relegated the achievement of socialism to the distant future and considered it less important than the other tasks facing the young state.[7] While Ben-Gurion frequently articulated the hope that "the day will come when a socialist state will be built in Israel," he tended to invoke such sentiments in order to postpone specific questions of socialism.[8] Ratifying the status quo, Mapai's 1951 platform formally accepted the existence of private capital alongside its collective enterprises.[9] That year, Ben-Gurion's proposed "minimum educational program" for Israeli schoolchildren paid scant attention to socialism.[10] These changes did not go unnoticed. They led some within the movement to complain that their socialist slogans were now empty of any content.[11] Undeterred, Ben-Gurion eventually openly disassociated himself from socialism, arguing that "our generation has little to learn from socialism and the classical socialists of the nineteenth century."[12] By 1967, he would even argue that the term "socialist-Zionism" was "meaningless."[13]

Evolution at Work: Explaining the Eclipse of Labor Zionism's Class Mission

Each of the three explanations of change under consideration offers a different expectation of the direction, timing, and process of this transformation. Rational adaptation expects to see a shock to the world that made continued adherence to a class-based ideology impossible or nonsensical. Once this realization sinks in, rational adaptation predicts that the new reality-conforming ideology would be articulated consciously and consistently. The Holocaust and routinization following Mapai's achievement of political dominance are sometimes used to explain the onset of this change.[14] As the actual timing of the change demonstrates, the transformation in the Labor Zionists' vision of their mission took place before either of these events. The evolutionary dynamic shows, moreover, that the achievement of Mapai's dominance was the consequence of the shift and not its trigger. The 1920s did include a number of other shocks, namely, the massive immigration of middle-class Jews to Palestine starting in 1924, and the 1926–27 recession, which fit the onset of this change. However, because Labor Zionist leaders reacted to these events from within their socialist perspective rather than by seeking to eliminate it, the actual process of this shift does not correspond to the expectations of rational adaptation.

Elite imposition, on the other hand, expects the eclipse of socialism to have taken place because it benefited the leaders of the movement. Once initiated to capture the rewards available on the economic right of the political spectrum, the nonsocialist perception of national mission would have been articulated consciously and consistently as the leaders, who profited from the ideological change, imposed it on the movement.[15] Ben-Gurion's role in moderating the socialist views of every party he was associated with makes elite imposition especially plausible. Nonetheless, this mechanism cannot account for the delay between the onset of change in the 1920s and its completion in the 1950s. If elite imposition really accounted for this shift, we would have expected it to spread much more quickly given Ben-Gurion's towering influence. Moreover, the inconsistency of the transformation and the mixed ideological messages articulated by the movement's leadership throughout this period also undermine the plausibility of an intentional change imposed from the top down.

The empirical benchmarks of the transformation correspond most closely to the expectations of the evolutionary dynamic. Driven to unify the movement and gain control of the World Zionist Organization (WZO) by new political threats and exogenous shocks in the 1920s, the leaders of the Labor movement began to engage in tactical adjustments to their class-based message. Clearly understood as a shallow rhetorical reaction to the conditions they faced, these adjustments were initially intended to provide the lowest common denominator that would allow united action by a fractious Labor movement. The adjustment to the class message also enabled the cross-class alliance with, and eventual co-optation of, the middle-class General Zionist movement. As I will show below, the success of this alliance made the rhetorical softening of Labor Zionism's commitment to socialism too costly to abandon. As a result, the Labor movement eventually reinterpreted the once tactical muting of their class mission as the new ideological status quo.

The rhetorical modulation that (in retrospect) undermined Labor Zionism's class message emerged in the 1920s as the movement began to grapple seriously with the question of how to unify its fractious components. By the mid-1920s, its two main factions, Hapoel Hatzair (the Young Worker) and Ahdut Haavoda (Labor Unity), understood the benefits of coordinated action but still disagreed on crucial ideological issues. Unlike Ahdut Haavoda, Hapoel Hatzair opposed any strict interpretation of Marxist ideology and downplayed the principle of class warfare. Formal cooperation between the two factions depended on bridging this ideological gulf—or at least papering it over.

The adjustment of Ahdut Haavoda's class rhetoric provided a way to do so. Its downplaying of the need for class warfare was explicitly portrayed as a pragmatic, short-term initiative undertaken for the express purpose of co-opting the less orthodox segments of the Labor movement. As part of his campaign to elicit support for the union with Hapoel Hatzair, Ben-Gurion argued in 1928 that they should not fear its (relatively) "bourgeoisie nature," and that any apparent straying from the socialist path was only temporary. Once Hapoel Hatzair's followers arrived in Palestine they would, he predicted, inevitably join forces with the working class on its terms.[16] Nonetheless, opposition by truth-telling socialists to the ideological modulation needed to solicit the support of less doctrinaire factions delayed the actual unification of these two parties for a number of years despite its clear political benefits.[17]

Once initiated, however, the muting of the emphasis on class warfare had at least one unanticipated advantage. Not only was the united Labor movement a stronger political force, but reducing the emphasis on class conflict placed it in a position from which it could credibly attempt a cross-class alliance with the middle-class General Zionists. In the mid-1920s, the General Zionists were the strongest party in the Zionist world. They enjoyed the legacy of having been founded by Theodor Herzl, the first prophet of

Zionism. Their leader at the time, Chaim Weizmann, was the undisputed voice of Zionism. Most importantly, they controlled the funding apparatuses of the World Zionist Organization. As a result, an alliance with them would provide significant material advantages to the Labor Zionist movement.

The emergence of the Revisionist Zionists as a distinct organization in 1925 reinforced the incentives of the Labor movement to reach out to the General Zionists. The Revisionists were overtly hostile to the Labor movement and its socialism. Labor, in turn, saw the Revisionists as the Jewish manifestation of the global rise of fascism and resisted them accordingly. The emergence of Revisionist Zionism was particularly threatening to the Labor movement because it raised the specter of a middle-class alliance between the Revisionists and the General Zionists that could marginalize Labor Zionism.

An alliance with the General Zionists, however, was impossible as long as they felt threatened by the working-class message of the Labor Zionists. The tacit bargain that eventually enabled the cooperation between these movements involved the General Zionists' acceptance of the political leadership of the Labor movement. In return, the Labor movement abandoned, at least rhetorically, the struggle against capitalism and the existing social order.[18] The General Zionist movement was willing to enter into this alliance because Weizmann concluded that private capital would not invest in Palestine until the needed infrastructure was already in place and that the collective enterprises of the Labor movement were the most likely vehicle for constructing this infrastructure.[19] Both sides benefited. "The bourgeoisie had the assurance of dealing with an abstract form of socialism that did not threaten its existence, that never demanded the 'socialization' of private property, that never interfered with its economic activities, and that in fact consolidated its status because of the major part it played in the economy as a whole. The labor movement gained the bourgeoisie's cooperation in the area it believed was the most important: the financing of the agricultural settlement that was conquering the land."[20]

While Mapai "jettisoned the identity of national and working class interests as an operative premise of its politics,"[21] it did not abandon its socialism all at once, or even intend this "jettisoning" as a permanent renunciation of socialism. Rather, the Labor movement did what it needed to do in order to gain control of the WZO so that it could address its immediate financial crisis and accomplish its class mission.

The recession that engulfed Palestine in 1926 hit the Labor movement especially hard. The impending bankruptcy of some of the movement's most important enterprises, especially Solel Boneh (its construction arm), and the movement's relative inability to respond to the economic needs of its settlements, made the leaders of the Labor movement acutely aware that somebody else controlled the funding stream of the World Zionist Organization. In 1927, Berl Katznelson excoriated the failure of the Labor movement to cooperate with (and thereby attempt to control) the middle class. Such cooperation, he admitted, "entails concessions, compromises, coalition; a list of not so pleasant matters. But when one sees the necessity of the task, *one does not run away from it.* ... We did not understand that we were obligated to go to the fourth aliyah [i.e., the middle-class immigrants who came to Palestine in the mid-1920s], to take care of its problems and to conquer it."[22]

Other leaders of the movement also acknowledged the explicitly tactical character of the adjusted class claims. Responding to the criticism from socialist truth tellers that the move "from class to nation" diluted their class-based interests, Chaim Arlozorov argued that they were not "speaking of blurring the socialist face of our project. [We are] speaking of [appealing to] classes that should naturally be our allies, and we are giving them to our enemies who use them against us." Continuing Arlozorov's argument, in 1932, Ben-Gurion contended that to make the Labor movement truly dominant it was necessary to appeal to a broader audience (explicitly including the petite bourgeoisie), and not just to "pioneers." Unless the Labor movement toned down its exclusivist class-based message, he argued, it risked "needlessly" alienating the middle class. He asked rhetorically: "Is it necessary that everybody who is not part of the working class oppose us?"[23]

Ben-Gurion explicitly defended some of his more controversial overtures to the middle class in terms of short-term practical and political necessities. For example, in 1934, Ben-Gurion and Jabotinsky hammered out an agreement intended to resolve the growing animosity and violence between their two movements. Ben-Gurion defended his concessions on key labor issues by arguing that adhering to a strict collectivist doctrine would make it impossible for them to increase their electoral support or co-opt smaller parties. Specifically, he contended that rejecting binding labor arbitration (his main concession in this agreement) would prevent the formation of crucial alliances with most of the other parties in the Zionist movement, including the Religious and General Zionists.[24]

In a later, equally controversial context, Ben-Gurion argued that Mapai should allocate some of the immigration certificates it controlled—certificates that granted legal immigration to Palestine in the 1930s—to petit bourgeois immigrants and to those who were destined to become private farmers (that is, to General Zionists) rather than to members of the Labor movement. While this implied a reduction in the relative number of Labor supporters in Palestine, he considered the action necessary to convince the General Zionists that Mapai was a friend of the middle class. Responding to the intense resistance that this proposal generated within the party, Ben-Gurion insisted that it was simply a practical step and did not represent an ideological shift of any kind.[25]

Three factors helped transform what had been a temporary adjustment made for particular short-term goals into the new orthodoxy: the need to respond to internal criticism, the secession of these critics from the movement, and the success of the tacit bargain with the General Zionists. The move from class to nation generated considerable opposition within Mapai. The truth tellers on this issue included the remnants of Mapai's more strident socialist components and the group that would go on to become Faction B. In 1934, the truth tellers were strong enough within the movement to scuttle Ben-Gurion's agreement with Jabotinsky, largely for reasons of socialist doctrine.[26] As part of the response to the socialist objections of these truth tellers, the consensus builders castigated attempts to pursue class interests as narrow, particularistic agendas that undermined the national cause.[27] The advocates of the modulation recast class warfare and the framing of politics through the interests of the working class as threats to the power of the movement and to the national interest (both achieved and outstanding) rather than as ideals they should uphold.

The relative weight of the focus on the nation over class shifted in 1944 when Faction B split from Mapai to form its own independent party. Faction B consistently subordinated nationalist goals to class interests—even when the cost was great. Its class interests prevented it from forming a common front with the Revisionists against the Peel partition plan. In 1939, this segment of the movement hindered Ben-Gurion's pursuit of the support of American Jewry in part because it desired closer relations with the Soviet Union instead. In 1942, Faction B's socialism even led it to reject Mapai's coordination of enlistment in the British army during World War II and cooperation with the Revisionists in the fight against the Nazis. After formally splitting from Mapai, Faction B even returned to the name of the more socialist segment of the Labor movement: Ahdut Haavoda. The (new) Ahdut Haavoda returned to the (old) class message.[28] The exodus of this last bastion of truth tellers from the party left few with any standing or organization to contest the institutionalization of the shift away from socialism.

Finally, the shift from class to nation helped Mapai gain power. Since its dominance depended on resources from the Jewish middle class in the Diaspora and the perception that the Labor movement was working for the general interest rather than for a particular class, the shift from class to nation was difficult to abandon. The initially tactical muting of class interests removed one of the lingering obstacles to closer cooperation with American Jewry, who were deeply skeptical of class-based politics. The economic dependence of the Zionist enterprise on American Jews made the Labor Zionist leadership leery of attempting to build a socialist state even after independence because they feared that doing so would limit American support and undermine their efforts to absorb Jewish immigration.[29]

The Labor movement's initial engagement in the ideological modulation "from class to nation" to strengthen the worker's role in society and to protect its collectivist approach runs counter to the explanations offered by both rational adaptation and elite imposition. As I noted above, two shocks could have plausibly triggered this ideological change: the influx of middle-class Jews that began in 1924 (known as the Fourth Aliyah in Zionist historiography) and the economic downturn in 1926–27. While both shook the socialist foundation of the Labor movement, in both cases Labor leaders believed that their actions fortified their socialist goals. There is no evidence that they intended to dismantle their socialism in response to these events.

The wave of immigrants that arrived between 1924 and 1928 added approximately 72,000 largely middle-class Polish Jews to the 90,000 members of the Yishuv (the Jewish community in Mandatory Palestine). Given the significant demographic shift in the class structure of the Yishuv toward the middle class that resulted from this influx of immigrants, it would have been rational for the Labor movement to consciously shift its message in response. Nonetheless, rather than accommodating the new arrivals, the leaders of the Labor movement reacted to the vast immigration of middle-class Jews to Palestine and the growth of private enterprise with defiance, insisting that the project of building a socialist society in Palestine would not be derailed.[30]

Similarly, while the 1926 recession convinced the Labor movement that it had to gain control of the WZO, this economic development did not lead Labor Zionists to turn away from their socialist vision. In fact, Ben-Gurion interpreted the economic downturn as proof that the bourgeoisie approach to settling Palestine was untenable, rather than as a failure of socialism.[31] Not everybody in the Zionist world shared this assessment. The (General Zionist-led) Zionist Executive dispatched an "experts commission" to investigate the root causes of the economic problems in Palestine. This commission concluded that the collectivist and socialist approach of the Labor movement bred an environment hostile to private capital and thereby to development. It recommended replacing collectivist farming with an individualistic and capitalist agriculture based on free enterprise and private industry. It specifically targeted the Histadrut as the biggest obstacle to economic progress and sought, generally speaking, to neuter the Labor movement by depriving it of resources.[32] The Labor movement thus entered the political fray with vigor because it sought to protect its collectivist approach from what it called a "capitalist offensive," not because socialism no longer made sense. In fact, the Labor movement sought to strengthen the workers' movement by achieving the "hegemony of the workers" in the Zionist movement. In a representative statement, Berl Katznelson concluded: "There is no future for Zionism unless it is conquered by the Labor movement, and no other way for the worker: Labor must take over the Zionist movement completely so that our spirit prevails in the economy and in cultural affairs."[33]

To be sure, one could massage a rational adaptation story to fit the empirical account. Such an explanation would focus on Ben-Gurion's famous pragmatism and argue that he rationally adapted to a context where socialism was unrealistic early in his political career. From this perspective, his articulations about the long-term desirability of a socialist society are just sophisticated ploys designed to reduce the political cost of abandoning the socialist goal. This is surely a possibility. Indeed, Ben-Gurion's very real pragmatism makes focusing on him an especially hard case for the evolutionary dynamic precisely because he is likely to be an early adapter.

Two concerns weaken the plausibility of this otherwise convincing story. First, the need "to mask" his adaptation implies that not everyone within the movement rationally adapted at the same time. This variation is problematic for an orthodox theory of rational adaptation because, as I outlined in the introduction, it assumes that the shock has to be so catastrophic that everybody has to adapt. Rational adaptation models that allow for variations in the sensitivity to changes in the reality, and therefore for different propensities for adaptation, address this concern. However, it is still not clear that the classless message was more rational than the class-based one. While the collapse of the Soviet Union may make this appear self-evident in retrospect, socialism's stock was rising around the world in the 1920s. As a result, it is not at all obvious that abandoning socialism at that historical juncture would have been rational.

Second, even Mapai's famous pragmatism plays a more complicated role than is usually assumed. As we saw above, the leaders of the Labor movement appealed to pragmatism to resolve the apparent contradictions between their ideology and their political positions. Their political positions, they argued, did not represent an ideological change. Rather, they reflected tactical modulations intended to fulfill the traditional ideological imperative by bringing about the worker's political supremacy. Faced with accusations of ideological deviance, they retreated to the claim that ideology was, in any case, secondary. The appeal to pragmatism is thus itself as much of a rhetorical strategy as a fundamental characteristic of the Labor movement. Rational adaptation theories of change have difficulty disentangling these two uses of pragmatism.

Moreover, as others have noted, rather than the expected sharp break with the previous ideology that rational adaptation (and elite imposition) expect, the move "from class to nation" was characterized by a gradual "shift to the right."[34] This was also true of Ben-Gurion who, along with other leaders in the movement, continued for some time to offer mixed messages.[35] Anita

Shapira even described Ben-Gurion's shedding of Marxist ideology as taking place "unconsciously, almost casually."[36] The resulting inconsistency further weakens the plausibility of the claim that it was an intentional or calculated transformation imposed from above. More generally, to the extent that the Labor movement did not tackle the significant ideological issues involved in the unification of its ranks and in the close cooperation with the middle class directly but found practical ways to accommodate conflicting ideological imperatives, it is difficult to speak of conscious ideological change—of either the rational or the venal variety.

Religion in the Public Realm

Abandoning the Creation of a Secular Society

The Labor Zionist mission of normalizing the Jewish nation also involved its secularization. For some, secularization was a corollary of their socialism. For most, it was based on their rejection of "exilic life," including, inter alia, a rejection of rabbinic Judaism and the religious practices that had developed since the Roman expulsion of the Jews from Palestine. The distinction between "Jews" and "Hebrews" that was used at the time reflected Labor Zionism's conception of Judaism as a secular nationality rather than a religion. As Amos Elon noted, the Labor Zionist "pioneers called themselves 'Hebrews,' not Jews. The pioneer was a *Poel Ivri* (*Hebrew* Worker). His union was the *Histadrut Ha'ovdim HaIvrriim B'Eretz Israel* (Confederation of *Hebrew* Workers in Eretz Israel). In the 1930s and early 1940s most settlers still campaigned not for a Jewish, but for a 'Hebrew' state. Thousands of middle-aged sabras remember marching through the streets in anti-British demonstrations chanting the slogan, *Aliya Chofshit! Medina Ivrit!* (Free Immigration! A Hebrew State!)."[37]

As part of this conception, the Labor Zionist movement initially rejected the demands made by the Religious Zionists to color the public realm with a religious hue. Despite formal agreements between the Zionist Organization and the Religious Zionist movement requiring the observance of Jewish dietary restrictions and the Sabbath laws, most Labor-affiliated settlements did not do so. Well into the 1930s, Labor-run kitchens refused, *as a matter of principle,* to follow the Jewish dietary laws (kashrut).[38]

At the same time, while the Labor movement was strongly anticlerical, with the exception of parts of the kibbutz movement, it was not necessarily hostile to religion per se. Many of its leaders were educated in traditional religious schools and carried this legacy forward in their thinking and reference points, if not in their daily lives. They were also firmly grounded in their ethnic identity as Jews and accepted the claim that religious practice had safeguarded the Jews' collective existence in the past. The leaders of the Labor Zionist movement did not believe, however, that religion was particularly relevant to the process of building the new Jewish society in Palestine. In fact, they saw the building of a modern national community as a functional replacement for religion.

In this vein, the Labor movement consciously attempted to imbue religious symbols with secular nationalist meaning. For example, they selected Saturday as the weekly day of rest, but on the grounds that it was socially progressive, not because it was the Fourth Commandment. In fact, Rachel Yanait's description of the Sabbath as a day of general rest and recuperation, including dancing, literary readings, hiking, and milking is literally sacrilegious.[39] The Labor Zionist movement also invested religious holidays such as Hanukah, Sukkot, Passover, and Shavuot with secular nationalist meanings. The Bible itself was both elevated as a way to "skip over" rabbinic Judaism and secularized as a historical text or a tour book rather than venerated as divine revelation.[10]

This dual attitude toward religion was clearly articulated by Yanait, who, when asked how they maintained their link to Jewish tradition, responded:

> If you mean the tradition of religious customs, attending synagogue, and prayer, the pioneers mostly do not observe these, but all of us observe the foundation,... the dedication bordering on self-sacrifice, the tie to the land, the enthusiasm and the dedication to reestablishing the homeland anew, to reviving our tongue, and to creating a normal national life—is this not the real religion of the young generation?... And the content of our religion since time immemorial was not just the belief in a single God, but also [a belief] in the revival of the Hebrew nation and in his eternal link with the Land of Israel...[We] maintain the content and renew the form.[41]

Some have interpreted this duality as meaning that Labor Zionists applied merely a thin veneer of secularism over a fundamentally religious conception of mission. From this perspective, their eventual acceptance of a religious cast to the public realm involved no transformation at all.[42] This interpretation is problematic for two reasons. First, the use of the existence of change as evidence that the Labor Zionism was not secular in the first place relies on the incorrect assumption that deeply seated ideological positions cannot change. Second, this reasoning also mistakenly assumes that because Labor eventually modified the secularizing component of its national mission, such a change was inevitable. Labor Zionism's anchoring of some of its claims in religious symbols made it difficult to completely disconnect its nationalism from religion, but there was nothing inevitable about its willingness to allow the entry of religion into the public realm.

The "veneer" argument is also not particularly helpful in understanding the parallel transformation that took place in the mission of Revisionist Zionism. Unlike their counterparts in the Labor movement, most leaders of the Revisionist movement did not have a traditional religious background. There was little, in other words, to apply a veneer to. Moreover, as part of their pursuit of "monism"—a nationalism undiluted by potentially conflicting (especially socialist or religious) imperatives—they "did not feel that there was any organic connection between Zionism and religion," and feared that it diluted the will to nation.[43] The leaders of the Revisionist movement initially viewed the Jewish religion as little more than the preservative of the national pathos in the dark period before the national awakening. Jabotinsky believed that once the nation of Israel returned to its land, religion would no longer fulfill even this task; Halachic laws would become obsolete just as the specialized economy of the ghetto would disappear.[44]

Reflecting the Revisionists' secular nationalist understanding of religion, Betar's educational guidelines referred to the Bible as "the most original work that reflects our national spirit across the generations," explaining:

> The Bible is a fountain of national education, and a national education is not complete...without knowledge of the Bible. We must instill in the members of Betar the sublime and hidden foundations in the Israeli prophecy, its great moral and national value, its influences and foundations, and for this purpose it will be necessary to give selected chapters and sections of the Bible that deal with national moments. *God forbid that we should overwhelm the Betar member with a flow of mere sayings, which may fatigue and bore him. It is forbidden to heap mere chapters [with no purpose]. It will be required to only pick those which are appropriate for the achievement of our educational mission.*[45]

In this vein, Betar's chief educator made no distinction between religious, partisan, and political holidays. His list of the festivals to be commemorated by the movement included biblical holidays (such as the three pilgrimage festivals), historical holidays that have been assimilated to religious tradition (such as Hanukah and the commemoration of the destruction of the second Temple), days on which sacrifices were made in the Temple, recent nationalist anniversaries (such as the deaths of Theodor Herzl and Max Nordau, the Balfour Declaration, and the battle at Tel Hai), and Arbor Day. All of these were equally important.[46] The list of holy days adopted by Betar, instructively, left out some of the most important religious holidays, including the Jewish New Year (Rosh Hashanah) and the Day of Atonement (Yom Kippur).

While Jabotinsky appreciated the role of religion as a source of the social contract, he clearly rejected the notion that religion ought to play a role in the public realm. The liberal strands of his thought promoted a view of religion as a private affair. He also feared that making any concessions to the religious would undermine Zionism's argument that the Jews were a nation and not merely a religious community. At least once he even floated the possibility of taxing religious Jews in order to distance "this barren element" from the nationalist project.[47] In a 1935 letter to Ben-Gurion, Jabotinsky expressed his contempt for the religious and for their attempts to impose religious control over the public realm. He indicated his willingness to agree to the establishment of a "state of the pious in which I would be forced to eat Gefilte fish from morning to night" if it would hasten the establishment of a Jewish state. "But," he asserted, "[only] where there is *no* other way." He continued: "Even worse: A 'Yiddishite' state, which is the end of all the magic of the desert for me; if there is no other way—I agree. And I will leave a will for my sons to undertake a rebellion; but on the envelope I will write: 'Open five years after the christening of the Hebrew state.'"[48]

The ambivalence, not to say distaste, regarding a religious public realm has been replaced in both the Labor and the Revisionist Zionist movements with an affirmation of the role of religion in governing significant aspects of public life. For the Labor movement, this shift began in the 1930s. One of the first indicators that Labor Zionists were willing to allow a religious cast to some aspects of the public realm came in a 1933 debate over the Religious Zionists' demand that institutions receiving support from the Zionist Organization—that is, all settlements and Histadrut enterprises—observe the Sabbath and maintain kosher kitchens. Berl Katznelson, in formulating the Labor movement's response, designed a compromise in which Labor Zionist communities would commit to not working on the Sabbath, but that no one would actually enforce this commitment. While this response ensured that there would be no actual change in the lives of the settlers, it was widely understood and criticized within the Labor movement as conceding the principle of religious influence in the public realm.[49]

By 1947, the Labor movement was willing to concede more than mere principle. In the "status quo" letter, Ben-Gurion committed to turning over formal control of important aspects of the public realm to the religious. This letter promised the Executive Committee of Agudat Israel, a non-Zionist Orthodox Jewish party, that the status quo of the relationship between religion and the state that existed during the British Mandate would continue after independence. Concretely, this meant that state institutions would maintain dietary restrictions, that Saturday would be the official day of rest, that personal status issues would remain under religious jurisdiction, and that religious educational institutions would maintain their autonomy. Unlike the compromise formulated by Katznelson in 1933, this concession carried practical consequences and was enshrined in legislation after the founding of the state.

Mapai's changed attitude toward the place of religion in society was also evident in its withdrawal from the secularization of religious symbols, and to a certain extent, a return to their traditional religious meanings by the mid-1940s.[50] Reflecting its changing attitudes toward religion, as well as more mundane political considerations, the Labor movement established a religious workers' faction within the Histadrut in 1944 and even created religious schools within the Labor-run educational stream.[51]

The analogous transformation in the Revisionists' view of the role of religion in the public realm did not take place until the mid-1950s. At this time, there was a rather sudden quantitative and qualitative intensification of the Revisionists' willingness to increase the role of religion in the public realm. As part of this intensification, Betar paid significantly more attention to issues of religion and state at its 1957 convention than it had since the establishment of the state. In 1958, Begin suddenly began to declare frequently that for Jews, religion and nationality were the same. Begin and Herut also began to emphasize their respect for tradition and for the chief rabbis.[52] During this period, Herut changed its position on a number of highly symbolic issues that were, not coincidentally, crucially important to the Religious Zionists. Herut made the recognition of the Orthodox monopoly on conversion in Israel its official position only in 1958, and Begin started to make this argument in earnest in the 1960s![53] For the first time, Herut's sixth national convention (1961) substantively addressed issues of religion and state, and, also for the first time, its decisions accorded this issue its own distinct section. The leaders of the movement decided, again for the first time, to highlight their "religion" plank (itself unchanged since the 1930s), to ensure that the movement was represented in public religious bodies, to establish a special department of propaganda directed at the religious public, and to support the establishment of religious institutions by members of the movement.[54] By the early 1970s, Begin even argued that despite its earlier advocacy of civil marriage, Herut now supported the Orthodox monopoly on marriage and divorce in Israel.[55] The religious turn was so complete that Yitzhak Shamir eventually declared that "there will never be a party of the right [wing] that will be antagonistic to the Jewish tradition." He even appropriated the Religious Zionist "tricolor," arguing that "the nation of Israel, the land of Israel, and the Torah of Israel are one."[56]

Evolution at Work: Explaining the Acceptance of a Religious Public Realm

On its face, the parallel transformations of the Labor and Revisionist movements increase the likelihood that both rationally adapted to a shared new environment. If an exogenous shock changed the world in such a way that the pursuit of a secular public realm became irrational, we would expect to see something like this. However, the variation in the timing of the shifts in the ideology of the Labor and Revisionist movements complicates the attempts to account for them in terms of rational adaptation. If the two movements were adapting to the same new reality, why is there a twenty-year gap between the onset of change in the Labor movement's conceptualization of mission and that in the Revisionists'? It is possible that Labor Zionists are systematically more rational than Revisionist Zionists, but there is little theoretical or empirical ground for such an assumption.

Rational adaptation provides a problematic explanation for the details of each individual case as well. There is no shock whose timing is consistent with the Revisionist's change in mission. For Labor Zionism, most appeals to rational adaptation identify the Holocaust or the immigration to Israel of Jews from the Middle East and North Africa as the realties that triggered its growing acceptance of religion.[57] Certainly, the destruction of the great learning centers in Europe awakened more than a little bit of sympathy among the Labor Zionist leadership for Orthodox Jewry. The Holocaust also reinforced Labor's belief that the religious were a dying breed. Both of these factors could plausibly have made the Labor movement more willing to accede to the demands of the religious. The new immigrants from the Middle East and North Africa, for their part, tended to be more traditional than Israelis as a whole. As a result, it is possible that the Labor movement "turned, somewhat reluctantly, towards the wider common denominator of all Jewish groups, namely Jewish tradition," in order to appeal to them.[58] While these arguments point to the powerful role of exogenous shocks in reinforcing a transformation that was taking place (in this case by weakening the vehemence of the secularist truth tellers in the party), both of these commonly cited shocks occurred after the change began. Neither the Holocaust, of which the Labor movement learned in 1942, nor the mass immigration, which took place in the early 1950s, can account for the onset of change in the 1930s.

In both of these cases, elite imposition is more plausible, though for different reasons. Labor Zionism's nuanced relationship to the role of religion suggests that the Labor movement might have been open to increasing religion's role in the public realm under the right circumstances. For the Revisionists, the plausibility of elite imposition rests on Begin's personal sympathy for religious tradition. This explanation assumes that as he came to power within the movement, his view of the appropriate role of religion in the public realm displaced the earlier secularism.[59] Indeed, the openness with which Begin tacked toward the religious in the 1950s matches the expectation of elite imposition.

However, while elite imposition might account for the variation between the two movements in the timing of the transformation, it can offer only a weak explanation for the timing and direction of each individually. Since Begin came to power in the early 1940s, why did the transformation in the mission of Revisionist Zionism not begin until the mid-1950s? Nor can elite imposition, which assumes an intentional modification of the fundamental ideology, account for the inconsistent and explicitly tactical character of the change. In Mapai's case, it is not immediately obvious why elite imposition would lead movement leaders to shift toward the demands of the religious rather than away from them. In fact, the secularists to the left of Mapai were more numerous and powerful in the early years of the state than the religious. An electoral calculus, then, ought to have moved Mapai toward the position of the secularists. In any case, there is little evidence that the acceptance of a religious role in the public realm was intended as a permanent and significant ideological shift. Indeed, Mapai's initial accommodation of religious demands understood them as just that: a short-term accommodation rather than an intentional narrowing of ideological differences.

Ultimately, the empirical record of both of these transformations is more consistent with the expectations of the evolutionary dynamic. The transformation in Labor's secularizing mission began with their co-optation of the Religious Zionists in the 1930s—a political project that came at the price of what they saw as temporary concessions allowing some religious influence over the public realm. These concessions became institutionalized because they generated benefits that made reversing them increasingly less likely. The story of the change in Revisionist ideology is similar. The Revisionists also embarked on what they understood as tactical concessions to the religious in order to build an alliance that would serve as a credible alternative to Labor's political domination. Their success in weakening the "historic alliance" led to the institutionalization of the new view within the movement that religion had an appropriate role to play in the public realm.

Something for Nothing? Labor Zionism's Acceptance of a Role for Religion in the Public Realm

The cadence of the acceptance of a role for religion in the public realm in Mapai's sense of national mission is linked to the success of the "historic alliance" and to the outcome of the intramovement struggle over this question. As we saw above, in the early 1930s, Mapai sought to create and maintain a coalition that would establish itself at the head of the Zionist enterprise and enable Mapai to chart the course of the nationalist alliance. To do so, the Labor movement needed to co-opt the Religious Zionists. Labor's inclusion of them in the Zionist Executive in 1935 and the adjustment of the view of the appropriate role of religion in the public realm laid the groundwork for this cooperation.

Significant parts of the Labor movement opposed the co-optation of the Religious Zionists. The secularists within the movement viewed Judaism in purely national terms. They wanted to separate religion and state and resisted making any overtures to the religious. Others within the Labor movement saw little value in Judaism without religious values and sympathized with many of the demands of the Religious Zionists. Between them stood the consensus builders on this issue. They sought a partial, tactical accommodation with the religious that would ensure the support of the religious for the more critical aspects of Labor's nationalist project. For them, religion was simply not that important. Since they assumed that it would inevitably become irrelevant, they saw no reason to waste any energy actively opposing it.[60]

In the 1930s, the secularist truth tellers clearly dominated the movement. In fact, it was the political cost of their continuous, even malicious provocations of religious sensibilities that led Katznelson to formulate the 1933 compromise noted earlier. By the mid-1940s, however, the balance of power among the various views of the role of religion had shifted in favor of the consensus-building approach taken by Katznelson and Ben-Gurion. Their success in framing Labor's position enabled the cooperation between the Religious Zionists and the Labor movement to deepen.

Labor Zionist leaders consistently understood and defended the resulting deviations from the pursuit of a secular public realm as both temporary and not very important in comparison with the other political battles—with the Revisionists, the British, and the Arabs—that consumed them at the time.[61] Thus, in 1933, Ben-Gurion argued that the movement should accede to the demands of the religious on the largely symbolic issue of maintaining kosher kitchens because Mapai was "not interested" in engaging in this fight at that moment.[62] In other words, the short-term political cost of alienating the Religious Zionists in the midst of their fight with the Revisionists and their struggle for control of the WZO was too high. In 1939, Berl Katznelson again argued that maintaining their alliance with the Religious Zionists depended on accommodating some of their demands. He warned that the resistance to this strategy by the truth tellers within the movement damaged Labor's credibility and risked abandoning a significant group of potential supporters to their political rivals.[63] This was not an empty fear. There were many within Mizrachi who were very sympathetic toward the Revisionist point of view. Not only were many Irgun members also part of Mizrachi, but as late as 1945 there were still attempts to create an alliance between the two movements that would more effectively compete with the Labor-dominated coalition.[64]

The concessions to the religious promoted by the consensus builders were politically expedient. The consensus builders within Mapai also believed that these accommodations would be temporary. They assumed that over time the secular national component of Jewish identity would triumph over the religious component. Ben-Gurion, especially, believed that the disappearance of Orthodox Judaism was an inevitable consequence of modernity. He argued that it was preferable to have this process take place gradually with a minimum of conflict rather than through open confrontation.[65] The belief that the religious were a dying breed helps explain how two personalities such as Ben-Gurion and Yitzhak Greenboim, with so little personal sympathy for religious tradition, approved the institutionalization of religious control over parts of the public realm, in the "status quo" letter.

A proponent of rational adaptation might point to this belief and argue that Ben-Gurion rationally adapted to a new reality but erred in his evaluation of the world. In other words, what we have here is rational adaptation, but with a bounded rationality. Ben-Gurion certainly underestimated religion's staying power. The appeal to a bounded rational adaptation, however, cannot account for the fact that the architects of these changes understood them as short-term tactics and not as fundamental ideological changes. In this particular case, Mapai's leaders understood the religious concessions in the status-quo agreement as required to prevent Agudat Israel from undermining the appearance of a united Jewish front before the UN in 1947.[66] Even the leaders of Agudat Israel recognized that the "status quo" letter was a tactical gesture by Mapai. In fact, Agudat Israel's leadership decided to toe the Zionist line and not publicly oppose the establishment of the state *despite* the letter's purely tactical character.[67] Labor leaders, for their part, viewed this price as negligible both in comparison with the potential achievement of a state and because they assumed the "status quo" letter was written in disappearing ink. They believed that they were getting something for nothing: short-term concessions to a disappearing segment of the population in exchange for their support for maintaining Mapai in power and achieving its other nationalist goals.

Ben-Gurion openly acknowledged the tactical character of their concessions to the religious. For example, speaking of the decision to allow immigrants from Yemen to be educated by the Religious Zionists rather than in Labor's own schools, Ben-Gurion argued that the religious attitudes and practices of the immigrants "need[ed] to be respected." This "respect," however, was explicitly intended to make the pious immigrants "comfortable" so that they would be open to indoctrination in other, more important realms.[68]

The tactical concessions made to the religious came under constant attack from the secularist wing of the party, especially after the formation of the state, when they became enforceable by its coercive power. These truth tellers argued that the alliance with the religious contradicted their ideals of creating of a modern enlightened state with real freedom of conscience, tolerance, and gender equality. Some argued that the coalition with the religious was even laying the "clerical foundations" for a theocracy "without anyone paying attention" to this development.[69] However, when Faction B and the Kibbutz movement split from Mapai in 1944, they took many of the vehement anticlericalists with them. This undermined the ability of any remaining truth tellers within Mapai to contest the adjusted ideology from becoming gradually institutionalized as the new ideological status quo.

The consensus builders suppressed the dissent by the remaining critics within the movement by equating criticism with disloyalty and accusing them of putting their own selfish interests above those of the nation.[70] The consensus builders also argued that the secularist aspect of Labor Zionist ideology, the creation of a new "free" Jew, was less important than other goals, especially those of Jewish immigration and support of the state by Diaspora Jews. Thus during the debate over whether or not Israel should adopt a constitution the consensus builders argued that taking an explicit stance on the role of religion in the public realm might lead to fragmentation in the Jewish world at a time when its united support was critical. They worried that the separation between religion and state that the truth tellers demanded would alienate parts of the Jewish Diaspora (particularly in the United States). In this context, they argued that a studied evenhandedness and even concessions to the religious were worth the price.[71] Maintaining their tactical arguments in the face of vehement secularist opposition was not easy. As a result, the once tactical purpose of the ideological modulations was reinterpreted as a goal in its own right. The short-term concessions to the religious became a principled stance taken in the best interest of the nation.

Moreover, as we saw above, the alliance between the Religious Zionists and the Labor movement succeeded in achieving the latter's political aims. The Labor movement's ability to lead the Zionist movement was predicated on maintaining quiet on the "religious front." Its position at the helm of the nationalist alliance paid dividends, which only increased after the establishment of the state. As a result, the tactical concessions made to get there became difficult to abandon. As part of this process, the original vision of a secular public realm was marginalized within the movement. It became so marginal that no one resuscitated it even after the alliance between Labor and Religious Zionism broke down.

From Hating Gefilte Fish to Eating It Up: Revisionist Zionism's
Acceptance of a Role for Religion in the Public Realm
As we already noted, the fact that Begin was personally much more sympathetic to religion than Jabotinsky makes disentangling elite imposition and

the evolutionary dynamic particularly challenging in this case. Certainly, the frequent declarations of the Revisionist movement's "respect for tradition" became a regular feature of its articulations after Begin came to the helm. This was most clearly visible in the context of the Revisionist youth movement, Betar. For example, Betar's 1944 summer camp included "streets" named after not only Revisionist figures like Jabotinsky and Klausner, but also Rabbi A. I. Kook, the patron saint of Religious Zionism. This particular camp was also the first in which a synagogue complete with its own Torah scrolls was erected. After Begin became the leader of Betar, the rhetoric of its members consistently began to feature religious messianic terms such as "the eternal promise to the eternal nation" and "the kingdom of Israel."[72] The apparent increase in religiosity was evident elsewhere as well. Indeed, in the early days of Herut, Begin called for Israel to be ruled according to religious law.[73] The Revisionist movement even went so far as to portray itself as more faithful to religious values than the Religious Zionists.[74]

It is also true that the most radically secularist wing of the Revisionists, those who had, since the 1940s, strongly agitated for a completely secular state, were marginalized after Begin's emergence as the leader of the movement. This wing of the movement included, among others, Hillel Kook, who argued that the Hebrew state should have no official religion and castigated the call for a Jewish commonwealth as little more than a call for the establishment of a theocratic state. "We want Palestine," he concluded, "as a free state and not 'a Jewish state.'" Eri Jabotinsky, the son of the movement's founder, even demanded that the Knesset cafeteria serve nonkosher food.[75] The marginalization of this wing of the party after 1949 certainly contributed to the sense that the Revisionists under Begin were becoming more sympathetic to religious tradition.

In reality, however, Begin and the Revisionist movement did not go beyond an articulation of a generic "respect for religion" before the mid-1950s. As late as 1952, Begin's thorough discussion of his worldview and national mission did not even address the role of religion in the public realm. In fact, he mentioned religion only peripherally—as providing the inspiration for social justice, democracy, and individual liberty.[76] Similarly, the Irgun limited its comments on religion to promising religious freedom and setting the Jewish holy days as state holidays.[77] The "Jewishness" of the state sought by the Revisionists was conceptualized in terms of an ethnic Jewish majority rather than in any religious sense.

During the early years of the state, issues of religion and the appropriate Jewishness of the state were conspicuously absent from Herut's proclamations and internal discussions. For example, Begin's speech to the first Herut National Council and the political resolutions it adopted made no mention of Israel as a Jewish state other than in the sense of providing a safe haven for Jews. Herut's second and third conventions also devoted only minimal space to issues of religion and state. While at least one person in Herut's Central Committee suggested that it base the state's constitution on religious law, the constitutional arrangement that it ultimately proposed did not reserve any role for religion. Nor was religion mentioned in the proposals for how to organize the newly constituted Herut movement or for how to focus its activities.[78]

The positions Herut took on domestic policies in 1949 and 1951 also reflected its liberal treatment of religion.[79] Herut's vision of the appropriate relationship between religion and the state was captured in its proposed version of "Basic Law: The Law of the Rights of Man and the State," which accorded Judaism "a special, though equal, place among the religions and the beliefs" because of its role in maintaining the historical continuity of the nation. This "special place," however, did not translate into any religious prerogative in the public realm other than the setting of the Jewish holy days as the state holidays. Herut rejected any religious coercion, advocated complete individual freedom of conscience and religious association, and even called for civil marriage.[80]

Only Rabbi Mordechai Lisman, the token ultra-Orthodox member of the Central Committee, consistently raised religious issues. His lament that Herut's views alienated many potential supporters among the Orthodox underscores the secular position of the Revisionists at the time. In 1954, he even complained that the Party Center provided no information on religion or the religious aspect of the views of the Revisionists.[81] The secularity of Herut and the meager attention it paid to religious matters even led some at its 1958 convention to complain and to call for the establishment of a separate department that would deal with issues of religion and state.[82]

Even the apparently greater tendency toward a public role for religion demonstrated by Betar was mostly superficial. The "religiosity" of the Betar camp in 1944 was more likely a reaction to the significant influx of religious youth into the movement than an indication of a real ideological shift.[83] In 1950, the Betar Congress decided that the education of the youth movement's members should be directed toward the secular goals of liberating the entire homeland, the ingathering of exiles, sport, and the creation of a free citizen. The role of the Jewish tradition was relegated to one of a number of "sites of inspiration." Only in 1953, was the Bible as a source of education brought to the forefront.[84] Given the fact that Begin became the leader of Betar in Palestine in 1943 and of the Irgun in 1944, the delay of the onset of change in the role assigned to religion undermines explanations based on the difference between the inclinations of Begin and Jabotinsky.

The internal justifications for the religious turn also complicate the assumption that the transformation in the role assigned to religion in the public realm was intentional. A 1948 memo from the Herut Secretariat justified the hints at religious sympathies because they "enabled the entire nation to fight in our ranks, whether they were the students of the yeshivot [religious schools] or those of the General [secular] schools....As a result of this—*since we are on the verge of extensive work in preparation for the elections,* which may cause the breaking of the Sabbath—we must warn our members to take all the possible precautions to prevent any transgression of the laws of Israel."[85]

The debates over the so-called pig laws in 1956 and 1962 exposed the tactical rationale for the promotion of this ideological variant. The 1956 law, which validated municipal regulations banning the breeding and trading of pork, generated a great deal of opposition within Herut's rank and file because they saw it as an instance of religious coercion. Led by Begin, however, the consensus builders within the leadership argued that Herut should support the law for both principled and opportunistic reasons.[86] Unable to convince the truth tellers, who continued to adhere to Jabotinsky's notion of religious liberty, Begin asked them to refrain from openly demonstrating their opposition. He feared that the implication that they "support pigs will cause serious damage to the chances of the movement in the future. According to my estimate, of the 107,000 votes we received, this issue is the most cherished principle, perhaps more important than any other, of no less than 60,000. And if we harm their most cherished principle, we will lose an opportunity."[87]

In July of 1956, when this debate took place, Begin and the consensus builders were unable to impose their view on the entire movement. As a result, Herut abstained during the vote on the law. The public rationale for Herut's position, however, was explicitly designed to appeal to the religious despite its (in)action. Herut decided to declare that it would abstain because the law *did not go far enough* in banning pigs from Israel (because it still allowed municipalities some discretion).[88]

The main difference between the tactical appeals to the religious in the late 1940s and those that took place in the late 1950s and early 1960s was that the latter worked. The earlier attempts failed to drive a wedge between the Religious Zionist movement and the Labor Zionist movement or to attract many Orthodox to the Revisionists' banner. By the early 1960s, the "historic alliance" between Labor and Religious Zionism was collapsing. The greater religious strictness of the rising Young Guard of the Religious Zionist movement made them less willing to compromise with the secular majority. The parallel decline of the concept of "Torah and Labor" within Religious Zionism also meant that the Young Guard no longer saw any ideological commonalities with the secular socialist-Zionist movement.

[handwritten margin notes:] Herut abstaining from pig laws / clever move

the latter appeals to religion (1950-60) worked

less willingness for religious and secular to compromise

As a result, they increasingly perceived the coalition with Mapai in terms of immediate utility, rather than as the pursuit of a common social agenda.[89]

The adjustments to the Revisionist position on issues of religion and state capitalized on the widening gap between the Labor and Religious movements. Internally, however, the debate over the extent of religious influence in the public realm between the Revisionist truth-telling (secularist) and consensus-building ("sympathetic") wings continued in the 1950s and early 1960s on topics ranging from the regulation of autopsies to the recognition of non-Orthodox streams of Judaism in Israel. Even those sympathetic to the religious view tended to combine principled arguments with tactical electoral considerations. Until the mid-1960s, the Revisionist movement frequently split the difference between the different views on the issue within it by declaring its support for the religious position but abstaining during the actual vote.[90]

After 1973, the Likud's alliance with Gush Emunim drove the Revisionists closer to the Religious Zionists' view of the role of religion in the public realm. This alliance was initially based explicitly on the Likud's and Gush Emunim's shared desire to extend Israeli control of the territories, not on a fundamental agreement on matters of religion and state.[91] Still, maintaining it required both Gush Emunim and the Revisionists to make rhetorical adjustments in those basic claims that did clash. As we saw in chapter 2, Gush Emunim muted its claim to the Land of Israel from "the River of Egypt to . . . the River Euphrates." For the Revisionists, the alliance with Gush Emunim reinforced the tactical appeal to the religious that Begin initiated in the mid-1950s. The alliance between the Revisionists and the Religious Zionists became so close that observers began calling it a "natural alliance"—in much the same way that others once referred to the alliance between Labor and Religious Zionism—ordaining the emergence of a "neo-Zionism."[92]

As in other cases of change driven by the evolutionary dynamic, two developments reinforced the institutionalization of this neo-Zionism in place of the movement's original mission. First, the truth tellers lost the intramovement battle. Second, the tactical adjustment proved politically successful. The secularist wing of the Revisionist movement interpreted the tactical modulations that moved the movement closer to the religious in the 1950s as a violation of the "monist" principle. Many of the Revisionist intelligentsia who opposed the move even angrily left Herut and political life as a consequence.[93] By 1977, the secularist wing of Herut had clearly lost, and Begin's government excluded its most prominent representatives. This exodus left few with any standing within the movement to disagree with Begin on this score. While the Liberal Party members that were part of Gahal and then of the Likud relayed some of their objections, by the 1970s, they were too weak within the combined party to counter the religious turn.

Second, the "bargain" made with the Religious Zionists generated significant electoral returns. The Likud's showing in the 1974 elections vindicated the tactical rapprochement with the religious. Begin even argued that Herut must "respect the religion and tradition in Israel," not just out of an intrinsic respect for religion, but "out of respect for what lifted us up [i.e., gave us so many votes].... They are the source of our strength."[94] Like Jabotinsky, Begin emphasized national rather than theological reasons for this stance, but this rationale did not mask the effect of increasing the role of religion in the public realm, which was evident in Herut's new positions. The combined support of large segments of the religious public and of the more traditional Mizrachi voter is one of the reasons for the Likud's political dominance over the past thirty years. The success of the alliance with the Religious Zionists made it increasingly costly for the Revisionists to return to the old liberal delineation of the very limited role of religion in the public realm.

It is important, however, not to press the extent of this change in the Revisionist Zionist understanding of national mission too far. Today's Revisionists certainly accept a role for religion in the public realm as inherently good. For the most part, however, they have not accepted the Religious Zionist premise that normalizing the Jewish people and their state is undesirable or impossible. Some within the movement did go this far. They overtly sought to replace the old Revisionist mission of normalizing the Jews with the Religious Zionists' mission of preserving the uniqueness of the Jewish people.[95] This segment of the Revisionist movement failed in its bid to take over the movement's reins and transform its mission in this way. As a result of its failure, and enraged by Begin's signing of the Camp David Accords, many members of this faction left the Likud.[96] As a result, mainstream Revisionism continues to adhere to the Zionist mission of normalization, even though it allows religion an explicit role in the public realm.

A Case of Elite Imposition

The Subordination of the State of Israel to the Land of Israel

The Religious Zionists' sense of national mission differed radically from that of either the Labor or the Revisionist movement. To begin with, the Religious Zionists rejected the need to create, and even the possibility of creating, a new secular Jew. For them, religion was at the core of both the individual and the national Jewish existence. They also rejected the notion that it was possible to normalize a nation defined as exceptional by the Almighty. Certainly, when Religious Zionism first emerged, it embraced the nationalist program entirely on pragmatic grounds: a Jewish state would be the most effective way to save Jews from persecution. By the 1920s, however, the Kookist view of Zionism as a divinely inspired step in the mystical progress toward redemption eclipsed this perspective. As part of the divine plan, Zionism, and the state Zionists dreamed of, acquired deep theological significance. Rabbi A. I. Kook envisioned "our state, the State of Israel, [as] the pedestal of God's throne in this world." He argued that "Zionism is a heavenly matter," and that "the state of Israel is a divine entity, our holy and exalted state!"[97]

The state's theological status as signaling the "dawn of our redemption" was enshrined in the prayer for the state of Israel adopted by the Chief Rabbinate in 1948. Rabbi Zvi Yehuda Kook sanctified the actions and instruments of the state as well: "The holiness of the divine service, the service of the Temple, is extended to the work of the state as a whole, both practical and spiritual, both public and private."[98] He declared: "The tank is sacred. The military uniform is a holy vestment." Even the jails in Israel were "holy prisons."[99] The sanctity of the state of Israel was taken for granted; it was an ontological principle, disconnected from both the personal piety of its citizens and the actions of its leaders.[100]

As a signal of the "dawn of redemption" and an active participant in bringing it about, the state was to be protected and nurtured, even at the cost of other cherished ideals. In accordance with this order of priorities, the leadership of the Religious Zionist movement explicitly articulated its willingness to withdraw from parts of the Land of Israel if it would benefit the state.[101] This did not mean, importantly, that the Religious Zionists did not sincerely believe that the land itself was sacred. They did. Until the early 1970s, however, this belief did not translate into an all-consuming concern with the land or how much of it was under Israeli control. As we saw in chapter 2, after the establishment of the state, the Religious Zionist movement all but stopped addressing the issue of borders. Where the movement dealt with this issue, it was inevitably as a secondary matter, subordinated to the movement's concern with extending the influence of religion in the public realm. The negligible weight of the Land of Israel in Religious Zionist programmatic essays, the issues Religious Zionists used to mobilize their constituency, and the topics the movement's leaders chose to speak about during movement conventions at the time clearly reflected this order of priorities.[102]

The political platforms of the Religious Zionists also reflected this ranking. As late as 1965, the NRP's platform said little about borders or the Land of Israel, and even placed the "security and foreign policy" section after those dealing with the status of the Rabbinate in Israel, Sabbath observance, outlawing pork, autopsies, missionaries, religious councils, the "who is a Jew" question, education and culture, and the construction of old-age homes.[103] The correspondence, writing, and instructional materials of Bnei Akiva also reflected its primary concern with issues of religion and state rather than with the sanctity or extent of the land.[104]

since 1970s: territorial concerns have come back into play

This order of priorities has been inverted. Since the 1970s, Religious Zionism has increasingly subordinated the needs of the state to the imperative of extending Jewish control over the Land of Israel. The inversion of Religious Zionism's ideological priorities was initially accomplished by significantly raising the theological importance of the land, to the extent that Gush Emunim elevated the wholeness of the land over personal piety as the harbinger of redemption.[105] Representatives of Gush Emunim argued that settlement, not the religious cast of the public realm, or even the existence of the state of Israel, was the condition for the survival of the Jewish nation.[106] The theological importance of the land led Yehuda Elitzur to argue: "Just as there is no Judaism without God and without the choosing of Israel, there is no Judaism without the land of Israel."[107] Rabbi Mordechai Bruyer went so far as to argue: "Even the monumental tiding of the creation of the world...did not come for its own sake, but only to establish the right of the nation of Israel to its land. This is also the case for the commandments. The commandments have no value in and of themselves, they are only the key to the land of Israel."[108]

The theological importance of the state necessarily suffered by comparison. The Religious Zionists still considered the state sacred, but this sanctity was transformed from an ontological principle—emanating from its very existence—to a conditional one. The state was holy, according to the new calculus, only to the extent that it fulfilled its assigned role in the process of redemption. This implied that the state had no right to withdraw from the territories, even if its leaders and population believed that it was in the best interest of the state, and regardless of the legitimacy of the decision-making procedure. Reversing Israel's hold on the territories became tantamount to the heresy of reversing the process of redemption. The ultimate value ascribed to the settlements fostered a shift in the way in which Religious Zionism viewed the state. In the eyes of the settlers, the state increasingly became merely a source of material resources rather than the central and monopolistic symbol of the collectivity.

Explaining the Subordination of the State of Israel to the Land of Israel

This ideological shift is the product of elite imposition. The transformation began in the late 1960s and early 1970s, reached a turning point in 1973, and was largely completed by 1977. This timing does not match the expectations of rational adaptation. It is not obvious why adaptation to the 1967 war, the closest shock to the onset of change, would include the desanctification of the state. After the war, Religious Zionists believed that the process of redemption was well underway and that the state was fully playing its part. The process of change does not match the expectations of the evolutionary dynamic either. The existing leadership of the movement did not drive this change as the evolutionary explanation expects. Those articulating the change were not in a position of leadership within the movement to make the kinds of alliances that are at the heart of the evolutionary dynamic. There is also no evidence that the shift originated as a tactical adjustment for short-term political gain. In fact, the transformation came at the expense of the proven political benefits of the alliance with the Labor movement. Gush Emunim shifted the movement's ideology *despite* the danger that they would lose their seat at the decision-making table, not to gain access to it. The one alliance that might have contributed to this shift, the one that developed between the Likud and the Religious Zionists, was already premised on their agreement that Israel should control the territories. As a result, there was no need to adjust their claim of the sanctity of the land for its sake.

Rather, this ideological shift was part of the takeover of the movement's leadership by Gush Emunim and the Young Guard. This new cadre came to the table with a preexisting, coherent set of ideological standards that it used to distinguish itself from the traditional leadership. As it took control of the movement, it successfully imposed its ideological positions on most of the movement.[109]

As we noted earlier, the Young Guard and Gush Emunim were more theologically doctrinaire than the leadership they replaced. They rejected the grand bargain crafted with the Labor movement in the 1930s and 1940s and blamed it for artificially limiting the influence of Religious Zionism to issues of religion and state. They argued that as the one true representation of the nation, Religious Zionism should forcefully engage in the political struggle for power and present itself as a full-fledged "alternative to rule" rather than as a permanent junior partner in the coalition. Going even further, Gush Emunim framed the intra-Israeli battle over the future of the territories as part of the battle between authentic and false Zionisms.[110]

The reunion with the biblical heartland after the 1967 war certainly placed the issue of the Land of Israel back on the Religious Zionist agenda. The conquest of the West Bank and Gaza Strip reinforced the Young Guard's argument that the Religious Zionist movement should address itself to all areas of life, including, prominently, "foreign policy and security" issues. The messianic fervor that swept through the movement in the wake of the war did not, however, automatically turn its traditional order of priorities on its head. A year later, the emphasis in the movement's convention was still firmly on religious issues even as the pressure to expand the scope of the issues to include security and territorial ones increased. Even in 1973, the topics the NRP leadership chose to report on to their convention focused on religious issues. Issues of religion and state remained their central concern.[111]

In fact, the NRP did not even establish a "working group" to formulate its policy toward the territories until 1969, and the movement's new position vis-à-vis the territories was not officially enunciated until 1973. Part of the reason for this delay was the internal disagreement over what stance to take. The movement's traditional leadership was largely, if reluctantly, willing to part with most of the territories (with the exception of Jerusalem) in the context of peace treaties with Israel's neighbors. This position, importantly, did not imply that they accepted Israel's 1949 borders as appropriate. Their territorial moderation stemmed from their belief that where the interests of the state conflicted with their other aspirations, the former ought to take precedence. The Young Guard, which challenged the leadership, made an adamant and unyielding call for the annexation of these parts of the "liberated land of Israel" to the state.

The increasing influence of the Young Guard was already evident in 1969 when the party's platform, for the first time, devoted a prominent section to matters of the land.[112] The intramovement struggle between these perspectives was not settled until 1973, when the Young Guard took control of the movement's governing bodies. Only then did the NRP add the clause rejecting "any plan that contains a ceding of part of historic Eretz Israel, our patrimony" to its platform. To its historical call for peace with Israel's neighbors, presumably including Jordan and Lebanon, the NRP added an affirmation of its belief in the promise that the entire divinely promised patrimony would be settled.[113] The victory of the Young Guard's view was not a foregone conclusion; the new clause was adopted by a majority of a single vote.[114] Once in place, however, it very quickly became the dominant position within the movement.

Reflecting the rise of the Young Guard and Gush Emunim to power within the movement, by 1974, the relative effort expended by Religious Zionist MKs on religious issues slowed down enough to merit notice by the movement's newspaper.[115] By 1978, only a single speaker in that year's NRP convention raised the condition of religious affairs in the state as an issue. The rest spoke of the territories.[116] In 1992, a propaganda kit explicitly acknowledged the relative subjugation of other issues to the territorial one (though this was justified on practical rather than on ideological grounds).[117] The concern with settlement in the territories above all else became so ingrained that a National Religious Party MK responded to a request that the party deal more extensively with social issues by saying that "it won't look authentic."[118] As the new leadership increasingly set the ideological tone of the movement and came to control its institutions this new order of priorities became more widely entrenched.

Evolution Interrupted

The history of the transformations in the sense of mission articulated by the Israeli nationalist movements contains at least two notable instances in which new ideological variants were introduced for tactical political reasons but substantive ideological transformations did not follow: (1) the apparent acceptance of a religious role in the public realm by the Revisionists in the 1930s, and (2) the Religious Zionist retreat from the goal of a theocracy. At first glance, the fact that the origins of these variants are consistent with the expectations of the evolutionary dynamic but their end is not challenges the plausibility of an argument based on the unguided institutionalization of adjustments introduced for short-term political gain.

A closer look, however, shows that these would-be changes illustrate the important role played by the institutional frameworks in which new variants are embedded in bringing about substantive ideological transformation. These institutional frameworks provide a concrete vehicle that engages in the political struggle. The fate of the new ideological variants is then tied to the fortunes of these institutional vehicles and their ability to succeed politically. When these vehicles stall, the tactical adjustments fade with them. The unpredictable results of the political contests in which these vehicles engage reinforce the contingency involved in the evolutionary dynamic.

A Case of Early Failure

As we saw above, the Revisionist movement accepted a role for religion in the public realm in the late 1950s and early 1960s. This was not, however, the first time that Revisionist rhetoric opened the door for such an ideological shift. Already in the 1930s, the Revisionist movement engaged in an overtly tactical adjustment that, had it succeeded, might have led away from their monism at that juncture. This adjustment took place in the context of the increasing acrimony between the Labor and Revisionist movements and the wider struggle between the New Zionist Organization (NZO) and the World Zionist Organization (WZO). Trying to increase his base of support, Jabotinsky turned to the largely Orthodox Polish middle class. While Jabotinsky did not change his basic attitude toward clericalism, he dropped his objections to forming tactical alliances with the religious at that point. In order to enable closer cooperation with the non-Zionist Agudat Israel and the Religious Zionists, he added a "religion plank" to the Revisionist constitution calling for the "cultivation of religious tradition." Hoping to attract Agudat Israel, in 1937, Jabotinsky even appeared to retreat from his view that religion was a private matter: "I believe that the day is coming when the spirit of the masses will demand the revival of a direct link between religious inspiration and the concrete common life of the state and society. And it will be proven to the world that this can come about only with full adherence to the exalted principles of liberty, democracy, and social justice."[119]

Even those who argued that the Revisionists were always sympathetic to the idea of a religious role in the public realm recognized the overtly tactical character of this appeal.[120] Jabotinsky himself justified the inclusion of the "religion plank" to his secularist son by arguing that they should harness the "moral force" of religion. He continued: "There is no doubt that we will have trouble with the Haredi [i.e., the ultra-Orthodox] partners, but...I am sure that we will be able to limit this fundamental fanaticism within appropriate limits."[121]

The ideological adjustment made to cooperate with the religious is exactly the kind of variation that the evolutionary dynamic predicts could lead to substantive transformation. Yet, as we saw above, the Revisionist movement's view of the public realm remained decidedly secular well into the 1950s. The evolutionary dynamic helps us understand why. It expects ideological transformation to stem from the success of a tactical adjustment in achieving the goals for which it was deployed. In this case, Jabotinsky's ideological modulation was never institutionalized because the attempted alliance with the Orthodox in general, and with the non-Zionist Agudat Israel in particular, failed to materialize. The failure to construct an alliance based on this adjustment meant that there was no opportunity for the adjusted variant to prove its political worth. Nor was there an institution whose survival depended on the continued salience of this modulation. As a result, there were few short-term incentives for the Revisionists to continue articulating it. While the Revisionist movement maintained the "religion plank" as a low-cost appeal to the religious public, no change in its sense of mission took place.

This failed transformation also challenges the logic of elite imposition. Jabotinsky was the undisputed leader of the Revisionist movement. If any leader was able to do as he wished with a movement's ideology, it was Jabotinsky among the Revisionists. Yet, in this case, he tried to modify their ideology and failed. The elite's search for power is certainly a credible explanation for why politicians would engage in ideological modulations in the first place. However, while we can reasonably expect politicians to engage in tactical rhetorical modulations in a constant search for workable formulations, relatively rarely do these modulations amount to substantive ideological change. This case of early failure reminds us that elite imposition often neglects to account for the variation in the ability of elites to impose their view on the movement.

A Case of Late Failure

The ups and downs of the Religious Zionists' pursuit of a theocracy as the ideal form of state also illustrate the close link between the success of the institutional arrangement in which a new ideological variant is embedded and the success of that variant. Since the victory of the Kookist branch of the movement, the meaning of a "Jewish state" was impossible to comprehend within Religious Zionism as anything other than a state ruled according to the Halacha (Jewish religious law). Rabbi A. I. Kook even argued that the goal of a state ruled by Halacha was ontologically built into the political aspirations of the Jewish nation and could not be denied.[122] Indeed, the idea that the Torah and religious laws should govern all social, political, and economic activity was part of Hapoel Hamizrachi's "Holy Rebellion" and an explicit part of its program.[123] Mizrachi's goal was no different. Rabbi Meir Berlin, one of its leaders, argued that the plan of the Religious Zionists was "to conquer Judaism, Jewish life, to impose the spirit of the Torah on the marketplace, on the public, on the state."[124] In fact, in its memorandum to the Partition Commission in 1938, Mizrachi explicitly laid out its plan for a theocratic state.[125] In this vein, representatives of Religious Zionism in the 1930s and 1940s repeatedly emphasized that they were less concerned with the personal fulfillment of the religious commandments by individuals than with the public realm—with establishing a "Torah state."[126] This was the very issue that they used to distinguish themselves from the non-Zionist Agudat Israel. Unlike Agudat Israel, which was happy to insulate itself, the Religious Zionists argued:

> [We] cannot be satisfied by allowing the religious Jew to live a life of religion as an individual in the Hebrew state but leaving the regulations of the state, its laws and institutions, to the extent that they generally touch upon the public life, without any national religious character....The Mizrachi aspires not just to ensure a religious life for religious Jews, but also to have all public life and the formal institutions in the Hebrew state arranged according to the foundations of the Hebrew law and the laws of Israel that are sanctified in the life of the nation and in the Torah of Israel.[127]

By the early 1950s, however, the concept of a Torah state was clearly pushed aside as a topic for practical discussions. The establishment of the

National Religious Front by the Religious Zionists and Agudat Israel was one of the first indicators that this shift was underway. While Agudat Israel (temporarily) acceded to the categorization of the state as the "dawn of the redemption," it remained steadfastly opposed to the attempt by anyone other than the Messiah to bring about a Torah state. Not only was the leadership of the Religious Zionist movement willing to accept this stance, but the issue did not play a significant role in the eventual breakup of the National Religious Front. The tepid response to Rabbi Maimon's 1950 proposal to renew the Sanhedrin (a religious council empowered to rewrite religious law) also indicated the retreat of the ideal of the Torah state. Convening the Sanhedrin was seen as the theological requirement for operationalizing a Torah state, because only such a body would be empowered to update Jewish religious law to deal with issues of modern sovereignty. Not only was this proposal dismissed by the Religious Zionist establishment, but it was rejected with a deafening silence. It elicited virtually no discussion or debate.[128] Finally, the willingness of the Religious Zionist movement to agree to a constitution that, from its perspective, guaranteed the secularity of the state also suggests that the salience of the quest for a "Torah state" had waned.[129]

In 1956, the declaration of the basic principles of the NRP as formulated in its founding convention did not include a call for a Torah state.[130] Although a die-hard minority of truth tellers held to it, the goal of arranging every aspect of social, political, and economic life in the state according to religious law gave way to the more limited goal of "shaping the character of the state according to the light of the Torah" and influencing the piety of individual Jews.[131] In 1962, Zerach Warhaftig argued that the ideal of a theocracy belonged in the realm of dreams.[132]

Up to this point, the characteristics of this transformation follow the pattern of the evolutionary dynamic. For all of its ideological and religious utility, the pursuit of a theocracy posed a practical problem for the Religious Zionist movement. As the truth tellers within the movement argued, their commitment to a Torah state obligated them to bring all aspects of life under religious jurisdiction. The consensus builders within the movement, however, hesitated to do so. They feared that overtly pursuing a theocracy would antagonize the Labor movement and jeopardize their participation in the ruling coalition it led. They based their concern on the Religious Zionists' relative weakness within the Yishuv and, as importantly, within the ruling coalition, where they faced a secular, even anticlerical majority. The consensus builders argued that breaking with the Labor Zionist movement would risk the loss of access to state resources, the closure of their educational system, and, potentially, the permanent separation of religion and state. This cost, they contended, was too high; especially since they had not yet worked out the Halachic details involved in establishing a Torah state.[133]

Instead, the consensus builders offered an interim strategy according to which the movement would focus its energies on "shaping the character of the state" in a religious direction. As Warhaftig argued, unlike Agudat Israel, the Religious Zionists could not quixotically demand "all or nothing." Rather, they should "fight over each and every clause in order to insert the maximum religious elements into the Constitution." "We have to present the program in an acceptable way," Warhaftig noted. "We have to ensure that our fight will be a real fight."[134] Both Haim Moshe Shapira and Warhaftig maintained that the demand for a Torah state was naive and even detrimental to the Religious Zionist movement and that it would get more by demanding less.[135] Chief Rabbi Herzog set the tone of this strategy in his reasoning that while the Religious Zionists should ultimately seek the establishment of a theocracy, realpolitik constraints dictated that they settle for less in the short term.[136] This strategy converted the vision of a Torah state to a nonoperational slogan, enabling the commitment to it as a long-range vision while not undermining the alliance with the Labor Zionists in the present.[137]

The unintended institutionalization of this once tactical approach was at least partly a function of the need to respond to the constant and repeated attacks by its opponents within the Religious Zionist movement, as well as by Agudat Israel.[138] The truth tellers in the movement criticized this tactic as effectively abandoning the original vision. They interpreted the political leadership's pragmatism as conceding the very essence of the movement rather than as a strategy for its gradual fulfillment.[139] In response, the consensus builders...agreed! They argued that the tactic of religious legislation was not intended to bring about the incremental fulfillment of the vision of the Torah state.[140] Rather, they tended to justify it in explicitly tactical terms, usually as a function of Religious Zionism's political weakness.[141] One of the critics of the drive to institute religious legislation commented that while the movement influenced the personal piety of Jews in the state, it did almost nothing "to prepare and to propose to the state institutions a system of Torah laws for the arrangement of the social, economic, and political life between the state and its residents, [and] among men."[142] In response to these attacks, the consensus builders increasingly defended their modest religious claims and reluctance to pursue a Halachic state as necessary for "the unity of the nation."[143] In other words, the once tactical and temporary mission was now justified as required for the pursuit of other ideological goals (whose importance was elevated for this purpose). The success of this tactical adjustment in attaining the material goals of the Religious Zionist movement, including, most prominently, a burgeoning autonomous educational system, reinforced this bait and switch. These inducements were sufficient to lead scholars to conclude that the Religious Zionists had traded their ambition to extend religion into the public realm for the ability to defend their particularistic interests.[144]

These responses reinforce the notion that the leaders of the Religious Zionist movement initially conceived the shift away from the pursuit of a Torah state as a temporary measure. In fact, conforming to the inconsistency expected in the evolutionary dynamic, movement forums and the articulations of some of the same leaders who initiated the tactical ideological stance continued to feature the mission of a Torah state.[145]

The rise of the Young Guard and Gush Emunim and the corresponding breakdown of the "historic alliance" with the Labor movement interrupted the institutionalization of the shift away from the pursuit of a theocracy. Mapai's positions in the 1950s and 1960s on a number of religiously sensitive issues—including the proposed recognition of non-Orthodox conversion, the "who is a Jew" question, and the possibility of civil marriage—generated a great deal of resentment among Religious Zionists. This resentment weakened the political standing of the consensus builders within the movement. As a result, the new variant of the mission did not develop a constituency entrenched enough to defend it.[146]

As in other cases of change by an evolutionary dynamic during this period, the original ideological formulation remained available within the Religious Zionist movement's repertoire of ideological positions. Indeed, the Young Guard resuscitated the ideal of the Torah state as part of its challenge of the movement's leadership. It accused the movement's traditional leadership of insufficient piety. On the eve of the NRP's third party convention, Zvulun Hammer castigated the NRP's traditional leadership for not making enough progress toward the establishment of a theocratic society. In the name of the Young Guard, he demanded the creation of a "master-plan for the creation of a Torah state" that would provide "national religious answers to the problem of religion, society, and politics, [and] a religious approach to military and economic problems."[147] Returning to the arguments made by the truth tellers fifteen years earlier, the Young Guard (and later Gush Emunim) consistently called for a Torah state.[148]

The new leaders of Religious Zionism rejected the notion that the benefits of the adjusted ideology were worth the ideological cost, thereby undermining the process of positive returns that was underway. They explicitly accused the "religious legislation" approach and the nearly exclusive emphasis on religious issues of costing them votes.[149] They also perceived the bargain made with Labor—including the move away from the Torah state as an operational goal—as having limited the growth and influence of the Religious Zionist movement. They saw the compromises made by the older generation not as an attempt to protect the religious community, but as selling out.[150]

Their success in replacing the traditional leadership at the helm of the movement enabled this ideal to reemerge. As the consensus builders lost political power within the Religious Zionist movement, the tactical change they implemented ceased to be supported and the original ideological mission arose in its place. There have been suggestions that since the decline of Gush Emunim the pursuit of this ideal has once again correspondingly declined.[151] It is too soon to tell. At the very least, however, it is clear that a struggle is taking place within Religious Zionism between an increasingly religiously doctrinaire view and a desire for a theocracy and the opposite tendency of Religious Zionists to merge into mainstream Israeli society. Chapter 6 takes up aspects of this struggle in greater detail.

● ● ●

Renan was right. The perceptions of the national mission, of the kind of society nationalists want to create, are as fundamental an aspect of their ideology as borders or membership boundaries. He also correctly observed that even these deeply seated ideals are subject to change—even if he overestimated the frequency of such transformations.

The evolutionary dynamic accounted for the declassicization of a socialist movement and the "religious conversion" of two secular nationalist movements. The evolution of these missions was the by-product of the various grand alliances between nationalist movements that also accounted for the shifts in the visions of the homeland explored in chapters 1–3. That the evolutionary dynamic can account for the related changes in different dimensions increases its plausibility as an explanation of how nationalism changes more generally.

This chapter also demonstrates that the evolutionary dynamic does not explain everything. Elite imposition accounted for a transformation in the ideology of one of the movements. Even so, unlike the conventional elite imposition thesis, where existing elites impose a new ideological position on the movement, this transformation was the product of a new cadre who came to power within the movement and imposed their vision as the dominant one. Change was therefore as much the product of elite replacement as of elite imposition.

The implications of transformations in mission that (a) can take place and (b) do so largely through the evolutionary dynamic extend beyond considerations of nationalism. The contemporary debate over how democratic states should cope with the rise of religious fundamentalism hinges on our assumptions about if, and how, such movements change their most radical beliefs. The notion that basic beliefs cannot change, and the conclusion that therefore they must be fought at every turn, find little empirical support.

Nationalists, who tend to believe their ideology as deeply as anyone, did change the fundamental ways in which they perceived the desired public realm of their society. This was also true of religious nationalists. Elite imposition appears to offer a more likely avenue of change, but it depends on the emergence of a new leadership cadre to do so. The changes in the missions articulated by the Zionist movements show that change can also occur as the result of tactical adjustments made by radical movements for mundane reasons. Drawing such movements into the political game may be the best way of encouraging such adjustments, though it offers no guarantees. Whether a tactical adjustment actually leads to change, and whether or not such a change would be moderating or radicalizing, depend on the character of the "bargain" among movements and the short-term political success of these adjustments.

5

Arabs and Diaspora Jews in Israeli National Identity

Nationalism defines the criteria for inclusion in the political community and for exclusion from it. Linguistic, racial, religious, ethnic, and territorial criteria have all been used as more or less explicit rules for inclusion and exclusion. In the Israeli case, the Labor, Religious and Revisionist Zionist movements have consistently articulated an ethnic definition of the nation—one that included all Jews wherever they might live, and excluded the local Arab population. These movements' definition of the appropriate membership in the nation's *state,* however, was not static. Each of the Zionist movements initially believed that all Jews appropriately belonged in the Jewish state. They saw exile as spiritually debilitating, and Jewish life in it as inherently physically precarious. Since survival in exile was ultimately impossible, they expected all Jews to eventually become members of the nation-state. The Zionists, however, had a problem. Despite their claim to speak for the entire Jewish nation, it was not at all clear that the "entire Jewish nation" wanted to join them. In the context of this tension, the Labor Zionist movement's conception of appropriate membership in the state shifted from including all Jews to excluding the Jewish communities in the West, especially in the United States. The first part of this chapter shows that the evolutionary dynamic better accounts for the timing, direction, and process of this transformation than the alternative explanations.

The second part of the chapter deals with the other main axis of the membership dimension in Israeli nationalism: the place of Palestinian Arabs in the Jewish state. As a general rule, despite having civil and political rights, Palestinian Arab citizens have not been integrated into the definition of the appropriate membership in the state. The symbols of the state—the anthem, the flag, the celebration of the "nation's birthday," and days of commemoration—visibly exclude the Arabs from the collectivity. Indeed, for many in Israel the terms Israeli and Jew are synonymous. The ethnic definition of appropriate membership articulated by the Zionist movements persisted despite tremendous pressure by the international community, political opportunity, and the desire to reconcile the tension between this exclusion and their democratic self-image. Why did these pressures not lead to change despite the expectations of rational adaptation and elite imposition? The experience of the Labor Zionist movement shows that political incentives and new realities did lead to rhetorical adjustments, but not to substantive ideological change. As in the explanation of the dogs that didn't bark in chapter 4, here too the failure to create a political vehicle based on these tactical adjustments was critical. The absence of such a vehicle, whose success might have been subject to increasing returns, mediated the effects of both external pressures and political opportunities.

Diaspora Jews in Labor Zionist Ideology

From Eradicating Exile to Saving the Dispersion

The nationalist mission of the Labor Zionist movement (and of all the Zionist movements) was missing one main ingredient: Jews. As a result, Labor Zionism, like its counterparts, defined the "ingathering of the exiles" and the eradication of the Diaspora as its most important missions. The sine qua non of normalizing the Jews required their territorial concentration in an independent state. In line with this imperative, the Zionist movements evaluated virtually every aspect of life by its effect on the potential immigration of Jews to the Land of Israel. In fact, Jewish existence in the Diaspora was so denigrated within Mapai that, as Shlomo Kaplansky accurately complained, it tended "to claim the absolute sovereignty of [the Jews in Palestine] over the Diaspora, and to speak arrogantly of 'domination,' 'hegemony,' and 'control' when we ought to be cooperating with the Diaspora and exchanging ideas."[1]

Kaplansky's view, once barely heard within the Labor movement, is now the mainstream view. A number of overlapping terminological shifts reflected the acceptance of the Diaspora's continued existence. Starting in the early 1940s, Mapai's leaders began to refer to American Jews as "allies," "partners," or "friends," rather than as part of "us."[2] In a wider, but related, shift, Ben-Gurion also began to distinguish between "Jews" and "Zionists." He expected the latter to personally fulfill their Zionism by immigrating to Palestine. Just "Jews" were not obligated to do so. By the 1950s, Ben-Gurion was also careful to speak of the "ingathering of exiles" rather than of the "ingathering of *the* exile." The shift to individuals from the Jewish collectivity minimized the mission of eradicating the Diaspora.[3]

By then, the notion of "exile" itself, with all of its negative connotations, was already waning. Even symposia devoted to encouraging Jewish immigration, where we might have expected the negation of the Diaspora to last the longest, began to speak in terms of "tfuzot" (dispersions) rather than "galut" (exile). In 1967, one Labor activist noted that the term "galut" already sounded odd.[4] This terminological shift recategorized Jewish communities outside Israel. While Labor Zionism once saw them as existing in a kind of purgatory, it now considered these communities as viable and legitimate entities. Jews in the dispersion could still become members of the political community constructed by the Labor movement if they made the individual decision to immigrate to Israel, but they were no longer automatically included in it en masse.

The increasing emphasis on the distinctiveness of the Jewish community in the Land of Israel also reflected the exclusion of Diaspora Jews from membership in the state. Thus Ben-Gurion argued: "Here in the country there is a Jewish community that is different from all the Jewish communities in other countries, because the *community here* is a *nation,* with all the explicit markers that every independent nation that is rooted in its land has."[5] The ubiquitous notion that Jews, coming from a variety of places and communities, needed to be "melded into a nation," and that a "common national basis" had to be "created," contributed to the differentiation between the "nation in Zion" and Jews outside it.[6] Fighting against this trend, Yitzhak Greenboim wanted to call the state "the state of the Jews" rather than "Israel," because the latter risked exacerbating the differences between Israelis and Diaspora Jews.[7]

The 1950 "exchange of views" between Jacob Blaustein and Ben-Gurion made the exclusion of American Jews from Mapai's definition of the appropriate membership in the state explicit. Blaustein, who headed the American Jewish Committee (AJC)—the most important non-Zionist organization of American Jews—demanded, and received, a declaration from Ben-Gurion that Israel did not speak for all Jews, and that its leaders would not call for the eradication of the American Jewish Diaspora. The recognition that American Jews who might immigrate to Israel would do so of their own free will rather than as the fulfillment of an obligation to return to the homeland conceded that American Jews did not live in "exile." This "exchange of views" became a formal statement of policy in 1961 and was reaffirmed by subsequent prime ministers in 1963 and 1970.[8]

By the 1960s, a wide range of Mapai's leadership explicitly articulated the difference between "Jews" and "Israelis." In 1962, Abba Eban insisted that there was a reciprocal relationship between Israel and the dispersion and argued that there is an Israeli nation that is "not identical" with the Jewish one. Moshe Sharett developed the distinction between the Jewish people and the Israeli nation: the term "nation," he argued, delineates a people with a territorial-political existence. For that reason, he explained: "I do not hold that all the Jews are a single nation. I argue that the Jews are a single people."[9] By the 1980s, the terms with which the minority that still objected to this shift voiced its complaints showed how far the change had progressed. Arye Harel declared in 1982: "What hurts me, [what] really shocks me, is not the surrender to an outside power, but the lack of Zionism in the Jewish nation. We are accepting it as a given that the state of Israel is a private affair of the three million Jews that are here. We are surrendering to [the belief] that others will not come."[10]

The exclusion of Western, especially American, Jews from the definition of appropriate membership in the nation-state was evident in the role that Mapai's leaders assigned to them. The appropriate role of American Jewry (as a community) was recast as maintaining personal ties with the state, remaining Jewish, and supporting the new state from *the outside,* rather than as immediately returning to the homeland.[11] Mapai's leaders wanted to educate Diaspora Jewry "so that it will understand its duty and will willingly accept upon itself the large part, relatively speaking, of the huge and tremendous burden" of supporting the state.[12] Put another way, "we need Zionists, but so long as they remain citizens of the United States, Australia, South Africa, they are not citizens of Israel. They would not get rights in the state, but as for obligations—they must feel themselves as if they were citizens of Israel."[13] Moshe Sharett even placed this external support on par with actual physical participation in the establishment of the state of Israel.[14] Ben-Gurion compared the extent of the Diaspora's appropriate membership in the Jewish state to the bond existing between Ireland and an Irishman who "is tied to the tradition of his nation and wishes well to the land of his tradition."[15] The extent of this link is a far cry from the obligation once placed on Diaspora Jews to return to the homeland.

This transformed notion of membership went hand in hand with a transformed sense of the national mission articulated by Mapai. If Diaspora Jews were no longer considered automatically part of the political community, the mission of eradicating the exile was less tenable.[16] Indeed, at least as applied to Western, particularly American, Jews, Mapai's mission shifted to one focused on *preserving* the nation in exile. On occasion, this shift even devolved to the argument that the Diaspora was responsible for its own survival, with the state of Israel only playing a supporting role.[17] Indeed, Israel's concern with the fight against Jewish assimilation in the Diaspora assumed the continued existence of those communities, their legitimacy, and the desirability of maintaining their vitality.[18]

Mapai's platforms clearly display this shift. As late as 1949, Mapai's platform still declared that "the yearned-for era of the ingathering of the exiles has begun" and listed the ingathering of exiles as the first of the three significant tasks now facing the state. More concretely, the 1949 platform promised that the "central efforts of the state will be directed to the eradication of the exile and to the rapid transfer of the masses of Israel to their land."[19] By 1951, however, this commitment was gone. In fact, Mapai now declared that among its foreign policy goals was "concern for the equality of Jews in every country" and a commitment to "nurturing the tie with the Jewish community around the world and to the deepening awareness of the unity of the Jewish nation in the dispersion [!] and its historic partnership." The next plank, in a not so thinly veiled appeal to American Jews, called for "the mobilization of massive help on a global scale—in treasure and knowledge—for the combined process of the return of masses of Jews to their land and to the flowering of the desert." While the ingathering of exiles remained important, the platform mirrored the rhetorical shift from the use of the term "exile" to the less pejorative term "dispersion." Even the rationale for the project of the ingathering of exiles betrayed a retreat from the notion that every Jew should immigrate to Israel. Mapai now viewed "the ingathering of the exiles, the building-up of the country, and the steadfastness in defense of the state as the three central tasks of [this] generation that ensure the existence, safety, and future of every man [sic] in Israel and also the existence, safety, and future of the state of Israel and *of the Jewish nation around the world.*"[20]

By 1955, Mapai's declaration that the state embodied the messianic wishes of generations of the Jewish people for redemption and the ingathering of the exiles was blandly interpreted as meaning that the state should nurture the link between Jews in the world and the state. In 1965, the Labor Alignment's platform for the 6th Knesset affirmed both that the state was primarily concerned with Jews (not necessarily with citizens) and, as importantly in this context, that the Jewish nation outside of Israel had an independent existence. By the 1980s, despite the obvious continued existence of Jewish communities (in fact, of most Jews) outside the state of Israel, Shimon Peres could claim: "We are a nation which is moving from a situation of the ingathering of the exiles to the melding of the exiles." In so doing, he openly sidelined the mission of ingathering the exiles. Labor Alignment's 1981 platform spoke of the "mutual dependence" of the state and Diaspora Jews. In 1984, the party's listing of its "central goals" neglected to mention the ingathering of the exiles.[21] This did not mean that the party no longer wanted Jewish immigration. It did. The failure to appeal to this once central mission does suggest, however, that its salience had been reduced.

Evolution at Work: Explaining the Shift from Eradicating Exile to Saving the Dispersion

Each of the alternative explanations of change has different expectations about when and how these changes in membership boundaries and national mission would have taken place. Rational adaptation expects the transformation to follow an exogenous shock that made the pursuit of the eradication of the Diaspora irrational. The most likely such shock was the founding of the state. Its establishment certainly increased the meaningfulness of the distinction between Jews who were in it and those who were not. Israeli Jews now not only spoke a different language but also had a flag, currency, passports, and all the accoutrements of statehood that distinguished them from Jews elsewhere. Ben-Gurion's statist view—his zealous protection of the state's prerogatives and his efforts to entrench the state—was certainly consistent with deepening this distinction. Moreover, after independence, Mapai's leaders openly recognized that if all American Jews immigrated to Israel, they would no longer have the access to the capital that they needed to accomplish the two most pressing tasks of the state: its physical defense and the absorption of the massive influx of Jews that doubled the Jewish population of the state between 1949 and 1953.[22]

At least five issues complicate the ability of rational adaptation to the poststate reality to account for this change. First, the shift in Mapai's conception of membership started in the early 1940s, before the establishment of the state. As a result, this new reality could not have triggered the change. Second, there were other, equally significant exogenous shocks that pointed in the opposite direction. For example, the Zionists interpreted the Holocaust and its liquidation of Europe's Jewish communities as vindicating their goal of eradicating the exile. That Jewish life proved impossible in the most enlightened states, especially in Germany, with its well-integrated and assimilated Jewish population, they argued, meant that life in exile anywhere was untenable. Especially when people's propensity to emphasize confirming information and discount disconfirming information is factored in, the appeal to rational adaptation cannot account for why the implications of the ideologically confirming reality of the Holocaust (exile is impossible) would be ignored in favor of the disconfirming reality of the state (exile is a permanent reality).

Third, the ambivalence of the world Jewish community toward the Zionist project was nothing new. Only a small percentage of Jews who migrated during the prestate period ended up in Palestine—and arguably even fewer were motivated by nationalism. The vast majority of Jews—in Europe and the Middle East, as well as in the United States—were at best ambivalent and often hostile to Zionism. The fact that only a small minority of Jews worldwide wanted to immigrate to Israel bedeviled Zionism from the time of its emergence. The reality, in other words, was clear for all to see for a long time before the change began.

Fourth, all Zionist movements experienced this reality simultaneously. However, only the Labor movement changed its position on this score at this time. This variation suggests, at the very least, that something else contributed to this transformation. Finally, if adaptation to a new reality really drove this change, we would have observed a more consistent transition in the pattern of articulation than actually took place. Rather than a sharp or smooth transition, the Labor Zionist movement continued to articulate the old notions of mission and membership in a wide variety of forums, even as the new variants were gaining strength. For example, despite the promises made in the Ben-Gurion–Blaustein exchange, Ben-Gurion and other Labor Zionist leaders continued to include, in their overall pattern of articulation, calls for the eradication of the entire exile and the claim that Israel spoke in the name of all Jews.[23] Far from adapting to the growing gulf between Israelis and Diaspora Jews, Mapai's leaders were greatly concerned about its presence and worked hard to ameliorate the situation.[24]

It is possible that Mapai's leaders simply changed their minds about the appropriateness of including American Jews in the Jewish state. However, not only is the likelihood of this explanation weakened by the inconsistent process of the transformation, but it engages in an assumption about the beliefs of the Labor Zionist leaders that is completely unnecessary. This shift can be explained even if the Labor Zionist leaders (initially) maintained their commitment to eradicating the exile.

Such an evolutionary story begins with the Labor Zionist drive to secure the support of American, especially non-Zionist, Jews for their state-building project. Mapai's leaders sought to harness their financial support and their (perceived) political influence on the American government.[25] Non-Zionist American Jewish influence over the distribution of funds collected from American Jewry for use overseas had resulted in a steep decline in the proportion of funds going to Palestine. In 1938, Palestine received about 36 percent of the funds collected in the United States, but in 1940 this proportion dropped to 20 percent.[26] Mapai's belief that the reviled Revisionists were making inroads among the American public and American donors also spurred the effort to build a closer alliance with American Jewry.[27] The attempt to include American Jews in the nationalist alliance that the Labor movement was crafting in the 1940s accounts for the timing of the transformation.

To secure the support of American Jews, Mapai had to engage in a tactical adjustment to its articulation of mission and membership that could accommodate the two basic demands of American Jews: (1) that their continued existence in the Diaspora be recognized as legitimate, and (2) that they be excluded from the scope of appropriate membership in the state so as to avoid accusations of dual loyalty. Ben-Gurion's exceptional courting of the *non-Zionist* Jews at the expense of cooperating with the American Zionists demonstrates the tactical political rationale behind this adjustment. Presumably, securing the latter's support would not have required any ideological modulation, since they already shared the Zionist goal. However, Ben-Gurion increasingly devalued the American Zionist Organization, partly because its members were not fulfilling what he saw as their obligation to immigrate to Palestine and partly because they tended to support the rival General Zionist party. Ben-Gurion's decision to privilege American non-Zionists also reflected his belief that they had more influence in American policy-making circles than American Zionists.[28]

The way in which the related distinction between "exile" and "dispersion" was mapped onto the Jewish world supported the tacit trade-off between the (non-Zionist) leaders of American Jewry and the Labor movement. The Labor Zionists did not cease to think in terms of exile. They did, however, limit its application to Jews in the Displaced Persons camps in Europe, behind the Iron Curtain, and in the Arab states. The "dispersion," by contrast, referred to Western, especially American, Jews, who were thus excluded from the definition of the appropriate membership in the state.

While Ben-Gurion and Katznelson were willing to make this concession already in 1939, they faced significant internal opposition. The truth tellers, again clustered in Faction B, continued to include American Jews as appropriately members of the state and insisted on demanding their immigration to Palestine. This faction of the Labor movement opposed the reliance on American Jews partly because of its adherence to a more radical socialist stance and its desire to foster closer relations with the Soviet Union. Through 1941, the truth tellers were stronger than the consensus builders who supported the co-optation of American Jews. However, once Faction B split off from Mapai in 1944, no serious opposition remained within the movement that could object to the inclusion of American Jews within the nationalist alliance and their attendant exclusion from the state.

A number of other factors also contributed to the undirected institutionalization of the exclusion of American Jews from the scope of the appropriate membership in the state. Foremost among these was the mutually beneficial character of the arrangement. Non-Zionist American Jews fended off the threat Israel posed to their American identity, and Mapai secured the financial resources it needed to establish the state, entrench the state's defenses, and undertake the ingathering of the Jewish communities that it still considered to be in exile. Both reflecting the changes in membership and mission and reinforcing them, by the late 1950s, Mapai increasingly emphasized religion rather than the state of Israel as the element shared by all members of the nation.[29] The rise of the view that religion rather than the state served as the glue holding Jews together meant that Diaspora Jews could remain part of the nation without membership in the state. Finally, the exclusion of Diaspora Jewry from the Labor Zionist view of the state's appropriate membership boundaries was also reinforced by the exclusion of the Arabs. The desire to exclude the Palestinian refugees from the state's body politic drove Mapai's decision to limit voting rights to those who were physically in the state, even though this excluded most of the Jewish nation.[30] The success of the tactical adjustments to Mapai's conception of mission and membership regarding American Jews was reinforced by the poststate reality. As a result, over time the concern with saving Jews in the dispersion replaced the mission of eradicating the exile.

The Exclusion of Palestinian Israelis: A Test of Rational Adaptation and Elite Imposition

The continuous exclusion of local (and later citizen) Palestinians from the definition of the appropriate membership boundaries of the state de-spite ample pressure provides another test of the plausibility of the alter-native explanations of ideological change. Elite imposition and rational adaptation expect this pressure to have induced the Zionists to recast their notion of the appropriate membership in the state. This expectation would be especially plausible in the case of the Labor Zionist movement, whose ideological flexibility and self-image as a social democratic movement make it the most likely to respond to external pressure and changed elite incen-tives on this dimension. Nonetheless, even it did not change its answer to the question 'Who are we?' in response. The Labor movement did react, but the tactical adjustments to its articulation of the appropriate membership in the state never led to substantive ideological change. The circumscribed response to the pressures and opportunities to change its definition of the appropriate membership in the nation's state highlights the limitations of these pressures and opportunities to account for change directly.

The tactical reaction to these pressures was evident after 1925, when Ben-Gurion and the leaders of the Labor movement began to argue that "Eretz Israel will be for the Hebrew nation and for the Arabs who reside in it."[31] The Labor movement combined this formulation with occasional

calls for parity in the political roles of Jews and Arabs and for institutional-
izing Palestine's binational character.[32] Rather than striving for a state that
would belong solely to the Jews, these calls appeared to reflect the addition
of a civic element to the ethnic definition of membership boundaries that
they had articulated up to that point.

There is little question that this was a tactical step. Labor Zionist leaders
recognized the reality that the Jews were a very small minority in Palestine
and that they would benefit from group-based power-sharing arrangements
as long as that continued to be the case. The leaders of the Labor movement
were also moved to add this civic tinge because they believed that the way
they treated the Arabs (or, more properly, the way they *said* they would
treat the Arabs) would set a precedent for the treatment of Jews around the
world. Finally, this tactical step was also motivated by a concern with maintaining world public opinion on their side.[33]

That the mainstream of the movement no longer called for "parity" once
a Jewish majority became plausible reveals the tactical and instrumental
character of this modulation. The lack of accusations of ideological deviance or internal dissent of the kind that we saw on other issues also suggests
that no one took this modulation seriously enough to complain. The criticism that did exist came from the other direction and held that more should
be done to integrate the Arabs. Mapai's leaders, however, tended to belittle
these complaints and dismiss them out of hand.

While adjustments originally intended as temporary tactical measures can
unintentionally become the new orthodoxy, this particular rhetorical shift
was not translated into behavior or institutionalized as the new ideological
status quo. In fact, all of Mapai's actions at the time pointed in the opposite direction. Mapai was concerned with creating a community that was
as distinct as possible from that of the Arabs in Palestine. Some, including
Ben-Gurion, saw separation from the Arab population—even on a village-
by-village level—as *the* condition for the success of the Zionist project.[34]
Ben-Gurion's rejection of attempts to organize Arab workers in the 1920s
and early 1930s shows that even Mapai's socialism remained predicated on
an ethnic definition of membership. He argued: "We would like to have a
socialist regime, we would like to set up a commune.... [But] we have no
special interest in a socialist regime or a commune in this country, if those involved are not Jewish workers. We did not come here to organize anything,
and we did not come here to spread the socialist idea among anyone. We
came here to create a home and a place of work for the Jewish people."[35]

There was certainly an economic logic to the creation of a segregated
and segmented society.[36] As Dov Hoz noted in his testimony before the Peel
Partition Commission, such segregation was also explicitly intended to

tactical step
of
accepting
Arabs as
Israelis

not taken
seriously
&
no one
opposed

ethnic
membership

limit the kinds of marketplace interactions that (they worried) might have led Jews and Arabs to form a common identity.[37]

The reality of the nationalist conflict in Palestine also placed would-be advocates of the civic adjustment in a weak political position. The self-reinforcing organization of Jews and Arabs against one another created an environment in which it was difficult for a notion of membership that crossed these lines to gain traction. Even the potential inclusion of "individual Arabs" in the Israeli nation became increasingly untenable after the 1936 Arab Revolt because it became difficult for Mapai's leaders to deny that they were facing a competing nationalist movement. As a result, the belief that the Arabs could join the Jews as partners, even junior partners, in the formation of a new society all but disappeared.[38] As Shabtai Teveth noted, the Arabs in Palestine could be granted civil rights in a Jewish state without endangering the Jewish claim to self-determination if they were only a branch of the larger Arab people. However, the recognition of a distinct Palestinian nationalism would have required recognizing the right of Arabs in Palestine to self-determination.[39] The identification of Arab resistance to Zionism as nationalist also increased the salience of the ethnic definition of membership, because it fostered the construction of the conflict in zero-sum terms. Even if these realities were not enough to hinder the institutionalization of the rhetorical modulation as the new orthodoxy, the fact that it was not embedded in any institutions or alliances meant that there was little that could be politically selected for success. In other words, there was nothing at stake in the domestic political game that could reinforce and promote the articulation of the civic notion of membership at the expense of the ethnic one.

The establishment of the state of Israel provided an even stronger opportunity for rational adaptation to lead to a change on this issue than did the context in the 1920s. Once again, the Labor Zionist movement felt itself under a great deal of pressure to include Arabs in its articulated notion of the appropriate membership boundaries. Some of this pressure came from the international community, which intended that both the Arab and the Jewish states created by the 1947 partition plan would be democratic. Given Israel's desperate quest for international acceptance at the time, Mapai's leaders repeatedly argued that overtly discriminatory policies against the Arabs would undermine Israel's position in the world and deepen its isolation.[40] The fact that the Arabs formed an overwhelming majority in the region and the ensuing belief that Israel would need to maintain good relations with the neighboring states in order to survive reinforced these positions. As in the 1920s, Mapai's leaders also felt obligated to treat the Arab minority justly for fear of sparking anti-Semitism elsewhere.[41] Finally, at least some within the Labor movement took the rhetoric of equality seriously and believed in the intrinsic value of democracy. For all of these reasons, formal civic and political rights were awarded to Arabs who were within the area under Jewish control at the end of the fighting in 1949.

Even this, however, did not force Mapai to include citizen Palestinians in their definition of the appropriate membership in the state. Mapai merely shifted its strategy to one that acknowledged the Arabs' formal rights but limited their influence over the crucial questions affecting the direction of the state. In what is perhaps the most overt indicator of this strategy, while citizen Arabs were granted the right to vote, the military administration imposed on the Arab areas of the state restricted the freedoms of movement, association, and organization that were needed for the real exercise of political participation. The desire to minimize the influence of the Arabs was also clearly, but more subtly, evident in the internal debate within Mapai over whether the state of Israel should have a constitution or a series of more malleable "Basic Laws." Instructively, both sides marshaled the political neutering of the Arabs in support of their position. Advocates of a constitution argued that the political system should be solidified before the proportion of Arabs in the state increased (because of their higher birthrate), and their influence grew. Opponents of a constitution argued that the increased flexibility permitted by "Basic Laws" would allow them to change the rules of the political game as the proportion of Jews increased (because of the expected waves of Jewish immigration).[42]

Mapai's goal was to make the exclusion of the Arabs from full membership in the state less overt. Thus Yitzhak Ben-Zvi argued: "With the establishment of the government we will need to take care of the 500 [thousand] Arabs that will be in the Jewish state—schools, medical assistance, fulfilling their needs, and collecting taxes from them. In these conditions it is clear that the government cannot be comprised automatically from members of the [Zionist] Executive Committee and the [Jewish] Agency—*but they need to ensure that, when the time comes, it will appear as a Deus ex Machina.*"[43] Meir Argov's portrayal of Mapai's general strategy was particularly revealing. He argued: "[Citizen Arabs] sit in the Knesset, and they do not have all the rights. They do not enter all the committees. We do not let them get into all the committees, not the Budget Committee and not the Foreign Affairs and Security Committee... because we outsmarted them.... The fact is that they do not enter. They also do not enter the army, and no one suggests that we do that. They do not enter the administration in the state, and that is an open secret."[44]

Mapai leaders also worked to minimize the access of citizen Arabs to the resources of the state by, among other things, farming out aspects of the welfare state to the Jewish Agency. As a "private" organization, the Jewish Agency was not limited by the formal promise of equal treatment that restricted the actions of the state. Ben-Gurion explicitly articulated Mapai's effort to bypass its expressed commitment to formal equality in his reasoning for opposing state aid to large families:

> The problem of the birthrate in Israel is not the problem of all of its residents, but only the problem of the Jewish community. For this reason it cannot be resolved by the government. In the state of Israel there is equality of rights for all citizens without distinction of nationality. This is a Jewish state... but only in the matter of immigration to the country does the law distinguish between Jews and non-Jews.... In all other matters there is full and complete equality, and if the government would encourage [population growth] through special aid to families with many children, the aid would mainly go to Arab families... Only the Jews need encouragement to raise the birthrate, and for that reason the government cannot deal with it; if the encouragement of the high birthrate will be a government function, all of the money earmarked for this purpose will go only to Arabs... for this reason the encouragement of a higher birth-rate needs to be taken care of by the Jewish Agency or a special Jewish organization.[45]

The continued predominance of the ethnic definition of appropriate membership in the state was also plainly evident in the Labor movement's willingness to engage in a trade-off between territory and demography. The desire to ensure that control of the polity would be securely in Jewish hands contributed to Israel's readiness to forgo conquering parts of the homeland that were densely populated with Arabs. As Ben-Gurion put it, "Land which has Arabs on it and land which has no Arabs on it are two completely different kinds of land."[46] It was presumably for this reason that he did not regret the failure to conquer the Triangle in the Galilee in 1949.[47] This trade-off was again evident in 1956. Even if Ben-Gurion only hit upon demography as an excuse not to annex the Gaza Strip when faced with insurmountable international pressure, this argument struck a receptive chord within the movement. The main opponents of annexing the Gaza Strip argued that it would create a "nightmare"; that "the Arab population of Israel would suddenly jump to 500,000, half a million Arabs, we will arrive at a situation where a quarter of the population would be Arab and 30 members of the Knesset would be Arabs."[48] The dominant position was articulated by Shimon Peres, who argued that the Arabs in the "western land of Israel" not under Israeli control were "absolutely superfluous in the state of Israel." "What would we do with them?" Peres asked. "Do we need a million and two hundred thousand Arabs among us?"[49] While not everyone within the Labor movement reached the same conclusion about the desired future of the Gaza Strip, they all made the same demographic calculation: those who favored annexing it argued that they should do so "with all its troubles"; others assumed that a large proportion of the Arab population of the Gaza Strip would be moved elsewhere.[50]

The strategy of excluding the Arabs from positions of influence extended to membership in Mapai itself. Instead of allowing citizen Arabs into the party, their political participation was funneled through a series of easily controlled patronage-based "sister-parties." Their eventual inclusion in the party did not come about because the majority within the Labor Zionist movement changed their conception of the desired membership. Rather, like the opening of the Histadrut to the Arabs, it was politically motivated—intended to counter the inroads made by Mapam and the Communists among the citizen Palestinian population and its radicalization—and calculated to continue the political emasculation of the Arab population.[51] In fact, each step in the process was presented as necessary to continue the control of the Arabs rather than as a step toward their integration. At each step, proponents of greater inclusion argued that doing so would not undermine the Jewish and Zionist character of the party.[52]

Nonetheless, by the early 1960s, there were signs that the series of tactical changes that increasingly opened the party to Arabs, and the formalization of Arab rights in the state, affected the notion of the appropriate membership boundaries of the state, at least for some within the movement. Years ahead of the rest of the movement, Labor's Youth Faction began to discuss openly the possibility of including Arab youth.[53] The next time the question of maintaining the segmented structure or integrating Jews and Arabs came up—in the context of a 1962 petition by Arabs who wanted to participate in a seminar offered for Mapai youth leaders—the party, for the first time, opted for integration.[54]

It is certainly possible that this trend toward a greater integration of Palestinian citizens and the broadening of the definition of appropriate membership could have continued. The change at the top of the Labor movement, including the retirement of Ben-Gurion, who had been one of the main opponents of integration, certainly reinforced the position of advocates of fuller integration. That the carriers of this change tended to be the movement's Young Guard and the locus for much of the change was located in their institutions suggests that a generational dynamic further reinforced these factors.

However, the exogenous shock of the 1967 war halted this trend, at least for a while. The sudden control over more than one million additional Palestinians undermined the sense of demographic security that had enabled part of the Labor movement to expand its notion of the state's appropriate membership. In a reprise of the territory/demography trade-off, the desire to keep the state's Arab population as low as possible was (and still is) the main argument marshaled by those who were willing, with varying degrees of reluctance, to part with the West Bank and Gaza Strip. Golda Meir summarized the dominant position in the wake of the 1967 war. Echoing Peres's argument from a decade earlier, she argued that they wanted "more or less secure borders, maximum security, as much as possible that the border will be far from what it was on June 4th [1967], and somehow that the Arabs won't stay with us."[55] This became the semiofficial position of the Labor party in the 1970s. The party explicitly stated that "one of the principles for the drawing of the border will be that most of the Palestinian population will be on the border's eastern side."[56]

The terms with which it rejected Begin's autonomy plan also reflected the Labor movement's continued exclusion of the Arabs from the definition of the state's appropriate membership boundaries. While some distinguished between citizen and noncitizen Arabs, their critique overtly emphasized Labor's adherence to the principle of uninational control of the state. Begin's plan was thus castigated as fostering a binational state because it opened the door for the naturalization of Arabs living in the territories and therefore undermined Israel's Jewish majority.[57]

In the post-1967 context, the integrationists voiced their positions, but statements and policies that reflected the continued exclusion of the Arab population from the Labor movement's definition of the appropriate membership in the state continued to dominate.[58] In 1968, citizen Arabs were literally written out of the covenant creating the unified Labor Party. While an early draft of this agreement spoke of the "citizens of Israel," Reuven Barkat, Mapai's general secretary, objected to the phrase's implied inclusion of non-Jews. During the same meeting, Shimon Peres objected to the call for "the integration of non-Jewish citizens in *all* aspects of life," arguing: "This is not correct and we do not want it. We do not want to let them in the army. Why should we say something that is not true? I propose to write: the integration of non-Jewish citizens in the life of the state."[59] His proposal was accepted.

[margin note: Shimon Peres: he don't want Arabs in all aspects of life]

The mid-1970s still saw similar objections. For example, the wording in the proposed 1977 platform that called for the Arabs' "integration in [the party's] institutions and their participation in decisions in an appropriate representation" was removed from the final version because it was pointed out that Labor did not really intend to fully integrate Arabs into the party and its decision-making apparatuses. Even Raanan Cohen, who argued repeatedly for the inclusion and integration of citizen Palestinians, still felt the need to qualify his statement by stating that he did not call for integration in all the movement's decision-making institutions.[60] In 1985, Peres explicitly argued: "In addition to being a social-democratic party, we are also a nationalist party. That is, we are a party that is concerned with sustaining

[margin note: Even integrationists did not want full integration]

the Jewish nation.... We are concerned not just with the land, we are also concerned with the nation. We are concerned not only about the borders of the state, but also with the character of the state."[61] In 1987, Shimon Peres still called for the same delegation of state services to nonstate agencies that Ben-Gurion advocated in 1969.[62] The Labor Party also continued to speak of a "demographic problem," not just in the state as a whole, but also in each region, especially in the Galilee and the Negev.[63]

Whereas previous instances of ideological transformation tended to be marked by the opponents of a modulation leaving the party, in this case it was those who more fully accepted the citizen Palestinians as appropriately part of the state who tended to leave the Labor movement for parties to its left. The withdrawal of the proponents of the integrationist trend from the ILP also contributed to the failure of the integrationist view of the appropriate membership to spread.

Tactical political calculations—bred by the competition for the votes of Palestinian Israelis in the context of a Jewish public evenly divided over the future of the territories—appeared to breathe new life into the integrationist trend in the 1980s.[64] Indeed, in the aftermath of the 1984 elections, the Labor party (among others) was more solicitous of the Arab population than in the past. Moreover, during Peres's time in the rotating premiership (1984–86), the Labor-led government undertook a number of symbolic and actual steps to increase the integration of Israeli Arabs, ranging from the introduction of the first stamp honoring Israeli Muslims, recognition of Um-el-Fahm's long-stalled application for municipal status, and a freeze on the demolition of illegal structures in Arab villages. A series of reforms initiated under the Labor Party's new slogan "Integration of Minorities" culminated in the 1986 closure of the successor to the Arab Department and the placing of the majority of Arab localities under the jurisdiction of Labor Councils in neighboring Jewish areas. Shimon Peres declared to both Jewish and Arab audiences his belief that changes in Arab-Jewish relations in Israel were in the offing. He told a Jewish audience in 1985: "The intention is...to incorporate Arabs and Druze in the decision-making establishment, so that they can express their views before decisions are made and I am certain this is a development in the right direction."[65] In direct contradiction to his position in 1968, the guidelines that Peres wanted to use for the government he hoped to establish in 1990 explicitly articulated the goal of integrating Arabs into all areas of the state.[66] Rabin's 1992 government, which relied on the support of six Palestinian Knesset members, appeared to usher in a period of liberal political reform inside Israel as it pursued the least discriminatory policy toward Palestinian citizens that Israel had ever known.

At the same time, the Labor Zionist movement also understood its own integrationist drive in the 1980s partly as needed to protect the Jewish and

Zionist character of both the movement and the state. Labor Zionists were particularly concerned with driving a wedge between citizen and noncitizen Arabs and with providing a safety valve for the frustrated youth and educated population of citizen Arabs.[67] An internal Labor Party review made the tactical character of much of this reform explicit when it concluded that "integration" would close a potential opening for the Communists by weakening their local party activists.[68]

These tactical changes, however, did not have a chance to become institutionalized. This was partly because Rabin's heavy-handed response to the first intifada strongly curtailed the desire of Israeli Arabs to move toward Labor as part of their strategic voting.[69] More fundamentally, the integrationist rhetorical and policy modulations were not embedded in a bargain— tacit or otherwise—between the Labor movement and citizen Palestinian groups. As a result, these modulations were not subject to a process whereby they would be reinforced by political success.

Paradoxically, the Oslo Accords closed the door on the possibility that (at least this round of) the tactical rapprochement with Israeli Palestinians would become institutionalized. As in the past, the Labor movement justified the territorial concessions it was willing to make in terms of maintaining the ethnic conception of membership in the state. The use of this rationale—that withdrawing from the territories was good because it preserved the fundamental Zionist goal of a Jewish majority—made it difficult to simultaneously integrate citizen Arabs as appropriately part of the state. The principle that citizens constitute the state, which, in turn, acts on their behalf, clashed with the principle that the state of Israel ought to serve (primarily) the needs of the Jewish population. This helps explain the apparent paradox that the increasing willingness to disengage from the territories and the increasing willingness to countenance the emergence of a Palestinian state was correlated with a *decreasing* acceptance of citizen Arabs as appropriately part of Israeli society.[70]

· · ·

While the definition of the appropriate membership in the nation did not change for any of the movements examined, the evolutionary dynamic accounted better than the alternative explanations for the empirical benchmarks of the exclusion of American Jews from the definition of the appropriate membership in the state articulated by Labor Zionists. At the same time, Labor Zionism's resistance to integrating citizen Arabs into its conception of the appropriate membership of the state demonstrated that even relatively pragmatic nationalist movements are unlikely to modify their ideology as a direct response to external constraints and political incentives.

The Labor movement did repeatedly engage in tactical rhetorical adjustments in response to external pressures. These, however, were never placed in a position that could have led to positive returns. That is, there was never a short-term political incentive to transform the rhetorical adjustments into anything substantive. This helps explain why no change took place. The absence of change on this axis of the membership dimension of the national community was not inevitable. At each juncture there was a political contest within Mapai between those who favored greater integration between Jews and Arabs and those who opposed it. For most of Israeli history, the integrationists lost this intramovement struggle. Certainly, a different sequence of events might have led to a different result. In this case, however, outside pressures did not lead to change, despite being exactly the kinds of shocks and incentives that scholars of nationalism assume serve in that capacity.

[Margin handwritten notes: no incentive for Labor Party to transform adjustments into institutions = NO CHANGE]

6

Ongoing Transformations
of Israeli Nationalism

In the summer of 2005, Israel "disengaged" from the Gaza Strip and demolished four settlements in the West Bank. Protestors against the disengagement burned Israeli flags, stoned Israeli soldiers, and compared the state of Israel to Nazi Germany. The traumatic events of the summer of 2005 suggest that there are a number of currently ongoing changes in Israeli nationalisms. The fact that the heirs of the Revisionist movement drove the disengagement raises the possibility that the Revisionists are in the process of accepting the principle of partition. In the language of nationalism more generally, their definition of the appropriate extent of the homeland may be shifting yet again.

A second ongoing shift is evident in the mission of Religious Zionism. Many of the most vocal protestors against the disengagement were Religious Zionists who had viewed the state as marking the dawn of redemption. Their actions suggest that, for at least some within Religious Zionism, the state and its paramount symbol, the IDF, are so profane that they can be physically attacked rather than revered. In a related, but analytically distinct, shift the secular Zionists, who were once seen as partners in the work of bringing the Messiah, are increasingly categorized as foreign, or even as indistinguishable from the most despised of Jewish enemies.

To explore these changes, we must deviate from the approach taken so far in this book. Until now, our exploration of the ability of alternative explanations to account for changes in Israeli nationalisms has been explicitly backward-looking; it assumed that the ideological transformations are largely completed and that we can confidently identify the empirical benchmarks of change. However, as noted in the introduction, evolution has no end (at least as long as it is characterized by variation, retention, and competition). The evolution of Israeli nationalism, in other words, does not end at the conclusion of this book. Because these cases are still very much in process, the task of definitively comparing the empirical benchmarks of these changes (if they continue) with the expectations of the alternative mechanisms must be left to future scholars. Taken with the appropriate caveats, however, the processes of these changes thus far appear to reinforce the lessons learned in earlier chapters about the role of the evolutionary dynamic and elite imposition.

The Likud's Acceptance of Partition?

From the "Whole Land of Israel" to a "Two-State Solution"

Despite the elimination of the claim to the East Bank of the Jordan from their conception of the homeland, the Revisionists remained territorially hawkish. As we saw in chapter 3, for nearly forty years, the Revisionist movement constantly called for deepening Israel's control of the West Bank and the Gaza Strip. More recently, however, the heirs of the Revisionist movement have been widely and routinely articulating positions that were once anathema to the movement, including partition of the land between the river and the sea and acceptance of a Palestinian state. Most concretely, Revisionist Zionists (those in the Likud and, later, those who left it to form Kadima) enacted this acceptance of partition in the construction of the "separation barrier" in the West Bank and in the withdrawal from the Gaza Strip.

Such positions are not just the province of long-time moderates in the movement. Erstwhile hard-liners such as Benjamin Netanyahu and Ariel Sharon have also adopted them. In the fall of 2009, Netanyahu openly accepted a two-state solution (at least in principle). However, a shift in his attitude had been evident since the mid-1990s. While he publicly deplored the Oslo Accords as appeasement not seen since Munich, and cast Shimon Peres as Neville Chamberlain, Netanyahu was nonetheless willing, at least privately, to accept the Oslo Accords as early as 1994, and did so openly by 1996.[1] As prime minister, Netanyahu even handed over additional parts of the homeland to the Palestinians in the Wye and Hebron agreements. There are also indications that he came to terms with the establishment of a Palestinian state. Hinting at this possibility, David Bar-Ilan, Netanyahu's senior policy adviser and leading ideological aide, stated that "a Palestinian state with strictly defined, limited sovereignty—including demilitarization—is something Israel may be able to accept, especially since partition already

[margin handwritten note: Revisionist now moving toward accepting Palestinian state]

exists today and the notion of "Greater Israel" is no longer possible."[2] Some commentators have even concluded that Netanyahu no longer believes that Israel *should* or could hold the West Bank in its entirety, even if he wants to delay partition as much as possible and to leave as much of the area in Israel's control.[3] Indeed, David Bar-Ilan noted: "I think in general he [i.e., Netanyahu] is no longer (in favor of) a whole-land-of-Israel movement. I don't think he feels that there is any chance of the Land of Israel remaining completely under the exclusive rule of Israel."[4] The tepid, indeed almost hushed reaction to these comments within the movement suggests that this view was widely shared by others in the Likud.[5]

Even Ariel Sharon, the "father" of the settlement movement, came to accept the establishment of a Palestinian state in the mid-1990s.[6] By 1999, the main difference between him and Ehud Barak on the question of partition was not one of quality—both accepted the concept of a Palestinian state—but one of quantity: Barak was willing to withdraw from 90 percent of the West Bank, and Sharon from less than 45 percent.[7] Sharon, who condemned the Oslo Accords as "an agreement that no longer exists," nevertheless articulated a willingness to make "painful concessions" for the peace that he promised, and even orchestrated the actual withdrawal of Israeli settlements from the Gaza Strip.

The Likud's shift to the left did not go unnoticed within the Revisionist movement. In response, Benjamin Begin left the party to found a movement that, in his view, would remain true to Revisionist Zionist principles. The ideological hard-liners that remained within the Likud, including Uzi Landau and Moshe Arens, challenged Netanyahu for leadership of the party in 1999. Arens, who contested the Likud primaries, articulating their traditional rejection of partition, netted only the twenty-sixth spot on their list. Among other things, his poor showing implies the reduced salience of this view among the party faithful. This pattern was repeated in 2002, when Sharon, who presented a relatively more moderate program than Netanyahu, won the primary with 56 percent of the vote.

Explaining the Likud's Acceptance of Partition

The apparent acceptance of partition among the Revisionists is still in progress. As a result, there is no guarantee that it will actually culminate in a substantive ideological shift. Nonetheless, to this point, the timing, direction, and process of the Likud's acceptance of partition are consistent with a change driven by an evolutionary dynamic. In an effort to solve local political problems and to maintain their old ideology, Likud leaders shifted the rationale they used to justify Israeli control of the territories from one based on ideological considerations to one based on a security argument.

However, as the meaning of "security" in Israel became understood in terms of personal safety rather than national security, the security argument became more consistent with partition than with Israeli control of the territories. Trapped by its reliance on the political benefits of being "strong on security," the Likud grudgingly, but increasingly, accepted the principle of partition.

As we saw above, the Likud, and Herut before it, traditionally based its claim to the territories primarily on nationalist and emotive rather than instrumental criteria. Security was a consideration, but it was always secondary to principle—to the right of the Jews to the entire land. The distinction many Likud leaders drew between the West Bank and Gaza Strip on the one hand, and the Sinai Peninsula and Golan Heights on the other, displayed the primacy of the ideological claims over security considerations when it came to the former territories. For example, in 1974 David Magen proposed that the Revisionists make it clear that, unlike the West Bank and Gaza Strip, which could never be relinquished because they are an integral part of the homeland, the refusal to retreat from the Sinai Peninsula and the Golan Heights was based entirely on security concerns.[8] Menachem Begin himself, when he set the limits of compromise as the boundary of Mandatory Palestine, allowed for the possibility of compromise over the fate of the Sinai Peninsula and the Golan Heights, but not the West Bank or Gaza Strip.[9]

Unlike the ideological and theological claims to the Land of Israel as the birthright of the Jewish people, the security argument posited that Israeli control of the Golan Heights, Sinai Peninsula, West Bank, and Gaza Strip was the best way to guarantee the security of the state of Israel. In its original guise, the security argument predicted that holding onto the territories would prevent the next war. Israel's manifest size and strength after the 1967 war, the argument held, would deter future attack by the Arab states, since they now had no chance of destroying it. When that prophecy failed in 1973, the argument was modified. Rather than preventing additional war, the security argument was transformed to claim that another war with the Arabs was inevitable and that therefore military considerations (strategic depth, holding the high ground, etc.) made Israeli control of the territories of paramount importance.[10]

By the early 1990s, the Likud's rejection of the Oslo Accords was largely couched in terms of this security discourse rather than in the traditional ideological terms. Representatively, Netanyahu framed his rejection of the Oslo Accords entirely in terms of the physical danger posed to Israel and its citizens. Nearly "all his arguments were instrumentalist, not expressive. Not in the name of ideology, but in the name of security did Netanyahu promise that the future generations of Jews would 'pursue the trial of history' against Rabin and his ministers."[11]

The rise of the security argument within the Likud did not reflect a decline of ideology. The security discourse was a politically convenient way with which to maintain the ideologically based rejection of partition. It provided a useful cover for the ideological claim to the land because it offered a solution to the double bind in which the Likud found itself. Externally, the Likud was caught between the public's clear demand for an end to the conflict with the Palestinians (implied in Rabin's victory and consistently in survey data since the first intifada) and the ideological need to reject partition as the way to do so. Internally, the Likud had to reconcile conflicting reactions to the Oslo Accords. Some within the movement argued that they should accept the accords and modify their platform accordingly. Others rejected any "effort to be fashionable" by tinkering with their ideology.[12]

Highlighting the security dimension over the ideological claim to the land provided a way for the Likud's leadership to navigate these conflicting pressures. It allowed them to rhetorically accept the ends of the Oslo Accords (thereby appealing to the median voter and to internal moderates) while simultaneously rejecting the means for getting there (thereby mollifying the truth tellers and maintaining the status quo of Israeli control of the territories). Such an instrumental use of the security argument is consistent with the ways in which it had been previously used within the Likud.[13] In this case, focusing on the security dimension allowed the Likud to frame its rejection of the agreement with the PLO as a rejection of its particular technical insufficiencies rather than an outright rejection of an accommodation with the Palestinians, with the same result. This was Sharon's explicit aim in the early 1990s. He argued that while the goals of the Likud's platform should remain unaltered, "one could exploit the tools [it provides] better and sometimes change them" in order to make the platform serve as a blueprint for a solution to the Palestinian problem, ensure Israeli sovereignty over the territories, and restrict Arab autonomy so that it would not be a source of danger.[14]

The Likud's slogan "Peace with Security"—used first in the 1996 elections and in some guise in every campaign since then—epitomized the appeal to the center and the blurring of the Likud's claims using the security argument. In 1996, a representative Likud advertisement made a highly emotional appeal "to the nation not to abandon the peace process, 'even with heavy hearts and while choking back our tears.' However, it defined peace as contingent on the assurance that 'parents would be able to part from their children in the morning without fear.' In this the government had failed." Instead, the Likud promised: "We shall bring Peace with Security."[15] The security argument, in other words, served as the bridge from the right wing to the middle of the Israeli political spectrum. Indeed, Netanyahu probably utilized the security rhetoric instead of an ideological discourse for this reason. As one of his senior advisers noted, whatever Netanyahu's convictions, he realized that security was a winning issue, whereas ideology was not: "We don't win when we talk about settlements and ideological issues, but rather when we talk about security."[16]

This tactic was successful because it was also consistent with the changing social basis of the Likud's support and its reliance on what Ehud Sprinzak called the "soft right."[17] The Likud's middle-class base of support is not interested in the "Greater Israel" ideology. They are disillusioned with the prospects of making peace with the current Palestinian leadership and largely seek an end to the threat from terrorist attacks.[18] The other pillar of Netanyahu's support, the ultra-Orthodox, could also accept the security argument more easily than an ideological appeal for the continued control over the territories. To the extent that they addressed the question of the territories largely through the prism of *pikuah nefesh*—the principle in Jewish law that saving a life trumps other religious obligations—they were able to accept the security argument as contributing to this principle.

The usefulness of the security discourse in appealing to the median Israeli voter and in glossing over the internal disagreements within the Likud does not necessarily mean that its advocates abandoned the old ideological rejection of partition, though it clearly shows their conclusion that it was politically unwise to articulate it. Indeed, there is little evidence that the main leaders of the Likud, including Netanyahu and Sharon, changed their minds at this point in history.[19] The use of the security argument did allow the Likud, however, to mask its *continued fidelity* to the ideological belief that the West Bank and Gaza Strip were appropriately part of the state of Israel. Those within the Likud who may have adapted to the new reality—such as Meir Shitreet and Dan Meridor—were either marginalized within the movement or left it for parties that more explicitly endorsed partition.

The security argument worked. It brought the Likud back to power in 1996. The argument had, however, some unanticipated consequences as the meaning of security in Israel increasingly focused on personal safety rather than national security. This redefinition of the meaning of "security" in Israeli society was partially a response to the new geopolitical context of the 1990s. Israelis began to feel reasonably certain about Israel's survival. In contrast to the existential dread that permeated Israeli discourse since the establishment of the state, in the late 1980s, as much as 89 percent of the Israeli population expressed the belief that Israel's long-range existence was assured, with 74 percent assessing as nonexistent or low the probability that the state of Israel would be destroyed.[20] The fall of the Soviet Union, which further undermined the claim that Israel's immediate neighbors posed a threat to its existence, bolstered this feeling.

Israeli society was also simultaneously undergoing a cultural process of individualization. The idealization of the "collective ethos" of the earlier heroic epoch was being replaced by an emphasis on individual welfare and achievement.[21] This was true in the realm of security as well. Terrorist violence, especially after the Oslo Accords, was interpreted as an attack on the personal safety of the Israeli population, not as an attempt to destroy the state.[22] In 2002, concern with personal safety was so widespread that one survey found that 92 percent of Israelis feared that either they or a member of their family would fall victim to a terrorist attack.[23]

In this context, the security argument was reconfigured to claim that if the territories were relinquished, there would be no way to provide for the *personal* security of Israeli citizens. Israeli control of the territories was important, in other words, not because it protected the state from invasion, but because it allowed Israel to conduct more effective police work. The Likud and Netanyahu modified the security discourse to take advantage of this picture. Following the wave of suicide bombings and kidnappings in 1994, Likud leaders proclaimed that instead of receiving peace in exchange for land, Israel was receiving increased terror.[24] In 1996, while Peres's campaign focused on Labor's peace policy, Netanyahu emphasized the threat to personal security.[25]

The Likud, in other words, did not just deploy the argument that the Oslo Accords undermined the security of the state of Israel (though they did that as well). More prominently, they emphasized the danger posed to *individual* Israelis.[26] Speaking to a joint session of the US Congress on July 10, 1996, Netanyahu argued: "We must have a peace based on security for all. We cannot, and I might say we dare not, forget that more men, women, and children have lost their lives through terrorist attacks in the last 3 years, than in the entire previous decade.... Security is the first pillar. There is no substitute for it."[27]

The security that Netanyahu had in mind is clearly personal rather than national. As he argued in a Knesset speech later that year,

> At the top of our [i.e., the Likud's] priorities would be the return of our real rather than pretend security.... And I think that the most important thing is that the citizens of Israel that today live in fear—this government is a government of fear, a government that has brought about an unprecedented collapse to an unheard-of low in the personal security of each and every citizen—Israeli citizens that live in fright, afraid to take their children to kindergarten, afraid to get on a bus, afraid to go to the mall, will know that in thirty days a government will be created that will return security to this nation and the confidence that they have lost.[28]

The individualization of the security argument reflected in Netanyahu's rhetoric was both politically powerful and ideologically problematic. To the extent that free Palestinian movement into Israel made it easier to carry out terrorist attacks, the prevention of this movement posed an obvious alternative to Israeli control of the territories as a way of reducing the threat. Indeed, "We Are Here and They Are There" became an increasingly popular slogan. If the interaction between Israelis and Palestinians was the problem, one solution was to separate the populations, and, as a by-product, the land on which they sat. The security argument now became more consistent with partition than with maintaining Israeli control of the territories. Once this took place, the political benefits of being identified as pro-security increased the returns to supporting the principle of partition rather than continued Israeli control of the territories.

The Scud missiles that rained down on Israel during the first Gulf War also reduced the plausibility of the claim that the territories provided much strategic safety. Iran's ballistic capabilities and nuclear ambitions only reinforce this lesson. As a result, separation between the Jewish and Palestinian populations—initially a Labor idea—was taken over by the Likud.[29] The implied erection of a permanent border was anathema to the Likud, whose cardinal tenet involved blurring the Green Line. However, the security argument was too good a political card to throw away. As a result, even opponents of separation, such as Netanyahu and Sharon, eventually endorsed it. Thus even before he voted for unilateral disengagement, when Netanyahu was prime minister, he instructed the Israeli military to prepare plans for a physical separation of Israelis and Palestinians.[30] Ariel Sharon also initially opposed the construction of a security barrier because it would leave a large number of Israelis on the other side and because it would signal to the Palestinians that Israel was willing to give up on the territory east of the fence. By 2001, however, Sharon agreed to the construction of exactly such a wall.

Netanyahu and Sharon attempted to square the circle by portraying the separation barrier as solely a security measure and denying that it was a border of any kind or that it had any long-term political implications. The Israeli public, however, was skeptical of these claims. The May 2002 Peace Index Poll found that while 36.7 percent of Israelis believed that these measures were merely a security measure, 43 percent believed that such measures would determine the eventual border between Israel and the Palestinian state. Sharon himself probably did not believe these claims, as his office considered the potential of removing those settlements that remained on the other side of the barrier.[31]

Sharon's creation of Kadima in 2005 organized those within the Revisionist movement who had more fully accepted the principle that the security of Israelis required territorial compromise as a separate party. Kadima's victory and the seeming electoral eclipse of the remnant of the Likud in the

2006 elections suggested that the political returns to supporting the principle of partition would continue to drive the secular Israeli Right to the left. The likely role of the evolutionary dynamic in driving this transformation means, however, that politics could reverse the process as well. Indeed, these returns largely dissipated in the wake of allegations of corruption among Kadima's leadership, the widely perceived mismanagement of the war in Lebanon in 2006, and the failure of the Kadima-led government to respond effectively to the rocket attacks from the Gaza Strip.

The corruption allegations tarnished Kadima's brand and forced it to expend political capital that might have been turned toward further territorial withdrawals. The perception in Israel that the Kadima-led government botched the war in Lebanon, and its impotence in the face of the rocket fire from Gaza, also undercut the argument that it was possible for Israel to provide an answer to security challenges in the wake of territorial withdrawals. The lesson drawn (rightly or wrongly) by many Israelis from both Lebanon and Gaza is that territorial withdrawal does not necessarily bring with it higher levels of personal security. Since the provision of this security underwrote the increasing returns to partition within the Likud, its evaporation meant that the logic of the security argument rocketed back to supporting occupation rather than territorial compromise. The impact of factors unrelated to the ideological conflict within the movement (in this case run-of-the-mill corruption) in shifting the balance of power within the Revisionist movement from those articulating a vision of the homeland that accepted partition to their opponents illustrates the more general lesson that the fate of ideological variants is often decided by random, even mundane events, unrelated to the actual ideological change.

In this sense, the rocket fire from the Gaza Strip undermined the acceptance of partition within the Likud. The rocket attacks shifted the focus of personal security in Israel, at least in the Israeli south, from a fear of suicide bombers to a fear of the seemingly equally random and unpredictable rockets. Since the Israeli withdrawal from the interior of the Gaza Strip did little to stop the flight of these rockets, the argument that territorial division would bring security became harder for Israeli politicians to sustain, and therefore is less likely to be made in the future. This accounts for both the decline of the Israeli left and the resurgence of a territorially recalcitrant Likud. In the 2009 elections the Likud's campaign returned to the notions of "autonomy" (in the guise of an "economic peace") and Israeli control of the territories. This too is a contingent and potentially mutable stance. (Netanyahu's recent endorsement of the principle of a two-state solution provides some evidence of the current flux in the Likud's territorial positions.) Nonetheless, the role of the evolutionary dynamic suggests that the success of any reconciliation enabled by ideological change is more closely related to its ability to harness the domestic political logics within Israeli and Palestinian societies than to exogenous shocks.

Since this transformation is not yet complete, it is impossible to rule out completely the alternative explanations. Nonetheless, rational adaptation and elite imposition cannot account for the timing, direction, and process of change to date as well as the evolutionary dynamic. A number of different versions of rational adaptation have been offered in an attempt to explain the Right's move to the left. Some have argued that this shift reflects an adaptation to the reality of having to rule Israel in the post-Oslo context. Sharon himself justified his apparent change of heart with the claim that "there are things you see from here [i.e., as prime minister] that you don't see from there." According to the commentator David Makovsky, the combined pressure of needing to maintain good relations with the United States and the Arab world, Israel's economic dependence on the global economy, and a growing belief that halting the peace process would not halt the violence forced Netanyahu to moderate his views. Some in US policy-making circles also articulate this view. As one US official put it, speaking of Netanyahu, "You can be an ideologue in the opposition. But when you are a prime minister, you have to adjust your ideological underpinnings. The world is putting tremendous stock in these talks. You cannot ignore this reality without a paying price in Israel's standing."[32]

Another version of the rational adaptation argument holds that the shift to the left is the consequence of the realization that it was impossible to preserve the whole land of Israel as a democracy with a Jewish majority.[33] This trade-off between democracy, demography, and territory was evident in Sharon's 2005 speech in which he stated: "We never forgot that this is our country and we never gave it up. Nevertheless for peace we are willing to give up part of our right. When we had to choose between the completeness of the land without a Jewish state or a Jewish state without the completeness of the land, we chose a Jewish state."[34] Ehud Olmert, Tsipi Livni, Dan Meridor, and Tzahi Hanegbi, all right-wing members of the "fighting family," have also come to accept the primacy of the demographic threat. Tsipi Livni, reflecting on her personal transformation, stated: "I came to understand that I cannot have it all, that Jabotinsky's ambition that 'the son of Arabia, the son of Nazareth, and my son could live in comfort' cannot happen, no matter how painful it is.... This is what I think. If we want to uphold democracy and a Jewish majority here, there is no way to avoid dividing this land."[35]

Members of the Right certainly invoke the demographic argument to defend once heretical positions, and recognition of the tension between demography and territory may explain the change experienced in the ideology of select individuals. However, on the movement level, the story of rational adaptation does not account for the variation in the timing of change (both between the Likud and other movements exposed to the same reality and within the Likud itself), its substantive direction (if the crux of the issue was the demographic balance, why did the transformation lead to a withdrawal from Gaza with its 1.5 million Palestinian inhabitants rather than from the West Bank with its population of 2.4 million, or both?), or the inconsistency displayed by Likud leaders on the future of the territories.

The timing of the Likud's realization that maintaining the whole land of Israel is inconsistent with maintaining a Jewish state is problematic from the perspective of a mechanism of rational adaptation because others reached this conclusion much earlier despite being subjected to exactly the same reality. As we saw above, the Labor movement had been making this argument in general since the establishment of the state and had specifically applied it to the territories since the 1970s. It is, of course, possible that the Likud's ideological commitment to the whole land of Israel required a more significant exogenous shock to be overcome than that of the Labor movement. This possibility, however, rests on the implicit assumption that the depth of love for the homeland systematically varied between these two movements or that the leaders of the Labor movement were more rational than their counterparts in the Likud (or both). These additional assumptions may or may not be true, but an evolutionary dynamic can account for the timing of the change without resorting to them in the first place.

In any case, the leaders of the Revisionist movement recognized as early as 1967 the threat to Israel's Jewish majority that resulted from the conquest of the territories.[36] This recognition, however, did not lead to a change in the Revisionist vision of the appropriate borders. Rather, for most of its history, Revisionist Zionist thinking discounted the idea that there was a demographic threat to the Jewish majority. The Revisionists also argued that even if there was such a threat, it was nothing new. Rather, it was a permanent feature of Jewish and Zionist life. They routinely contended that the addition of the territories changed the demographic calculus only by a few years and that Jewish immigration to Israel would continue to ensure a Jewish majority.[37]

It is possible, as has been argued, that the first Palestinian intifada in 1987 fatally undermined this insistence, and that Likud leaders adapted to this new reality.[38] Here, however, the same problems with rational adaptation repeat themselves. The most prominent Likud leaders interpreted the intifada not as heralding the bankruptcy of the autonomy plan, but as confirming that peace with the Palestinians was impossible.[39] This is even the case for Netanyahu, who, as late as 1993, adhered to the traditional Revisionist Zionist rejection of the demographic threat, dismissing it as a "demographic demon."[40] If the Likud's ideological transformation was brought about by rational adaptation, why did some within the movement "recognize" the new reality after 1987 while others did not?

Here again, rational adaptation may be able to explain the variation between Netanyahu, for example, and earlier adapters in the Likud with the additional assumption that they vary in their personal sensitivity to exogenous shocks. However, not only is this assumption difficult to operationalize and verify, but, even if we allow for intra-Likud variation in sensitivity to new realities, we would still be unable to account for the inconsistency demonstrated by Likud leaders, including many of those driving this change. For example, Moshe Arens is sometimes identified as being among the first in the Likud to abandon the idea of "autonomy."[41] This did not mean, however, that he accepted the principle of partition. In fact, as noted above, as late as 1999, he based his primary campaign on the rejection of partition.

In terms of the assessment of the plausibility of the Likud's autonomy plan, nothing has happened in Israel or the territories to reverse the lesson of the intifada that the Palestinians would not settle for anything short of independence. If this realization motivated the Likud's shift to the left, why was the autonomy plan still being articulated by the leaders of the Likud, especially by Netanyahu? In an op-ed piece in 1994, Netanyahu argued that the Palestinians would accept autonomy if they knew Israel would not grant them an independent state.[42] Again, in a speech to the Likud Central Committee on May 21, 2002, long after the rational adaptation was to have taken place, Netanyahu called for the establishment of "security buffer zones opposite the main Palestinian population centers in order to seal off the free passage of Palestinians into our cities and towns," perhaps reflecting some acceptance of partition; but he still explicitly maintained the autonomy plan: "In any future agreement, if and when we get that far, I see self-rule in which the Palestinians will have the freedom to rule themselves. But to establish a state, with everything that that concept entails, with all the powers I have enumerated, which would endanger Israel's existence—that no."[43]

It is also possible that the Revisionist leaders were responding to the changed opinion of the Israeli public about Palestinian statehood and partition and imposing a new vision to take advantage of the new electoral incentives. Whereas the idea of a Palestinian state was once limited to the fringes of the Israeli political spectrum—in 1987 only 20 percent supported its establishment—today consistently more than half of the Israeli public does so. Even 27 percent of those who voted for the Likud and other right-wing parties in 1988 favored a compromise based on territorial withdrawal in exchange for peace. In more recent surveys, more than half of the Israeli public even believed that the creation of such a state was a just or very just cause.[44]

Undermining the plausibility of elite imposition in response to the new electoral incentives created by this shift in public opinion, however, the leadership of the Likud, especially Netanyahu, has vacillated in their pattern of articulation regarding partition and Palestinian statehood—sometimes endorsing them, and sometimes rejecting them—despite a rather constant position by the public.[45] The same inconsistency troubles accounts that point to an adaptation to the responsibility of sitting in the prime minister's office in the post-Oslo context or to international pressure. For example, Netanyahu's vacillations on this very question took place *after* he had already served one term as prime minister (1996–99). If the argument rests on the fact that one learns a new perspective with the responsibility of office, it is unlikely that those lessons are so easily forgotten.

Such inconsistencies raise the possibility that no real change in the Likud's ideological position occurred, and that the leadership just engaged in a tactical modulation of their rhetoric. Certainly political considerations played a role in the adoption of the critical slogan "Peace with Security." However, if the shift was merely rhetorical, we would not have observed the tangible real-world impact that it has had, including the handover of territory in the Wye and Hebron agreements, the evacuation of Israelis from the Gaza Strip, and the construction of the "security barrier." Moreover, while there may have been a political logic in moving to the center in pursuit of the median voter in the 1996 and 1999 elections under the direct election of the prime minister, such structural incentives for moderation expired when Israel abandoned this electoral experiment. That the Likud continued to maintain this shift suggests both that it is real and that it is driven by more than mere electoral calculations.

Religious Zionism's Changing Mission

The Twilight of the Dawn of the Redemption

The disengagement from the Gaza Strip generated its own particular iconography. Those opposing the disengagement donned orange Stars of David evoking the Holocaust, posted posters of Sharon as Hitler, and reenacted the frieze on the Titus Gate (commemorating the destruction of the second Temple) in Netzarim. These images forcefully brought the delegitimization of the state by parts of Religious Zionism to the attention of the wider public. These developments, however, were not unique. Nor were they the product of an understandable outpouring of emotion in the midst of crisis. They were also evident in an otherwise unexceptional afternoon in January 2006 when protestors stoned an Israeli military patrol, injuring Second Lieutenant Ariel Nusbacher. Two elements of this story distinguish it from the scores of back-page accounts of stone-throwing incidents in the West Bank. First, the lynchers were not Palestinian nationalists resisting an Israeli occupation, but

the religious ultranationalist Jewish settlers Lieutenant Nusbacher was sent
to protect. Second, in addition to sticks and stones, these Orthodox Jews
greeted Nusbacher and his patrol with the Nazi salute and cries of "Heil
Hitler."

The idea that the state of Israel was not sacred, that it did not actually
represent the dawn of redemption, and that therefore it was both profane
and disposable can be traced within Religious Zionism to the early 1980s.
This view takes the change in the Religious Zionist order of ideological
priorities—the subordination of the state to the land (chapter 4)—to its ultimate conclusion. Since the state's holiness was contingent on its maintaining control of the land, the fact that it relinquished parts of the homeland
in 1982, 1993, 1996, and 2005 provides definitive proof of its adultera-
tion. This segment of Religious Zionism thus sees the state of Israel as a
perhaps necessary, perhaps avoidable, dead-end; at best a stage on the path
to redemption whose time has passed. This message is encoded in calls to
"re-establish the Jewish state" or to "found a real Jewish state," both of
which imply that Israel is not really the Jewish state and thus cannot bear
the sanctity once applied to it.[46]

The discovery of the Jewish Underground in the early 1980s provided
one of the first clear indications that this variant existed within Religious
Zionism. This group engaged in a series of terrorist strikes across the West
Bank and was planning an attack on the Dome of the Rock when Israeli
security services apprehended it. The group's actions were criticized within
Religious Zionism precisely because they impugned the sanctity of the state.
Rabbi Yoel Ben-Nun, for example, argued that because the state of Israel
was sacred, rebelling against it by taking the law into one's own hands was
also a rebellion against God.[47] The terrorists did not disagree that they were
rebelling against the state, but rejected the notion that it was sacred.[48]

If in the early 1980s the Jewish Underground was a fringe group, a decade
later the logic they used to sanction their actions was evident even among
mainstream Religious Zionists. In the aftermath of the Oslo Accords, the
state of Israel was commonly compared to the Vichy regime and the pages
of *Nekuda* were filled with articles and letters to the editor delegitimizing the
state. Several Religious Zionist synagogues even ceased saying the prayer for
the state of Israel.[49] Prominent Religious Zionist rabbis called on soldiers to
disobey orders to evacuate Jewish settlements, and occasionally for outright
rebellion.[50] Israel soldiers, like Lieutenant Nusbacher, are not uncommonly
harassed and attacked by the very Religious Zionist settlers they are sent
to protect. The assassination of the state's elected leader, Yitzhak Rabin,
in 1995 represented its ultimate devaluation. These themes were repeated,
only with greater vigor and by a wider constituency, in the protests over the
2005 disengagement from the Gaza Strip. The iconography of the protests

demonstrated that a not insignificant segment of Religious Zionism held the state to be so blasphemous that it was socially acceptable to compare its soldiers to the Gestapo and to place its leaders in the pantheon of Jewish oppressors alongside Titus and Hitler.

The architects of this shift portray their efforts as a return to the values of Rabbi A. I. Kook and his stillborn attempt to create an alternative to the Zionist movement. These "post-Zionists" argue that Rabbi Kook erred in his decision to focus entirely on religious matters rather than pursuing a religious alternative to Zionism. The resulting dependence on the secular Zionist state rendered the protests of Religious Zionists predictably ineffectual. Some even applied this logic to Gush Emunim and the Yesha Council. They argued that these bodies were unable to meaningfully criticize or oppose the state because they accepted the Zionist premise and because they relied on it for their funding.[51]

Even more fundamentally this group contends that the ideological position that the state itself was sacred was harmful because it preemptively atoned for its sins. As early as 1985, Yehuda Etzion, writing from his prison cell, where he was serving a sentence for his role in the attacks on Arab mayors in 1982, derided the belief that the state itself represents a step in the process of redemption as giving the state carte blanche to do whatever it wants, even when this contradicts religious dictates.[52] Going one step further, Motti Karpel charged traditional Religious Zionism with misunderstanding the meaning of the phrase "the dawn of redemption." The excessive emphasis on the "certainty" that the state would serve in that capacity, he argues, left Religious Zionism and Gush Emunim unable to offer a real alternative to Zionism or to engage in truly meaningful action to reform it from within.[53]

The adherents of this view offer a way out of this trap by transcending Zionism with a movement that is "more authentically rooted in the Torah and the Land of Israel." They are explicit in their belief that the Zionist state-building project has reached the end of its usefulness. Since the state of Israel "does not meet the minimum demands of 'a Jewish state'" it is impossible to fix the secular Zionist "instrument" (for Redemption) and it should be replaced with a new one. This new tool is sometimes called the "Kingdom of David" or the "state of Judea."[54]

The proponents of this view see themselves as engaged in a bitter war "against all that the state of Israel is and represents today," and openly acknowledge that the state of Judea would be established on the ashes of the state of Israel. At the same time, perhaps as a nod to the coercive power of the state, they declare that they will not fight it directly.[55] As Etzion argued, while they do not accept the sovereignty of the state (much less its sanctity), "we are not speaking of direct rebellion, but of the building of a new, appropriate, sovereign building that will replace the current profane experience."[56] They remain loyal to the state only "in order to foment a revolution in it."[57] As this suggests, the proponents of this new mission no longer believe in the sanctity of the state or that they are continuing the project begun by Labor Zionism in any meaningful sense. They are revolutionaries engaged in a new, distinct project. This shift is so fundamental that it is no longer appropriate to call its adherents Religious "Zionists"; even they reject the label.[58]

not really Zionists

Explaining the Twilight of the Dawn of the Redemption

Religious Zionism's inability to fully contend with the implications of modern Jewish sovereignty contained the seeds for the potential desacralization of the state of Israel. The Chief Rabbinate's failure to deal with the fundamental moral assumptions at the heart of modern Jewish sovereignty resulted in a rigid system that did not enable either full identification with the state or the state's full integration into the world of Halacha (Jewish religious law). Religious Zionism's inability either to digest the state of Israel within the existing corpus of religious law or to completely disavow it created an unstable system whose eventual breakdown (because of the inevitable disjuncture between the dream and reality) fostered the devaluation of the religious value of the state.[59] Nonetheless, this precondition is not enough to explain why the change took place when it did. Why did an ideological structure solid enough to last for at least thirty-four years suddenly collapse? Nor can this account explain why it was only a segment within Religious Zionism that carried the declining sanctity of the state to its ultimate conclusion.

The onset of change in the early 1980s is consistent with the expectations of a shift driven by rational adaptation. Israel's withdrawal from the Sinai Peninsula in 1982 certainly shook Religious Zionism. In its wake, an increasing proportion of modern Orthodox youth began denying the religious importance of the existence of the state of Israel. Even at the theological center of Gush Emunim, the Merkaz Harav Yeshiva, many began to openly consider avoiding military service. What was once seen as an expression of national, even religious, duty was now openly dismissed as a waste of time.[60] It also became increasingly common during this period to hear the once sacred state of Israel equated with the British Mandate. This equation is consistent with the desacralization of the state, since Religious Zionist historiography understands the Mandate as having impeded the creation of the Jewish state and contributed to the Holocaust by limiting Jewish immigration.[61]

duty to the state: "a waste of time"

The direction of change, however, is not as consistent with the expectations of rational adaptation. It is unclear in what sense the desacralization of the state functioned to bring the movement's ideology into closer congruence with reality. Even from within the Religious Zionist paradigm, it would have been as rational to interpret the withdrawal from Sinai not as a retreat from redemption, but as one more of the "birth pangs of the Messiah." Such dialectical reasoning would have been quite consistent with the way in which Religious Zionism dealt with inconsistencies in the past.

The evolutionary dynamic does not fare any better in accounting for the empirical benchmarks of this change. The emergence of the notion that the state was not sacred does not appear to have begun as a tactical modulation intended for another purpose. Rather, the articulation of this view represents a purposeful and self-conscious challenge to the ideology of Religious Zionism from within. The proponents of this new view do not believe themselves to be engaged in tactical ideological adjustment; nor do they justify their positions in these terms. Indeed, they go so far as to argue that God is on their side and they are on God's side [62] They are also quite consistent in their pattern of articulation, displaying none of the vacillation that characterizes cases of change driven by the evolutionary dynamic.

All of this, however, is consistent with a process of elite imposition. As in the earlier case where elite imposition drove change, the ideological transformation is characterized by the attempt of a new cadre of aspiring leaders to impose their preexisting ideology on the movement. In this particular case, this group emerged in the early 1980s into the ideological space created by the "betrayal" of the withdrawal from Sinai and the death of Rabbi Zvi Yehuda Kook. His successor, Rabbi Avraham Shapira, who came to Merkaz Harav from a traditionally Haredi milieu, did not share the attention to the "process of redemption" that characterized Zvi Yehuda's thought. This made it possible for those who were inclined to devalue the instruments of redemption, including the state, to do so without sanction.[63]

Currently, the key manifestations of this group are found in the "Hardal" wing of Religious Zionism. Literally meaning "mustard," Hardal is the acronym of Haredi Leumi, or nationalist ultra-Orthodox. It connotes religious observance in the Haredi style combined with an uncompromising nationalist position as developed by the leaders of Merkaz Harav Yeshiva. The devaluation of the state of Israel by this segment of Religious Zionism lowered the barriers to cooperation with the ultra-Orthodox, who always denied that the state had any theological significance. Organizationally, the Hardal wing of the movement is concentrated in several overlapping organizations, including the National Union Party, the organizations that stemmed from Rabbi Meir Kahane's Kach (Thus) movement, and the Emunit movement. The political wing of the latter, Manhigut Yehudit (Jewish Leadership), openly argues that "Zionism is finished and only Judaism remains."[64] The Emunit movement also contains the remnants of Yehuda Etzion's Hai

Vekayam, which called for the establishment of "a ladder to ascend from Zionism and the state to the kingdom of the house of David,"[65] and the Zo Artzeneinu (This Is Our Land) movement. The proponents of this variant are also evident in the growing influence of the so-called hilltop youth and their supporters.

Originally relegated to the margins of the movement, the proponents of this movement have become a force within Religious Zionism. Estimating their precise strength, however, is challenging. On the one hand, the organization of the state of Judea did not appear to proceed beyond its "First Congress." Indeed, some have contended that this component of the Religious Zionist movement is small and losing its significance in the face of the broader, moderating trends within Religious Zionism.[66] This argument is undercut, however, by the fact that the graduates of the flagship Religious Zionist institution, the Merkaz Harav Yeshiva, are those who led the Haredization of Religious Zionism. The reaction of the (now) traditional leadership of Religious Zionism and Gush Emunim also suggests that they consider the Hardal a real contender for power within the movement. It apparently represented enough of a threat to be criticized within Gush Emunim as a "nationalist Neturei Karta,"[67] and to be subjected to what it called a "Bolshevik" campaign to silence it by the Gush Emunim establishment.[68] Despite the Hardal's complaints, the idea that the state of Israel was a failed experiment—usually because it was not based on a theological foundation—was quite common in the pages of *Nekuda* throughout the 1980s and 1990s. Mainstream leaders of Gush Emunim also articulated this claim.[69] In fact, by 1991, Yoel Ben-Nun even warned that the "state of Judea" ideology had moved from the margins of the movement to its center.[70] Still, in 1995 the notion that the state did not merit the label of the dawn of the redemption was popular enough that ideologues of Gush Emunim felt obligated to respond to it explicitly.[71] Other students of the radical Right in Israel concluded that this group plays an important role in the collective consciousness of the religious Right that is greater than their absolute numbers would indicate. More recently, Yuval Diskin, the head of Israel's General Security Services, noted that those who were once thought to be on the extreme fringe of the settler public are now the center for a segment of the settler public, and that the Yesha Council, the traditional leadership of the settlers, had little or no influence on the masses of youth who led the struggle over the partial evacuation of Amona.[72]

Consistent with the growth of the Hardal trend within Religious Zionism, in the mid-1980s and increasingly in the 1990s some within Gush Emunim began to offer olive branches to the Haredim in an effort to patch up the historically poor relations between them. Letters to the editor and articles in *Nekuda* began to argue that rather than vilify the Haredim, Religious

Zionists should see them as their natural partners.[73] The rehabilitation of the Haredim within Gush Emunim even included the emphasis of the former's nationalist, even Zionist, credentials. This included, amazingly, a Zionist reading of the ideology of Rabbi Bruyer himself.[74] Contributors to *Nekuda* began to argue that Gush Emunim and the Haredim shared a basic "Zionism" composed of the fundamental assumption that their existence in the Land of Israel was based solely on the legacy of the Jewish tradition.[75] Even articulations of the iconic Religious Zionist position that military service was as valuable as Torah study began to be criticized in Religious Zionist circles.[76] In 1992, some within the NRP even called for a covenant with the Haredim that would include changing their long-held position calling for the drafting of yeshiva students.[77] It even became not uncommon to see public articulations of the sentiment that the isolationist path of the Haredim was the right one, while the Religious Zionist attempt to cooperate with secular Zionism had been misguided.[78]

The shift is also closely tied to the growing social, cultural, and theological closeness between this segment of Religious Zionism and the Haredi world.[79] The decreasing cultural gap between Religious Zionism and the ultra-Orthodox world symbolized by the Hardal is evident primarily, though not exclusively, in the growing religious radicalization of the Religious Zionist movement.[80] This increased religious fanaticism was not limited to the margins of the movement but was spearheaded by the graduates and leadership of the Merkaz Harav Yeshiva. The conception of its leaders and students on issues such as the status of women, gender relations, secular studies, and military service became consistently closer to those articulated by the Haredim. The "Haredization" of Religious Zionism is also evident in the greater role assigned to rabbis (at the expense of the lay political leadership) in determining the NRP's positions on an increasingly wider range of issues. The desired proximity to the Haredim is even noticeable in their adoption of Haredi fashion.

In the wake of the Oslo Accords, ever-widening circles within Religious Zionism welcomed the common ground with the Haredim.[81] This development was heralded by a shift in the terms of the debate over the Land of Israel. During the earlier debates over partition, Religious Zionists rarely couched their opposition to partition in terms of Halacha. In the 1990s, Gush Emunim, the Emunit movement, and Religious Zionism more generally, tended to frame their opposition to partition in explicitly religious and Halachic terms.[82] The growing number of advertisements for Haredi singers and entertainers featured in *Nekuda* also suggests that the distance between these two communities had narrowed. These shows initially began as benefits to raise money to oppose the Oslo Accords and quickly morphed into fund-raising for settlement activity more broadly.

The growth of the Hardal is also evident in theological terms. Perhaps most significant is the spread of the Talmudic concepts of "Da'at Torah" (loosely meaning that the advice given by Torah scholars must be followed by observant Jews) and "Emunat Hahamim" (referring to the virtually unlimited authority granted to Torah scholars to determine religious law) into Religious Zionist discourse. These concepts have become codes eliciting unquestioning obedience to rabbinical authority. They are used to stifle debate and eliminate the need to have the opinions of the Torah sages substantiated. In an important sense, they depoliticize the discussion over the issues regarding which they are invoked by removing the possibility of disagreement. The adoption of these Haredi religious concepts in Religious Zionist discourse is part of the spread to Religious Zionism of the formalistic understanding of the Halacha that is prevalent in the Haredi world. This formalistic understanding places the moral authority of the religious jurist above that of the individual receiving the ruling, and thereby obligates the latter to obey. Indeed, one of the prominent usages of this reasoning was Rabbi Israel Rosen's appeal to Da'at Torah to justify the call to disobey orders and to eliminate objections to it.[83]

This cultural, social, and theological change lowered the barriers to cooperation between segments of the Religious Zionists and parts of the ultra-Orthodox world. The increasing closeness between them, in turn, reinforced the prominence of the ultra-Orthodox view of the state as profane and of the secular Zionists as apostates.

Many within Religious Zionism and even within Gush Emunim resisted the turn toward the Haredim and their increased influence.[84] Amnon Shapira, general secretary of Bnei Akiva, was worried by these developments and predicted that "the new term 'nationalist Haredi' will cause an unstoppable process" that will lead to "the negative element of anti-Zionism."[85] Yoel Ben-Nun even warned that the increasing Haredization of the national religious public was undercutting the latter's own existence.[86]

The concern engendered by the Haredization of Religious Zionism and its attendant shift in the view of the secular suggests that it is not marginal. As one measure of its spread, between 1955 and 1975 about 13 percent of modern Orthodox parents planned to send their children to ultra-Orthodox schools. In the early 1980s, this estimate stood at about 20 percent.[87] The increasing segregation between the modern Orthodox and secular Israelis in all realms of life also reflects the strength of the Hardal trend within Religious Zionism.[88]

The growing influence of those within the movement who seek to replace the state of Israel with a "real" Jewish state was especially visible during, and after, the disengagement from the Gaza Strip. Religious Zionist newspapers, blogs, radio outlets, and sermons repeatedly engaged in heated debates and anguished soul-searching over the question of the sanctity of the state. The very existence of this questioning, the need to justify what was once a foundational and taken-for-granted aspect of Religious Zionism, and the widespread perception of a crisis in the movement testify to the spread of the new variant of their nationalist mission. Even if the group articulating it is not yet powerful enough to take over the leadership of Religious Zionism as a whole, we can expect the struggle for control of what is left of Religious Zionism to continue. As this group succeeds, the mission of replacing the current state of Israel with a "real" Jewish state can be expected to become more widespread.

From National Unity to a Nation of Real Jews

A second, related transformation in the ideology of Religious Zionism is the apparent abandonment of the principle of cooperation with secular Jews as a good in its own right. This was one of the most important aspects that originally set Religious Zionists apart from the rest of observant Jewry. The latter, represented by Agudat Israel, rejected the Zionist enterprise on both practical and theological grounds. In practical terms, they feared that the pursuit of Jewish statehood would incite the non-Jewish world and lead to greater, not less, persecution. Theologically, they argued that Zionism was a heretical attempt to perform by human hands the mission—the ingathering of the Jews—that was God's alone.

Religious Zionism disagreed. Initially Religious Zionism did not assign any theological value to the Zionist enterprise. It saw the nationalist project as a practical measure—as the best way to save Jewish lives. This view was quickly eclipsed by that of the followers of Rabbi A. I. Kook, who saw the Zionist project in mystical and messianic terms. Since the world was on an inexorable march to redemption, Rabbi Kook argued that the secular Zionists were actually the unwitting agents of God, advancing the cause of redemption despite their secularism. He argued that the divine inner spark governing their actions would eventually and inevitably emerge. As a result, unlike Agudat Israel, which urged insulation from the secular Zionists lest they be contaminated, Religious Zionists embraced cooperation with the secular as part of the divine plan for redemption. This led Religious Zionism to foster an abiding concern for the "wholeness" and "unity" of the nation.

The belief in the intrinsic value of cooperating with secular Zionists even survived the rise of the Young Guard and Gush Emunim. In its early years, Gush Emunim continued to adhere to the goal of uniting the nation and to A. I. Kook's split-level theory of the secular Zionists. Indeed, members of Gush Emunim tended to reject the very concept of a "secular Jew." Yoel

Ben-Nun, for example, compared the secularity of the Zionist movement to a suit of clothes worn by the Jew when he leaves the ghetto, but which is mistaken for the man inside.[89] They even made a point of emphasizing their openness to the secular and their willingness to accept them into their settlements.

By the 1980s, however, it was clear that even within Gush Emunim, cooperation between religious and secular was based more on tactical and self-consciously short-term considerations than on genuine acceptance.[90] Despite Gush Emunim's calls for cooperation with the secular, its settlements commonly turned secular families away.[91] Building on the increasing segregation between religious and secular—in housing, the military, and the job market—some began openly calling for settlements that were populated only by Religious Zionists.[92] The increasing portrayal of "going with the secular" as a tactic whose usefulness has ended also reflects this reality.[93] By 1986, the increasing exclusion of the secular even led *Nekuda*'s editorial page to complain that Gush Emunim had changed from a movement that combined religious and secular to a religious movement.[94] In the early 1980s, however, this had not yet been transformed into a widespread exclusion of secular Israelis from the bounds of the "we."

This step is now apparently taking place. Since the mid-1980s, the political Left and secular Israelis have been portrayed as less Jewish, or even as not at all Jewish.[95] A growing trend within Religious Zionism rejected all Western culture and its offshoots (including, for some, Zionism), and that attitude all too easily slid into a rejection of the people espousing "Western," especially "humanist," values.[96] Some, especially, in the Emunit movement explicitly identify the Israeli Left with Christianity.[97] Consistent with this shift, Charles Liebman found that the perception of the secular as "goyim," hostile, and foreign, even anti-Semitic, was increasingly present in the daily language of the modern Orthodox.[98] Whereas the Haredim, especially, but not exclusively, Neturei Karta, had long used the term "Erev Rav" to describe the secular, thereby implying that they were not really Jewish, the term was now gaining acceptance among Religious Zionists as well.[99]

This segment of the Religious Zionist movement increasingly understands the unity of the nation not in terms of a bridge between the Haredim and the Zionists or between Right and Left, but instead as dependent on the wholeness of the land. According to this view, since the nation and its land are an ontological unity, harming the wholeness of the land is equivalent to harming the wholeness of the nation. As a result, the fight for the wholeness of the land, even if it appears to be dividing the nation, is actually the only way to achieve its unity. Moreover, since the land is a holy entity, then action taken for its wholeness is justified and absolves its doers, who partake in its holiness.[100] This dialectical logic has led parts of the Religious Zionist movement to abandon the mission of cooperation with the secular. Instead, the secular and the Israeli Left (first conflated and then accused of dividing the nation by seeking to divide the land) are increasingly excluded from the realm of legitimate partners and even of the "really Jewish."

The prevalence of the invidious comparisons between Israel and Nazi Germany, between the IDF and the Gestapo, and between Israel's secular leaders and Hitler, reflects the shift away from the mission of cooperating with the secular to bring about redemption to one that excludes them from the bounds of the community. As I mentioned above, the comparison overtly denigrates the character of the state and its actions. Implicitly, however, this comparison also says something about the character and identity of the actors involved. Since the Nazis are the antithesis of Jews, if the state's actions resemble those of the Nazis, then those who carry them out are, by implication, also the antithesis of Jews. This logic undergirded the slogan adopted by the organized protests against the disengagement from the Gaza Strip. Mass produced bumper stickers, graffiti on the walls of doomed houses, and young men and women carried out of their homes and synagogues cried: "A Jew does not expel a Jew." This was more than an appeal to the emotions and conscience of the soldiers carrying out the disengagement. It was also a declaration of faith. Since the protestors did not question their own Jewishness, and since Jews were in fact expelled, either the faith was wrong or those carrying out the expulsion were somehow not Jewish. The everyday language of this sector of Religious Zionism, in which Religious Zionists refer to themselves as "Jews," "good Jews," or "healthy Jews" in contrast to "Israelis," recalls and inverts the linguistic distinction between "Hebrews" and "Jews" promoted by early Labor Zionism (see chapter 4).

The excommunication of secular Israelis within Religious Zionism is still so much in process that disentangling the mechanisms driving it is problematic. Nonetheless, it appears closely associated with the same process of elite imposition implicated in the desacralization of the state. For this cadre of aspiring leaders, the belief in the bankruptcy of the Zionist project also meant the end of the historic partnership between religious and secular crafted by Rabbi Kook. In fact, as we saw above, the leaders of the Emunit movement blame this partnership for the failure to create a "real Jewish state." Motti Karpel, one of their chief ideologues, even accepted the basic Haredi critique of Zionism that called for insulation from the Zionists:

The truth is that already in those days when the Zionist idea crystallized, there were those who saw its fundamental problems and knew then that the day will necessarily come when it will reach a dead-end. There were many reasons for the criticism of the Greats from the religious world.... They warned back then that the Zionist idea will not be able to lead "the return to Zion" for long and will not be able to form the appropriate base for Jewish existence in the land of Israel.[101]

As with the other changes driven by elite imposition, to the extent that this segment of the movement succeeds in its attempt to take over Religious Zionism, the movement's answer to foundational questions will change as well. The implications of the Hardal's replacement of the principle of cooperation with the secular with a belief that they ought to be excluded from the political community is likely to have drastic consequences for Israeli society. At the very least, we can expect the growth of the Hardal variant of Religious Zionist ideology to generate greater conflict between the religious and secular in Israel over increasingly diverse aspects of the public realm.

Nationalism and the Question of Change

Despite repeated obituaries, nationalism continues to imbue politics with meaning. Nationalism determines who is included in and excluded from the political community, delimits the homeland in which daily political contestation takes place, and galvanizes its adherents in the service of a greater goal. People are willing to die for the nation and in the name of nationalism because it defines the basic bounds of political life. At the same time, the actual definitions of the political community offered by nationalism can, and do, change over time.

This duality—the combination of stability and change, of invention and of deep-seatedness—has been at the heart of the analytical debates over nationalism. Unable to reconcile both faces of nationalism, many scholars have opted, in effect, to emphasize one over the other. Too often, nationalism is assumed to be so malleable that it can be modified at the command of political elites or so rigid that only a significant exogenous shock can trigger change. Struggling with the problem that both perspectives are theoretically plausible and, in some cases, empirically accurate, Rogers Brubaker and Fredrick Cooper argued that we should jettison the concept of "identity" because "if identity is everywhere, it is nowhere. If it is fluid, how can we understand the ways in which self-understandings may harden, congeal, and crystallize?...If it is multiple, how do we understand the terrible singularity that is often striven for—and sometimes realized—by politicians seeking to transform mere categories into unitary and exclusive groups? How can we understand the power and pathos of identity politics?"[1]

duality of
primordial
and fluid
nationalism

Changing our terminology, however, is not enough. The problem is deeper than that. Both the conceptualization of nationalism as "as-if primordial" and the view that it is inherently fluid clearly capture part of the story. To gain analytical purchase on this duality we need to "harden" the soft constructivist notion of identity rightly criticized by Brubaker and Cooper. This does not require admitting some "essentialist" character of identity. (Doing so would repeat the mistake of privileging stability over fluidity.)

We can, however, accommodate nationalism's Janus face by subjecting our assumptions about the mechanisms that govern changes in the definition of the social (in this book, national) identity to systematic empirical scrutiny. Using the Israeli case, this book provided a two-step template for doing so. It first traced the transformations that took place along the basic ideological dimensions of nationalism articulated by the three most important Israeli nationalist movements. It then tested the ability of alternative explanations to account for the empirical benchmarks of these transformations. Table 3 summarizes the results.

On the territorial dimension of nationalist ideology, all three movements shifted their view of the appropriate borders of the homeland from one that, at the very least, included both banks of the Jordan River to a delineation of the homeland that does not extend beyond the river. This may seem like an esoteric tidbit given the current conflict over the land west of the Jordan River. If nothing else, however, the peace treaty between Israel and Jordan, which ended nearly fifty years of formal belligerency and repeated wars, would have been impossible without this transformation. In any case, the perception of the appropriate fate of the territories has also shifted. The Labor Zionist vision of the extent of the homeland contracted further and now conceives of the 1949 armistice borders (with minor modifications) as the appropriate ones for the state of Israel. Even the Revisionist Zionist movement appears to be in the midst of an analogous acceptance of the principle of partition of the land west of the Jordan.

The cherished national missions that galvanized millions to action also shifted over time. Among the most important were the eclipse of the Labor movement's socialism, the acceptance by the once secularist Labor and Revisionist Zionist movements of a role for religious law in the public realm, and the subordination of the state to the land by the Religious Zionist movement. These shifts have been crucial in shaping almost every aspect of Israeli society.

Israeli nationalism has also struggled to cope with the existence of a large minority population within the national state and a significant (indeed majority) of would-be co-nationals outside it. On the latter issue, the Labor Zionist movement modified its ideology to exclude Diaspora, especially American, Jews from the scope of those automatically categorized as co-nationals. On the other axis of national membership, however, no change

TABLE 3
Changes in Israeli Nationalisms (by date of onset)

Who?	Dimension	Where? Direction	When? Onset	When? Turning point	When? End	Mechanism
		Completed transformations				
Labor Zionism	Mission	From class to nation	1924	1944	1951	The evolutionary dynamic
Labor Zionism	Mission	Acceptance of a religious role in the public realm	1933	1947	1958	The evolutionary dynamic
Religious Zionism	Borders	From "the River of Egypt to...the River Euphrates" to the "whole land of Israel"	1937	1946	1951	The evolutionary dynamic
Labor Zionism	Borders	The elision of the East Bank	1937	1944	1946	The evolutionary dynamic
Labor Zionism	Mission	From ingathering the exiles to saving the exile	1939	1944	1956	The evolutionary dynamic
Labor Zionism	Membership	From including American Jews to saving them in exile	1941	1944	1958	The evolutionary dynamic
Labor Zionism	Borders	From the "whole land of Israel" to the 1949 armistice lines	1949	1973	1982	Rational adaptation
Revisionist Zionism	Borders	From "both banks of the Jordan" to the "whole land of Israel"	1955	1960	1982	The evolutionary dynamic
Revisionist Zionism	Mission	Acceptance of a religious role in the public realm (take 2)	1958	1974	1981	The evolutionary dynamic
Religious Zionism	Mission	Subordination of the state of Israel to the Land of Israel	1969	1973	1977	Elite imposition
		Ongoing transformations				
Religious Zionism	Mission	From preserving the unity of the nation to excluding the secular	1980	1985	N/A	Elite imposition?
Religious Zionism	Mission	The twilight of the "dawn of our redemption"	1982	1993	N/A	Elite imposition?
Revisionist Zionism	Borders	From the "whole land of Israel" to the 1949 armistice lines	1987	1996	N/A	The evolutionary dynamic?

has taken place. Each of the Israeli nationalist movements continues to articulate an ethnic definition of national membership that excludes Palestinian citizens from the answer to the question "Who are we?"

On its own, such a result might be interpreted as evidence for a primordial ontology of nationalism, one in which the answer to "Who are we?" is hardwired into nations. Such an interpretation, however, would inexplicably ignore the existence of change in the other dimensions of nationalism. This variation—the fact that some answers to foundational questions changed while others remained constant—reinforces the analytical importance of simultaneously accounting for the multiple dimensions of nationalist ideology. Arguments about the nature of nationalism that are based solely on one of these dimensions are likely to be missing part of the picture.

Advocates of primordial ontologies might still claim that this particular dimension is more fundamental to nationalism than the others, and that even if visions of the homeland and mission change, the notion of appropriate membership cannot. Not only is this assertion conceptually problematic; it is also difficult to sustain empirically. If nothing else, the American experience in which African Americans once constituted three-fifths of a person demonstrates that changes in the definition of national membership can occur. The absence of change in this aspect of Israeli nationalism is more likely to reflect the particular movements included in this study rather than an inherent feature of nationalism. Taken as a whole, the findings of this book contribute to the growing evidence that theories based on primordial ontologies of nationalism have little empirical traction. In this way, Israel joins the growing number of cases in which scholars have identified significant changes in the cardinal aspects of the nation and nationalism over time.

The most significant finding of the empirical test of the ability of alternative explanations to account for these changes is that an evolutionary dynamic accounted for most of the fundamental transformations in the meaning of Israeli nationalisms. Taken together, rational adaptation to new realities and elite imposition accounted for only four of the thirteen completed and ongoing changes in nationalist ideologies in the Zionist/Israeli context. In nine of the thirteen cases, however, the empirical benchmarks of change were more consistent with the expectations of an evolutionary dynamic (see table 3). Most of the changes that took place in Zionist/Israeli nationalisms are thus best understood as the undirected by-products of attempts by nationalist movements to resolve local political problems. When accomplishing these mundane political goals required bridging the significant ideological gaps that exist between rival nationalist movements over the very bounds of the political game, such cooperation led to temporary adjustments of the claims of the relevant movements. Sometimes, however, these adjustments succeeded too well. The political goals in whose name they were crafted carried significant rewards in terms of power and influence. Once achieved, maintaining these gains often depended on perpetuating the ideological variant that made them possible in the first place. In these cases, the articulation of the adjusted ideology increased at the expense of the old orthodoxy because there were increasing returns to the politically successful variants. These rewards made it harder to abandon the (once temporary) adjustment, even to the point of its reinterpretation as the right, true, and orthodox ideological position, regardless of the original intentions of those who promoted the adjusted claim.

This logic is identical to the logic that guides evolutionary theory. Restated abstractly, evolutionary theory predicts that when and where units are characterized by variation and retention, those variants that happen to be in a better position to survive the selection pressure exerted on them will spread at the expense of the other variants. Applied to the political realm, this logic offers a corrective to the assumption that change must be intentional. Just as the story of biological evolution claims that there does not have to be a guiding intelligence behind biological change (not that there cannot be one), so, in the political realm, the evolutionary dynamic implies that fundamental transformations in nationalist ideology do not have to be intentional (not that they cannot be).

Both exogenous shocks and elite innovation still play important roles in an evolutionary dynamic. Political movements and the domestic struggle for power among them cannot be disconnected from reality. Thus, even if the exogenous shocks that create new realities rarely cause change directly, they do affect the perception of the possible by the leaders of nationalist movements, shape the prospects of intramovement factions in their struggle for power, make the attempted formation of some alliances more or less likely, and promote the prospects of some political projects at the expense of others. New realities thus shape the political mechanism that "selects" among variants of nationalist ideology.

The central role played by politics in differentiating successful ideological variants from unsuccessful ones also emphasizes the fact that nationalist leaders are not passive observers of history. Acting in the world in which they live, responding to the political incentives they see, and reacting to the cognitive punches that pummel them, political entrepreneurs pursue their goals with relish and (occasionally) creativity. The resulting ideological modulations are the crucial source of variation on which the evolutionary dynamic relies, even if the actions of political entrepreneurs are not the primary engine of change.

All ideological modulations—made for any reason, including those made as rational adaptations to a new reality or as elite manipulations—are theoretically available to be "selected" (to succeed at greater rates than their alternatives) and to thereby become the new ideological standard. However, those made in the context of creating successful alliances between movements that differ on foundational questions are especially likely to lead to substantive change, because these alliances provide a tangible vehicle on whose success (which may or may not be related to the ideological adjustment) the new ideological variant can piggyback. As we saw above, the failure of the political vehicle in which the adjusted claim is embedded (or, indeed, the absence of such a vehicle) means that the ideological adjustment is less likely to benefit from a cycle of positive returns. If this is the case, the varying conception of nationalism that it embodies is likely to fade.

The evolutionary dynamic also offers a conceptually coherent way of reconciling the conflicting logics of rational adaptation (with its emphasis on stability) and elite imposition (with its emphasis on fluidity). Instead of assuming that nationalism is inherently either sticky or fluid, the evolutionary dynamic pegs the balance between stability and change to the cadence of domestic politics among rival nationalist movements. In the Zionist/Israeli context, we saw that changes to key ideological tenets took place more frequently than expected by those who treat nations "as if" they were primordial, but less often than predicted by those who emphasize their malleability. Over the eighty-year scope of this study there were ten completed and three ongoing changes in nationalist ideology distributed across three movements and three ideological dimensions. Change did take place. It was not rare, but neither was it constant.

The empirical findings of the test of the ability of alternative explanations to account for change also show that the common assumptions about how nationalism changes are much less powerful than conventionally assumed. As discussed in the introduction, rational adaptation tends to assume that the exogenous shock that triggers ideological transformation makes it very difficult for those experiencing it to resist adapting to the new reality. This fosters the related expectation that all the movements exposed to a particular shock would react, or at least experience pressure to react, simultaneously, and that this reaction would take place on the same ideological dimensions—namely, those affected by the new reality. The comparison of the processes of ideological transformation among nationalist movements that were located in the same historical and geographical context allowed us to test this expectation. Since all three movements shared the same reality, any significant "cognitive punch" ought to have left its mark on all of them. Concretely, this would have meant that all movements would have experienced change in the affected dimension at the same time. As table 3 shows, however, this was not the case. No single exogenous shock can plausibly be held responsible for the timing of change across the board. The process tracing of the individual cases of change showed, moreover, that the direction of the shifts that do cluster in time (and which, therefore, might lend support to the rational adaptation mechanism) is better explained by the unintended consequences of the short-term politics of alliance formation between rival nationalist movements than by any particular new reality.

Not only does rational adaptation fall short as an explanation for the aggregate pattern of stability and change, it also failed to drive change when it was most likely to do so: in the ideology of the famously pragmatic Labor Zionist movement. Mapai's pragmatism probably accounts for its willingness to engage in rhetorical ideological modulations relatively more frequently than the other movements examined. But the substantive content of its claims did not change so easily. The empirical benchmarks of change could be plausibly linked to a new reality in only one of the six transformations it experienced. Moreover, on the membership dimension, despite the creation of the new political reality in which, depending on the period, between 13 percent and 20 percent of the population was Arab and there was tremendous moral and international pressure, the Labor movement did not modify its ideology to include Arabs as appropriately part of the political community. The tendency to stretch Mapai's pragmatism from the tactical realm to the substantive one may be a function of the reliance on Mapai's (retrospective) willingness to subordinate its socialist goals to its nationalist aims. By itself, however, this willingness begs the question of the degree of Mapai's pragmatism when it came to compromising its other, *nationalist*, goals. If anything, the discarding of socialism suggests that its nationalist goals were especially sacrosanct. Moreover, politicians will usually rationalize changes in their ideologies (if they admit them at all) by blaming force majeure. That these justifications are usually offered in retrospect and not at the time of the actual modification should make us skeptical of most claims to "pragmatic adjustments to reality" by nationalist leaders. In many cases, the appeal to pragmatism appears as a post-hoc cover for the unguided evolution of nationalism.

Rational adaptation failed to trigger change even when the impact of the new reality was undeniable. The most significant shocks in the Zionist/Israeli context, including the Holocaust, the establishment of the state, and the 1967 war, did not usually lead to change. The Holocaust tended to reinforce the beliefs of the Zionists rather than lead to their reevaluation. To be sure, it made some more willing to consider short-term compromises, but the direction of these shifts was not necessarily consistent with the impact of the Holocaust. Even more problematic for explanations of change based on rational adaptation, most of the changes usually attributed to the Holocaust actually began before, or long after, its impact was felt.

The timing of the onsets and turning points of the ideological changes summarized in table 3 shows that even the establishment of the state of

Israel, and the inevitable routinization that followed, did not lead to a change on the main dimensions of nationalism (with one significant exception). Even the earthquake of the 1967 war, which was major enough to restructure Israeli politics around the territorial question, did not actually have the ideological effect commonly ascribed to it. The territorial maximalism that characterized the Likud and the Religious Zionists in the war's aftermath was not new. In fact, for the Revisionists, the expansion of the area under Israeli control actually covered up the *contraction* of the area they claimed as appropriately the nation's. The conquest of the territories allowed them to continue the exclusion of the East Bank of the Jordan from the definition of the "whole land of Israel" that began a decade earlier, while claiming fidelity to the old ideal. In the case of the Religious Zionists, the reunion with the biblical heartland and the old city of Jerusalem certainly rekindled the discussion of the appropriate borders and helped shift their mission to preserving Israeli control of the land. However, despite the radicalization represented by the rise of the Young Guard and Gush Emunim (Bloc of the Faithful), the post-1967 articulations of the appropriate borders of the nation-state were largely identical to those that preceded the war. In other words, the new reality created by the conquest of the territories did not bring about a change in the pattern of articulation regarding the appropriate borders of the state.

One might still argue that the results reflect a process of rational adaptation, but one based on a 'bounded' rationality. From this perspective, actors rationally responded to these (and other) shocks but misread reality. Bounded rationality certainly makes more sense than versions of rational adaptation that discount the role played by ideologies in interpreting the cognitive punches that pummel them, and thus their ability to subvert them or modify their impact. Nonetheless, the appeal to a bounded rational adaptation still cannot account for the evidence that these changes were not literally rational. Rational action starts from the premise that actors consciously calculate the costs and benefits of the alternatives available to them and opt for the alternative with the largest expected payoff. Bounded rationality would certainly explain miscalculations about the expected payoffs. It cannot account, however, for the fact that such a calculation did not appear to take place. Nationalist leaders did not know that they were playing this "game"; they did not think that they were fundamentally changing their ideology or that the new ideological variant was better than their old beliefs. They tended not to be concerned with such fundamental considerations at all. If they paid any attention to the fundamental ideological issues, they almost invariably saw the modulations that they engaged in as little more than short-term tactics intended to *preserve* their original ideology rather than modify it. The explanation of the shift in rational terms, as better than the old orthodoxy, only takes place retroactively. Analytically, emphasizing the rationality of change despite this complication ignores the reality that the ideological transformation that ultimately occurred was only one of the many possible changes that could have taken place.

The relatively weak explanatory ability of rational adaptation has far-reaching implications for the conventional periodization of history according to exogenous shocks. Given the very large number of significant changes to the reality in which nationalist movements function, it is always possible to retrospectively tell a story that appears to link a particular change with a particular shock. Such ad-hoc explanations may hide, however, the systematic processes at work if they do not actually account for all the relevant empirical benchmarks of change. In the Israeli context, this more rigorous approach showed that the key turning points in its nationalist history were more closely related to the prices exacted by the formation of successful alliances between movements with different answers to foundational questions than to exogenous shocks, including Israel's wars.

This does not mean that rational adaptation never happens. In the Israeli context, it accounted for one of the transformations in borders, boundaries, and mission. This instance provides empirical support for cascading models of transformation in which the sensitivity to exogenous shocks varies among individuals.[2] Rather than a universal "aha moment" across the population, only a segment of the movement rationally adapted to the new reality. Most of its leadership continued to articulate the previous version of the appropriate borders of the homeland despite the reality of the state's existence.

At the same time, the actual impact of new realities on the fundamental aspects of nationalism still depended on the political selection process. Early adapters could shift the pattern of articulation of the movement as a whole only to the extent that they were politically successful, maintained their leadership positions, and eliminated competing views. These apparently necessary conditions may be related to the new reality, but they do not have to be. In the one instance of rational adaptation in the Israeli context, local, contingent political factors played a more important role in the spread of the change than the exogenous shock that triggered the adaptation. Integrating the lesson from the evolutionary dynamic that politics exerts an important, perhaps even *the* important, selection pressure would improve the analytical utility of rational adaptation even if the evolutionary dynamic itself does not trigger the particular change under consideration.

Elite imposition played a slightly larger direct role than rational adaptation in causing transformations in nationalist ideologies: it accounted for the empirical benchmarks of one of the completed changes and is the most plausible explanation, to date, of two of the ongoing transformations. The importance of these instances notwithstanding, the relatively small explanatory power of elite imposition suggests that the expectation that nationalist leaders routinely manipulate nationalist ideology to suit their interests is too strongly stated.

Even when elite imposition was responsible for the changes that took place, it was not through the top-down imposition of a new ideology by existing leaders, as we might have expected. Rather, elite imposition took place when new elites, articulating different answers to foundational questions, took over a movement's leadership. When these more or less hostile takeovers succeeded, the movement as a whole came to articulate the new ideological perspective. Here again, local, often picayune politics, this time at the intramovement level, played the crucial mediating role of selecting between success and failure.

The relative empirical weakness of elite imposition is surprising given the low bar for its operation provided by the strongly hierarchical Revisionist movement, in which power and decision-making were highly concentrated in the hands of a charismatic leader. Revisionist Zionist nationalism, however, evolved rather than changing in response to elite imposition. Moreover, even when a highly mobilized group self-consciously and intentionally imposed its new ideological variant on a movement, it could not do so at will. As we saw in chapter 2, Gush Emunim's failure to impose its territorial vision on the rest of the Religious Zionist movement, despite Gush Emunim's successful modification of the way Religious Zionism understood its national mission, suggests that, in at least a subset of cases, the evolutionary dynamic can trump the concerted efforts of political leaders whose activities point in different directions.

Another implication of the finding that mundane domestic politics exerted the most important selection pressure is that, at least for the study of nationalism and change, we should frame the analysis at the level of the nationalist movement. Framing the analysis at this level rather than at the more conventional "national" or individual level takes advantage of the fact that the most consequential political competition takes place within nationalist movements and among them. This is not to say that competition does not take place at the other levels. It does. Individuals compete for the survival of their beliefs, and the national idea (however defined) competes with other—religious, imperial, local, and so on—forms of identification and social organization. The nested character of political phenomena like nationalism allows us, however, to choose the level of analysis where invariance emerges, where the "confusion, noise, or random variation at one level resolves itself into systematic patterns."[3] Framing the analysis at the level of the nationalist movement allows us to resolve the sometimes apparently random and inconsistent actions of individual political entrepreneurs into a systematic pattern of change. Such a frame for analysis allows us to navigate between the twin dangers of a priori limiting too much the potential variation in the ways in which the nations are imagined and of taking such variation too far.

The important role of mundane domestic politics also implies that big outcomes are not necessarily the result of big causes. This conclusion challenges the frequent argument, made using Martin Seliger's distinction between fundamental and operative aspects of ideology, that all ideological change remains at the operative or tactical level. According to this view, fundamental ideological tenets, by definition, cannot change. Empirically, however, such change does take place. The evolutionary dynamic shows how. Because they are subject to the increasing returns to short-term political success, small modifications to the operative ideology can lead to the transformation of fundamental ideological tenets.[4]

The evolutionary dynamic's explicit attention to variation means that it is well placed to explain the waxing and (potential) waning of nationalism, as well as change in its meaning. While this book argues for the plausibility of the evolutionary dynamic in accounting for change in the meaning of nationalism once it was created, there is no reason a similar logic could not account for its origins. Nationalism emerged from a contest with other ways of organizing society and continues to face challenges to its supremacy. Looking into the future, the evolutionary dynamic predicts that, facing competition from religious fundamentalisms and supranational entities such as the European Union, the continued appeal of nationalism depends on the undirected by-products of the political contests between advocates of these different ways of organizing political society.

Finally, two notes of caution: despite its utility, the evolutionary dynamic is not an analytical panacea. To begin with, it is inherently backward-looking. Given a range of variation, it can identify the changes only ex post facto. Even if we could identify all of the factors that exercise selection pressure, the dominant role played by politics means that change is inherently chaotic. Simply put, there is no way to know ex ante who will win the political battles within and among nationalist movements that determine the fate of ideological variants. As a result, while we might use the evolutionary dynamic to predict the kinds of struggles that are likely to take place and their potential by-products, we should resist the temptation to use it to predict the outcomes of those struggles.

The evolutionary dynamic is also limited to those times and places characterized by variation in the answers offered to foundational questions, competition among the movements offering these different answers, and retention of the ideals they espouse. Where and when any one of these criteria is missing, the evolutionary dynamic cannot account for change. Even if these conditions hold, the evolutionary dynamic may not actually account for all changes. In the Israeli case, for example, intentional mechanisms drove nearly a third of the instances of change (completed and ongoing). It is possible that this distribution of mechanisms reflects the distribution more broadly. While there are good theoretical reasons to think that the evolutionary dynamic is likely to play some, perhaps significant, role in explaining foundational changes elsewhere, there is no way to know what the distribution of explanations for changes in the meaning of nationalism is more broadly without replicating the empirical testing of mechanisms in a wider array of contexts.

Evolving Nationalism in Other Contexts

To illustrate the potential portability of the evolutionary dynamic, the next two sections briefly sketch ways in which it might be used to explain ideological transformations in Palestinian and Turkish nationalism. Such deeply divided societies represent arenas in which the evolutionary dynamic is likely to operate because, by definition, no single definition of the nation-state reigns, and, as a result, their nationalisms are likely to be characterized by variation, competition, and retention. Returning to a theme raised in chapter 4, a third section suggests that the evolutionary dynamic may be useful beyond the context of nationalism and outlines some of its implications for engaging with religious fundamentalist movements.

Palestinian Nationalism

Even as all Palestinian nationalist movements share a desire for independence, they are divided by substantial disagreements over the extent and character of the longed-for state. This variation—along with the influence of foreign powers, geographical dispersion, and mundane personal ambitions—shapes an intense Palestinian politics. Given the existence of variation, retention, and competition among rival Palestinian nationalist movements, the evolutionary dynamic is well poised to explain the past transformations in the definition of the appropriate membership of the Palestinian nation and the contours (but not the outcomes) of the struggles over the relationship between Palestinian nationalism and Arab nationalism, the appropriate role of the Palestinian Diaspora in a Palestinian state, and the appropriate role of religion in the public realm, among other transformations.

The evolutionary dynamic also appears to offer a better potential explanation than the alternatives of the acceptance of a two-state solution by the historically dominant Palestinian nationalist movement. Most explanations of this shift in the area claimed as appropriately part of the nation's state attribute it to rational adaptation. Indeed, many of the individuals who were part of it portray their change of heart (in retrospect) as an adjustment to the reality of Israel's existence.[5] However, a more systematic exploration of the ability of rational adaptation to account for the timing, direction, object, and process of the change from the claim of the entire British Mandate to a claim of the West Bank and Gaza Strip reveals some unresolved questions.

The timing of the change poses a particular problem for an explanation based on rational adaptation. If the transformation was a response to the reality of Israel's existence, what accounts for the lag between its creation in 1948 and the onset of change in the 1970s? In other words, why did the rational adaptation not begin in the aftermath of the Nakba (the catastrophe) in 1948–49? It is hard to imagine a greater exogenous shock than the destruction of nearly 430 Palestinian villages and towns; the expulsion, flight, and dispersal of their populations; and the concomitant establishment of the state of Israel on the ashes of the Palestinian dream. Nonetheless, as in the case of the Holocaust for the Zionist movements, there is little evidence that the Nakba triggered a transformation in the ways in which Palestinian nationalists viewed the extent of their homeland. Indeed, with the notable exceptions of the Palestinian Communist Party and those Palestinians who became Israeli citizens, none of the Palestinian nationalist movements accepted the partition in 1949. If anything, the formative experience of exile had the opposite effect, giving birth to the notion of *sumud* (steadfastness) and a more militant and active pursuit of nationalist goals by Palestinian movements.

It is of course possible that other shocks triggered the acceptance of partition. Potential candidates include Israel's invasion of Lebanon and the exile of the Palestinian leadership to Tunis in 1982, the fall of the Soviet Union, and the repercussions of the first Gulf War. Even if we granted that these smaller shocks could trigger what the big one could not, they occur too late to account for the onset of the transformation. While the 1967 war is closer to the timing of the onset of change, the fact that the PLO adopted a different formula in its wake, that of a "secular democratic state" that maintained the claim to the entire territory of "historic Palestine," undermines the war's plausibility as the trigger of change in the acceptable borders of the Palestinian state.

Even if an exogenous shock could be found that accounted for the timing and direction of change, an explanation based on rational adaptation would still be challenged by the fact that even once the change began, only some Palestinian nationalists, led by parts of Fateh and the Democratic Front for the Liberation of Palestine (DFLP), appeared to adapt to the reality of Israel's existence. One does not have to go the ranks of the Islamist opposition to find variation in the object of change. Significant segments of the PLO continued to oppose the willingness to settle for "partial liberation" even as an intermediary step. Rational adaptation cannot explain the existence and strength of the Rejection Front, led at the time by the Popular Front for the Liberation of Palestine (PFLP), without making the unsustainable assumption that the rationality of the members of the PFLP and the Islamists systematically differs from that of the members of Fateh and the DFLP.

The actual process of change also seems to be more consistent with the expectations of the evolutionary dynamic than with those of intentional mechanisms. Rather than an open and consistent transformation, the acceptance of a truncated Palestine took place haltingly, unevenly, and over the course of fifteen years. The presumed architects of the change (especially Yasser Arafat) were notoriously inconsistent both in their articulation of support for a two-state solution and in their actions. As Rashid Khalidi asked,

> If the Palestinians had adopted diplomacy as their main means of struggle by the late 1970s, why were they still apparently attached to the rhetoric of armed struggle over a decade later? Even after the PLO abjured violence in 1988...there still appeared to be some reticence on its part on this score, raising questions about Palestinian good faith....If the Palestinians wanted to make peace with Israel within its 1967 frontiers, why were militant Palestinian groups killing Israeli civilians within these borders? If the problem was occupation (and not the existence of Israel itself) why was the occupation itself not the sole target of Palestinian attacks?[6]

While these inconsistencies may have their own guiding logic, it is difficult to make them congruent with a rational mechanism of ideological change. Some have tried to do so by arguing that the leaders of the PLO are somehow constitutionally unable to make the switch and fully accept the end of the armed struggle against Israel. Thomas Friedman, for example, argued that Arafat could not descend from the heights of revolution to the mundane grind of governance.[7] In a similar vein, Rashid Khalidi answers his own questions with the conclusion that the PLO leadership did not "understand the limits of violence....Given their age, their background, and their experiences, the PLO leadership was manifestly incapable of undertaking such a transformation."[8]

Unfortunately, the absence of reason that this attributes to the PLO's leadership is inconsistent with the notion that they were "rationally" adapting. As importantly, this answer also makes an unnecessary assumption about their mind-set. While this assessment of the psychology of the PLO's leadership may be true, actually verifying it requires the kinds of clinical insight into their thoughts and personalities that are not usually available to scholars of nationalism. In any case, as we have seen, the evolutionary dynamic does not need to assume anything on this score one way or another. Other things being equal, we should prefer the mechanisms that require fewer unverifiable assumptions.

The evolutionary dynamic can incorporate the inconsistencies in the pattern of articulation and between actions and words because it does not expect a consistent transformation. In terms of the timing of change, the evolutionary dynamic would expect the onset of the transformation to correspond to the articulation of ideological adjustments in response to the political necessities of the time. Perhaps the claim that King Hussein staked to the West Bank in March 1972 and the rising influence of the West Bank and Gaza Palestinians within the PLO prompted its leadership to emphasize their claim to the territories at the (unintended) expense of the claim to all of Palestine. Indeed, the resolutions of the 12th Palestinian National Council (PNC) in 1974 reflected this mix of pressures in the council's call for the establishment of an "independent combatant national authority for the people over every part of Palestinian territory *that is liberated*."[9] As Muhammad Muslih notes, this was a dramatic, if subtle, break from the PNC's previous position, given "the repeated and vociferous rejections of the 'ministate' [idea] and the principle of partition, even as an interim stage."[10]

Consistent with the expectations of the evolutionary dynamic, this adjustment was not understood at the time as a significant ideological change. Rather, its advocates portrayed it as a short-term tactical measure, while the end goal remained "the liberation of all Palestinian soil." The "constructive ambiguity" of the formula used in 1974 initially allowed the competing movements within the PLO to interpret it in different ways. As we saw in the discussion of Israeli nationalisms, such ambiguity could have masked the movement of the national goalposts. Thus, by 1977, for the first time, the PNC resolutions did not mention the idea of "total liberation." Instead, the PNC called for an "independent national state on their own land." By 1981, the PNC resolutions called for "the establishment of their own independent state on the soil of the homeland under the leadership of the PLO."[11] The notion that the end goal of Palestinian nationalism was a Palestinian state, even if on only part of the homeland, was becoming entrenched within the movement. In the aftermath of the first Gulf War, when the position of Fateh's leadership became dependent on the projection of a moderate image, this once-tactical adjustment became even more widespread. The spread throughout the movement of the idea that the Palestinian state could be constituted in part of the homeland was not inevitable. To increase the confidence that the evolutionary dynamic actually accounted for this, the political struggles between the consensus builders that advocated this adjustment and the truth tellers who opposed it would have to be traced (both within Fateh and between it and rival nationalist movements).

It is of course possible that the inconsistencies between the PLO's rhetoric and action reflect an underlying reality in which its acceptance of a two-state solution is merely a sophisticated ploy to cover an ongoing desire to replace Israel with Palestine. While further research needs to be carried out in order to judge the empirical veracity of this possibility, the discussion so far raises two relevant points. First, even if it is accurate, this observation does not undermine the relative merit of the evolutionary dynamic to account for change, since it posits that there is nothing to explain. Second, and more important, the evolutionary dynamic suggests that initial motives are not the most important determinants of fundamental change in the meaning of nationalism. To spread within the movement, perhaps to the point of becoming the new orthodoxy, the initially tactical adjustment has to achieve the short-term political goals in whose name it was crafted and its proponents have to defeat its opponents within the movement. That is, foundational change may take place regardless of the desires of the leaders who introduce the adjusted version of their claims.

One might apply a similar perspective to the recent apparent willingness of Hamas to accept the existence of Israel within the June 4, 1967, borders. These rhetorical modulations do not reflect a principled acceptance of Israel. They are intended for external consumption and to maintain Hamas's position vis-à-vis Fateh in the context of a Palestinian public that (still) overwhelmingly supports a two-state solution. The evolutionary dynamic suggests, however, that Hamas's intentions are not a good predictor of the ultimate outcome. Its refusal to recognize Israel may change in the long run despite its current intentions if it achieves the short-term goals whose pursuit led to this adjustment. The likelihood of the evolution of Hamas's vision of the homeland will increase if the adjustment is anchored in a vehicle (perhaps a Palestinian national unity government) whose political success would provide positive returns to the once-tactical position.

Turkish Nationalism

Turkey's nationalism has also been characterized by variation, competition, and retention. Territorially speaking, the extent of the homeland has at times and for some movements included all the lands of the Ottoman Empire, Cyprus, the Hatay region (now in Syria), and/or parts of the Caucasus, the lower Volga, and the Crimea in addition to the Anatolian peninsula. Conflicts over the appropriate membership in the Turkish political community most often erupt in the context of the Kurdish question, but various Turkish nationalist movements have articulated a Sunni definition of membership (which excludes the large Alevite minority), as well as Pan-Ottoman, Pan-Islamic, and Pan-Turanic varieties. This variation, and the open competition in the post–World War I period and again since the transition away from one-party rule beginning in 1950, raise the possibility that an evolutionary dynamic played a role in at least some of the changes in these dimensions.

A particularly interesting payoff of considering Turkish nationalism in light of the evolutionary dynamic is the latter's potential to illuminate aspects of the changing place of religion in Turkish national identity. Turkish nationalism, at least the version promulgated by Mustafa Kemal Atatürk, was fiercely secularist. Atatürk famously equated religion with backwardness, and the Kemalists attempted to eliminate religion as a factor in the public realm. They eradicated the caliphate, instituted the Western calendar in place of the Islamic one, and even replaced the sacred Arabic script with the Latin alphabet. Still today, the Turkish army—an institution that periodically intervenes in Turkish politics—sees itself as the guardian of Kemalism and its attendant secularism. How is it, then, that in Turkey of all places, a religious nationalist movement has dominated the country's politics for the last decade?

The conventional analyses of Turkish politics and society attribute the rise of Turkish political Islam to a swing of the pendulum from the Kemalists to the Islamists, with the latter simply gaining power at the expense of the former.[12] While there is certainly something to this story, to the extent that this explanation reifies both sides, it overlooks the important changes that have taken place in both the Islamist and the Kemalist versions of Turkish nationalism. Unlike their counterparts in the 1920s, the Islamists today no longer consider the appropriate extent of their political community to include all Muslims, but only those in the Anatolian peninsula. Contemporary Kemalism is also not identical to its former self, as it no longer articulates the same Westernizing, modernizing, and secularizing mission that it once did.

The reigning portrayal of these shifts as the products of the wholesale replacement of one ideology by another overstates the case. This perspective leads to the expectation that the shift in the Islamist ideology is simply a function of the Kemalists' success in imposing a new Turkish identity in place of the old Ottoman and Islamic one. Indeed, the victory of the Kemalists was nearly as complete as political victories can be. The Islamists, however, did not conclude that the Kemalists were right after all and therefore adopted the secularist ideal. They did, however, adopt the Kemalist notions of Republican membership in the polity.[13] Rational adaptation cannot account for change in one ideological dimension and the simultaneous stability in the other dimensions of nationalist ideology, since the impact of the Kemalists on all facets of Turkish nationalism was equally strong. While further research is needed to substantiate the hypothesis, the evolutionary dynamic raises the possibility that, like the reaction of the Revisionist Zionists to the victory of the Labor movement, the Islamists might have adjusted

(margin notes) Kemalists to Islamists ↓ both have undergone changes

Islamists accepted Kemalist idea of membership ↓ short-term tactic part of their ideology as a short-term tactic needed to stay alive in difficult circumstances. As this modulation succeeded, their survival and ability to pursue their religious nationalist mission became dependent on accepting the Republican notion of membership.

Explaining any transformation in the ideology of the dominant Turkish nationalist movement is also difficult for both elite imposition and rational adaptation mechanisms. From the perspective of the former, it is not clear what benefit would accrue to leaders already at the top for adopting a more open attitude toward religion in the public realm when the legitimacy of the regime was partly based on its claim to modern secularism. From the perspective of the latter, it is not obvious what exogenously derived new reality would force a greater acceptance of religion in the public realm.

The evolutionary dynamic raises the possibility that the onset of this transformation lies in the unintended consequences of the 1974 coalition between the Republican People's Party (RPP, the party founded by Atatürk) and the National Salvation Party (NSP, the main Islamist party at the time). From a strict Kemalist perspective, this was an odd alliance. However, the cooperation between the political heirs of Atatürk and the Islamists was not a sign of the former's increased religiosity. It was a tactical reaction to the perception that the RPP had moved too far to the left with its adoption of a social democratic platform. Facing a choice between a coalition with the socialists, which would have reinforced this perception, or with the Islamists, who were not associated with the Left, the RPP opted for the latter. This fostered, perhaps unintentionally, a more tolerant attitude toward politicized Islam. The fact that the Islamists were virtually the only group in Turkish society not tainted by the violence of the late 1970s further widened the space created for religion in the public realm. The military's 1982 affirmation of Islam as the social glue of Turkish society thus makes sense, because Kemalism had already been modified to allow much more space for religion in the public realm than its earlier secular crusaders did.[14] Moreover, the nationalization of "traditional" religious practice and the military's use of religion to reintegrate Turkish society in the early 1980s legitimated the notion that it was possible both to be a good Turk and to allow religion into the public square.[15] While the evolutionary dynamic has the potential to provide a more nuanced explanation of this shift than the alternatives, additional work is still necessary to determine if it actually does so.

Evolving Fundamentalism

One of the nonnationalist contexts in which the evolutionary dynamic may be useful is the question of how democratic states should cope with the rise of fundamentalist movements. Here too the evolutionary dynamic helps us disentangle two equally plausible intuitions. On the one hand, it makes sense that movements will moderate their ideologies as a result of political engagement. Since politics is the art of the possible, even fundamentalists will choose among various parts of their agenda, effectively sidelining some demands in favor of other, perhaps more moderate ones. This plausible notion, however, contradicts the equally intuitive one, raised by Crawford Young among others, that "mobilized identities alter less readily than do unmobilized ones";[16] and its more radical corollary (underlying the Bush Doctrine) that since such movements are unlikely to change fundamental aspects of their ideology, they have to be fought at every turn.

The evolutionary dynamic helps us reconcile these logical but contradictory perspectives. It suggests that radical movements are unlikely to moderate their views in response to exogenous shocks like a military defeat by an outside power. At the same time, it also complicates the argument that democracies should co-opt fundamentalist movements into the political game. Participation in politics does increase the likelihood that movements will engage in what they believe are temporary, even insincere adjustments of their basic claims. If these adjustments pay political dividends, they may eventually displace the original version, thereby engineering an actual ideological transformation. However, the probabilistic character of this dynamic means that political engagement on its own does not guarantee that change will take place. Actual transformation depends on the inherently chaotic and contingent political prospects of the consensus builders within these movements and of the movements that then articulate these adjustments. Nor does political engagement guarantee that change will necessarily lead to moderation; the direction of change depends on the particular character of the variant that emerges. (An adjustment undertaken to enable an alliance with more radical rivals, for example, is unlikely to lead to moderation.) Finally, the multidimensionality of identity politics also suggests that even if democratic engagement leads to change in one ideological dimension, it is unlikely to do so in all of them. In the Israeli case, for example, the alliance between secular nationalists and religious nationalists did lead to the latter's moderation of the territory they claimed as the homeland. In return, however, they were able to impose their religious influence on the public realm. To the extent that such trade-offs are not uniquely Israeli, they suggest that the "democratic cure" may have potentially severe side effects.

Evolving Nationalism and Conflict Resolution

The resolution of nationalist conflicts (as opposed to their management) requires changing precisely the kind of deep-seated ideological beliefs that this book explored. Most conflict resolution approaches, however, assume that such changes come about through a process of rational adaptation. Uri Savir, former director general of Israel's Foreign Ministry and one of the architects of the Oslo Accords, articulated this common belief when he explained that the role of peacemaking is to reset "perceptional clocks" in order to counteract the "psychological jet lag" of long-standing perceptions.[17] The findings of this book suggest, however, that at the very least the relationship between peacemaking and perceptual change is reciprocal: ideological change may have to begin (usually because of unrelated, or at least not necessarily related, domestic political dynamics) before peacemaking can succeed.

More broadly, the demonstration that nationalist movements tend not to be rationally adaptive organisms automatically reacting to their environment undermines conflict-resolution strategies that are based on the assumption that rational adaptation drives change. Similarly, the related logic that only a series of costly defeats can convince a nationalist movement to relinquish cherished claims may make intuitive sense, but its underlying assumption that the mechanism that brings this about is a purposive and rational adaptation to a changing reality does not necessarily hold. For this reason, policies such as the settlement project in the territories and the wall currently being built by Israel—whatever their impact on the probability of a political settlement between Israelis and Palestinians—are unlikely on their own to lead to a changed image of the appropriate territorial borders of the nation-state held by either Israeli or Palestinian nationalists.

This helps explain the inconsistent record of partition in resolving nationalist conflicts. By itself, partition (as any exogenous shock) is unlikely to drive change. Combatants and rival nationalist movements are likely to continue to desire the amputated land and to wait for the opportunity to liberate it. Where domestic politics, however, leads to short-term adjustments of territorial claims that are consistent with the new territorially possible borders and that succeed in achieving their shorter-term aims, the shape of the homeland can change. This process took (and is still taking) place among Israelis and Palestinians. The transformation of what the combatants involved in a nationalist conflict see as "the land" over which they are fighting undermines the refrain that we heard from Ben-Gurion and Said at the beginning of the book. Whatever obstacles exist to making peace between Israelis and Palestinians, the immutability of the homeland is not one of them. To be sure, the potential for change does not make peace between Israelis and Palestinians inevitable. It does, however, make it possible.

In fact, the dominance of the evolutionary dynamic can even serve as a source of guarded optimism in this regard. Scholars, pundits, and politicians routinely argue that the resolution of deeply entrenched inter- and intra-national conflict can only be accomplished "after the passing of generations." This pronouncement depends on the hidden assumption that the ideological change that is required for the real resolution of conflict over foundational issues necessarily takes a long time and that reality has to change before ideology does. As table 3 shows, however, this intuitive assessment underestimates the actual pace of ideological change. At least in these instances, ideological change took place in a much shorter time span than that between different generational cohorts. While there is no doubt that generational replacement (like any exogenous factor) can reinforce ideological transformation, it is not required to bring it about. Instead, where nationalism evolves, the pace of change is more closely linked to the rate at which alliances between movements with different answers to foundational questions are formed, achieve their short-term political goals, and marginalize the internal opponents of the modulations needed to make these alliances possible.

The role of the evolutionary dynamic in bringing fundamental changes about in the Israeli context also suggests, however, that if support for a two-state solution does not become a successful political strategy, its advocates are likely to lose the political contest. To the extent that this takes place, alternative Palestinian and Israeli visions of the homeland that are less conducive to a peaceful resolution of the conflict between them are likely to become more prominent. On the Israeli side, if Israelis lose hope that the painful acquiescence in the two-state solution will provide a secure and demographically Jewish Israel, opponents of the two-state solution will gain strength. This may account for the rise in the popularity of unilateral actions in place of a negotiated settlement. On the Palestinian side, if the equally painful acceptance of a truncated Palestine by the PLO does not actually lead to the establishment of a Palestinian state, we can expect it to be challenged by other alternative map images of the homeland. Indeed, the rise of Hamas, on the one hand, and the apparent resurgence of the "secular democratic state" idea, on the other, suggest that this might already be taking place.

In any case, the evolutionary story does not stop here. In fact, it has no end. The answers to the foundational questions defining the political community will continue to evolve in Israel and elsewhere. The direction in which they go depends on the everyday politics of the people whose imagination is up for grabs.

Notes

Nationalism, Change, and Evolution

1. Cited in Segev, *One Palestine, Complete*, 116.

2. Edward Said, "The One-State Solution: Why the Only Answer to Middle East Peace Is Palestinians and Israelis Living as Equal Citizens under One Flag," *New York Times Magazine*, January 10, 1999.

3. A limited sample might include the following: the change in the definition of national membership in France and Britain, which originally excluded Protestants and Catholics, respectively, to a civic, territorial definition (at least as the ideal) (Marx, *Faith in Nation*); the change in German national identity from an identity based mainly on culture to one in which racial codes were more prominent, and then back again (Eisenstadt and Geisen, "The Construction of Collective Identity"). The shifting role of race in defining national membership in the United States (Basson, *White Enough to Be American?*); the changes in the geographical scope of the German, Spanish, and Armenian homelands (Llobera, *The God of Modernity*, Lang, *Armenia*); and the exclusion of Bangladesh and Pakistan, once an integral part of India, from the claims of Indian nationalists (Nanda, "Nehru, the Indian National Congress and the Partition of India").

4. A partial exception to this trend is Brubaker, *Nationalism Reframed.* The inattention to mechanisms of change is not unique to scholarship about nationalism. It also characterizes studies of social boundaries more generally. See Tilly, "Social Boundary Mechanisms"; Lamont and Molnar, "Study of Boundaries in the Social Sciences."

5. Amos Oz, "Behind the Sound and Fury," *Tikkun*, 1998: 57, original emphasis.

6. The so-called Uganda proposal was a short-lived idea floated by British Colonial Secretary Joseph Chamberlain to provide a refuge for the Jews in part of today's Kenya. While the 1903 Zionist Congress decided to explore the issue, opposition by the Zionists within the Congress was so strong that little came of the idea. The 1905 Zionist Congress formally rejected the idea.

7. I say "more or less" because there is a consensus within the Labor movement that any agreement with the Palestinians should involve some limited modifications of the armistice line.

8. Medding, *Mapai in Israel;* Gorni, *Ahdut-ha-avodah* [Ahdut Haavoda]; Shapiro, *Formative Years of the Israeli Labor Party;* Ben-Avram, *Miflagot u-zeramim politiyim bitkufat ha-bayit ha-le'ummi* [Political Parties and Organizations during the British Mandate for Palestine]; Avizohar, *Be-re'i saduk* [Broken Mirror]; Sternhell, *Founding Myths of Israel.*

9. Ben-Hur, *Kol yachid hu melech* [Every Individual a King].

10. Shavit, *ha-Mitologyot shel ha-yamin* [The Mythologies of the Zionist Right Wing], 207.

11. Shapiro, *Road to Power,* 2.

12. Rael Jean Isaac, quoted in Peleg, *Begin's Foreign Policy, 1977–1983,* 31. See also Mark Segal, "Herut Brings Down the Roof," *Jerusalem Post,* July 8, 1966.

13. Smith, "Gastronomy or Geology?" 4. Smith cites the work of Karl Deutsch, Elie Kedourie, J. H. Kautsky, Hugh Seton-Watson, Tom Nairn, and Charles Tilly as falling into this category. Other examples include Smith, *Theories of Nationalism;* Gellner, *Nations and Nationalism;* Anderson, *Imagined Communities;* Connor, "A Nation Is a Nation"; Greenfeld, *Nationalism;* Alter, *Nationalism.*

14. Adler, "Cognitive Evolution," 55. For more general instances of this assumption, see North, "Transaction Cost Theory of Politics"; Krasner, "Approaches to the State"; Eagleton, *Ideology: An Introduction,* 30–31; Seliger, *Ideology and Politics;* Eckstein, "Culturalist Theory of Political Change"; Tilly, "Social Boundary Mechanisms." For a more nuanced perspective that still falls within this broad approach, see Hall, "Policy Paradigms, Social Learning, and the State."

15. For examples of the use of globalization or industrialization, see Gellner, *Nationalism;* Hechter, *Internal Colonialism;* Ram, "Postnationalist Pasts"; Greenfeld, *Nationalism,* 490; Peled and Shafir, "Roots of Peacemaking," 394; Aharoni, "Changing Political Economy of Israel"; Nitzan and Bichler, "From War Profits to Peace Dividends"; Scholte, "Geography of Collective Identities in a Globalizing World." For a critique of the use of globalization or industrialization in the end of ideology debate, see Arian, *Ideological Change in Israel.* For examples of the use of demographic changes in this capacity, see Deutsch, *Nationalism and Social Communication;* Brubaker, *Citizenship and Nationhood in France and Germany,* 125; Banton, *Racial and Ethnic Competition.* For the use of superpower diktats in this capacity, see Meyer et al., "World Society and the Nation-State"; Raanan, *Frontiers of a Nation;* Galnoor, *Partition of Palestine,* 41. For examples of the use of war or catastrophe in this capacity, see Schuman and Rieger, "Historical Analogies, Generational Effects, and Attitudes toward War"; Haas, *Nationalism, Liberalism, and Progress;* Liebman and Don-Yehiya, *Civil Religion in Israel,* 223; Ram, "National, Ethnic, or Civic?"; Baumel, "Bridging Myth and Reality"; Smooha, "Implications of the Transition to Peace."

16. Introduction to Hobsbawm and Ranger, *Invention of Tradition,* 13. Hobsbawm's claim is relatively nuanced. He notes that "conscious invention succeeded mainly in proportion to its success in broadcasting on a wavelength to which the public was ready to tune in." Hobsbawm, "Mass-Producing Traditions," 263; see also 307. For other examples, see Lustick, *Unsettled States, Disputed Lands;* Price, "Race and Reconciliation in the New South Africa"; Seliger, *Ideology and Politics,* 248–51; Sewell, "Ideologies and Social Revolutions."

17. Wallerstein, "Construction of Peoplehood," 77.

18. Thompson, "Nations, National Identities, and Human Agency," 24.

19. Wodak et al., *Discursive Construction of National Identity,* 4.

20. Banton, *Racial and Ethnic Competition,* 100. For other examples from a variety of perspectives, see Hobsbawm and Ranger, *Invention of Tradition;* Hawkins, "Discovery of Rural England"; Haas, "Reason and Change in International Life"; Hardin, *One for All;* Guha, *Dominance without Hegemony.*

21. This point was made by Seliger, *Ideology and Politics,* 172.

22. For example, Michael Hechter speaks in terms of the "blurring" of cultural identities and the "gradual replacement" of local cultures by a national one but does not elaborate how "blurring" or "gradual replacement" take place. Hechter, *Internal Colonialism,* 5. Ranajit Guha discusses Indian nationalism as "maturing" but does not specify what this means. Guha, *Dominance without Hegemony,* 150. Victor Kiernan, too, extrapolates a process of ideological

"blending" but does not suggest how this might take place. Kiernan, "State and Nation in Western Europe," 32. Margaret Canovan argues that change takes place as a result of "myriad acts and opinions," but does not explore what these acts might be. Canovan, *Nationhood and Political Theory,* 55. Because she does not delve into the mechanisms of change, she makes such statements as "Nationhood is always fluid" (80), which in large measure conflict with her rejection of subjectivist conclusions. Aletta Norval argues that "changes in political frontiers result from complex processes of interaction of different and opposing discourses," but does not identify what these "processes of interaction" might be. Norval, "Social Ambiguity and the Crisis of Apartheid," 122.

23. Billig, *Banal Nationalism,* 139, original emphasis.

24. Canovan, *Nationhood and Political Theory.*

25. See, for example, Banton, *Racial and Ethnic Competition;* Banton, "Modeling Ethnic and National Relations"; Posner, *Institutions and Ethnic Politics in Africa;* Hardin, *One for All;* Laitin, "Hegemony and Religious Conflict"; Laitin, *Identity in Formation;* Bates, "Modernization, Ethnic Competition, and the Rationality of Politics."

26. For example, even David Laitin's excellent study of identity formation frames the choices available to the populations he studies as either to "assimilate into a cosmopolitan culture or to seek fulfillment as a member of a separate nation." The option of redefining the content of "Estonian," for example, is not commonly available. Laitin, *Identity in Formation,* 245 n. 6.

27. See, for example, Bates, "Modernization, Ethnic Competition and the Rationality of Politics"; Trevor-Roper, "Invention of Tradition"; Rogowski, "Causes and Varieties of Nationalism"; Gagnon, "Ethnic Nationalism and International Conflict"; Van Evera, "Hypotheses on Nationalism and War"; Snyder and Ballentine, "Nationalism and the Marketplace of Ideas"; Hroch, "From Ethnic Group toward the Modern Nation"; Laclau and Mouffe, *Hegemony and Socialist Strategy;* Meadwell, "Breaking the Mould?"; Sollors, *Invention of Ethnicity;* Snyder, *From Voting to Violence;* Hobsbawm, "Mass-Producing Traditions"; Breuilly, *Nationalism and the State.*

28. For different versions of this critique, see Smith, "Culture, Community, and Territory"; Anno, "Collective Identity as an 'Emotional Investment Portfolio,'"; Giuliano, "Who Determines the Self?"

29. Dawkins, *Selfish Gene;* Dennett, *Darwin's Dangerous Idea,* 343–44.

30. Kohn, "Nature of Nationalism," 1009; Berger and Luckmann, *Social Construction of Reality.* For a recent exploration of the implications of the contested character of identity, see Abdelal et al., *Measuring Identity.*

31. Billig, *Banal Nationalism,* 85; Sayyid, "Sign O' Times"; Calhoun, "Nationalism and Ethnicity"; Brubaker, *Nationalism Reframed,* 63 n. 12.

32. Anderson, *Imagined Communities,* 86, 159; Chatterjee, *Nation and Its Fragments.*

33. Hobsbawm, *Nations and Nationalism since 1780;* Brubaker, *Citizenship and Nationhood,* 163; Gelvin, *Divided Loyalties.*

34. Kedourie, *Nationalism;* Smith, *Theories of Nationalism.* For a review of the literature on civic and ethnic conception of the nations, see Smith, *Stories of Peoplehood,* 74–77.

35. Price, "Race and Reconciliation in the New South Africa"; Citrin et al., "Is American Nationalism Changing?"; Doak, "What Is a Nation and Who Belongs?"; Varshney, "Contested Meanings"; Hutchinson, *Nations As Zones of Conflict.*

36. Baldwin, "Power Analysis and World Politics."

37. Smith, *Stories of Peoplehood,* 92.

38. Thompson, "Nations, National Identities, and Human Agency," 24. For less radical versions of the search for the "microfoundations" of national identity, see Laitin, *Identity in Formation;* Wodak et al., *Discursive Construction of National Identity.*

39. The division between "truth tellers" and "consensus builders" is borrowed from Lustick, *For the Land and the Lord.*

40. For a discussion of ideologies as subject to increasing returns, see Denzau and North, "Shared Mental Models"; Pierson, "Increasing Returns, Path Dependence, and the Study of Politics."

41. This is also the logic that underwrites Ann Swidler's observation that "bursts of ideological activism occur in periods when competing ways of organizing action are developing or contending for dominance." Swidler, "Culture in Action," 279.

42. The mistaken interpretation of evolution offered by Social Darwinists misses both of these points.

43. The probabilistic character of evolution makes it difficult to predict particular outcomes. The exploration of ideological change in this book skirts this problem by focusing on the processes of transformation rather than their particular outcomes. The empirical benchmarks that I use to judge the relative plausibility of alternative explanations are benchmarks of processes rather than point predictors of particular events.

44. For a particularly strident example of this criticism, see Lewontin, Rose, and Kamin, *Not in Our Genes*.

45. Dennett, *Darwin's Dangerous Idea*, 318, 319.

46. Burian, "Adaptation: Historical Perspectives," 8.

47. For discussions of this methodology, see King, Keohane, and Verba, *Designing Social Inquiry*, 11–12, 109–12; Ragin, "Turning the Tables"; McKeown, "Case Studies and the Limits of the Quantitative Worldview." A similar methodology is also used in the context of debates about change in biological evolutionary. See Gould, "Tempo and Mode in the Macroevolutionary Reconstruction of Darwinism."

48. For examples of its use, see Greenfeld, *Nationalism*; Laclau, *Making of Political Identities*; Billig, *Banal Nationalism*; Smith, *Stories of Peoplehood*; Brecher, *Decisions in Israel's Foreign Policy*; Kimmerling, "Sociology, Ideology, and Nation Building"; Khalidi, *Palestinian Identity*.

49. Elon, *The Israelis*, 192–93.

50. Eban, *Personal Witness*, 301.

1. Labor Zionist Mapping of the Homeland

1. Anderson, in turn, bases his insight on the work of the historian Thongchai Winichakul. Anderson, *Imagined Communities*, 173–74, 175.

2. While the exact eastern border was variously interpreted within the Zionist movement as the Hejaz Railway or the Euphrates River, these differences were mainly tactical in nature regarding how to get as much as possible from the international community rather than representing ultimate goals. Raanan, *Frontiers of a Nation*; Galnoor, *Partition of Palestine*; Naor, *Eretz Yisrael ha-shelemah* [Greater Israel], 21.

3. Ben-Gurion and Ben-Zvi, *Eretz Yisrael ba-'avar uva-hoveh* [The Land of Israel in the Past and in the Present].

4. See David Ben-Gurion, "The Rights of the Jews and Others in Eretz Israel," "On the Borders of Eretz Israel," and "Our Political Path after the Events," in Ben-Gurion, *Anachnu u-shcheneinu* [Us and Our Neighbors].

5. The Zionist National Assembly in March 1920, quoted in Attias, *Sefer HaTeudot shel haVa'ad Haleumi leKnesset Yisrael B'eretz Yisrael: 1918–1948* [The Book of Documents of the National Assembly in Israel: 1918–1948], 16. The claim to Transjordan was also affirmed in the 12th (1921) and 13th (1923) Zionist Congresses. Galnoor, *Partition of Palestine*, 41; Katz, *Jabo—biyografyah shel Ze'ev Jabotinsky* [Jabo—A Biography], 589.

6. Bar-Gal, *Moledet ve-ge'ografyah be-me'ah shenot hinukh tsiyoni* [Homeland and Geography in a Hundred Years of Zionist Education]; Selushtz, *Ever ha-yarden* [Transjordan]; Jewish Agency Executive, meeting protocol, Central Zionist Archives (hereafter cited as CZA), S100/22b (October 3, 1937).

7. Ilan, *ha-Nisyonot li-rekhishat adamah ule-hityashvut Yehudit be-ever ha-Yarden ha-mizrahi, 1871–1947* [Attempts at Jewish Settlement in Trans-Jordan, 1871–1947]; Shapira, "Parashat ha-optzia al admot ha-emir Abdalla be-Ghur-el-Kabd" [The Option on the Emir's Land at Ghur-el-Kabd].

8. Levi Shkolnik (Eshkol) in Mapai Center, *Center Bulletin* #1(19), The Moshe Sharett Israel Labor Party Archives (hereafter cited as LPA), 2–2-1933–7 (April 24, 1933). See also Ilan, *Attempts at Jewish Settlement in Trans-Jordan*, 375–77; Mapai Center, meeting protocol, LPA, 2–23-1933–4 (February 5, 1933); Mapai Center, "Meeting with the Mapai Delegates to the Zionist Congress, Representatives of Branches in the Country, and Other Guests," LPA, 2–23-1933–5 (July 29, 1933); Jewish Agency Executive, meeting protocol, CZA, S100/14b (May 7, 1933); Jewish Agency Executive, meeting protocol, CZA, S100/15b (December 11, 1933).

9. David Ben-Gurion to Mapai, letter, LPA, 2–932-1933–4 (October 28, 1934). For other examples of Ben-Gurion's claim to Transjordan in the early 1930s, see his recollection of his talks with Malcolm MacDonald in 1931, Musa Alami in 1933, and George Antonius in 1936. Ben-Gurion, *Medinat Yisrael Ha-mechudeshet* [The Restored State of Israel], 56, 884. See also Hattis, *Bi-National Idea in Palestine*, 100; Bar-Eyal, "Eretz Hermonim ve-negev, yam u-midbar" [Land of Hermons and Negev, Sea, and Desert]; Teveth, *Ben-Gurion and the Palestinian Arabs*, 34–35; Avizohar and Bareli, *Akhshav o le-olam lo* [Now or Never], 80 n. 17.

10. Mapai Center, *Center Bulletin* #1(19), LPA, 2–2-1933–7 (April 24, 1933).

11. Mapai Center, protocol, LPA, 2–23-1933–4 (February 5, 1933). See also Mapai, "Protocol of 11th Mapai Party Council," LPA, 2–22-1937–20 (January 22–23, 1937).

12. Rachel Yanait, conversation with Mr. Doni, LPA, 2–201-1937–8 (May 19, 1937). See also Zionist Congress, *The Newspaper of the Congress: The Formal Organ of the 20th Zionist Congress, Zurich*, no. 1, LPA, 2–602-1937–10 (August 8, 1937); Berl Katznelson, address at the National Council of the Party in Tel Aviv about the Report of the Peel Commission, LPA, 2–2-1937–13 (July 10, 1937); Berl Katznelson, speech at the Unification Council in Zurich, LPA, 4–6-1936–126 (August 5, 1937); Yitzhak Tabenkin in Yishai, *Si'atiyut bi-tenu'at ha-'avodah* [Factionalism in the Labor Movement], 46; I. Lofben, "The Party Council," *Hapoel Hatzair*, July 20, 1937; see also the discussion in Mapai Central Committee, meeting protocol, LPA, 2–023-1937–16 (April 10, 1937); Mapai, "Protocol of 12th National Convention Dealing with How to Proceed after the Publication of the Peel Report," LPA, 2–22-1937–22 (July 9–11, 1937).

13. The theory of stages was a common thread among those who accepted the principle of partition but who still explicitly claimed Transjordan. Mapai Central Committee, protocol, LPA, 2–23-1937–16 (April 10, 1937). For a discussion of Ben-Gurion's theory of stages, see Shalom, "Emdot be-hanhagat ha-medina be-sugiyat ha-status-quo ha territoriali be-shanim ha-rishonot she leachar milhemet ha-atzmaut" [Positions of the Leadership of the State on the Issue of the Territorial Status Quo in the First Years after the War of Independence]; Bialer, "David Ben-Gurion veMoshe Sharett: Hitgabshut shtei orientatziot mediniyot-bitchoniyot bahevra hayisraelit" [David Ben-Gurion and Moshe Sharett]; Teveth, *Ben-Gurion and the Palestinian Arabs*, 187–90; Ben-Gurion, *Restored State of Israel*; David Ben-Gurion, diary entry, LPA, 2–201-1937–8 (May 15, 1937); Mapai, "Protocol of 12th National Convention," LPA, 2–22-1937–22; Mapai Central Committee, protocol, LPA, 2–23-1937–16 (April 10, 1937); Segev, *One Palestine, Complete*, 403; Jewish Agency Executive and the Political Committee of the Zionist Executive Council, meeting protocol, CZA, S100/24b (June 12, 1938); Ben-Gurion, quoted in Avizohar and Bareli, *Now or Never*, 80 (originally in a Mapai Council meeting, August 9, 1947) and 264 (originally at a Mapai Central Committee meeting, December 3, 1947).

14. Mapai Central Committee, protocol, LPA, 2–23-1937–16 (April 10, 1937), original emphasis; see also David Ben-Gurion, speech at the meeting of the Political Committee, LPA, 2–201-1937–8 (April 24, 1937).

15. Zionist Congress, *The Newspaper of the Congress: The Formal Organ of the 20th Zionist Congress, Zurich*, no. 5, LPA, 2–602-1937–10 (August 10, 1937), original emphasis.

16. Ben-Gurion in Mapai, "Protocol of 12th National Convention," LPA, 2–22-1937–22, original emphasis. Ben-Gurion reiterated this position in his address to the Mizrachi Convention. Finbron, *Devar anshe-shem 'al tokhnit ha-halukah* [Words of Notable People about Partition]. See also Shertok (Sharett) in Mapai Central Committee, meeting protocol, LPA, 2–23-1937–17 (July 5, 1937).

17. David Ben-Gurion to the Zionist Executive, letter, LPA, 2–201-1937–8 (June 22, 1937).

18. See, for example, Ben-Zvi and Berl Loker, respectively, in Mapai Central Committee, meeting protocol, LPA, 2–23-1938–19 (May 17, 1938).

19. Colonial Office Great Britain, "Palestine Royal Commission: Minutes of Evidence Heard at Public Sessions," Colonial no. 134 (1937), 60; Mapai, "Protocol of 11th Mapai Party Council," LPA, 2–22-1937–20.

20. Mapai, *Intelligence Reports,* LPA, 4–006-1936–327 (1938–1939).

21. Mapai leaders knew of the persecution of European Jewry as early as 1941 but tended to dismiss the scale of the news from Europe until the fall of 1942, when the first group of Holocaust survivors reached Palestine. Shapira, *Berl,* 318.

22. See Ben-Gurion, quoted in Avizohar, "Tochnit ha-medina etzel Ben-Gurion beshlav 'hazionut halochemet'" [Ben-Gurion's Militant Strategy for the Creation of a Jewish State], 126–27 n. 101.

23. Pinchas Lubyanker (Lavon), "Things Said at Explanation Meetings: The Questions That Are in Dispute," *Hapoel Hatzair,* August 3, 1944, my emphasis.

24. Shlaim, *Collusion across the Jordan,* 80; Sharett, *Besha'ar ha-ummot: 1946–1949* [At the Gate of Nations: 1946–1949], 50, originally on March 28, 1946.

25. Avizohar, "Ben-Gurion's Militant Strategy for the Creation of a Jewish State"; Galnoor, *Partition of Palestine,* 280; Shlaim, *Collusion across the Jordan,* 79; Zionist Organization, *Congrezion,* no. 11, LPA, 2–602-1946–15 (December 22, 1946); Heller, "Ha-mediniyut ha-tzionit ve-tochniyot ha-haluka shel E"I be-shnot ha-40" [Zionist Policy and the Partition Plans in the 1940s].

26. Ben-Gurion, "Zionist Policy"; Ben-Gurion, *Restored State of Israel,* 311, originally in October 31, 1948; Manor, "Dimuyim kabalat hachlatot ve-hizun hozer be-mediniyut ha-huts ha-Yisraelit" [Comparisons of Decision-Making and Feedback of Israeli Foreign Policy], 27, 47 n. 77; Mapai Center, Department of Diaspora Affairs and the Halutz, "Letter to Representatives," LPA, 2–2-1949–55 (May 6, 1949); Mapai Knesset Faction, "Protocol of Meeting with Party Center," LPA, 2–11-1949–1 (July 22, 1949).

27. Mapai Center, Propaganda Department, "Divrei Haverim: For Information and Internal Elucidation," LPA, 2–002-1947–37 (July 10, 1947); also Avizohar and Bareli, *Now or Never,* 64.

28. Sharett, *At the Gate of Nations,* 75, originally on June 17, 1947.

29. Galnoor, *Partition of Palestine,* 287; Mapai Center, Department of Diaspora Affairs and the Halutz, "Letter to Representatives," LPA, 2–002-1947–37 (December 10, 1947); Mapai Center, Organizing Committee for the Party's Branches in the Kibbutz Hameuchad, letter to the branches, LPA, 2–002-1947–37 (September 9, 1947).

30. See, for example, Mapai Center, meeting protocol, LPA, 2–23-1948–49 (May 11, 1948). See also the discussions in the Mapai Center on January 8, 1948, and in the Mapai Secretariat meetings on October 11, 1947, and October 21, 1947, in Avizohar and Bareli, *Now or Never,* 99, 177, 179, 287, 293, 490–91. See also Moshe Shertok (Sharett), "Speech at the Zionist Executive Council," *HaOlam,* August 26, 1948. During the government's meeting on August 1, 1948, Greenboim objected to Ben-Gurion's definition of "our country" as the land west of the Jordan—for him even this was too much. Ben-Gurion, *Restored State of Israel,* 249.

31. Examples of each can be found, respectively, in Mapai Council meeting, August 9, 1947, and Mapai Secretariat meeting, October 11, 1947, in Avizohar and Bareli, *Now or Never,* 80, 177.

32. Mapai Council, February 7, 1947, in Avizohar and Bareli, *Now or Never,* 332.

33. Mapai Center, September 2, 1947, in Avizohar and Bareli, *Now or Never,* 82.

34. Ben-Gurion, *Restored State of Israel,* 270, originally in September 1948.

35. Mapai, "Protocol of the 37th Party Council" LPA, 2–11-1949–21 (January 12–13, 1949).

36. See Sharett's testimony before the Anglo-American Commission of Inquiry on March 26, 1946; his address before UNSCOP on June 17, 1947; his speech to the "parallel committee" of the UN General Assembly on October 17 and November 24, 1947; and his comments to

the UN Security Council on February 27, 1948. Sharett, *At the Gate of Nations*. Golda Meir, in Avizohar and Bareli, *Now or Never*, originally in a Mapai Center meeting, September 2, 1947; Ben-Gurion and Ben-Zvi in Mapai Secretariat, meeting protocol, LPA, 2–24-1947–19 (June 11, 1947).

37. Shalom, "Positions of the Leadership of the State on the Issue of the Territorial Status Quo"; Peri, *Between Battles and Ballots*, 58.

38. Manor, "Dimuyim ve-kabalat ha-hlatot be-nose ha-gevulot bi-mediniyut ha-huts ha-Yisraelit, 1948–1973" [Images and Decision Making on the Boundaries Issue in Israeli Foreign Policy in the Years 1948–1973].

39. Mapai Center, "Letter to Representatives," LPA, 2–2-1949–55 (May 6, 1949).

40. Sharett, *At the Gate of Nations*, 304.

41. Mapai Knesset Faction, "Protocol of Meeting with the Party Executive," LPA, 2–11-1949–1 (July 28, 1949); Mapai Secretariat, "Protocol of Meeting with the Knesset Party Faction," LPA, 2–11-1950–8 (June 18, 1950).

42. See Sharett's report to the Provisional Government on November 4, 1948, and his report of Israel's position during the second truce in July 1949. Sharett, *At the Gate of Nations*, 264. The former instance is cited in Ben-Gurion, *Restored State of Israel*, 313. The same was true of Ben-Gurion's address to the graduates of the first graduating class of IDF company commanders. See Ben-Gurion, 316.

43. Shlaim, *Collusion across the Jordan*, 371, originally in December 22, 1948; Shalom, "Positions of the Leadership of the State on the Issue of the Territorial Status Quo," 127; Sharett, *At the Gate of Nations*, 368; Mapai Knesset Faction, meeting protocol, LPA, 2–11-1953–26 (November 10, 1953); Mapai Center, "Letter to Representatives," LPA, 2–2-1949–55 (May 6, 1949).

44. Quoted in Shalom, "Positions of the Leadership of the State on the Issue of the Territorial Status Quo," 144, original emphasis. See also Bar-On, "Status-quo lifnei o achrei?" [Status Quo Before—or After?]; Manor, "Images and Decision Making on the Boundaries Issue."

45. For example, Ben-Gurion and Sharett in Shalom, "Positions of the Leadership of the State on the Issue of the Territorial Status Quo," 127, 130; Mapai Knesset Faction, protocol, LPA, 2–11-1949–1 (July 28, 1949).

46. Shlaim, *Collusion across the Jordan*, 610–11; Bar-On, "Status Quo Before—or After?"

47. Dayan, *Story of My Life*, 215.

48. Miron, "Teuda be-yisrael" [A Document in Israel]; Naor, *Greater Israel*, 43 n. 57. There were, however, instances where territorial maximalists did imply that Transjordan was appropriately part of the Land of Israel. See, for example, Tabenkin, *Lekah sheshet ha-yamim* [The Lesson of the Six-Day War]; also Efraim Ben-Haim, "Temura ve-sikui" [Change and Possibility], 227.

49. Alterman, "Shalom ke-tahlit ve lo ke-tahlif" [Peace as the Substance and Not as an Alternative], 63–64, my emphasis.

50. ILP Center, meeting protocol, LPA, 2–24-1972–100 (September 9, 1972).

51. Beilin, *Mehiro shel ihud* [The Price of Unity], 61.

52. Chug Leshiluv of the ILP Center, "Proposal of the Workgroup for Peace and Security Policy: 2 Nations in 2 States," LPA, 2–14-1971–78 (March 1971); ILP Etgar (Challenge) Ideational Circle, "Platform for Discussion," LPA, 2–14-1972–79 (1972). Yehoshua Palmon in Central Ideational Circle, "Protocol of the Meeting of the Committee for Arab Affairs," LPA, 2–14-1970–49 (June 24, 1970); Maarach Leadership, meeting protocol, LPA, 2–28-1976–8 (May 19, 1976).

53. Mapai Secretariat, meeting protocol, LPA, 2–24-1968–93 (April 21, 1968). This became the official position in 1971. See ILP Convention, "Thinking Group of Socialist Zionism Recommendations," LPA, 2–21-1971–106 (February 1971).

54. Allon, *Kelim shluvim* [Communicating Vessels], 155, originally in November 1977; Allon in ILP Convention, meeting protocol, LPA, 2–21-1977–121 (February 24, 1977); ILP Center, The Preparatory Committee, Subcommittee for Political Matters, meeting protocol, LPA, 2–921-1976–341 (January 14, 1977); Allon, "Israel and the Palestinians"; Abba Eban,

working paper, LPA, 2–921-1976–431 (June 17, 1976). For other examples, see The Circle for Discussion of Problems of Society and State in the ILP, circular, LPA, 2–14-1974–75 (1974); M. Carmel in Maarach Leadership, protocol, LPA, 2–28-1976–8 (May 19, 1976); ILP Etgar (Challenge) Ideational Circle, "Platform for Discussion," 1972, LPA, 2–14-1972–79.

55. Avizohar, "Ben-Gurion's Militant Strategy."

56. Ben-Gurion, Ba-ma'arakhah [In the Struggle], 44, originally on October 15, 1942.

57. Ben-Gurion, In the Struggle, 144, original emphasis. For other acknowledgments of the tactical character of this maneuver, see Ben-Gurion, 69; Mapai, "The Zionist Political Plan of Mapai," LPA, 2–932-1945–75 (1942); Mapai Center, Ahdut Haavoda: The 5th Congress of the Party, at Kfar Vitkin, 1942 (Tel Aviv, 1943).

58. Galnoor, Partition of Palestine, 278. See also Beilin, Price of Unity; Yishai, Factionalism in the Labor Movement.

59. Ben-Gurion, In the Struggle, 102–7, originally in a Mapai Council meeting, January 1944.

60. Morris, "He'arot al ha-histografya ha-tsionit ve-ra'ayon ha-transfer ba-shanim 1937–1947" [Comments on Zionist Historiography and the Idea of Transfer in the Years 1937–1944], 196.

61. Heller, "Zionist Policy and the Partition Plans in the 1940s."

62. Originally on September 27, 1948. Quoted in Ben-Gurion, Restored State of Israel, 291.

63. Ben-Gurion, Restored State of Israel, 54. Even Ben-Gurion occasionally implied that Transjordan was distinct from the "Land of Israel." See "The Hebrew and the Arab Worker" and "Memo to the Shaw Commission" in Ben-Gurion, Us and Our Neighbors. There were also other instances of Labor leaders distinguishing between the Land of Israel and Transjordan as early as the late 1930s. See Dov Hoz's May 14 and 15, 1937, reports of his meetings with representatives of Abdullah. Avizohar and Friedman, Iyunim be-tokhniyot ha-halukah, 1937–1947 [Studies in the Palestine Partition Plans, 1937–1947].

64. Mapai Center, protocol, LPA, 2–23-1933–4 (February 5, 1933); Mapai Center, Center Bulletin #1(19), LPA, 2–2-1933–7 (April 24, 1933).

65. Mapai Center, Center Bulletin #1(19), LPA, 2–2-1933–7 (April 24, 1933); Mapai Executive, "Meeting of the Coalition Parties in the Zionist Executive," LPA, 2–23-1933–4 (January 24, 1933). Ben-Zvi in Mapai Center, protocol, LPA, 2–23-1933–4 (February 5, 1933).

66. Mapai Center, Center Bulletin #1(19), LPA, 2–2-1933–7 (April 24, 1933); Mapai Executive, "Meeting of the Coalition Parties," LPA, 2–23-1933–4 (January 24, 1933); Shlaim, Collusion across the Jordan, 49.

67. Shapira, "Option on the Emir's Land at Ghur-el-Kabd," 319–20, 330.

68. Eban, Personal Witness, 88. For an explicit articulation of this strategy, see Ben-Gurion, speech, LPA, 2–201-1937–8 (April 24, 1937).

69. See, for example, Heller, "Zionist Policy and the Partition Plans in the 1940s"; Kolatt, "Pulmus ha-haluka be-tnuat ha-avoda" [The Debate on Partition within the Labor Movement].

70. Zionist Organization, "Meeting of the Limited Zionist Executive Committee," LPA, 2–601-1938–15 (January 1, 1938). For other examples of the late claims of the original map image, see Mapai, "Protocol of 13th Party Council," LPA, 2–22-1939–26 (April 14, 1939); Joseph Bertz, "Twice in Transjordan," HaPoel Hatzair, April 21, 1939; Ilan, Attempts at Jewish Settlement in Trans-Jordan, 300; Bar-Eyal, "Land of Hermons and Negev, Sea, and Desert"; Shaked, "Eretz Moledet—Eretz Yisrael" [Land of Homeland—Land of Israel], 104.

71. In 1943, Ben-Gurion still defined the "historic borders of the land of Israel" as the borders of the Balfour Declaration, explicitly including Transjordan. Ben-Gurion, "Zionist Policy," 21, 29. He was also careful to speak of the "western Eretz Israel" and to highlight that he believed Transjordan to be part of the land (even if it had been temporarily cut off). Mapai Center, Ahdut Haavoda: The 5th Congress of the Party, at Kfar Vitkin, 1942. See also Ben-Gurion in Zionist Organization, Congrezion, no. 11, LPA, 2–602-1946–15 (December 22, 1946); Mapai Center, "Letter to Representatives," LPA, 2–2-1949–55 (May 6, 1949); see also Ben-Gurion's letters to De Gaulle in June 1960 and December 1967, quoted in Ben-Gurion, Restored State of Israel, 839–51. Ben-Zvi termed Etzel's reference to a state on both sides of the Jordan as "absurd" because it limited immigration, not because it was wrong. While Ben-Zvi was willing

to settle for less in the present, he asserted: "Of course, in the far future, for the days of the Messiah, I will not give up on Shchem nor on Transjordan." Mapai Secretariat, meeting protocol, LPA, 2-24-1947-19 (June 11, 1947). For examples of the claims to the area up to the Litani, see the discussion of Ben-Gurion and Allon in Manor, "Comparisons of Decision-Making and Feedback of Israeli Foreign Policy"; Manor, "Images and Decision Making on the Boundaries Issue." Other exceptions included occasional calls to take the Litani River because of Israel's water needs. In 1956, Ben-Gurion suggested that the Christian areas of Lebanon south of the Litani be annexed to Israel. Bar-On, "Status Quo Before—or After?" See also Peres in Golan, *Shimon Peres,* 79. In 1967 the IDF was authorized to conquer Southern Lebanon up to the Litani in the event that Lebanon entered the war. Oren, *Six Days of War.* For a short period between June 1956 and March 1957, the claim to the Sinai Peninsula became dominant within the party's leadership. Manor, "Images and Decision Making on the Boundaries Issue."

72. There is some evidence to suggest that this reshuffling was accomplished not by the founding of the state per se, but by the UN partition plan itself. For instance, the tacit alliance between Ben-Gurion and Abdullah, which allowed the latter to move into the territories west of the River Jordan, even if intended as a temporary measure to allow Israel to avoid fighting on its eastern front, indicated some acceptance of the UN-drawn border with Jordan. Moreover, for a period in early 1948, Ben-Gurion and Sharett saw the Arab part of Palestine as a prize with which to tempt Abdullah to break ranks with the Arab League and cooperate with Israel. Even Mapai's calls for increased settlement in early 1948 (that is, before the official establishment of the state) largely followed the lines of the areas allocated to the Jewish state by the UN. Shlaim, *Collusion across the Jordan,* 147–50; Pappe, "Moshe Sharett, David Ben-Gurion, ve- 'ha-optzia ha-falastinit,' 1948–1956" [Moshe Sharett, David Ben-Gurion, and the "Palestinian Option," 1948–1956]; Mapai Center, Department of Diaspora Affairs and the Halutz, "Letter to Representatives," LPA, 2-002-1948-41 (March 3, 1948); Mapai Center, Propaganda Department, "Divrei Haverim: For Information and Internal Elucidation," LPA, 2-932-1948-24 (February 20, 1948). That the acceptance of this division was still a contentious issue is suggested by Ben-Gurion's decision not to share his grand plan about the division of western Eretz Israel and Jerusalem with the Cabinet or the military command. Peri, *Between Battles and Ballots,* 58.

73. Bar-On, "Status Quo Before—or After?"

74. Berl Loker in Mapai, *7th Convention of the Party,* LPA, 2-21-1950-29 (August 15–18, 1950).

75. Mapai, "Protocol of the 37th Party Council," LPA, 2-11-1949-21 (1949).

76. Ben-Gurion was, however, "willing to sign a peace agreement with the Arabs for the next one hundred years on the basis of the status-quo." Quoted in Bar-On, "Status Quo Before—or After?" 72.

77. The West Bank and Gaza Strip were excluded from a list of the country's regions in a 1954 seminar for youth movement instructors. At the same time, they distinguished between, but did not define, the country's natural, historical, and political borders. Mapai Center, Youth Department, "Seminar for Youth Instructors at Beit Berl—5th Cycle," LPA, 2-932-1954-107 (1954).

78. Sharett, "Israel and the Arab World—War and Peace," 8, originally in 1957.

79. Eban, *Personal Witness,* 188–89.

80. Quoted in Beilin, *Price of Unity,* 63.

81. Lavon, *Al 'arakhim u-nekhasim* [On Values and Assets], 134, originally in 1948.

82. Shlaim, *Collusion across the Jordan,* 438, originally on April 12, 1949. The theme that increasing Israel's Jewish population was more critical for the strength and survival of the state than its exact borders was frequently repeated by Ben-Gurion. Bar-On, "Status Quo Before—or After?"; Bar-On, "Small Wars, Big Wars; Manor, "Images and Decision Making on the Boundaries Issue." See, for example, Mapai Center, "Letter to Representatives," LPA, 2-2-1949-55 (May 6, 1949).

83. Mapai Secretariat, meeting protocol, LPA, 2-24-1967-91 (September 24, 1967).

84. Beilin, *Price of Unity.*

85. Mapai Central Ideational Circle, protocol, LPA, 2–24-1967–33 (December 23, 1967); Alignment, "Platform for the 7th Knesset," LPA (1969); ILP Center, meeting protocol, LPA, 2–23-1971–102 (March 17, 1971); ILP, "The Oral Torah," LPA, 2–14-1972–79 (attached to ILP decisions from its 1971 convention) (September 11, 1969); ILP Center, meeting protocol, LPA, 2–23-1973–108 (November 28, 1973); Alignment, "Platform for the 8th Knesset," LPA (1974); Mapai Secretariat, protocol, LPA, 2–24-1968–93 (April 21, 1968); Allon, *Communicating Vessels,* 112, originally in June 1973; ILP Center, Preparatory Committee for the ILP Convention, "Materials from a packet for the ILP Subcommittee for Political Matters," LPA, 2–21-1977 (1976); ILP, "Decisions of the Second Convention," LPA, 2–21-1977–122 (February 22–24, 1977); Alignment, "Platform for the 9th Knesset," LPA (1977); ILP Center, "Decisions," LPA, 2–23-1978–118 (April 19, 1978).

86. ILP Center, The Preparatory Committee, Subcommittee for Political Matters, meeting protocol, LPA, 2–21-1977–133 (January 7, 1977).

87. The four variants of the argument were often interwoven. For examples of their deployment, see Mapai Knesset Faction, meeting summary, LPA, 2–11-1965–152 (September 10, 1967); Mapai Central Ideational Circle, protocol, LPA, 2–14-1967–34 (November 25, 1967); Mapai Central Ideational Circle, protocol, LPA, 2–24-1967–33 (December 23, 1967); ILP Secretariat, meeting protocol, LPA, 2–24-1968–94 (November 14, 1968); ILP Secretariat, meeting protocol, LPA, 2–24-1968–95 (December 1, 1968); ILP Secretariat, meeting protocol, LPA, 2–24-1971–99 (November 9, 1972); ILP Center, protocol, LPA, 2–24-1972–100 (September 9, 1972); ILP, "Propaganda Policy for the 1973 Elections: Proposal for Action Plan for the 8th Knesset," LPA, 4–15-1973–5 (1973); Maarach Leadership, protocol, LPA, 2–28-1976–8 (May 19, 1976); ILP Convention, protocol, LPA, 2–21-1977–121 (February 24, 1977); National Conference of Activists to Renew the Shape of Israeli Society, protocol, LPA, 2–23-1979–120 (September 25, 1979); ILP Center, meeting protocol, LPA, 2–23-1979–120 (December 30, 1979); ILP, "Background Materials for the 3rd ILP Convention," LPA, 2–21-1981–138 (February 1981); ILP Center, "Decision," LPA, 2–32-1982–124 (September 12, 1982); Alignment, "Platform for the 11th Knesset," LPA (1984); Alignment, "Platform for the 12th Knesset," LPA (1988). See also Allon, *Communicating Vessels,* 114 (originally in June 1973), 161–62 (originally in November 1977), and 192 (originally in July 1979); Etgar Ideational Circle of the Israel Labor Party, Discussion Summary, LPA, 2–14-1972–79 (March 7, 1973); Abba Eban, "A New Look at Partition," *Jerusalem Post Weekly,* June 25, 1976.

88. ILP Center, Subcommittee for Political Matters, meeting protocol, LPA, 2–921-1976–341 (January 14, 1977). Allon articulated this position as far back as 1972. See ILP Secretariat, protocol, LPA, 2–24-1971–99 (November 9, 1972). For other examples of the injection of this moral argument, see Allon, *Communicating Vessels,* 161–62, originally in November 1977; ILP Center, "Proposal of the Forum on the Autonomy," LPA, 2–23-1976–119 (February 18, 1979). Abba Eban and others made very similar arguments in ILP Center, meeting protocol, LPA, 2–23-1981–124 (April 29, 1982); Alignment, "Platform for the 10th Knesset," LPA (1981).

89. ILP Center, protocol, LPA, 2–23-1979–120 (December 30, 1979).

90. Alignment, "Platform for the 11th Knesset," LPA (1984), my emphasis.

91. Haim Ramon and Motta Gur in ILP Center, meeting protocol, LPA, 2–23-1991–145 (March 27, 1991).

92. Throughout this period, Labor leaders consistently tried to maximize Israel's territorial gains, even in the context of a potential withdrawal from the territories. For example, in 1984, they called for a solution that would leave the Jordan Valley, including the northwestern corner of the Dead Sea, Gush Etzion, the environs of Jerusalem, and the southern part of the Gaza Strip as part of Israel. Alignment, "Platform for the 11th Knesset," LPA (1984).

2. Religious Zionist Mapping of the Homeland

1. See, for example, Zionist Congress, *Newspaper of the Congress,* August 8, 1937, LPA, 2–602-1937–10; Zvi Yehuda Kook, "Innocent We Shall Be—in Torah and in Country," *Hatzofe,*

November 1, 1946; C. P. Tkorsh, "Not Masada and not Vichy—but Yavne," *Hatzofe,* October 14, 1946; Executive Council of Hapoel Hamizrachi Organization in Eretz Israel, circular, The Jonah Kirshenbaum Archive for the Study of Religious Zionism (hereafter cited as RZA), Hapoel Hamizrachi, 26 (August 25, 1938); Hamizrachi Organization in Eretz Israel, *Report to the 9th Convention* (1947); Bnei Akiva Educational Department, "An Instructional Plan on the Topic of 'Our Right to Eretz Israel,'" RZA, Bnei Akiva in Eretz Israel, 107/2 (April 1974); Ariel, *Atlas Eretz Yisrael* [Atlas of the Land of Israel], 7; Bnei Akiva in Israel Instructional Department, "Eretz Hemda: An Instructional Plan on the Topic 'Our Right to Eretz Israel,'" RZA, Bnei Akiva instructional materials, 77 (1992).

2. Even discerning scholars accepted the premise that the territorial claims lay outside the reach of history. Anthony Smith used the "scriptural promise" delimiting the appropriate territory of the Jewish nation as a paradigmatic example of geographic taken-for-granted ness, akin to the geographical isolation of islands. Smith, "Culture, Community, and Territory," 454. In literature that deals specifically with Religious Zionism, see Schwartz, *Eretz ha-mamashut veha-dimyon* [Land of Reality and Imagination]; Sprinzak, *Ascendance of Israel's Radical Right,* 109, 113.

3. See Elitzur, "Gvulot ha-aretz be-masoret yisrael" [Borders of the Land in the Tradition of Israel]; Naor, *Greater Israel,* 17–19; Ariel, *Atlas of the Land of Israel;* Ariel, *Eretz yarden ve-hermonim* [The Land of Jordan and Hermon]. Some within the movement distinguished between the borders of the "land of Canaan" and the "Land of Israel;" others argued that the extent of the Land of Israel was coextensive with the area actually settled by Jews. Shapira to S. Z. Kahana, letter, The Jabotinsky Institute in Israel (hereafter cited as JI), H1/6/5 (November 27, 1956); Schwartz, *Land of Reality and Imagination,* 29, 189.

4. Yosef Burg in NRP, "Protocol of the 5th NRP Convention and the 16th Convention of Hapoel Hamizrachi (1978)," in *Between Convention and Convention: In Days of Test and Action* (Religious National Movement Convention, 1986), 88.

5. Raanan, *Gush Emunim,* 86–89; Elitzur, "Borders of the Land"; Ariel, *Land of the Jordan and the Hermon.*

6. Torah and Labor Leadership, *Igeret le-birur shealot hatziunut ve-ha-yishuv* [Letter for the Clarification of Questions of Zionism and the Yishuv], 14–16; Shraggai, "Hazon ve-hagshama" [Vision and Fulfillment]; Judah L. Fishman, "Israel and Its Land," *Hator,* March 3, 1922.

7. Hapoel Hamizrachi Executive Committee, "Protocol of the Testimony of the Chief Rabbinate before the Technical Committee," circular, RZA, Hapoel Hamizrachi, 25 (July 27, 1938). See also Meir Berlin in Zionist Congress, *Newspaper of the Congress,* August 8, 1937, LPA, 2-602-1937-10; S. Z. Shraggai, "Towards the Twentieth Zionist Congress," *Netiva,* July 5, 1937; S. Z. Shraggai, "Against Partition—For a State," *Hatzofe,* June 26, 1938; Reuven Gafni in Executive Council of Hapoel Hamizrachi Organization in Eretz Israel, circular, RZA, Hapoel Hamizrachi, 26 (August 25, 1938); Yaacov Moshe Harlap, cited in Berlin, *Kol Haaretz* [The Entire Land], originally on July 21, 1937; Mizrachi, "Memorandum on the Inclusion of Acre in the Borders of Eretz Israel," Ginzach Haziyonut Hadatit, 141 (August 31, 1938); and Herzog in Hapoel Hamizrachi Executive Committee, circular, RZA, Hapoel Hamizrachi, 25 (July 27, 1938).

8. Jewish Agency Executive, meeting protocol, CZA, S100/20b (November 1, 1936). See also Hapoel Hamizrachi Executive Committee, internal circular, RZA, Hapoel Hamizrachi, 26 (August 11, 1938); Avraham Yaacobus, "The Solution of the Eretz Israeli Problem," *Hatzofe,* January 30, 1938; Meir Berlin to the Hapoel Hamizrachi Executive Committee, letter, RZA, Merkaz Olami of Mizrachi, 110 (July 8, 1941).

9. Cited in Berlin, *The Entire Land,* 96, originally in *Hatzofe,* September 1937. Others recalled the tearing of Transjordan from the land, but treated the "Land of Israel" as if it did not include the East Bank of the Jordan. For example, Shraggai in Berlin, *Kol Haaretz,* originally in *Hatzofe,* September 14, 1937.

10. Hapoel Hamizrachi, *Digest of Events for Week of Jan. 6, 1939–Jan. 12, 1939,* RZA, Hapoel Hamizrachi, 289 (January 1939), my emphasis.

11. Hapoel Hamizrachi Executive Committee, "Protocol of Meeting with Chaim Weizmann and a Summary of the Zionist Executive Council Meeting," circular, RZA, Hapoel Hamizrachi, 55 (March 15, 1945).

12. Hava Ulman, "Derech ha-mizrachi likrat hamedina (1945–1946)" [The Way of Mizrachi toward the State (1945–46)], 96. See also Hecht in Hapoel Hamizrachi Center, meeting protocol, RZA, Hapoel Hamizrachi, 129 (October 8, 1946).

13. Heller, *Birth of Israel*, 124.

14. Hamizrachi Organization in Eretz Israel, *Report to the 9th Convention*, 66. See also H. Avraham, "Testimony—Accusation," *Hatzofe*, March 8, 1946; Shraggai, *Al ha-tsiyonut ha-datit* [On Religious Zionism]; Kook, "Innocent We Shall Be."

15. Shapira in Hapoel Hamizrachi Center, meeting protocol, RZA, Hapoel Hamizrachi, 130 (January 19, 1947); Warhaftig in Vaad Leumi Leadership, meeting protocol, RZA, Zerach Warhaftig unit, 79 (May 12, 1948); Zerach Warhaftig, *Memo to the Members of the Vaad Leumi Leadership regarding the Treaty of Friendship between England and Transjordan*, RZA, Zerach Warhaftig unit, 79 (1948). Gold cited in Schwartz, *Land of Reality and Imagination*, 180.

16. Shraggai to Meir Berlin, letter, Ginzach haZionut haDatit at Mosad Harav Kook, 282 (September 10, 1947). Elsewhere, however, Shraggai continued to claim both banks of the Jordan as late as 1956. See Schwartz, *Land of Reality and Imagination*, 139.

17. "With the Annexation to Transjordan," editorial, *Bamesila, the Journal of the Mizrachi Histadrut in Israel,* May 1950.

18. H. Holander, "Review of the Situation in Our Movement," *Bamesila,* January 1950.

19. See Warhaftig in Government Meeting, "Protocol about the Future of the Territories," RZA, Zerach Warhaftig unit, 9/3 (December 26, 1967); Zerach Warhaftig, address at a Bnei Akiva convention, "Infect All the Youth with Your Actions," RZA, Warhaftig 198/1c (April 26, 1970); Warhaftig in Bnei Akiva, "Protocol of the 11th Convention," RZA, Bnei Akiva in Eretz Israel, 117/2 (1970); Yitzhak Rephael in Hatzofe, "Symposium with the Heads of the NRP," RZA, Warhaftig Papers, 255/1a (1975); NRP Propaganda Department, "Chapters from What Is Occurring in the Movement and Its Institutions," RZA, publications annex, box 192 (August 1967).

20. NRP, "Platform for the 11th Knesset," RZA, Hapoel Hamizrachi, 263 (1984); NRP, "Platform for the 12th Knesset," RZA, Hapoel Hamizrachi, 263 (1988). Also NRP, press release, RZA, NRP Spokesman, 118b (June 7, 1985); *Nekuda* 93 (1985).

21. Haffner and Schremer, *ha-'Am veha-arets* [The People and the Land].

22. Bnei Akiva, "Shvilei hadracha for the Ma'alot tribe," RZA, Bnei Akiva in Eretz Israel (March–April, 1949). See also Bnei Akiva, "Decisions of the World Meeting," RZA, Bnei Akiva in Eretz Israel, 38/1 (September 30, 1954).

23. Bnei Akiva, "Shvilei hadracha for the Nitzanim tribe," RZA, Bnei Akiva in Eretz Israel, box 8 (1961).

24. Mizrachi and Hapoel Hamizrachi, *21st World Convention, June 19–24* (Jerusalem: World Center of the Mizrachi and Hapoel Hamizrachi, 1968), 15.

25. Mizrachi and Hapoel Hamizrachi World Center, *Report to the 21st Convention*, RZA (1968), my emphasis. See also S. Z. Shraggai at the same event.

26. Rosen, "Am Yisrael, le-Eretz Yisrael al pi torat Yisrael" [Nation of Israel to the Land of Israel], 123.

27. "Hatzofe Symposium 1974," *Hatzofe*, September 13, 1974.

28. Y. Rephael, press release, RZA, NRP and Hapoel Hamizrachi, 47 (February 27, 1971). See also Haim Pikersh, "The NRP in the Battles of Religion and State: A Conversation with Zvi Bernstein, General Secretary of the NRP," *Hatzofe*, September 13, 1974; Zvi Bernstein, elections radio broadcast, RZA, NRP in the Knesset, 133 (1973).

29. Mizrachi and Hapoel Hamizrachi, *21st World Convention*, 165–166, my emphasis. For similar comments, see "Political and Security Problems in the Light of Judaism: Interview with Dr. Z. Warhaftig," RZA, Warhaftig, 255/1a (1970), originally in *Hatzofe;* Yehoshua Shemesh, "Interview with Dr. Zerach Warhaftig: We Should Not Assume That the USSR Will

Reach Full Involvement in the Middle East," *Hatzofe*, May 11, 1970; NRP, *The Essence of Peace: Things Said at the NRP Leadership Meetings of September 7 and 24, 1970* (NRP Information Department, 1971), 17; Shaul Schiff, "Conversation with MK Dr. Zerach Warhaftig: The Religious-National Public Is Fighting for the Wholeness of the Torah, the Nation, and the Land," *Hatzofe*, August 16, 1974; Zerach Warhaftig, "Political Strength and Spiritual Strength," *Hatzofe*, June 9, 1978.

30. Warhaftig in N. Golan, "Conversation with Zerach Warhaftig: The Strengthening of the NRP is a Guarantee of Preserving Its Achievements," *Hatzofe*, June 22, 1984.

31. Mizrachi and Hapoel Mizrachi, "Declaration of the 21st World Convention," RZA, Mizrachi World Center, 47 (1968), my emphasis.

32. Cited in Segal, *Ahim Yekarim* [Dear Brothers], 232, my emphasis.

33. For examples, see Bnei Akiva, "Decisions of the 13th Convention," RZA, Bnei Akiva in Eretz Israel, 213/3 (1976); MK Ben-Meir in State of Israel, *Divrei HaKnesset* (March 5, 1975), and in NRP Knesset Faction, press release, RZA, NRP in the Knesset, 136/1 (March 2, 1977); see also NRP, *Between Conventions—Summary of a Period—Report to the 5th NRP Convention*, RZA (1978); "Wide and Crowded Settlement," editorial, *Hatzofe*, December 5, 1975; NRP, "Platform for the 9th Knesset," RZA, Hapoel Hamizrachi, 263 (1977); NRP Information Department, "Positions of the Religious National Movement," RZA, NRP Spokesman, 118a (April 24, 1987); NRP Information Department, "Positions of the Religious National Movement," RZA, NRP Spokesman, 118a (May 5, 1987); NRP, *There Is a Zionist Answer [to the Intifada]*, election pamphlet, RZA, Political General Secretary, 108 (1988). Also Cohen, *Ha-Mafdal* [The NRP], 23; Ben-Aharon, *Tsiyonut har ha-bayit* [Temple Mount Zionism], 188.

34. See, for example, M. Hazani in "Hatzofe Symposium 1974."

35. NRP, "Decisions of the 3rd NRP Convention," RZA, Publications appendix, 192 (1969), my emphasis; Hamizrachi and Hapoel Hamizrachi World Center, *The World Meeting of the Young Guard* (1969), my emphasis; Hatzofe, "Political and Security Problems in the Light of Judaism," 1970, RZA, Warhaftig, 255/1a. See also Rosen, "Nation of Israel to the Land of Israel."

36. Raanan, *Gush Emunim*, 191; Shaul Yahalom, "What's New in the Movement: Awareness of the Liberation of Areas of Eretz Israel," RZA, NRP and Hapoel Hamizrachi, 47 (September, 1970); Avner Shaki, press release, RZA, NRP and Hapoel Hamizrachi, 46 (October 20, 1969), my emphasis. See also NRP, *Summary of a Period—Report to the 3rd NRP Convention* (1969); Movement for a Religious-National Renewal—NRP, pamphlet, RZA, NRP and Hapoel Hamizrachi, 24 (1970s); NRP, "Protocol of the 5th NRP Convention."

37. Such statements became integrated into NRP platforms between 1973 and 1992.

38. NRP, elections broadcast, RZA, NRP and Hapoel Hamizrachi, 11 (October 22, 1969).

39. NRP, "Advertisement in Maariv," RZA, NRP and Hapoel Hamizrachi, 57 (October 21, 1969), original emphasis.

40. Al Hamishmar correspondent, "NRP Chairman: Slim Chance That We Will Establish a Coalition with Labor," *Al Hamishmar*, April 21, 1992, my emphasis.

41. Hanan Porat, "Two Minutes with the NRP on Arutz 7," RZA, NRP Spokesman (May 31, 1992), my emphasis; Shaul Yahalom, "Two Minutes with the NRP on Arutz 7," RZA, NRP Spokesman (June 1, 1992); NRP, "Electioneering Broadcast on Mishdar Boker, Reshet B, Kol Israel," RZA, NRP Spokesman (June 10, 1992).

42. See, for example, the images in NRP, "Kit for the Explainer to the 13th Knesset Elections," RZA, NRP Spokesman, 120/1 (1992).

43. One change that did take place after 1967 was a not too common tendency to identify the Golan Heights with the Bashan. Bnei Akiva in Israel, "Decisions of the 12th Convention," RZA, Bnei Akiva in Eretz Israel, 69/3 (1973).

44. Bnei Akiva, "Decisions of the 16th "El Ami" Convention," RZA, Bnei Akiva in Eretz Israel, 213/3 (1986); Bnei Akiva in Israel, "First Steps in Group B—An Annual Program of Instruction for Education Enrichment," RZA (1986); Neamanei Torah ve Avoda, *le-nohah ha-haslama ba-yahas la-aravim* [Given the Escalation regarding the Arabs], originally in a report in *Hatzofe*,

November 14, 1984. See also Bnei Akiva in Israel, "Bnei Akiva after the Six-Day War," RZA, Bnei Akiva in Eretz Israel, 20/3 (1970).

45. Bnei Akiva in Israel Instructional Department, "Eretz Hemda," RZA, Bnei Akiva instructional materials, 77 (1992), my emphasis.

46. Bnei Akiva, "Protocol of the 11th Convention," RZA, Bnei Akiva in Eretz Israel, folder 117/2 (1970), my emphasis. Instructively, the objections to changing the youth movement's name were based on the failure to gather all Jews in Israel and not on the reasoning that they did not actually control the entire land.

47. NRP, press release, RZA, NRP Spokesman, 10/2 (May 22, 1995).

48. For explorations of Gush Emunim, see O'Dea, "Gush Emunim"; Raanan, *Gush Emunim;* Sprinzak, "Gush Emunim"; Weissbrod, "Gush Emunim Ideology"; Aran, "From Religious Zionism to Zionist Religion"; Goldberg and Ben-Zadok, "Gush Emunim in the West Bank"; Lustick, *For the Land and the Lord;* Aran, "The Father, The Son, and the Holy Land"; Heilman, "Guides of The Faithful."

49. Lustick, *For the Land and the Lord,* 168–169.

50. See, for example, Amital, *ha-Ma'alot min ha-ma'amakim* [Upwards from the Depths], 12; Cohen, *The NRP,* 23; Nativ, "Kiddush ha-Shem," [The Sanctification of God before the eyes of the (foreign) nations], 502; Ben-Aharon, *Temple Mount Zionism,* 188; Seden, "Aspiration to peace and our national morality."

51. See, for example, Yochanan Fried in Daniel Ben-Simon, "Foreign Fire," *Haaretz Supplement,* April 21, 1986. See also Israel Meidad, "The Mount Takes Precedence over the Temple," *Nekuda* 89 (1985); Shimon Klein, "Eretz Israel Can Emerge Stronger from the Peace Process," *Nekuda* 169 (1993); Avraham Shavot, "In the Midst of a Hundred Years War," *Nekuda* 170 (1993); Yaacov Halamish, "To save Zionism from Itself," *Nekuda* 175 (1994).

52. See, for example, editorial, *Nekuda* 75 (1984); editorial, *Nekuda* 97 (1986); Moshe Shapira, "Under the Rule of the Mandate," *Nekuda* 155 (1991–2); Avraham Wacman and Elisha Haas, "Salvation [yesha] to the Eastern Spine," *Nekuda* 162 (1992); Hillel Weiss, "Yesha as a Laboratory for a National Utopia," *Nekuda* 162 (1992).

53. See, for example, the lead editorial in Nekuda, "Sharon's Accusation," *Nekuda* 71 (1984): 2. See also "Better Late Than Never," editorial, *Nekuda* 155 (1991–2).

54. "Dangerous Elections," editorial, *Nekuda* 129 (1989); Moshe Simon, "The Wholeness of the Land Supersedes the Sanctity of Life," *Nekuda* 135 (1989); editorial, *Nekuda* 138 (1990); Shlomo Baum, "The Fact that Arik Sharon Claims That Jordan Is Palestine Is Not Reason Enough to Reject This Correct Idea," *Nekuda* 149 (1991); Yair Dreifus, "Compromise or Suicide," *Nekuda* 177 (1994); editorial, *Nekuda* 178 (1994).

55. Uri Ariel, "Settlement and Aliya," *Nekuda* 107 (1987): 40; Benny Katzover, "The End of the Intifada, Encouraging Enlarging the Jewish Family, a Revolution in Settlement, Encouraging Arab Emigration, Extending Israeli Sovereignty over All the Land of Israel," *Nekuda* 130 (1989); Yitzhak Armoni, "The Way of Kaleb ben-Yefuneh," *Nekuda* 130 (1989); Benny Katzover, "The Jews Are Coming, the Arabs Are Going," *Nekuda* 145 (1990); Yaacov Sagiv, "The Myth Lives On," *Nekuda* 145 (1990); Benny Katzover, "A Promising Future," *Nekuda* 147 (1991); an open letter for the new year from the chief rabbis, Mordechai Eliyahu and Avraham Shapira, *Nekuda* 134 (1989); Yitzhak Levi, the general secretary of the NRP, in *Nekuda* 150 (1991); "Forward with Courage," editorial, *Nekuda* 167 (1993).

56. "Cancel the Advice of Our Haters," editorial, *Nekuda* 171 (1993), my emphasis. See also Seden, "Aspiration to Peace and Our National Morality," 38.

57. See, for example, the images in *Nekuda* 72 (1984); *Nekuda* 77 (1984); Yesha Council, "Yesha Pamphlet to Encourage Aliya," *Nekuda* 115 (1987); *Nekuda* 138 (1990); Ezra Zohar, "Towards the War of Independence (Economic and Political)," *Nekuda* 152 (1991); Elyakim Haetzni, "Not to Enable the Zionist State to Betray Zion," *Nekuda* 163 (1992); *Nekuda* 163 (1992); *Nekuda* 166 (1993); *Nekuda* 167 (1993); *Nekuda* 175 (1994).

58. For example, editorial, *Nekuda* 125 (1988). Mordechai Gafni, "Right-Left, Right-Left, In-Place, March!" *Nekuda* 141 (1990); letter to the editor, *Nekuda* 172 (1993). Also Benny Katzover, "To Institutionalize...Not Too Much," *Nekuda* 100 (1986).

59. See, for example, "Didn't Learn, Didn't Forget," editorial, *Nekuda* 79 (1984); Klein, "Eretz Israel Can Emerge Stronger from the Peace Process"; "The Condition for an Alternative," editorial, *Nekuda* 184 (1995); "There Won't Be a Separation," editorial, *Nekuda* 185 (1995).

60. See Yesha Council, "Open Letter to Peres and Shamir," *Nekuda* 82 (1985); See also Friedman, *Zealots for Zion,* 178; Yoel Ben-Nun, "Not to Anger and Not to Get Angry," *Nekuda* 68 (1984); Uri Orbach, "One Bank to the Jordan," *Nekuda* 95 (1986); Moshe Shabat, "Return to the 1922 Partition," *Nekuda* 121 (1988); Dan Bari, "If to Negotiate Then with the PLO," *Nekuda* 119 (1988); Amiel Unger, "Cujus Regio Ehus Religio," *Nekuda* 119 (1988); "The Political Message Is Paralysis," editorial, *Nekuda* 126 (1989); Dan Bari, "To Rebuild Anew the National Camp," *Nekuda* 126 (1989); Yitzhak Blot, "The Palestinians Need to Be Given the Right to Self-Determination Now," *Nekuda* 138 (1990); Amiel Unger, "Point of Fact," *Nekuda* 164 (1992); Amiel Unger, "A Point to the Heart," *Nekuda* 169 (1993); Baum, "The fact that Arik Sharon claims that Jordan is Palestine."

61. There were precedents for this argument in Religious Zionism. For example, Aharon Cohen in NRP, *Essence of Peace,* 86; also Aharon Cohen in Aharon AbuHazira, speech at a NRP Leadership meeting on the government's policy, the Rogers plan, etc., RZA, NRP and Hapoel Hamizrachi, 12 (1970s); Yehuda Ben Meir in State of Israel, *Knesset Protocols* (December 2, 1975); Sarit Fox, "Avner Shaki, Mearbel Tamlilim" [Avner Shaki Word Mixer], *Maariv,* June 3, 1988.

62. For the argument that the appeal to the "Jordan is the Palestinian state" argument was mainly polemical and that most Gush Emunim ideologues refrained from engaging in it because it implied ceding the claim to the East Bank, see Lustick, *For the Land and the Lord,* 107, 149.

63. Elyakim Haetzni, "Back to the Truth," *Nekuda* 139 (1990): 23.

64. NRP, press release, RZA, NRP Spokesman, 9/2 (October 17, 1994).

65. Editorial, *Hatzofe,* July 12, 1994. See also *Hatzofe,* July 18, 1994; July 22, 1994; July 25, 1994; July 26, 1994; October 2, 1994; October 14, 1994; October 18, 1994. See, for example, Yosef Shapira, "On Our Agenda," *Hatzofe,* July 22, 1994; *Hatzofe's* Washington correspondent on July 29, 1994.

66. Shulamit Mustik, "It Was Hard to Tell If It Was a Dream or a Reality," *Hatzofe,* August 9, 1994.

67. Shulamit Mustik, "Zerach Warhaftig: I've Dreamt of a Peace Agreement with Jordan My Entire Life," *Hatzofe,* October 26, 1994.

68. See the editorials in *Hatzofe* on July 22 and 26, 1994.

69. Ram Aviram, "The Agreement with Jordan and the Political Range in Israel," *Hatzofe,* July 29, 1994.

70. See the reactions of the NRP MKs in Aviram, "The Agreement with Jordan"; Shulamit Mustik, "The NRP Says Yes … But, to the Peace Agreement with Jordan: A Party in a "Trap"," *Hatzofe,* October 28 (Supplement), 1994. Some of the exceptions include Yigal Ariel, "Who Needs the Patrimony?" *Hatzofe,* August 12, 1994; Israel Ariel, "Transjordan—The Halachic Perspective," *Hatzofe,* August 19, 1994; Azriel Ariel, "Transjordan Is Part of the Land of Israel," *Hatzofe,* October 21, 1994; Yitzhak Deutsch, "Necessity but Not Happiness," *Hatzofe,* October 26, 1994; Hanan Porat, "Why I Abstained," *Nekuda* 182 (1994); Hanan Porat, interview, *Yoman Moreshet,* Reshet A—Israel Radio, RZA, NRP Spokesman, 85 (October 25, 1994); Yoel Ben-Nun, "To Get Out of the Abyss of Rejection and Desperation," *Nekuda* 182 (1994). Shaul Yahalom in State of Israel, *Divrei Haknesset: Government Announcement of a Peace Treaty between Israel and the Hashemite Kingdom of Jordan* (October 25, 1994).

71. NRP announcement in *Hatzofe,* October 25, 1994

72. See Yitzhak Levy, "The Peace Agreement—Between Reality and Desire," *Hatzofe,* October 28, 1994; Mustik, "NRP Says Yes … But"; Ben-Nun, "To Get Out of the Abyss of Rejection and Desperation."

73. Mustik, "NRP Says Yes … But"; Aviram, "Agreement with Jordan."

74. Ariel, "Transjordan is Part of the Land of Israel." Apparently, Hanan Porat consulted with "Torah Sages" who instructed him to abstain from voting for the treaty. However, the

NRP as a party did not include the rabbis in its discussions or its decision to support the treaty. The NRP received an anonymous fax on the last day of its deliberations outlining the objections of some (apparent) rabbis, which it effectively ignored. Mustik, "NRP Says Yes...But."

75. The silence about the agreement to relinquish the claim to the patrimony east of the Jordan was noted by the few who publicly opposed the treaty on this basis, as well as by those who supported it, but who did so with a heavy heart. See, respectively, Ariel, "Transjordan"; and Deutsch, "Necessity but Not happiness."

76. See, for example, Judah Fishman in Mapai Central Committee, protocol, July 5, 1937, LPA, 2–23-1937–17; Herzog in Hapoel Hamizrachi Executive Committee, circular, July 27, 1938, RZA, Hapoel Hamizrachi, 25; Hapoel Hamizrachi, "Recommendations to the "Technical Committee" of the Peel Commission," RZA, Poel Mizrachi 25 (July 3, 1938).

77. See, for example, Hamizrachi and Hapoel Hamizrachi, "Meeting Protocol of the Delegation to the Zionist Congress," RZA, World Zionist Organization and Mizrachi, 36/1 (December 10, 1946).

78. Hapoel Hamizrachi Executive Committee, *Hapoel Hamizrachi 1942–1949: Summary of Activity for the 10th Convention* (Jerusalem: Executive Committee of Hapoel Hamizrachi in Israel, 1949).

79. Hapoel Hamizrachi Center, protocol, RZA, Hapoel Hamizrachi, 129 (October 8, 1946); Moshe Meiri, "The Political Battle and Ways of Political Struggle," *Hatzofe,* October 27, 1946; Daniel, *ha-Sar Hayim-Mosheh Shapira* [Minister Haim Moshe Shapira].

80. Hapoel Hamizrachi Center, protocol, RZA, Hapoel Hamizrachi, 129 (October 8, 1946); Ulman, "The Way of Mizrachi toward the State"; Hamizrachi and Hapoel Hamizrachi, protocol, RZA, World Zionist Organization and Mizrachi, 36/1 (December 10, 1946).

81. Hapoel Hamizrachi Executive Committee, circular, RZA, Hapoel Hamizrachi, 292 (November 30, 1947).

82. Naor, *Greater Israel,* 124, 298. Naor notes even a basic geographic-religious education was missing from Religious Zionism at the time (299). This was even noted within the movement. See, for example, Shapira, "Under the Rule of the Mandate"; Israel Harel, "An Iron Curtain Splits Jerusalem: An Interview with Rabbi Israel Ariel," *Nekuda* 159 (1992).

83. Quoted in Eve Cohen-Pinchas, "Gush Emunim: The First Decade (2)," *Nekuda* 71 (1984). The Nahal is an IDF infantry brigade that combines military service with the establishment of new agricultural settlements in outlying areas.

84. MK Pinchas Sheinman in Hatzofe, "Symposium: Where Is the National Religious Movement Headed?" RZA, Warhaftig, 255/1a (1977).

85. Quoted in Galnoor, *Partition of Palestine.* 282. See also Geula Bat-Yehuda, *ha-Rav Maimon be-dorotav* [The Times of Rabbi Maimon], 544–45; Ulman, "Way of Mizrachi towards the State."

86. The modified position was expressed in a letter dated October 14, 1947. Quoted in Goldsheleg, "Two letters of Rabbi Meir Bar-Ilan." For Bar-Ilan's (Berlin) rejection of the argument that a safe haven justifies partition, see his statement in Zionist Congress, *Newspaper of the Congress,* August 8, 1937, LPA, 2–602-1937–10; Berlin, *The Entire Land,* 88, originally in *Hatzofe,* September 5, 1937. See also Yaacov Moshe Harlap, cited in Berlin, *The Entire Land,* originally on July 21, 1937; Meir Berlin to the Mizrachi Delegation to the 22nd Zionist Congress, letter, RZA, Mizrachi World Center, 12 (1946).

87. Hapoel Hamizrachi Center, protocol, RZA, Hapoel Hamizrachi, 129 (November 18, 1946).

88. NRP Information Department, *The Sinai Episode: Discussions, Thoughts, Conclusions* (Tel Aviv: NRP, 1957).

89. See, for example, Mizrachi Hapoel Hamizrachi—The World Movement of Religious Zionism, "Movement Constitution," RZA, World Mizrachi Center, 62 (after 1967); S. Israeli, a member of the high religious court in the Jerusalem, in Association for Religious Councils in Israel, *Nes ve-ma'ase be-shlavei ha-geula* [Miracles and Actions in the Steps of the Redemption], 19, 25; NRP, "Decisions of the 3rd NRP Convention," RZA, Publications appendix, 192 (1969).

90. Berlin, *The Entire Land*. In a 1947 letter to the American consul, Berlin argued that the borders of the Land of Israel are clearly articulated in Numbers, chapter 32 (which speaks of the East Bank of the Jordan, but not, interestingly, of the land all the way to the Euphrates). Goldsheleg, "Two Letters of Rabbi Meir Bar-Ilan."

91. The United Religious Front was a short-lived alliance between the Religious Zionists and the ultra-Orthodox.

92. For example, Judah Maimon (Fishman) did so in 1954 and again in his 1956 address to the NRP's unification convention. NRP, *Report of the Founding Convention of the NRP*, RZA, Hapoel Hamizrachi, 249 (June 20, 1956); Bat-Yehuda, "Torat Eretz Yisrael shel ha-Ramban be-machshevet ha-techiya," [The Ideology of the Ramban in the Thought of the Revival]; Yitzhak Refael, editorial, *Sinai* 61 no. 2–4 (1967). See also NRP, "Deputy Minister Dr. Ben-Meir: There Are Principles on Which One Does Not Compromise," press release, RZA, NRP and Hapoel Hamizrachi, 30 (August 25, 1969); Warhaftig in Shaul Schiff, "Is the Government Authorized to Decide on a Withdrawal," *Hatzofe*, November 15, 1985.

93. See, for example, Geula Cohen, "Eye to Eye: Interview with Zerach Warhaftig," *Maariv*, March 26, 1971; Mustik, "Zerach Warhaftig."

94. Bnei Akiva in Israel Instructional Department, "Eretz Hemda," RZA, Bnei Akiva instructional materials, 77, 50 (1992).

95. Kook, "Mizmor yud'tet shel medinat Yisrael" [Psalm 19 of the State of Israel], 66–67.

96. Don-Yehiya, "Yetzivut u-temurot be-mifleget mahane" [Stability and Change in a Camp Party].

97. Galili, *Kera' ben ha-kipot* [A Rift among the Religious], 22. A similar sentiment was articulated by Yehuda Zolden, a leader of the settlement movement, in the same volume, p. 27

98. See, for example, Yoel Ben-Nun in Galili, *Rift among the Religious*, 69–70. Also Yoel Ben-Nun, "To Extend Sovereignty Now over the Jewish Settlement," *Nekuda* 160 (1992); Yoel Ben Nun, "Without Force We Are Likely to Lose Everything," *Nekuda* 171 (1993).

99. Quoted in Peleg, *Begin's Foreign Policy*, 184, originally in *The Jerusalem Post*, March 27, 1983.

100. Schwartz, *Land of Reality and Imagination*, 122; Sprinzak, *Ascendance of Israel's Radical Right*, 46, 114, 303; Naor, *Greater Israel*, 150 n. 154, 195, 224; Lustick, *For the Land and the Lord*, 107–8. See, for example, Zvi Yehuda Kook, "The Oath of Fathers and the Conquests of Sons," *Hatzofe*, December 22, 1975; Kook, "Between a Nation and Its Land"; editorial, *Tsfiya* 2 (1985); Dov Lior, "'Ger Toshav' and Its Definition in Our Time," *Tsfiya* 2 (1985); Elihu Avihail, "Divine Providence Is Pushing Us," *Tsfiya* 2 (1985); Ilan Tor, "The Land of Israel—For Israel Alone," *Tsfiya* 2 (1985); Ariel, *Atlas of the Land of Israel*; Shaviv, *Eretz nahalah* [A Land of Settlement]; Ben-Nun, "Not to Anger and Not to Get Angry"; Yehuda Shaviv, "A Positive Expression of Fanaticism," *Nekuda* 116 (1987); Yoel Ben-Nun, "Only a National Consensus Will Prevent the Slide to a General War," *Nekuda* 118 (1988); Yoel Ben-Nun, "The Time of Summary and Conclusions Has Come," *Nekuda* 123 (1988); Ben-Nun, "To Extend Sovereignty Now." See also Yochanan Fried, quoted in Raanan, *Gush Emunim*, 184. In 2000, Motti Yogav, the new general secretary of Bnei Akiva, still claimed Lebanon as part of the Land of Israel. Cited in Greenfield, *Cosmic Fear*. Uriel Tal, "The Nationalism of Gush Emunim"; Ariel, *Atlas of the Land of Israel*.

101. Zertal and Eldar, *Lords of the Land*, 263.

102. Quoted in Lustick, *For the Land and the Lord*, 107.

103. Ibid., 84–85.

104. Shapira, letter, November 27, 1956, JI, H1/6/5.

105. NRP Information Department, *Sinai Episode*.

106. Government Meeting, protocol, RZA, Zerach Warhaftig unit, folder 9/3 (December 26, 1967). See also Mizrachi and Hapoel Hamizrachi, *21st World Convention, June 19–24, 1968*. 164–166; NRP Knesset Faction, press release, RZA, NRP in the Knesset, 138/1 (March 20, 1979); N. Golan, "Conversation with Dr. Warhaftig: It Is Time to Focus Inwards,"

Hatzofe, August 4, 1981; Warhaftig, *Hamishim shanah ve-shanah* [Fifty Years, from Year to Year], 293.

107. Hatzofe, "Symposium," RZA, Warhaftig Papers, 255/1a (1975); Zvulun Hammer, "Why I Voted against the Interim Arrangement in Sinai," RZA, NRP in the Knesset, 350/1 (n.d.); Raanan, *Gush Emunim,* 191; NRP, *Essence of Peace;* Rephael, press release, RZA, NRP and Hapoel Hamizrachi, 47 (February 27, 1971).

108. NRP Knesset Faction, press release, RZA, NRP in the Knesset, 137 (September 27, 1978); NRP Knesset Faction, press release, RZA, NRP in the Knesset, 138/1 (March 20, 1979); NRP Knesset Faction, press release, RZA, NRP in the Knesset, 137 (December 28, 1977); Azrieli, *Dor ha-kipot ha-serugot* [The Knit Kippa Generation]; Sprinzak, *Ascendance of Israel's Radical Right,* 77.

109. See, for example, Haim Druckman, cited in Naor, *Greater Israel,* 268, 214–19. See also the responses of Hanan Porat, Yoel Ben-Nun, Moshe Zvi Neria (the founder of the Bnei Akiva Yeshivot), and others. The claim to Sinai was repeatedly articulated in *Nekuda,* as well as in *Artzi* 2 (1982) and 3 (1983).

110. Segal, *Dear Brothers,* 135.

111. Bnei Akiva, "Decisions of the 15th Convention," RZA, Bnei Akiva in Eretz Israel, 213/3 (1983).

112. See, for example, Hazani in Hatzofe, "Hatzofe Symposium 1974." According to Azrieli, Zvulun Hammer also warned against this possibility. Azrieli, *Knit Kippa Generation.*

113. Naor, *Greater Israel.* See *Artzi.*

114. See, for example, editorial, *Tsfiya* 2 (1985)

115. Sprinzak, *Ascendance of Israel's Radical Right,* 114. Some went further and distinguished between the Land of Israel and Southern Lebanon. See David Rozensweig, "The War for Peace in The Galilee: Wrong Address," *Nekuda* 67 (1983).

116. Cited in Naor, *Greater Israel.* See also Yoel Ben-Nun, "The State of Israel against the Land of Israel?" *Nekuda* 72 (1984).

117. Ben-Nun, "State of Israel Against the Land of Israel?" 31. See also Naor, *Greater Israel.*

118. Cited in Naor, *Greater Israel.* See also the letter of introduction by Avraham Shapira in Ariel, *Land of the Jordan and the Hermon.*

119. For example, Avi Gisar in Galili, *Rift among the Religious,* 36; also Uzi Kelcheim, cited in Lustick, *For the Land and the Lord,* 107. For Kook's position, see Naor, *Greater Israel,* 165 n. 157.

120. See *Nekuda* 83 (1985). Yoel Ben-Nun and Moshe Levinger even proposed seeking a de facto agreement with Syria in order to stabilize Israel's northern border. Lustick, *For the Land and the Lord,* 149.

121. See, for example, Karpel, *Ha-mahapekhah ha-emunit* [The Emunit Revolution].

3. Revisionist Zionist Mapping of the Homeland

1. See, for example, Greenberg, "Shir tfelia le-meshichat ami" [Song of Prayer], 156.

2. Jabotinsky, *Shirim* [Songs], 201–2. The translation is from Betar, *Songs of Betar,* JI, B186 (1960). Reprinted courtesy of the Jabotinsky Institute in Israel.

3. See Ze'ev Jabotinsky, "What New Zionism Stands For—Draft by V.J.," JI, A1/7/238 (1925); Jabotinsky, "Class Problems," in *Ba-derekh la-medinah* [On the Way to the State].

4. B. Lubotsky, "About the Future," JI, B8C/9/2 (1936).

5. Ze'ev Jabotinsky, "What We Stand For: An Outline of the Revisionist (Activist) Programme," JI, A1/7/19 (1926). While Jabotinsky complained privately about Britain's 1922 decision to split Transjordan from Palestine, he did not go so far as to protest it by resigning from the Zionist Executive. For two different explanations of this, see Katz, *Jabo,* 520–23; Nedva, "Churchill and the Borders of the Land of Israel."

6. See, for example, New Zionist Organization, *Memorandum on the Partition of Palestine Submitted to the Permanent Mandates Commission,* JI, A1/4/37 (July, 1937). See also

M. A. Perlmutter, "Notes at the Margins of Days," *Hayarden*, July 23, 1937; Betar Galilee Gdud, "BaSherut," JI, B8C/8/12 (1937); *Hayarden*, October 8, 1937; Y. Klausner, "Open Letter," *HaMedina*, September 6, 1937. On at least one occasion, however, Yosef Klausner distinguished between the Land of Israel and Transjordan. See Yosef Klausner, *HaGesher: Leaflet for matters of enlistment and Betar in Eretz Israel*, JI, B2/24 (July 6, 1937).

7. Great Britain, "Palestine Royal Commission: Minutes of Evidence Heard at Public Sessions," 369.

8. Ze'ev Jabotinsky, "Jabotinsky on Partition," *Hayarden*, August 6, 1937.

9. Cited in Katz, *Jabo*, 1001–2. There is some evidence that Jabotinsky was beginning to change his mind shortly before his death. He apparently told Berl Katznelson that he would not oppose the creation of a Jewish state in part of Eretz Israel as long as the rest would remain in its "present condition" and not be given to an Arab state. Mapai Center, meeting protocol, LPA, 2–23-1939–26 (September 21, 1939).

10. Betar Leadership, "Call to All Betarists and to All Hebrew Youth," JI, B2/18 (July 4, 1937), original emphasis.

11. Betar, *1944 Camp Pamphlet, Wall Posters, etc.*, JI, B8C/9/5 (various). See also Betar, *Betar Educational Materials*, JI, B8C/9/1 (various); Stein-Ashkenazi, *Betar be-Eretz Yisrael* [Betar in the Land of Israel], 166–67; and a 1941 book of "Palestine geography" for American Betarists: Ben-Horin, *Land of Israel*, 7.

12. Betar, *Left of the Jordan*, 2.

13. Irgun Zvai Leumi, *Memorandum to the United Nations (in Irgun Zvai Leumi Speaks to the United Nations: Will There Be War or Peace in Palestine)*," JI, K18/13/2 (April 21, 1947), 1, 3.

14. Irgun Zvai Leumi, *Report of Conference between Representatives of UNSCOP and the Commander and Two Other Representatives of the Irgun Zvai Leumi (in Irgun Zvai Leumi Speaks to the United Nations: Will There Be War or Peace in Palestine)*," JI, K18/13/2 (June 24, 1947).

15. Irgun Zvai Leumi, announcement, JI, K8/1/8 (1947); Irgun Zvai Leumi Diaspora Headquarters, announcement, JI, K8/1/8 (September 5, 1947); Staff, "Report of Altman News Conference," *Hamashkif*, October 20, 1947, Central Committee of the Revisionist Zionist Organization in EI, "Response to the UN Vote of 29 November," *Hamashkif*, December 1, 1947; Irgun Zvai Leumi, "Declaration of the Irgun Zvai Leumi," JI, H1/1/1 (June 15, 1948); Irgun Zvai Leumi, "UNSCOP and Begin Meeting," June 24, 1947, JI, K18/13/2. Some have argued that this was merely a declarative position (e.g., Preuss, *Begin ba-shilton* [Begin: His Regime], 132.) At the very least, however, the British took it seriously enough to pressure Arab leaders not to support the mufti's declaration of a Palestinian government. See Shlaim, *Collusion across the Jordan*, 298.

16. Bercovici and Wolfson, *Packet about the Irgun*.

17. Irgun Zvai Leumi, "UNSCOP and Begin Meeting," JI, K18/13/2 (June 24, 1947).

18. Begin, *Revolt*, 24–25.

19. Central Committee of the Revisionist Zionist Organization in EI, "Response to the UN Vote of 29 November"; "Revisionist Memorandum That Would Have Been Submitted to UNESCO," *Hamashkif*, July 17, 1947; Y. Bader, "The Last Week of the UN Commission," *Hamashkif*, July 11, 1947; Staff, lead article, *Hamashkif*, July 16, 1947; "The Negotiations over the Pieces," editorial, *Hamashkif*, November 14, 1947; "If I Forget Thee Jerusalem!" *Hamashkif*, November 20, 1947; Y. Yerushalmi, "We Have Sinned against You Jerusalem!" *Hamashkif*, November 21, 1947.

20. Menachem Begin, "Speech of the Commander-in-Chief of the Irgun Zvai Leumi," JI, P20/11/1 (May 15, 1948), original emphasis; see also Menachem Begin, "Jerusalem Our Capital," JI, P20/10/19 (Summer 1948); Herut Movement, "Decisions of the First Convention," JI, H1/13/1/2 (30 June—3 July, 1949).

21. Naor, *Greater Israel*, 65.

22. Peter (Hillel Kook) Bergson to UN Secretary General, letter, JI, Kh/4/1/15 (July 9, 1946); Peter (Hillel Kook) Bergson to Dean Acheson, letter, JI, Kh/4/1/15 (January 7, 1946);

Hillel Kook, letter, JI, KH 4/1/7 (December 3, 1947); Eri Jabotinsky, "Jews and Hebrews," JI, A4/13/3 (1947); Hebrew Committee of National Liberation, cable, JI, Kh4/1/10 (October 9, 1946); Hebrew Committee of National Liberation, "*Proposal for the creation of a Hebrew republic of Palestine submitted to the UN Ad Hoc Committee on Palestine,*" JI, Kh4/1/7 (1947); Union of Zionist Revisionists—Jabotinsky's Movement, platform (1949).

23. For examples of these, see Mordechai Katz, "The Zohar in the Partitioned State," *Hamashkif,* December 19, 1947; Zeev Von-Weizel, "The Zionist Revisionist Movement on the Eve of a New Age in Zionism," *Hamashkif,* November 25, 1947; Zeev Von-Weizel, "Happiness in Agony," *Hamashkif,* December 1, 1947; Zeev Von-Weizel, "After the Happiness..." *Hamashkif,* December 5, 1947; Zeev Von-Weizel, "The Great Danger: Abdullah as Our Ally," *Hamashkif,* May 13, 1948. One of the very few indications that anyone in the Revisionist movement implicitly accepted the partition of the East Bank was found in a circular marked "absolutely internal" that discussed the numbers of Arab refugees. It listed Transjordan in the section "outside of the borders of Eretz Israel." Herut Department for Public Opinion Research, *General Circular No. 24,* JI, H1/4/19 (October 11, 1948).

24. See Shaviv in Herut, *Herut Documents,* JI, H1/1/1 (1948); Arye Altman in Herut Movement, "Materials related to the 3rd National Convention," JI, H1/13/3/1 (1954).

25. Menachem Begin, "Homeland and Freedom," JI, P20/12/15 (1948), original emphasis.

26. Herut Movement, Herut membership card, JI, H1/10/4 (1948).

27. See, for example, Menachem Begin, "Knesset Speech," JI, H2/9/1 (March 8, 1949); Menachem Begin, "The Victory of the Truth Will Not Be Delayed: Address to the National Conference of Betar," *Herut,* April 12, 1955.

28. Begin, *Hashkafat hayim ve-hashkafah le'umit* [Life View and National View], 43; Menachem Begin, "The Way of a National-Liberal Government: Opening Speech at the 5th National Committee of Herut, Nov. 24, 1958," JI, H1/13/5/3 (November 24, 1958).

29. Amman, the Gilead, and the Bashan are all on the East Bank of the Jordan River. Menachem Begin, "Knesset Speech," JI, P20/11/7 (November 9, 1949). For similar statements, see Begin, "Victory of the Truth"; Menachem Begin, "Who Gave You the Right?! Menachem Begin's Knesset Speech during the Debate on the 'Annexation of the Triangle,'" *Herut,* May 5, 1950; Begin, *Life View and National View,* 38, 51; Menachem Begin, "Sowed Deceit, Reaping Hostility," *Herut,* May 14, 1954; Menachem Begin, "Knesset Speech," JI, H2/9/2 (July 21, 1958); Betar Education Department, booklet, JI, B3–15/1 (1953); Aharon Propes and others in *The Fourth World Congress of Betar: Discussions and Decisions,* ed. Yosef Krost (Tel Aviv: Betar Department of Culture and Instruction, 1950), 5.

30. Herut Movement, "Decisions of the First Convention," JI, H1/13/1/2 (1949); Begin, speech, JI, P20/11/1 (May 15, 1948); Ben-Eliezer in Herut Movement, "National Council Meeting Protocol," JI, H1/11/6 (September 1954).

31. Herut Movement, "Announcement of the Irgun Zvai Leumi," JI, H1/1/1 (June 1948); Herut Movement, "Theses from M. Begin's Lecture on the Direction of Our Propaganda," JI, P20/12/1 (September 1948); Irgun Zvai Leumi, declaration, JI, H1/1/1 (June 15, 1948); Betar, *Decisions of the 6th World Congress of Betar* (Tel Aviv: Betar, 1953).

32. Menachem Begin, "Speech of Menachem Begin before the Masses of Jerusalem," *Hamashkif,* August 6, 1948. See also Herut Movement, Department for Public Opinion Research, JI, H1/4/19 (various); Begin, "Homeland and Freedom"; Begin, "Five Principles," *Herut,* August 27, 1948; Herut Movement, "To the Nation in Zion!" JI, H1/10/4 (1949).

33. Begin, "Five Principles."

34. Quoted in Bar-On, "Ha-bitchonism ve-mevakrav" [Bitchonism and Its Critics], 76.

35. Naor, *Greater Israel,* 98–99.

36. Herut Movement, "First National Council Meeting," JI, H1/11/1 (October 20, 1948).

37. Menachem Begin, speech given in Ramat-Gan, JI, P20/11/1 (August 19, 1948).

38. Herut Movement, "Decisions of the 2nd National Convention," JI, H1/13/2 (1951); Herut Movement, "Materials related to the 3rd National Convention, 1954," JI, H1/13/3/1.

39. Begin, "Victory of the Truth"; Begin, "Who Gave You the Right?!"; Begin, "Sowed Deceit, Reaping Hostility."

40. Herut Parliamentary Faction, protocol, JI, H2/1/5 (March 7, 1949); Begin, speech, JI, H2/9/1 (March 8, 1949); Menachem Begin, undated Begin speech in the first Knesset, JI, H2/1/4 (1949); Begin, "Victory of the Truth"; Begin, "Sowed Deceit, Reaping Hostility"; Herut Central Committee, protocol, JI, H1/2/4 (March 9, 1954); Ahimeir, *ha-Tsiyonut ha-mahpkhanit* [Revolutionary Zionism], 229–32 (in 1957).

41. See, for example, the reaction of Menashe Ben-Ari, Arye Altman's son, in Grossman, *Yellow Wind*, 102–3, 108–9.

42. Menachem Begin, "Those who Admit the Main [Point] of the Enemy," *Maariv*, September 22, 1972, my emphasis. Menachem Begin, "With Mixed Feelings…," *Maariv*, January 8, 1971; Menachem Begin, "The Right of the Jewish Nation to Eretz Israel Is Not Subject to Appeal," *Eretz Israel* (1972); see also Meridor in Gahal Knesset Faction, meeting protocol, JI, H2/2/10/2 (June 9, 1967); Menachem Begin, "The Nation and the People towards the Second Twenty-Five Years," *Eretz Israel* (1973); Menachem Begin, speech to the Center for the Study of Zionism, JI, P20/21/1 (November 28, 1974); Herut Central Committee, meeting protocol, JI, H1/2/21/2 (December 16, 1973).

43. Shamir in Misgav, *Sihot eem Yitzhak Shamir* [Conversations with Yitzhak Shamir], 22, 156; also Shmueli in Herut Central Committee, meeting protocol, JI, H1/2/24 (July 31, 1974). On at least one occasion Shamir stated that Eretz Israel is not entirely in Israel's hands, Misgav, 70, 103.

44. Netanyahu, *Makom Tachat Hashemesh* [A Place under the Sun], 25, my emphasis.

45. Menachem Begin, "Jew, Nation, and Religion: Knesset Speech on the Issue—Who Is a Jew," JI, P20/11/3 (February 9, 1970); Begin in Gahal Knesset Faction, meeting protocol, JI, H2/2/12 (August 12, 1970); Menachem Begin, "To a Confrontation without Credibility," *Maariv*, November 27, 1970; Menachem Begin, "Worry and Consolation: Following a Meeting with Youth in Haifa," *Maariv*, December 11, 1970; Menachem Begin, "Background Conversation—and the Background of the Conversation," *Eretz Israel*, April 1971; Menachem Begin, *Maariv*, July 19, 1974; Yitzhak Shamir, speech opening the Likud's 1988 election campaign, JI, H1/14/12/2 (September 6, 1988); Shamir in Herut Leadership Meeting, protocol, JI, H1/2/41/? (December 5, 1985); the Committee on Zionist Organization, Diaspora Jewry, and Immigration and Absorption of the 11th Herut Convention in Herut Movement, *11th National Convention*, JI, H1/13/11/31 (1972); Herut Central Committee, protocol, JI, H1/2/21/2 (December 16, 1973); Gahal Executive, meeting protocol, JI, H3/7/2 (August 21, 1973); Likud, "Platform for the 11th Knesset," JI, H1/19/1 (1984); Moshe Katzav and others in Herut Center, protocol, JI, H1/2/44 (April 24, 1988). Yitzhak Shamir in *Nekuda* 68 (1984).

46. For example, Herut Central Committee, announcement, JI, H1/2/18 (June 15, 1967). For a later example, see Shamir's statement that "we are determined that there will not be and there not arise any foreign sovereignty on any part whatsoever of Eretz Israel. We decided, we swore, and we made it so." Quoted in Naor, *Greater Israel*, 241.

47. Begin spoke of the "partition anew of Eretz Israel," or its redivision, or otherwise implied that it was currently whole in the following settings: Menachem Begin, "The Right Is Whole, the Wholeness Is the Right," *Maariv*, October 24, 1969; Gahal Knesset Faction, protocol, JI, H2/2/12 (August 12, 1970); Gahal Knesset Faction, "Proposals Raised during a Political Discussion," JI, H2/2/12 (October 13, 1970); Menachem Begin, speech at the Herut 10th National Conference, JI, H1/11/14 (November, 1971); Begin in State of Israel, *Divrei HaKnesset* (March 16, 1972), 1845; Menachem Begin, "Eretz Israel Is Ours: That Is Justice and We Will Insist on It," *Eretz Israel* (1973): 9; Menachem Begin, "Speculators upon You, Eretz Israel," *Maariv*, April 13, 1973; Menachem Begin, *Maariv*, July 6, 1973; Menachem Begin, "Leftism, Nationalism, and Chauvinism," JI, P20/10/5 (1973), 23; Begin, "The Right of the Jewish Nation to Eretz Israel Is Not Subject to Appeal"; Begin, "To a Confrontation without Credibility"; Menachem Begin, "Beyond the 5th of February," *Maariv*, February 5, 1971; Herut Movement, *11th National Convention*, JI, H1/13/11/31 (1972); Begin, "Nation and the People towards the Second Twenty Five Years"; Menachem Begin, "The Partition as Principle and Insult," *Maariv*, July 20, 1973; Herut Movement, "Protocol of the National Council," JI, H1/11/17 (September 1974); Herut Central Committee, protocol, July 31, 1974, JI, H1/2/24;

Menachem Begin, "For the Good of the People—For the Country," *Maariv*, August 3, 1973; Gahal Central Committee, meeting protocol, JI, H3/3/1 (August 3, 1970). See also Gahal Central Committee, meeting protocol, JI, H3/3/1 (December 11, 1969).

48. Gahal, "Platform for the 7th Knesset Elections," JI, H1/16/3 (1969), my emphasis. See also Mates Drobles, press release, JI, H2/6/3 (May 29, 1974); Chaim Korfo in Likud Movement, "Likud Unification Convention Materials," JI, H3/7/4 (May 10, 1981); Menachem Begin, speech at the "Unification Conference" of the Likud, JI, H3/7/3 (1981), 26; Likud Movement, *Unification Charter of the Likud*, JI, H3/7/4 (1981); Rephael Kotolovitch, the head of the Immigration and Absorption Department of the Jewish Agency, in Betar World Leadership, *Report to the 14th World Congress of Betar* (Jerusalem, 1982); Preparatory Committee of Political Issues, "Proposal to the 14th Herut Convention," JI, H1/13/14/11 (1979); Betar World Leadership, *Report to the 14th World Congress;* Moshe Katzav in Betar World Leadership, *Report to the 15th World Congress of Betar* (Maale Edumim, 1986); Shamir in Likud Movement, election pamphlet, JI, H1/14/11/9 (1984); Shamir and others in Herut Leadership Meeting, protocol, JI, H1/2/41/2 (December 5, 1985); Shamir in Misgav, *Conversations with Yitzhak Shamir,* 148; Shamir, speech, JI, H1/14/12/2 (September 6, 1988).

49. E.g., State of Israel, *Divrei HaKnesset* (March 16, 1972); Yoram Aridor, "Talking Points," JI, H1/10/30 (October, 1968); Herut Movement, "The Decisions of the 8th National Convention," JI, H1/11/13 (December 1967); Likud, "This Is Our Plan: Excerpts from the Principles and Lines of Action of the Likud," JI, H1/14/8/4 (1973); Gahal, "Platform for the 7th Knesset Elections," JI, H1/16/3.

50. Likud, "Election Advertisement Targeted at Religious Jews," JI, H1/14/12/8 (1988), my emphasis.

51. Preparatory Committee for Foreign and Security Affairs of Herut's 15th convention, meeting minutes, JI, H1/13/15/1/2 (February 6, 1986), my emphasis.

52. Menachem Begin, speech to the 9th Herut National Convention, May 1968, JI, H1/13/9/15 (1968). The Gahal platform similarly concluded that "our patrimony was liberated." Gahal, "Platform for the 7th Knesset Elections," JI, H1/16/3. Cf. Begin, "Who Gave You the Right?!"

53. Menachem Begin, "Overview of Foreign Policy Issues, Herut Center," JI, P20/11/4 (April 24, 1975).

54. Yoram Aridor, "Talking Points," JI, H1/10/30 (February, 1969); Begin, "Partition as Principle and Insult"; Menachem Begin, "Our Right to Eretz Israel: Lecture at a Gahal Center Meeting, November 20, 1968," *Hayom*, December 6, 1968; Menachem Begin, "The Future of Gahal," *Maariv*, July 16, 1971; Menachem Begin, "What Is a State—and What Is a Homeland?," *Maariv*, October 1, 1976; Begin in Herut Central Committee, protocol, JI, H1/2/24 (July 31, 1974); Gahal Central Committee, "Proposed Decision," JI, H3/3/1 (November 20, 1968); the Likud announcement against territorial compromise in Herut Central Committee, protocol, JI, H1/2/21/2 (December 16, 1973); Begin, quoted in Naor, *Greater Israel*, 292, originally in *Yediot Ahronot*, October 17, 1969; Shamir, quoted in Naor, *Greater Israel*, 240–41.

55. Likud, "Platform for the 9th Knesset," JI, H1/19/1 (1977); Likud, "Platform for the 10th Knesset," JI, H1/19/1 (1981).

56. Aridor, "Talking Points," JI, H1/10/30 (October 1968). This was also noted by Peleg, *Begin's Foreign Policy,* 14 n. 12.

57. Begin, speech, JI, H1/13/9/15 (1968); Naor, *Greater Israel,* 296.

58. Herut Central Committee, protocol, JI, H1/2/21/2 (December 16, 1973); Pichman in Herut Central Committee, meeting protocol, JI, H1/2/26 (April 24, 1975); Tuli Segel in Preparatory Committee for Foreign Affairs and Security for Herut's 13th National Convention, meeting protocol, JI, H1/13/13/6 (December 2, 1976).

59. Begin, cited in Beinin, "Political Economy and Public Culture"; Herut Central Committee, protocol, JI, H1/2/26 (April 24, 1975); Menachem Begin to Hillel Kook, letter, JI, P20/9/63 (May 24, 1946); Herut Central Committee, protocol, JI, H1/2/4 (March 9, 1954); Ben-Elissar in Ansky, *Mekhirat ha-Likud* [The Marketing of the Likud], 21; Benziman, *Rosh memshala be-mazor* [Prime Minister under Siege], 150; Aronoff, *Israeli Visions and Divisions,* 10.

60. Herut Central Committee, protocol, JI, H1/2/21/2 (December 16, 1973).

61. Gahal (meaning Ember) is the Hebrew acronym for Gush Herut-Liberalim, the Herut-Liberal Bloc. Gahal Knesset Faction, meeting protocol, JI, H2/2/11 (November 1, 1968).

62. Gahal, "Platform for the 7th Knesset Elections," JI, H1/16/3; Begin in Herut Central Committee, protocol, JI, H1/2/21/2 (December 16, 1973); Menachem Begin, "The Land, the Labor, and the Nation," *Maariv*, April 27, 1973; Begin, "To a Confrontation without Credibility"; Menachem Begin, "Transcript of Begin's Speech at the College of National Security," JI, P20/27/8 (August 11, 1982); Menachem Begin, "Realistic Foundations for a National Policy," *HaUma* 42 (1974); Herut Central Committee, protocol, JI, H1/2/24 (July 31, 1974); See also September 11, 1974, meeting; Menachem Begin, speech to the 11th National Moatza meeting, JI, P20/11/4 (September 29, 1974).

63. Gahal Central Committee, protocol, JI, H3/3/1 (August 3, 1970). The Allon plan proposed that the densely populated areas of the West Bank would be returned to Jordan, while Israel would continue to maintain control over a strip along the Jordan River. For details, see Allon, "Israel: The Case for Defensible Borders."

64. State of Israel, *Divrei HaKnesset* (March 16, 1972).

65. Herut Knesset Faction, meeting protocol, JI, H2/2/13 (March 15, 1972).

66. Herut Central Committee, meeting protocol, JI, H1/2/32/1 (January 8, 1978).

67. Cf. Begin, *Revolt*, 162; and Menachem Begin, *ha-Mered: zihkronotav shel mefaked ha-Irgun ha-tseva'i ha- le'umi be-Eretz Yisrael* [The Revolt: Memoirs of the commander of the Irgun in the Land of Israel], 220.

68. Herut Central Committee, protocol, JI, H1/2/21/2 (December 16, 1973), my emphasis. Also Begin, speech, JI, P20/21/1 (November 28, 1974); Begin in 13th Herut National Convention, "Protocols, Continuation," JI, H1/13/13/19 (January 1977).

69. Herut Central Committee, protocol, JI, H1/2/21/2 (December 16, 1973). While this is not the first time the idea was raised in Revisionist circles, it was the first time that it caught on. For an earlier instance, see Herut Movement, proclamation, JI, H1/10/10 (August, 28, 1955).

70. Nachson in 13th Herut National Convention, protocols, JI, H1/13/13/18 (January 1977); Segel and Hareven in Herut Central Committee, protocol, JI, H1/2/24 (July 31, 1974); Shamir in Misgav, *Conversations with Yitzhak Shamir*, 156; Netanyahu, *Place under the Sun*, 150–53, 155, 340–51; Papo in Preparatory Committee for Foreign and Security Affairs of Herut's 15th Convention, minutes, JI, H1/13/15/1/2 (February 6, 1986); Ariel Sharon in Herut Movement, *14th Herut national convention*, JI, H1/13/14/21 (June 1979); Herut Center, protocol, JI, H1/2/44 (April 24, 1988).

71. For example, Ben-Elissar, press release, JI, H1/10/29 (June 9, 1974); Ne'eman, *Mediniyut ha-reiya ha-mefukahat* [A Shrewd Policy], 54, originally in 1977; 168, originally in 1980; Herut Central Committee, meeting protocol, JI, H1/2/36 (August 24, 1980); Shamir in Herut Central Committee, protocol, JI, H1/2/36 (August 24, 1980); Yitzhak Shamir, "Speech Establishing the Likud as a Single Party," JI, H1/14/12/6 (August 25, 1988); Herut Center, protocol, JI, H1/2/44 (April 24, 1988); Freedman and Ortal in Preparatory Committee for Foreign and Security Affairs of Herut's 15th Convention, minutes, JI, H1/13/15/1/2 (February 6, 1986), Aharon Ben-Ami in Orbach, "One Bank to the Jordan," *Nekuda* 95 (1986), 30; Even Geula Cohen made this argument. See *Nekuda* 97 (1986); Geula Cohen, *On Right and On Left* (Reshet Bet of Kol Israel, August 22, 2002); Dekel in *Nekuda* 115 (1987). Dekel's statement is representative of the rising acceptance of "transfer" within the Revisionist movement and the assumption that this transfer would be to Jordan.

72. Preparatory Committee for Foreign and Security Affairs of Herut's 15th Convention, minutes, JI, H1/13/15/1/2 (February 6, 1986).

73. On at least one occasion, however, Netanyahu retreated from his consistent comments that Jordan was the Palestinian state. See Heral and Baltour Hakak, "The Government of the Retreat Must Be Defeated before 1996: An Interview with Benjamin Netanyahu," *Nekuda* 169 (1993).

74. *Maariv*, "Report about Herut Convention," *Maariv*, June 7, 1979; Menachem Begin, Opening speech to the 14th Herut Convention, JI, H1/13/13/6 (1979). Ilan Peleg suggests that

this change was not sincere, since Begin's hostility toward the Hashemite kingdom destroyed any possibility that he would invite Hussein to the Camp David negotiations. Peleg, *Begin's Foreign Policy,* 109. While possible, the unwillingness to invite Hussein to the talks could also reasonably be explained by Begin's unwillingness to deal realistically with the Palestinian problem, rather than as a reflection of his attitude toward Jordan.

75. Herut Central Committee, meeting protocol, JI, H1/2/34 (March 19, 1979), my emphasis.

76. See Herut Movement, "Protocols from the 14th National Convention," JI, H1/13/14/24 (June 1979). See also Gershon Solomon in Herut Central Committee, protocol, JI, H1/2/32/1 (January 8, 1978); Arens in Herut Central Committee, protocol, JI, H1/2/34 (March 19, 1979); Zipori in Herut Movement, *14th Herut National Convention,* JI, H1/13/14/21 (June 1979).

77. Herut Central Committee, meeting protocol, JI, H1/2/37 (November 19, 1981), my emphasis.

78. Begin, "Partition as Principle and Insult." Even Yochanan Bader, who as late as 1973 still agitated for the vision of both banks of the Jordan, wrote in 1974 that geographically the Jordan River is an ideal natural border, and called on the nation to stand on guard lest it be surprised by the redivision of Eretz Israel. Cf. Herut Central Committee, protocol, JI, H1/2/21/2 (December 16, 1973); and Yochanan Bader, "The Danger of Separation with Jordan," JI, H1/10/29 (July 2, 1974).

79. Netanyahu, *Place under the Sun,* 196; Shamir in Misgav, *Conversations with Yitzhak Shamir,* 66, 100; Shilanski made a similar statement in Herut Central Committee, protocol, JI, H1/2/32/1 (January 8, 1978).

80. Betar World Leadership, *Report to the 14th World Congress.*

81. http://www.betar.org.il/ideology/policy.htm (accessed April 12, 2009).

82. Likud English Division, "Judea and Samaria: Ten Thoughts," JI, H1/14/12/8 (1988).

83. Originally on June 5, 1991. Begin, *Kave imut* [Confrontations], 126–27.

84. Menachem Rahat, "The Likud to Rabin: We Will Vote for the Agreement with Jordan," *Maariv,* July 31, 1994.

85. The Likud's objections revolved around the unsettled issues of Jerusalem and the Palestinians. Arye Bender and Menachem Rahat, "The Knesset Supports Peace," *Hatzofe,* August 4, 1994; Israel Meidad, "Will They Forget Their Betraying Right Hand?" *Nekuda* 182 (1994).

86. Likud Knesset Faction, meeting protocol, JI, H2/2/25 (August 3, 1994); State of Israel, *Divrei HaKnesset* (February 1, 1995); State of Israel, *Divrei HaKnesset* (October 25, 1994).

87. For examples, see Herut Movement, "To the Nation in Zion!" JI, H1/10/4; Begin, *Life View and National View,* 34; Herut Movement, "Materials Related to the 3rd National Convention," JI, H1/13/3/1 (1954); Keren-Paz, "A Hagada of Independence Day," JI, B3/15/1 (1961).

88. Shapiro, *Road to Power,* 123.

89. This began, apparently, already in 1949. See, for example, Mapai Center, "Letter to Representatives," LPA, 2–2-1949–55 (May 6, 1949). See also Aran in Mapai, "Protocol of Meeting with the Press about the Upcoming Elections to the 23rd Zionist Congress and the 2nd Knesset," LPA, 2–13-1951–103 (1951); Sharett in Mapai, "Meeting of Lecturers about the Propaganda for the 23rd Zionist Congress Elections," LPA, 2–13-1951–104 (May 13, 1951). See also Weitz, "Road to the 'Upheaval.'"

90. Bnei Akiva Education Department, "Parties in Israel," RZA, Bnei Akiva in Eretz Israel, 85/1 (1961).

91. Shapiro, *Road to Power,* 116.

92. Shapiro, *Road to Power,* 123.

93. Naor, *Greater Israel,* 205; Shapiro, *Road to Power.*

94. Herut Central Committee, protocol, JI, H1/2/4 (March 9, 1954), my emphasis. This is not the very first time that Begin hinted that Transjordan was not part of Eretz Israel, but it is the first time that it formed part of a consistent pattern. In 1943, Begin placed Transjordan in the same category as the other countries in the Middle East: in the process of excoriating Soviet policy in the region, he stated that "Persia, Iraq, Transjordan, Yemen, Egypt, and co. are countries of poverty and mass hunger." Begin, "Russia and Zionism." In a never-published

article intended for an IDF magazine before the 1949 elections, Begin criticized the relations with Abdullah because they might allow the British to return to the region, not because they legitimated a foreign occupation of the homeland. Menachem Begin, "Article for BaMachane, Never Published," JI, P20/10/6 (1949).

95. Compare Begin, "*Speech*," JI, P20/11/7 (November 9, 1949), and Menachem Begin, "Knesset Speech," JI, H2/9/2 (October 18, 1955). For similar statements, see Menachem Begin, "Knesset Speech," JI, H2/9/2 (June 18, 1956); Menachem Begin, "The Right That Creates the Might," *Maariv*, May 11, 1973.

96. Shapiro, *Road to Power,* 116.

97. Cf. Herut Movement, "Elections Propaganda," JI, H1/14/4/3 (1959); and Herut Movement, "Herut Principles," JI, H1/14/5/7 (1961).

98. Herut Movement, "Elections Propaganda," JI, H1/14/5/4 (1961).

99. Betar, *Report to the 7th World Congress of Betar* (Tel-Aviv 1957), 11.

100. Betar, *Decisions of the 9th World Congress of Betar* (Jerusalem, 1962), 5.

101. Herut Movement, *Herut 6th National Convention,* JI, H1/13/6/7 (April, 1961).

102. There are a few oblique indications that some rational adaptation or routinization might have been taking place. Both a 1954 proposal that Herut's "branches in the Diaspora … be instructed to begin to speak and to explain the importance of the wholeness of the homeland," and Betar's 1956 decision to address the "problem" that some Betar members "do not understand the meaning" of Jabotinsky's song "The Left Bank of the Jordan," imply a declining salience of the original map image. Herut Central Committee, protocol, JI, H1/2/4 (March 9, 1954); Betar Education Department, *Instructional Packet No. 5,* JI, B3–15/1 (1956). There were also a few scattered and lonely notes in the statements to Betar's 4th Convention implying that Transjordan is not as important a part of Eretz Israel as the rest. See some of the speakers in Krost, *Fourth World Congress of Betar,* 30, 43, 77. While these references suggest that, at least in some quarters, the old map image was under some stress before the tactical modulation would have had any time to "filter down," they never progressed beyond the margins of the movement. This is also true for those who realized that they lost the battle for hegemony as early as the mid-1940s. They concluded that the Revisionist movement was "on its last legs" and argued that the NZO should be disbanded and the Revisionists should return to the Zionist institutions. This group, however, was soundly defeated by Begin's wing of the Revisionists, who remained outside the main Zionist institutions and therefore experienced little pressure to engage in even tactical ideological modulations in order to reenter mainstream Zionist politics. Stein-Ashkenazi, *Betar in the Land of Israel,* 304–6. The "Free Center" faction suffered the same fate in 1965.

103. Naor, *Greater Israel,* 91–92, 186, 289 n. 183; Shavit, *ha-Mitologyot shel ha-yamin* [The Mythologies of the Zionist Right Wing], 146; Begin, speech, JI, P20/27/8 (August 11, 1982).

104. Stein-Ashkenazi, *Betar in the Land of Israel,* 291.

105. For examples of scholars who point to the 1967 war as the key cause of ideological change in the realm of borders, see Vital, "Hagdarat ye'adim be-mediniyut hutz" [The Definition of Goals in Foreign Policy]; Sofer, *Begin: An Anatomy of Leadership,* 115; Barzilai, "Jewish Democracy at War," 187; Naor, *Greater Israel,* 65.

106. Herut Central Committee, protocol, JI, H1/2/18 (June 15, 1967); Rephael Bashan, "Interview with Menachem Begin," *Yediot Ahronot,* March 5, 1971; Menachem Begin, "Knesset Speech: You Don't Have a Majority in the Knesset for a Re-partition of Eretz Israel," *Jerusalem Post Advertisement,* January 22, 1974; see also the later debates in Herut Movement, "Protocol of the National Council," JI, III/11/17 (September 1974); Herut Central Committee, protocol, JI, H1/2/26 (April 24, 1975); Herut Central Committee, protocol, JI, H1/2/21/2 (December 16, 1973); Herut Central Committee, protocol, JI, H1/2/32/1 (January 8, 1978); Herut Movement, "Protocols from the 14th National Convention, June 1979," JI, H1/13/14/24. This was also the dominant position before the war. See Bader in Herut Central Committee, protocol, JI, H1/2/6 (August 12, 1956). See also Ze'ev Jabotinsky, "Testimony to British Parliament," JI, A1/4/37 (July 13, 1937).

107. Herut Movement, "Protocols of the 9th Herut National Convention," JI, H1/13/9/16 (May, 1968).

108. Sprinzak, *Ascendance of Israel's Radical Right,* 331 n. 336; Sella, "Custodians and Redeemers," 243. Begin, however, was not entirely consistent. On at least one occasion he implied that Sinai was part of the Land of Israel. "Interview with Menachem Begin," *Yediot Ahronot,* August 10, 1973.

109. Quoted in Misgav, *Conversations with Yitzhak Shamir,* 157.

110. The first claim is made by Preuss, *Begin.* The second claim is made by Brenner, *The Iron Wall,* 155; Peleg, *Begin's Foreign Policy,* 95; Naor, *Greater Israel,* 185; Galanti, Aaronson, and Schnell, "Power and Changes in the Balance between Ideology and Pragmatism." The final argument is made by Auerbach and Ben-Yehuda, "Attitudes towards an Existence Conflict," 338, 343; Naor, *Greater Israel.*

111. Shapiro's identification of 1959 as a turning point is a notable exception. However, Shapiro ignores the strategic implications of Begin's tactical machinations. Shapiro, *Road to Power.*

112. Yehiel Kadishai, personal communication, August 19, 2002.

113. Naor, *Greater Israel,* 65.

114. Mendilow, *Ideology, Party Change, and Electoral Campaigns,* 88. For others who credit the formation of Gahal with moderating aspects of Revisionist policy and ideology, see Dowty, *Jewish State,* 90; Aronoff, *Israeli Visions and Divisions,* 25–26; Sofer, *Begin,* 86; Peleg, *Begin's Foreign Policy,* 39; Aronoff, "Political Polarization"; Naor, *Greater Israel,* 80, 185.

115. Herut Movement, "Materials Related to the 3rd National Convention," JI, H1/13/3/1 (1954).

116. Various, "Talks between Herut and General Zionists," JI, H1/8/37 (1955–57).

117. Shapiro, *Road to Power,* 128.

118. Menachem Begin, "Begin's Closing Speech of the General Discussion of the 8th National Herut Convention," JI, H1/13/8/3 (1966); Menachem Begin, "About the Taken for Granted," JI, P20/10/18 (n.d.).

119. Examples of invocations of the old map image after the emergence of the new variant include Menachem Begin, "In the Congress and in the Knesset," *Herut,* May 11, 1956; Moshe Emanuel in Herut Movement, "Speeches during the 5th National Committee Meeting," JI, H1/13/5/3 (1958); Menachem Begin, "Knesset Speech," JI, H2/9/6 (December 6, 1966); Herut Movement, "The Political Decisions of the 1958 5th National Convention," JI, H1/13/5/4 (1958); Keren-Paz, "Hagada of Independence Day"; Esther Raziel-Naor, quoted in Naor, *Greater Israel,* 68; Menachem Begin, "The Wholeness of the Nation and the Wholeness of the Land: Speech at the National Council of the Herut Movement," JI, P20/11/3 (April 23, 1970); Herut Central Committee, protocol, JI, H1/2/4 (March 9, 1954); Ahimeir, *Revolutionary Zionism,* 228. Chaim Landau in Herut Movement, "Parliamentary Queries," JI, H2/3/4 (various); Hayom, "Report of a TV Interview with Menachem Begin," *Hayom,* January 8, 1969; Geula Cohen, "Face to Face with Minister Menachem Begin: Why I Am Sitting in a National Unity Government," *Maariv,* June 20, 1969; Moked TV Show, transcript, JI, P20/12/4 (January 22, 1970).

120. Begin, "Our Right to Eretz Israel."

121. Gahal Knesset Faction, "Leadership Meeting Protocol," JI, H/2/26 (August 30, 1967).

122. Menachem Begin, speech at the joint meeting of the centers of Herut and Liberals in Jerusalem," JI, P20/11/2 (June 27, 1967); Menachem Begin, speech at a Herut Rally, JI, P20/11/2 (October 23, 1967); Menachem Begin, lecture at Beit Brenner Club, JI, P20/21/1 (March 8, 1968); Begin, "Our Right to Eretz Israel."

123. Aridor, "Talking Points," JI, H1/10/30 (October, 1968).

124. Herut Movement, "Materials from National Convention," JI, H1/13/9/7 (1968); see also Begin, speech, JI, H3/7/3 (1981); Likud Party, "Likud's Platform for the 9th Knesset (English Version)," JI, H1/1/15 (1977).

125. Until 1978, the map of both banks of the Jordan was still engraved on the Herut Membership card. Meidad, "Will They Forget Their Betraying Right Hand?"

126. Naor, *Greater Israel,* 290–91. This explains the occasional reference to the division (or redivision) of "western Eretz Israel"—implying the continued existence of an "eastern" land of Israel. See Menachem Begin, "Dull-Sensed Rulers," *Maariv,* February 8, 1974; Begin, "Leftism, Nationalism, and Chauvinism," JI, P20/10/5, 23; Begin, "The Land, the Labor, and the Nation"; Begin, "For the Good of the People"; also the Likud's condemnation of Israel's acceptance of UN Resolution 242 in Likud Executive, meeting protocol, JI, H2/2/37 (October 20, 1973); Gahal, "Platform for the 7th Knesset Elections," JI, H1/16/3; Likud Movement, "Likud Platform for the 8th Knesset," JI, H1/14/8/4 (1973).

127. Yair Sheleg, "There Was Once a Movement," *Nekuda* 114 (1987): 59. See also Geula Cohen in Herut Central Committee, meeting protocol, JI, H1/2/21/1 (January 14, 1973); Schiff in Herut Movement, "Protocol of the National Council, September 1974," JI, H1/11/17; Shmueli in Herut Central Committee, protocol, JI, H1/2/24 (July 31, 1974).

128. Despite the decline of the salience of the "both banks of the Jordan" map image, Matityahu Drobles, then cochair of the World Zionist Organization's Settlement Department, invoked it in a 1991 interview with Robert Friedman. At the same time, he pushed off the actualization of the right to the East Bank to an indeterminate future: "I read the Bible. It doesn't talk about the borders of England. But Eretz Israel is in the Bible. According to the Bible, I have the right to the East Bank of the Jordan too. For my generation the West Bank is enough. As for the next generation, the East Bank is their problem." Friedman, *Zealots for Zion,* xxiv.

129. Herut Youth, proclamation, JI, H1/8/25/2 (April 11, 1982). A 1989 rally featured a banner with the original Herut map image. *Nekuda* 128 (1989).

130. Menachem Begin, "War of No Choice—or War of Choice," *Maariv,* August 20, 1982; Begin, speech, JI, P20/27/8 (August 11, 1982). Compare this statement with Betar's 1946 vow (see above) to fight for Transjordan. Arye Naor's comment that the second part of this statement generated great anger within Herut shows that, at least for some, the East Bank was still seen as part of the homeland (personal communication, May 2002). Other mentions of the East Bank include M. Eitan in Herut Central Committee, meeting protocol, JI, H1/2/38 (October 28, 1982); Bader in Peleg, *Begin's Foreign Policy,* 134 (the comment was made in 1985); Preparatory Committee for Foreign and Security Affairs of Herut's 15th Convention, minutes, JI, H1/13/15/1/2 (February 6, 1986); Papo in Herut Center, protocol, JI, H1/2/43/1 (July 12, 1987); Misgav, *Conversations with Yitzhak Shamir,* 9. Despite the glaring absence of "both sides of the Jordan" from most documents associated with this conference, the letterhead of the Israeli branch of Betar was still adorned in 1982 with the map including both Israel and Jordan. Also see some of the letters of congratulations to the Congress: Betar World Leadership, *Report to the 14th World Congress.*

131. Peleg, *Begin's Foreign Policy,* 96; Kadishai, personal communication, August 19, 2002.

132. Kadishai, personal communication, September 1, 2002.

133. Herut Movement, "Protocols of the 9th Herut National Convention, May 1968," JI, H1/13/9/16; 13th Herut National Convention, protocols, JI, H1/13/13/18 and H1/13/13/19 (January 1977).

134. Herut Central Committee, protocol, JI, H1/2/21/2 (December 16, 1973).

135. Yehoshua Doib in Herut Movement, "Speeches during the 5th National Committee Meeting, 1958," JI, H1/13/5/3.

136. Herut Movement, protocol, JI, H1/11/15 (September 1972). See also Frenkel in Herut Movement, "Protocol of the National Council," JI, H1/11/17 (September 1974).

137. Herut Central Committee, protocol, JI, H1/2/34 (March 19, 1979), my emphasis; Herut Movement, "Election Propaganda," JI, H1/14/10/12 (1981).

4. Transformations of the Collective Mission

1. Renan, "What Is a Nation?"

2. This was pointed out by Shapiro, *Formative Years of the Israeli Labor Party,* 245.

3. Cohen, *Zion and State*, 189.

4. Weissbrod, "From Labour Zionism to New Zionism"; Aronoff, *Israeli Visions and Divisions*.

5. Frenkel, Shenhav, and Herzog, "Ideological Wellspring of Zionist Capitalism."

6. Cohen, *Zion and State*, 205–6.

7. See, for example, David Ben-Gurion, "Speech at a Public Meeting," LPA, 2–13-1951–103 (March 31, 1951); David Ben-Gurion, "Zionei Derech," LPA, 2–21-1956–42 (May 1956).

8. Cohen, *Zion and State*, 204.

9. Ibid., 212. See also Khenin, "From 'Eretz Yisrael Haovedet' to 'Yisrael Hashniah.'"

10. David Ben-Gurion to Mapai Center, letter, LPA, 2–932-1951–69 (March 10, 1951).

11. Mapai Center, meeting protocol, LPA, 2–23-1953–61 (February 6, 1953); Mapai, "Symposium on the Ideological and Educational Activity of Our Movement at This Time," LPA, 2–14-1952–11 (April 14, 1953).

12. Quoted in Feldestein, *Kesher gordi* [Gordian Knot], 155.

13. Ben-Gurion, *Restored State of Israel*, 857, originally in a September 25, 1967, letter to Shimon Peres.

14. For the reliance on the Holocaust as the trigger of change, see Elon, *Israelis*, 39; Teveth, *Ben-Gurion and the Palestinian Arabs*, viii; Sternhell, *Founding Myths of Israel*, 225; Goldstein, "David Ben-Gurion and the Bi-National Idea," 466. For the assumption that the change was caused by routinization after Mapai's rise to dominance, see Weissbrod, "From Labour Zionism to New Zionism"; Goldstein, 466.

15. See, for example, Shapiro, *Formative Years of the Israeli Labor Party*; Sternhell, *Founding Myths of Israel*.

16. Avizohar, *Broken Mirror*, 78–80.

17. Mundane power conflicts and struggles for influence in the Histadrut also played a role in delaying the merger. Shapiro, *Formative Years of the Israeli Labor Party*, 163. See also Gorni, *Ahdut-ha-avodah* [Ahdut Haavoda]; Goldstein, *Mifleget po'ale Eretz Yisrael* [The Workers Party of the Land of Israel].

18. Sternhell, *Founding Myths of Israel*; Shalev, "Jewish Organized Labor and the Palestinians."

19. Weizmann, *Trial and Error*.

20. Sternhell, *Founding Myths of Israel*, 40.

21. Cohen, *Zion and State*, 7.

22. Quoted in Gorni, *Ahdut Haavoda*, 289, original emphasis.

23. Avizohar, *Broken Mirror*, 112, 108.

24. Ibid., 149–64.

25. Ibid., 113–15.

26. Ibid., 149–64. It is certainly possible that the ideological arguments made by opponents of the agreement were really a cover for the interests of the party apparatus and the Histadrut, whose power was threatened by Ben-Gurion's concessions. See, for example, Shapiro, *Formative Years of the Israeli Labor Party*, 247. However, because the interests of stakeholders in the Labor Zionist institutions and their ideological arguments coincided in this case, this episode cannot be used to discount either one.

27. See, for example, Mapai Center, *Ahdut Haavoda: The 5th Congress of the party, at Kfar Vitkin*, 1942.

28. Yishai, *Factionalism in the Labor Movement*; Gal, *David Ben-Gurion and the American Alignment for a Jewish State*.

29. Ben-Gurion, *Restored State of Israel*, 365.

30. Shapiro, *Formative Years of the Israeli Labor Party*. This was the subject of Katznelson's critique, cited above.

31. Gorni, *Ahdut Haavoda*.

32. Troen, "Frontier Myths and Their Applications"; Goldstein, *Workers Party of the Land of Israel*.

33. Quoted in Shapira, *Berl*, 159.

34. Sternhell, *Founding Myths of Israel.*

35. Late instances of the articulation of socialist goals include Mapai, *Leaflet for the 20th Zionist Congress,* LPA, 2–602-1937–11 (1937); Mapai Central Committee Announcements, "Protocol of the Meeting between Mapai and Hashomer Haaretzi about the Issue of Unification on April 8, 1937," LPA, 2–002-1937–15 (April 18, 1937); Mapai, "Protocol of 11th Mapai Party Council," LPA, 2–22-1937–20. In 1944, Ben-Gurion argued that the state, by itself, is not their end objective, because any ultimate goal would include a socialist society. Cited in Margalit, *Anatomyah shel smol* [Anatomy of the Left], 303–4; Mapai, "A Proposal for the Course of Study for Youth Group Leaders at Beit Berl," LPA, 2–932-1948–23 (1948); Mapai, "Protocol of the 37th Party Council," LPA, 2–11-1949–21 (1949); Mapai Knesset Faction, meeting protocol, LPA, 2–11-1949–1 (June 14, 1949); Mapai, "Elections Platform," LPA, 2–13-1949–50 (1949); Mapai, *7th Convention of the Party,* LPA, 2–21-1950–29 (1950); Mapai, *National Conference in Preparations for the Elections,* LPA, 2–13-1951–110 (July 6–7, 1951); Mapai Youth Center, "The Main Points of the Inter-Party Divisions in Israel," LPA, 2–13-1951–108 (June 20, 1951); Ben-Gurion, "Zionei Derech," LPA, 2–21-1956–42; Mapai Central Ideational Circle, protocol, LPA, 2–932-1954–107 (May 12, 1956); National Conference of Activists to Renew the Shape of Israeli Society, protocol, LPA, 2–23-1979–120 (September 25, 1979).

36. Shapira, *Berl,* 344–45.

37. Elon, *Israelis,* 329, original emphasis.

38. Ibid., 329.

39. Yanait, "Conversation," LPA, 2–201-1937–8 (May 19, 1937). See also Ben-Gurion, Lavon, and others in Mapai Center, meeting protocol, LPA, 2–23-1933–5 (November 21, 1933).

40. Canaani, *Ha-aliya hashniya* [The Second Aliya]; Don-Yehiya and Liebman, "Hafrada ben dat u-medina" [Separation between Religion and State]; Gorni, "Al 'nimoos' hevrati ve-interes leumi" [Social Manners, National Interest]; Don-Yehiya, "Hanukkah and the Myth of the Maccabees"; Zerubavel, *Recovered Roots;* Shapira, *Yehudim hadashim, yehudim yeshanim* [New Jews, Old Jews].

41. Yanait, "Conversation," LPA, 2–201-1937–8 (May 19, 1937).

42. See, for example, Kimmerling, *Invention and Decline of Israeliness,* 124–25; Sternhell, *Founding Myths of Israel.*

43. Schechtman and Benari, *History of the Revisionist Movement,* 235.

44. See Ze'ev Jabotinsky, "Islam"; Katz, *Jabo,* 943; Itizik Remba in Betar, *Report of the Third World Congress of Betar, 11–16 September, 1938, Warsaw,* JI, B2/32/1 (1938), 29; Shavit, *Mythologies of the Zionist Right Wing,* 217.

45. A. Remba, "Letter from Betar's Education Department," JI, B2/8/1 (December 15, 1936), my emphasis.

46. A. Remba, "Letter from Betar's Education Department Responding to Comments on the Letter of December 15," JI, B2/8/1 (December 30, 1936).

47. Katz, *Jabo,* 348–49; Schechtman and Benari, *History of the Revisionist Movement,* 236.

48. Ze'ev Jabotinsky to Ben-Gurion, letter, JI, A1/4/32 (May 2, 1935), original emphasis.

49. Mapai Center, protocol, LPA, 2–23-1933–5 (November 21, 1933).

50. The trend of the increased penetration of religious symbols into Israeli political culture continued in the 1950s and 1960s. Liebman, "Religion and Political Integration in Israel."

51. The Labor movement's ambivalence toward the religious faction is reflected in the fact that these schools were never fully funded. Kafkafi, "Ha-peshet ha-dati" [The Religious "Peshet"].

52. Shapiro, *Road to Power,* 124–25; Betar, *Report to the 7th World Congress.*

53. See Menachem Begin, "That a Judge May Sin," *Herut,* August 30, 1963; Herut Knesset Faction, meeting protocol, JI, H2/2/9 (July 5, 1965); Herut Knesset Faction, meeting protocol, JI, H2/2/12 (January 27, 1970); Begin, "Jew, Nation and Religion," JI, P20/11/3; Menachem Begin, "Approval and Negation in the Zionist Congress," *Maariv,* February 4, 1972; Menachem Begin, speech to the 13th National Convention of Herut, JI, P20/11/4 (January 2,

1977); Menachem Begin, "Notes of a Meeting between PM Begin and a Delegation of Conservative and Reform Rabbis in the Waldorf Astoria Hotel in NY," JI, P20/23/1 (July 24, 1977).

54. Herut Movement, *Herut 6th National Convention,* JI, H1/13/6/7 (April 1961).

55. Herut Knesset Faction, protocol, JI, H2/2/12 (January 27, 1970); Herut Knesset Faction, protocol, JI, H2/2/13 (March 15, 1972).

56. Misgav, *Conversations with Yitzhak Shamir,* 150, 196.

57. Shapira, *New Jews, Old Jews,* 274; Liebman, "Religion and Political Integration in Israel"; Kimmerling, *Invention and Decline of Israeliness,* 124–25.

58. Ram, "National, Ethnic, or Civic?" 409.

59. Shapiro, *Road to Power.*

60. Zameret, "Medina yehudit—ken" [Yes to a Jewish State]. See also the debates in Mapai Knesset Faction, meeting protocol, LPA, 2–11-1951–11 (February 20, 1951); Mapai, *National Conference,* LPA, 2–13-1951–110 (1951).

61. Gorni, "Social Manners, National Interest, and the Question of Coexistence," 275.

62. Mapai Center, protocol, LPA, 2–23-1933–5 (November 21, 1933).

63. Berl Katznelson, address to the 13th Council of Mapai, LPA, 4–006-1937–162 (April 14–16, 1939).

64. Genizi, "Nisyonot leshitoof peula be-mahane hayamin bein shtei milhamot ha-olam" [Attempts at Cooperation within the Right]; Ulman, "Way of Mizrachi toward the State."

65. Zameret, "Yes to a Jewish State." See, for example, Mapai, *National Conference,* LPA, 2–13-1951–110 (1951).

66. In 1937, Agudat Israel argued against partition (and independence) and for the continuation of the British Mandate because of its fear of a secular Zionist state.

67. Friedman, "The State of Israel as a Theological Dilemma," 181–83, 186.

68. Mapai Knesset Faction, "Protocol of Meeting with the Secretariat, and the Histadrut Executive about the Education in the Immigrant Camps Scandal," LPA, 2–11-1950–6 (January 26, 1950).

69. Mapai, "Protocol of 13th Party Council," LPA, 2–22-1939–26 (April 14, 1939); Z. Aronovitch in Mapai Knesset Faction, "Protocol of Meeting with Party Secretariat," LPA, 2–11-1949–2 (September 14, 1949); Mapai, "Protocol of the 37th Party Council," LPA, 2–11-1949–21 (1949); Mapai Knesset Faction Leadership, meeting protocol, LPA, 2–11-1950–10 (July 23, 1950); Mapai Knesset Faction, protocol, LPA, 2–11-1951–11 (February 20, 1951); Mapai Knesset Faction, meeting protocol, LPA, 2–11-1954–27 (July 20, 1954); Mapai Knesset Faction, protocol, LPA, 2–11-1949–1 (June 14, 1949); Mapai, "Material for a Campaign Lecture for the Histadrut Elections," LPA, 2–13-1944–64 (1944).

70. Aronoff, *Power and Ritual in the Israeli Labor Party.* For an example, see Mapai Knesset Faction, protocol, LPA, 2–11-1951–11 (February 20, 1951).

71. Zameret, "Yes to a Jewish State." For an example, see Mapai Knesset Faction, protocol, LPA, 2–11-1949–1 (June 14, 1949).

72. Betar, *Camp Pamphlet,* JI, B8C/9/5 (1944).

73. Begin, speech, JI, P20/11/1 (August 19, 1948); Herut Movement, *Election Leaflet,* JI, H1/14/1/1 (1949).

74. Herut General Secretariat, memorandum, JI, H1/3/1 (December 7, 1948); Herut Movement, "Herut Radio Announcement: From the 'Holy Cannon' to the Shaving of the Heads of Hebrew Soldiers," JI, P20/10/6 (August 9, 1948).

75. Hillel Kook, "Letter to Chaim Weizmann Calling for the Establishment of a Hebrew Republic in Palestine," JI, Kh4/1/6 (April 2, 1945); Sheleg, *ha-Datiyim ha-hadashim* [The New Religious Jews], 284.

76. Begin, *Life View and National View.*

77. Irgun Zvai Leumi, declaration, JI, H1/1/1 (June 15, 1948).

78. Herut Movement, *First National Council Meeting,* JI, H1/11/1 (October 20, 1948); Herut, *Herut Documents,* JI, H1/1/1 (1948); Herut Movement, "Decisions of the First Convention, 1949," JI, H1/13/1/2; Herut Central Committee, *Report to the Herut National Council,*

JI, H1/11/3 (August 1950); Herut Movement, "Materials Related to the 3rd National Convention, 1954," JI, H1/13/3/1.

79. Herut Movement, "Decisions of the First Convention, 1949," JI, H1/13/1/2; Herut Central Committee, *Report to the 3rd National Convention*, JI, H1/13/3/1 (1954). See also Herut Movement, "The Direction of Our Propaganda, 1948," JI, P20/12/1; Menachem Begin, "Guiding Lines for the Hebrew Domestic Policy: Opening Address to the First Herut Convention," JI, P20/10/8 (1949).

80. Herut Movement, "Proposed Law: Basic Law; The Law of the Rights of Man and the State," JI, H2/1/2 (March 2, 1949).

81. Herut Movement, *First National Council Meeting*, JI, H1/11/1 (October 20, 1948); Herut Movement, "National Council Meeting Protocol," JI, H1/11/6 (September 1954).

82. Herut Movement, "Speeches during the 5th National Committee Meeting, 1958," JI, H1/13/5/3.

83. Stein-Ashkenazi, *Betar in the Land of Israel*, 326–28.

84. Krost, *The Fourth World Congress of Betar*, 102–3; Betar, *Pamphlet Listing Decisions of 5th Congress*, JI, B3–19/2/1 (1951); Betar, "Decisions of the 6th World Congress."

85. Herut Movement, "Call to the Religious Voter," JI, H1/14/2/1 (1951), my emphasis.

86. Menachem Begin, "Knesset Speech on Pig Issue—Local Municipalities Law Debate," JI, H2/9/2 (July 25, 1956); Herut Knesset Faction, meeting protocol, JI, H2/2/2 (July 23, 1956).

87. Herut Knesset Faction, meeting protocol, JI, H2/2/2 (July 23, 1956).

88. Ibid.

89. Friedman, "ha-Mafdal be'tmura" [The National Religious Party in Crisis]; Ona, *Biderakhim nifradot* [In Separate Ways].

90. Herut Central Committee, protocol, JI, H1/2/6 (August 12, 1956); Herut Knesset Faction, protocol, JI, H2/2/9 (July 5, 1965); Herut Knesset Faction, protocol, JI, H2/2/13 (March 15, 1972).

91. See Herut Movement, "Protocols of the 9th Herut National Convention, May 1968," JI, H1/13/9/16; Herut Central Committee, protocol, JI, H1/2/21/2 (December 16, 1973); Begin, "For the Good of the People"; Herut Central Committee, protocol, JI, H1/2/24 (July 31, 1974); Likud Movement, "Likud's Internal Assessment of the 1973 Vote," JI, H1/14/8/9 (1974); Herut Knesset Faction, meeting protocol, JI, H2/2/47 (May 19, 1975); 13th Herut National Convention, protocols, JI, H1/13/13/18 (January 1977); Herut Center, protocol, JI, H1/2/44 (April 24, 1988).

92. E.g., Weissbrod, "From Labour Zionism to New Zionism"; Weissbrod, "Gush Emunim Ideology"; Liebman and Don-Yehiya, *Civil Religion in Israel*; Peleg, *Begin's Foreign Policy*; Sprinzak, *Ascendance of Israel's Radical Right*; Ram, "National, Ethnic, or Civic?"

93. Liebman and Don-Yehiya, *Civil Religion in Israel*, 71; Shapiro, *Road to Power*, 125–26.

94. Herut Central Committee, protocol, JI, H1/2/24 (July 31, 1974).

95. See Peleg, *Begin's Foreign Policy*, 56. Geula Cohen was perhaps the most vocal proponent of this new mission. See, for example, Likud Movement, press release, JI, H2/6/3 (March 15, 1976); Likud Movement, press release, JI, H2/6/3 (May 19, 1975); 13th Herut National Convention, protocols, JI, H1/13/13/18 and H1/13/13/19 (January 1977).

96. The party that members of the faction founded, Techiya, openly articulated their rejection of normalization.

97. Ravitzky, *Messianism, Zionism, and Jewish Religious Radicalism*, 82–83.

98. Ibid.

99. Daniel Ben-Simon, "Foreign Fire," *Haaretz Supplement*, April 21, 1986; Yitzhak Shilot, "The Merkaz-ist Revolution," *Nekuda* 181 (1994).

100. While this was the general view within Religious Zionism, not everybody subscribed to it. Rabbi Solobchek, for example, saw the state as a great divine message but did not subscribe to the view that the state itself marked the beginning of redemption. Naor, "Ribonut medinat yisrael ba-mahshava ha-yehudit-ortodoxit" [The Sovereignty of the State of Israel in Orthodox-Jewish Thought].

101. See, for example, Moshe Shapira in NRP, press release, RZA, NRP and Hapoel Hamizrachi, 45 (June 5, 1969); Warhaftig, *Fifty Years;* Warhaftig in Government Meeting, protocol, RZA, Zerach Warhaftig unit, folder 9/3 (December 26, 1967); Warhaftig in Mizrachi and Hapoel Hamizrachi, *21st World Convention, June 19–24, 1968,* 164–66; Yitzhak Refael in NRP, *Essence of Peace;* NRP, elections broadcast, RZA, NRP in the Knesset, 133 (1973); Yitzhak Rephael in Hatzofe, "Symposium," RZA, Warhaftig Papers, 255/1a (1975); Cohen, "Eye to Eye: Interview with Zerach Warhaftig."

102. See, for example, Shraggai, "Vision and Fulfillment"; Hapoel Hamizrachi, *Report of the 10th Convention of Hapoel Hamizrachi in Israel,* RZA, NRP in the Knesset, 2/1 (October 30—November 4, 1949); Mizrachi, *Report of the 18th World Congress of Mizrachi,* RZA, World Mizrachi Center, 39 (August, 1949); Mizrachi and Hapoel Hamizrachi, *Proceedings of the 19th World Convention,* Ginzach Hazionut Hadatit (1955); Hamizrachi Organization in Eretz Israel, *Report to the 12th Convention* (1956), 19; NRP, *Constitution,* RZA, NRP and Hapoel Hamizrachi, 4 (1956); NRP, *Report of the Founding Convention of the NRP,* RZA, Hapoel Hamizrachi, 249; World Mizrachi and Hapoel Hamizrachi Center, "Decisions," RZA, Mizrachi World Center, 57 (1957).

103. NRP, "Platform for the 6th Knesset," RZA, Hapoel Hamizrachi, 268, originally in *Hatzofe,* October 27, 1965. See also United Religious Front, "Platform for the Elections to the Constituent Assembly," RZA, Hapoel Hamizrachi, 263 (1949); Hapoel Hamizrachi, "Platform for the 2nd Knesset," RZA, Hapoel Hamizrachi, 263 (1951); NRP, "Platform for the 5th Knesset," RZA (1961); NRP, *Report of the 13th Convention of the Histadrut Hapoel Hamizrachi and the 2nd Convention of the Religious-National Party,* RZA, NRP in the Knesset, 2/1 (June 19–26, 1963); NRP, *In the Campaign of the Nation and the State (Remarks, Conclusions, Facts, and Documents): A Collection Presented to the Second NRP Convention and the 13th Hapoel Hamizrachi Organization Convention* (Tel Aviv, 1963); NRP, *Report of the 2nd Convention,* RZA, NRP and Hapoel Hamizrachi, publications annex, box 192 (1964).

104. See, for example, Bnei Akiva, "Protocol of the Second National Council," RZA, Bnei Akiva in Eretz Israel, 21/1 (September 1943); Bnei Brak Branch Halutzim Tribe, *Halutzim,* April-May 1944; Bnei Akiva, "Decisions of World Meeting, 1954," RZA, Bnei Akiva in Eretz Israel, 38/1; Bnei Akiva, "Decisions of the Sixth Convention of Bnei Akiva," RZA, Bnei Akiva in Eretz Israel, 38/1 (1956); Bnei Akiva, "Decisions of the 7th Convention," RZA, Bnei Akiva in Eretz Israel, 213/3 (1958); Bnei Akiva in Israel National Leadership, "The Aims and Ways of Education in Bnei Akiva: A Symposium," RZA, Bnei Akiva instructional materials, 350 (1960); Bnei Akiva Education Department, "Parties in Israel," RZA, Bnei Akiva in Eretz Israel, 85/1 (1961); Bnei Akiva, "Decisions of the 8th Convention," RZA, Bnei Akiva in Eretz Israel, 42/1 (1961); Bnei Akiva, "Decisions of the 9th Convention," RZA, Bnei Akiva in Eretz Israel, 213/3 (1964); Bnei Akiva, "Decisions of the 10th Convention," RZA, Bnei Akiva in Eretz Israel, 213/3 (1967).

105. Lustick, *For the Land and the Lord;* Aran, "The Father, the Son, and the Holy Land"; Naor, *Greater Israel,* 226; Schwartz, *Land of Reality and Imagination.*

106. See Fried, "Ma'avak hitnachalut shel gush Emunim" [Interview: Gush Emunim's Settlement Struggle]. See also Ben-Aharon, *Temple Mount Zionism;* Etzion, quoted in Segal, *Dear Brothers,* 279.

107. Elizur in Shaviv, *Eretz nahalah* [A Land of Settlement], 24.

108. Mordechai Bruyer, "Eineini mevin et kolot ha-yiush ha-bokeem me-shuroteinu" [I Don't Understand the Cries of Desperation Emerging from Our Ranks] *Nekuda* 184 (1995).

109. The role of Gush Emunim and the Young Guard in driving this change was recognized within the movement. For a view of the changed emphasis as positive, see Hammer in Hatzofe, "Symposium," RZA, Warhaftig Papers, 255/1a (1975). For critiques, see N. Golan, "Conversation with Zerach Warhaftig: The NRP—Real Loyalty and Devotion to Torah and State," *Hatzofe,* May 28, 1981; Golan, "Conversation with Zerach Warhaftig"; Moshe Ona, "Religious Zionism before a Decision on Its Fate," *Hatzofe,* September 26, 1984; Ona, quoted in O'Dea, "Religious Zionism Today," 113; Hanan Porat, "We Did Not Succeed, in a Wide Sense, to Be the Carriers of the 'Lights,'" *Nekuda* 100 (1986); Israel Rosen, in *Nekuda* 73 (1984).

110. Lustick, *For the Land and the Lord,* 89; Schwartz, *Land of Reality and Imagination,* 126.

111. The old order of priorities was still reflected in the late 1960s. See Mizrachi and Hapoel Hamizrachi World Center, *Report to the 21st Convention, 1968,* RZA. See also Gelnnan in Mizrachi and Hapoel Hamizrachi, *21st World Convention, June 19–24, 1968.* Their rejection of the Jaring initiative was the only issue that dealt with the land. NRP, *Between Conventions—Summary of a Period—Report to the 4th NRP Convention,* Mizrachi and Hapoel Hamizrachi (1973).

112. National Religious Front Hamizrachi—Hapoel Hamizrachi, "Platform for the 7th Knesset," RZA, Hapoel Hamizrachi, 263 (1969); NRP Information Department, "To the Explainer and the Activist, Chapter Headings no. 1," RZA, NRP and Hapoel Hamizrachi, publications annex, box 132 (1969); NRP, press release, RZA, NRP and Hapoel Hamizrachi, 46 (October 16, 1969); NRP, *Between Conventions—Summary of a Period.*

113. Compare the 1969 platform to those that followed it. National Religious Front Hamizrachi—Hapoel Hamizrachi, "Platform for the 7th Knesset; NRP, "Main Points of the Platform for the 8th Knesset," RZA, Hapoel Hamizrachi, 263 (1973); NRP, "Platform for the 9th Knesset.

114. Warhaftig, *Fifty Years,* 248.

115. Hatzofe, "Hatzofe Symposium 1974."

116. NRP, "Protocol of the 5th NRP Convention."

117. NRP, "Kit for the Explainer," RZA, NRP Spokesman, 120/1 (1992).

118. Bambi Sheleg and Yair Sheleg, "To Go on a New Path," *Nekuda* 162 (1992).

119. Ze'ev Jabotinsky to the Agudat Israel Convention, letter, JI, A1/2/27 (August 25, 1937).

120. See Remba, "Dat u-masoret he-hayav u-be-mishnato" [Religion and Tradition in His Life and Thought]. Perhaps for this reason, Shavit called it little more than a change of tone. Shavit, *Mythologies of the Zionist Right Wing,* 218.

121. Jabotinsky, "Letter to Eri Jabotinsky," 143–44.

122. Friedman, "State of Israel as a Theological Dilemma," 172. See also Cohen, *ha-Talit veha-degel* [The Talit and the Flag]; Salmon, "Dat umedinah ba-leumiyut ha-yehudit ha-modernit" [Religion and State in the Modern Jewish Nationalism]; Fishman, "'Torah and Labor'"; Naor, "Sovereignty of the State of Israel."

123. Fishman, "'Torah and Labor'"; Hapoel Hamizrachi, elections broadsheet, RZA, Hapoel Hamizrachi, folder 2 (1926).

124. Quoted in Liebman, "Hitpathut ha-neo-masortiyut bekerev yehudim ortodoxim be-Yisrael" [Neotraditional Developments among Orthodox Jews in Israel], 236. See also Mizrachi Organization, "Circular to National Committees," RZA, Merkaz Olami of Mizrachi, 9 (October 8, 1937); Berlin in Executive Council of Hapoel Hamizrachi Organization in Eretz Israel, circular, RZA, Hapoel Hamizrachi, 26 (August 25, 1938).

125. World Center of Hamizrachi, *Internal News no. 5,* Ginzach HaZionut Hadatit, 140 (August 31, 1938). See also Meir Berlin's testimony before the Partition Commission in Executive Council of Hapoel Hamizrachi Organization in Eretz Israel, circular, RZA, Hapoel Hamizrachi, 26 (August 25, 1938).

126. Bernstein, "Yesodot ve-maskanot" [Foundations and Conclusions]; Zvi Bernstein to Hapoel Hamizrachi Executive Committee, letter, RZA, Hapoel Hamizrachi, folder 50 (December 20, 1942); Bnei Akiva in Eretz Israel, "35—Definitions, Foundations, Lines of Development—Dedicated to the 35th Anniversary of the Mizrachi," RZA, instructional materials of Bnei Akiva in Eretz Israel, 336 (February, 1938); Shraggai, "Vision and Fulfillment"; Torah and Avoda List (Hapoel Hamizrachi), "Platform for the 20th Zionist Congress," RZA, Hapoel Hamizrachi, 268 (1937); Mizrachi, *Report to the 15th Mizrachi World Congress, Geneva,* RZA, Mizrachi World Center, 36 (August 9–13, 1939); Amiel, Bernstein and others in Hapoel Hamizrachi, "Protocol of the 8th Convention," RZA, Hapoel Hamizrachi, folder 225 (1942). Hapoel Hamizrachi, *Election Leaflet,* RZA, Hapoel Hamizrachi, folder 53 (1944); Hapoel Hamizrachi, *Election Leaflet,* RZA, Hapoel Hamizrachi, 53 (July, 1944); I.D.G,

"A Life of Torah in the Hebrew State," *Zeraim,* Tevet (1945); editorial, *Zeraim* (1945); S. Z. Kahane and others in Hapoel Hamizrachi, *Report of the 10th Hapoel Hamizrachi Convention* (Jerusalem: Hapoel Hamizrachi, 1949); C. P. Tkorsh, "A Torah State," RZA, Warhaftig, 109 (March 12, 1948). See also Bnei Akiva in Eretz Israel Educational Department, "Handbook for Instructors," RZA, Bnei Akiva in Eretz Israel instructional materials, 345 (May–June 1946).

127. Mizrachi Organization, "Circular to National Committees and Executive Committee," RZA, Merkaz Olami of Mizrachi, 9 (July 7, 1938). See also Hapoel Hamizrachi Executive Committee, circular, RZA, Hapoel Hamizrachi, 25 (July 27, 1938).

128. Warhaftig, *Fifty Years,* 313.

129. Far from demanding a theocratic constitution, the Religious Zionist movement limited its demands in 1949 to designation of the Jewish holidays as state holidays, state provision of religious needs (including kosher food in state institutions), religious control of personal status issues, and the autonomy of its educational system and of the Chief Rabbinate. Cohen, *Perakim be-toldot ha-tenu'ah ha-datit le'umit* [Chapters in the History of the Religious National Movement], 101.

130. See the RZA for the basic principles adopted on June 20, 1956.

131. See, for example, Shapira in Hapoel Hamizrachi, *Report of the 10th Hapoel Hamizrachi Convention,* 25.

132. Mizrachi and Hapoel Hamizrachi, *Proceedings of the 20th World Convention. August 19–23, 1962* (Jerusalem: World Center of the Mizrachi and Hapoel Hamizrachi, 1962), 316.

133. Rather than directly engage the truth tellers on this question, perhaps because they feared an explicit confrontation on theological grounds, which they were likely to lose, the consensus builders blocked the demands for a comprehensive discussion of the vision of the Torah state by "kicking it upstairs" to the Chief Rabbinate. The Chief Rabbinate, however, was not interested in taking up the challenge; it was also caught in the tension between religious imperatives and its dependence on the state for legitimization. As a result, it ignored the question of how to operationalize the vision of the Torah state. Cohen, *The Talit and the Flag.*

134. Warhaftig in Hapoel Hamizrachi Center, protocol, RZA, Hapoel Hamizrachi, 130 (January 19, 1947).

135. Cohen, *The Talit and the Flag,* 114–16. They also argued that, given the secularity of the nation, it was the most they could achieve. See, for example, Warhaftig in Mizrachi and Hapoel Hamizrachi, *Proceedings of the 20th World Convention, August 19–23, 1962;* Bernstein, "Achrit ke-resheet baspekleria shel zionut datit" [Last as First through the Prism of Religious Zionism]; Rosen, "Nation of Israel to the Land of Israel."

136. Achitov, "Lebetav ha-halachtiyim shel harav harashi Yitzhak Halevi Herzog be-'asor ha-rishon la-medinah" [The Halachic Considerations of Chief Rabbi Isaac Halevi Herzog in the First Decade of the State of Israel]. Zvi Yehuda Kook took much the same position. See Naor, "Sovereignty of the State of Israel."

137. Cohen, *The Talit and the Flag.*

138. That these attacks continued to take place is suggested by the constant defense of this tactic by leaders of the Religious Zionist movement. See, for example, Mizrachi and Hapoel Hamizrachi, *Proceedings of the 19th World Convention, 1955, Ginzach Hazionut Hadatit;* Ona, "Medinat Yisrael ve-golat Yisrael" [State of Israel and the Diaspora of Israel]; Hamizrachi Organization in Eretz Israel, *Report to the 12th Convention;* Warhaftig in NRP, *Report of the Founding Convention of the NRP, 1956,* RZA, Hapoel Hamizrachi, 249; Mizrachi and Hapoel Hamizrachi, *Proceedings of the 20th World Convention, August 19–23, 1962;* NRP Young Guard, *Conference on Religious-Secular Tension,* RZA, NRP and Hapoel Hamizrachi, 4 (October 26, 1963); NRP, *Report of the 2nd Convention, 1964,* RZA, NRP and Hapoel Hamizrachi, publications annex, box 192; Mizrachi and Hapoel Hamizrachi, *21st World Convention, June 19–24, 1968.*

139. For example, S. Z. Shraggai to Moshe Goldstein, letter, RZA, Hapoel Hamizrachi, 933 (December 17, 1953).

140. Some, however, did make this argument. For example, Moshe Zvi Neria, *Konters ha-vikuah* [Booklet of the Argument]. See also some of the speakers in Mizrachi, *Report of the 18th World Congress, 1949,* RZA, World Mizrachi Center, 39.

141. See, for example, Warhaftig in Symposium on Religion and State, protocol, LPA, 2–14-1962–23 (July 29, 1962); Zerach Warhaftig, "The Religion and the State," RZA, Hapoel Hamizrachi, 944 (March 30, 1962); Warhaftig, *Fifty Years;* Herzog in Achitov, "Halachic Considerations of Chief Rabbi Isaac Halevi Herzog."

142. Shraggai, "Le-heshbona shel haziyonut hadatit" [Balance Sheet of Religious Zionism], 246. See also Shraggai in NRP Information department, *Chapters in the Thought of the Movement: Report of the Ideological Conference within the Framework of the Council for Torah, Culture, and Spirit on Do the Changes in Our Days Require a Revision of the Fundamental Assumption of the Worldview of the Movement of Torah and Labor? And How Will We Ensure the Uniqueness of the Religious Society in the State?* RZA, Warhaftig, 198/1c (January 14, 1971). A general discussion can be found in Cohen, *The Talit and the Flag.*

143. Warhaftig, *Fifty Years,* 83–84, 99, 104.

144. For example, Don-Yehiya and Liebman, "Separation between Religion and State."

145. The leaders of the Religious Zionist movement, including the consensus builders, continually lamented the fact that Israel was not governed by the rules of the Torah. Mizrachi, *Report of the 18th World Congress, 1949,* RZA, World Mizrachi Center, 39; Shraggai in Hapoel Hamizrachi, "Protocol of 10th Convention," RZA, Hapoel Hamizrachi, 243 (October 31, 1949). See also United Religious Front, "Platform for the Elections to the Constituent Assembly"; United Religious Front, *Election Pamphlet,* RZA, Hapoel Hamizrachi, 292 (1949); United Religious Front, "Letter to the Religious Worker," RZA, Hapoel Hamizrachi, 292 (1949); Hapoel Hamizrachi, "Platform for the 2nd Knesset," RZA, Hapoel Hamizrachi, 263; Warhaftig in Mizrachi and Hapoel Hamizrachi, *Proceedings of the 20th World Convention, August 19–23, 1962,* 319; A. L. Gelman, *Declaration of the World Center of Hamizrachi, the Role of the World Center of Hamizrachi* (Jerusalem: Hamizrachi World Center, 1950); National Religious Central Ideational Circle, platform, RZA, Hapoel Hamizrachi, 263 (September–October, 1968). It also remained a goal articulated in Bnei Akiva's materials, alongside the new one. For articulations of the goal of a Torah state in Bnei Akiva after the tactical change began, see, Bnei Akiva, "Paths of Instruction for Ha'roeh tribe," RZA, Bnei Akiva in Eretz Israel, box 8 (n.d.); Bnei Akiva, "The Movement—A Plan of Instruction," RZA, Bnei Akiva in Eretz Israel, 72/1 (after 1956); Hatzofe, "Symposium on the Direction of Bnei Akiva," *Hatzofe,* April 24, 1967.

146. See the Religious Zionist accounts of the failure of the alliance with Labor in Bnei Akiva Education Department, "Parties in Israel," RZA, Bnei Akiva in Eretz Israel, 85/1 (1961); Daniel, *Minister Haim Moshe Shapira.*

147. Don-Yehiya, "Stability and Change in a Camp-Party," 49 n. 19.

148. Friedman, "National Religious Party in Crisis." See also Azrieli, *Knit Kippa Generation,* 25. Goldberg and Ben-Zadok, "Gush Emunim in the West Bank"; Raanan, *Gush Emunim;* Lustick, *For the Land and the Lord.* For examples, see Bnei Akiva in Eretz Israel Educational Department, "The State of Israel: Vision and Reality," RZA, booklet 331a (1985); Cohen, *Chapters in the History of the Religious National Movement;* Hatzofe, "Symposium: How We Are Fighting over the Character of the State," RZA, Warhaftig, 255/1a (September, 1973); Hatzofe, "Symposium," RZA, Warhaftig, 255/1a (1977); Rosen, "Nation of Israel to the Land of Israel"; Fried, "Interview: Gush Emunim's Settlement Struggle"; Bernstein, "Min ha-yesod" [From the Foundation]; Neria, "Ha mafridim bein torat Yisrael ve-medinat Yisrael" [Those Who Distinguish between the Torah of Israel and the State of Israel]; Moshe Zvi Neria, "The State in the Halacha: Chapters in the Worldview no. 314 by Bnei Akiva in Israel, in 1982," RZA, Bnei Akiva instructional materials, 511 (19/4 [1982]); Shraggai, "Balance Sheet of Religious Zionism." See also Yehuda Etzion and Yehuda Shaviv, cited in Sprinzak, *Ascendance of Israel's Radical Right,* 137, 256–57; and Etzion and Ben-Nun, cited in Segal, *Dear Brothers,* 112. Also, Haim Druckman, "The Meaning of Bnei Akiva Today," RZA, Bnei Akiva in Israel instructional materials, 120 (1992); NRP, "Platform for the 13th Knesset," RZA (1992); Bnei Akiva in Israel, "Israel and Torah—A Body and Soul," RZA, Bnei Akiva instructional materials (1989); Dan Bari, "To Uproot the Diaspora Renewing in Our Midst," *Nekuda* 103 (1985); Israel Rosen, "The Haredim (with the Help of the Likud and the Alignment) Have Begun to Take Over the Chief Rabbinate," *Nekuda* 152 (1991).

Even secular members of Gush Emunim called for a Torah state. Most prominent among these was Moshe Ben-Yosef (Hagar). See, for example, Moshe Ben-Yosef, "The Revolution Is on Break (and the Revolutionaries Are Busy in the NRP and in Techiya, or in Finding a Consensus with the Left)," *Nekuda* 139 (1990).

149. Ben-Meir in Hatzofe, "Symposium," RZA, Warhaftig, 255/1a (September 1973); a Hatzofe editorial in World Center of Mizrachi and Hapoel Hamizrachi, Information Department, Newspaper Collection no. 178, RZA, Bnei Akiva in Eretz Israel, 117/3 (June 12, 1963).

150. Friedman, "National Religious Party in Crisis."

151. See Sheleg, *New Religious Jews.*

5. Arabs and Diaspora Jews in Israeli National Identity

1. Quoted in Sternhell, *Founding Myths of Israel*, 127.

2. An early instance of this formulation is Levi Shkolnik (Eshkol) in Mapai, "Protocol of 13th Party Council," LPA, 2–22-1939–26. See also Mapai, *Conference on "Questions of Zionism in this period,"* LPA, 2–15-1940–7 (January 20, 1940); Ben-Gurion, "Zionist Policy"; Ben-Gurion, *Restored State of Israel,* 418–19, originally in 1943; Mapai Knesset Faction, "Protocol of Meeting with Party Secretariat," LPA, 2–11-1950–7 (March 12, 1950); Mapai, *Conference of Workers' Committees,* LPA, 2–15-1950–42 (July 16, 1950); Mapai, "Decisions of the 8th Mapai Convention," LPA, 2–21-1956–43 (1956); Mapai, *8th Mapai Convention—Second Session,* LPA, 2–21-1958–45 (May 15, 1958); The Ideational Circle of the Tzeirim, protocol, LPA, 2–14-1959–61 (December 19, 1959); Mapai and Mapam, "Text of Proposed Agreement in Negotiations between Them to Form the Alignment," LPA, 2–932-1968–456 (1968); Labor Party, *Israel Labor Party Constitution,* LPA, 2–932-1967–461 (January 21, 1968); Alignment, "Platform for the 8th Knesset, 1974"; ILP, "Decisions of the Second Convention," LPA, 2–21-1977–122 (1977); ILP, *"Background Materials for the 3rd ILP Convention,"* LPA, 2–21-1981–138 (1981); ILP Center, "Decisions and Proposals for the ILP 3rd Convention of the Subcommittee for Zionism and the Jewish Nation—Immigration and Absorption," LPA, 2–21-1981–138 (February 1981).

3. Gorni, *ha-Hipus ahar ha-zehut ha-le'umit* [The Quest for Collective Identity], 82–83; Feldestein, *Gordian Knot;* Weissbrod, "From Labour Zionism to New Zionism."

4. Mapai Central Ideational Circle, protocol, LPA, 2–7-1967–34 (November 25, 1967).

5. Ben-Gurion, *Restored State of Israel,* 75 (in the original only "nation" is emphasized), originally in August 1947. See also the debate in Mapai, *7th Convention of the Party,* LPA, 2–21-1950–29.

6. See, for example, Lavon, *On Values and Assets,* 29, originally in Histadrut Council Meeting, September 5, 1950; Alignment, "Platform for the 6th Knesset," LPA (1965).

7. Berry, *Hashivuto shel shem* [What's in a Name?], 103–4. For a different articulation of this fear, see Mapai, "Protocol of the Education Committee," LPA, 2–7-1948–2 (January 12, 1948).

8. Feldestein, *Gordian Knot,* 214.

9. Quoted in Gorni, *Quest for Collective Identity,* 127, 128.

10. ILP Center, protocol, LPA, 2–23-1981–124 (April 29, 1982). See also the discussion in ILP Third Convention, "Second Session, Protocols," LPA, 2–21-1981–138 (February 2, 1981).

11. Mapai Knesset Faction, protocol, LPA, 2–11-1950–7 (March 12, 1950); Mapai, *Conference of Workers' Committees,* LPA, 2–15-1950–42 (July 16, 1950); Mapai Center, meeting protocol, LPA, 2–23-1954–64 (July 15, 1954); Feldestein, *Gordian Knot.*

12. Berl Loker in Mapai, *Conference of Workers' Committees,* LPA, 2–15-1950–42 (July 16, 1950).

13. Berl Loker, speech at a seminar at Beit Berl, LPA, 2–13-1951–103 (March 29, 1951). Also in "The Elections to the 23rd Congress—A Zionist Test for Every Party," *Davar,* March 18, 1951.

14. Moshe Sharett, address at a public meeting in Yafo, LPA, 2–13-1951–104 (May 12, 1951).

15. David Ben-Gurion, speech to the 22nd Zionist Congress, LPA, 2–602-1946–15 (1946).

16. Shimoni, "Reformulations of Zionist Ideology," 25.

17. ILP, "Decisions of the Second Convention," LPA, 2–21-1977–122 (1977).

18. See, for example, Zalman Aran in Mapai, "Protocol of the 37th Party Council," LPA, 2–11-1949–21 (1949); Mapai Center, leaflet, LPA, 2–13-1948–34 (November, 1948); Mapai, "Platform for the 2nd Knesset," LPA, 2–13-1951–92 (1951); Mapai, *8th Mapai Convention,* LPA, 2–21-1958–45 (May 15, 1958). See also Shlomo Derech, the chairman of the Standing Committee on Ideology of the WZO executive. Derech, "Zionism as Ideology and Program." The appreciation for the Diaspora and its concerns further increased in the aftermath of the 1956 war, when Israel felt itself isolated in the international arena, facing opposition from both Eisenhower and the USSR. Liebman, "Yesodot mosariyim ve-smalim" [Moral and Symbolic Foundations].

19. Mapai, "Elections Platform, 1949."

20. Mapai, "Platform for the 2nd Knesset" (1951), my emphasis.

21. Mapai, "Platform for the 3rd Knesset," LPA (1955); Alignment, "Platform for the 6th Knesset" (1965); ILP Center, meeting protocol, LPA, 2–23-1984–126 (September 10, 1984); Alignment, "Platform for the 11th Knesset, 1984"; Alignment, "Platform for the 10th Knesset, 1981."

22. See, for example, Ben-Gurion, *Restored State of Israel,* 418–19.

23. Liebman, "Diaspora Influence of Israel." For other examples of inconsistent articulations of membership and mission, see Ben-Gurion, "Zionei Derech," LPA, 2–21-1956–42; Mapai, "Platform for the 3rd Knesset—English Version," LPA, 2–13-1952–240 (1955); Alignment, "Platform for the 6th Knesset, 1965"; Mapai, "Platform for the 4th Knesset," LPA (1959); Mapai, "Platform for the 5th Knesset," LPA (1961); ILP, *ILP Constitution,* LPA, 2–932-1967–467 (1967); Mapai and Mapam, "Text of Proposed Agreement," LPA, 2–932-1968–456 (1968); Alignment, "Platform for the 7th Knesset, 1969"; ILP Convention, "Thinking Group of Socialist Zionism Recommendations," LPA, 2–21-1971–106 (1971); ILP, "Decisions of the Second Convention," LPA, 2–21-1977–122 (1977); ILP, "Background Materials for the 3rd ILP Convention," LPA, 2–21-1981–138 (1981); Alignment, "Platform for the 10th Knesset, 1981"; Ben-Gurion, *Restored State of Israel.*

24. See, for example, Zalman Shazar in Mapai, *8th Mapai Convention,* LPA, 2–21-1958–45 (May 15, 1958); Abba Eban in Mapai Central Ideational Circle, protocol, LPA, 2–7-1967–34 (November 25, 1967); Yigal Allon in ILP Convention, protocol, LPA, 2–21-1971–103 (February 1971).

25. Ben-Gurion, *In the Struggle,* 44–45, originally on October 15, 1942.

26. Halperin, "Ideology or Philanthropy?"

27. See Elihu Golomb, quoted in Gal, *Ben-Gurion and the American Alignment,* 84.

28. Gorni, *Quest for Collective Identity;* Feldestein, *Gordian Knot.*

29. Liebman, "Religion and Political Integration in Israel"; Cohen, *Zion and State,* 247. See Mapai Center, protocol, LPA, 2–23-1954–64 (July 15, 1954); Mapai, *Mapai's 8th Convention,* LPA, 2–21-1958–48 (May 15, 1958); The Ideational Circle of the Tzeirim, protocol, LPA, 2–14-1959–61 (December 19, 1959); Allon in ILP Convention, protocol, LPA, 2–21-1971–103 (1971); ILP Center, "Decisions and Proposals for the ILP 3rd Convention of the Subcommittee for Zionism and the Jewish Nation—Immigration and Absorption," LPA, 2–21-1981–138 (1981); Rabin in ILP Center, meeting protocol, LPA, 2–23-1995–153 (February 16, 1995).

30. See Ben-Gurion, *Restored State of Israel,* 353–54.

31. One of the first instances is found in David Ben-Gurion, "The Hebrew and Arab Worker," in *Us and Our Neighbors,* ed. Ben-Gurion.

32. Hattis, *Bi-National Idea in Palestine,* 94; Goldstein, "David Ben-Gurion and the Bi-National Idea"; Ben-Avram, *Political Parties and Organizations,* 111.

33. Ben-Gurion in Jewish Agency Executive, meeting protocol, CZA, S100/24b (June 9, 1938); Ben-Gurion, "Zionist Policy." See also Lustick, *Arabs in the Jewish State;* Goldstein, "Were the Arabs Overlooked by the Zionists?"; Teveth, *Ben-Gurion and the Palestinian Arabs.*

34. See Ben-Gurion in Mapai, "Protocol of 12th National Convention," LPA, 2–22-1937–22.

35. Ben-Gurion, quoted in Sternhell, *Founding Myths of Israel*, 182–83, originally in 1931.

36. Shalev, "Jewish Organized Labor and the Palestinians"; Grinberg, *Split Corporatism in Israel*; Bernstein, "From Split Labor Market Strategy to Political Co-optation"; Bernstein, "Challenges to Separatism"; Shafir and Peled, *Being Israeli*, 41.

37. Great Britain, "Palestine Royal Commission: Minutes of Evidence Heard at Public Sessions," 234–35. See also Gorni, *ha-She'elah ha-'Arvit veha-be'ayah ha-Yehudit* [The Arab Question and the Jewish Problem], 285.

38. Kolatt, "Ha-tenuah ha-tsiyonit veha-aravim" [The Zionist Movement and the Arabs], 247–50. Not everybody within Mapai agreed with the conclusion, but the influence of these outliers was minimal. See the objections raised by Agassi and Abba Hushi, among others, in Mapai Central Committee, protocol, LPA, 2–23-1937–16 (April 10, 1937); Mapai, "Protocol of 11th Mapai Party Council," LPA, 2–22-1937–20.

39. Teveth, *Ben-Gurion and the Palestinian Arabs.*

40. E.g., Ben-Zvi in Mapai Knesset Faction, "Meeting with the Party Secretariat," LPA, 2–11-1950–8 (July 9, 1950); Mapai Knesset Faction, protocol, LPA, 2–11-1951–11 (February 20, 1951).

41. Yishai, *Factionalism in the Labor Movement*, 45. See Ben-Gurion in Avizohar and Bareli, *Now or Never*, 264, originally in December 1947; Sharett, *At the Gate of Nations*, 149, originally in 1947; Y. Halperin in Mapai, "Protocol of the Education Committee," LPA, 2–7-1948–2 (January 12, 1948). Some also used this logic to justify awarding Arabs the right to vote. Mapai Knesset Faction Leadership, "Meeting Protocol with Mapai MKs in the Law Committee," LPA, 2–11-1950–10 (October 23, 1950); Mapai Knesset Faction, protocol, LPA, 2–11-1950–8 (July 9, 1950); Mapai Knesset Faction, protocol, LPA, 2–11-1951–11 (February 20, 1951).

42. Mapai Knesset Faction, protocol, LPA, 2–11-1949–1 (June 14, 1949).

43. Originally in a Mapai Secretariat Meeting, October 11, 1947. Quoted in Avizohar and Bareli, *Now or Never*, 183, my emphasis. See also the debate in Mapai Secretariat, protocol, LPA, 2–11-1950–8 (June 18, 1950); Mapai Knesset Faction, protocol, LPA, 2–11-1950–8 (July 9, 1950).

44. Mapai, "Meeting Protocol of the Committee for Foreign Affairs," LPA, 2–7-1958–67 (January 1, 1959).

45. Ben-Gurion, *Restored State of Israel*, 886.

46. Quoted in Shlaim, *Collusion across the Jordan*, 456.

47. See Ben-Gurion's diary, June 26, 1949, quoted in Shlaim, *Collusion across the Jordan*, 503. This was not the case, however, for Jerusalem or the Gaza Strip. Regarding the latter, Sharett noted that only a minority wanted to avoid conquering it in 1948–49 for demographic reasons, while the majority was willing to do so. Mapai Secretariat, protocol, LPA, 2–11-1950–8 (June 18, 1950).

48. Sharett in Mapai, "Foreign Affairs Committee Meeting Protocol," LPA, 2–7-1956–64 (December 19, 1956). Sharett had expressed his opposition to conquest of the Gaza Strip for demographic reasons already in June 1955. Manor, "Images and Decision Making on the Boundaries Issue," 100 n. 135.

49. Mapai, *Meeting of the Young Guard with Shimon Peres*, LPA, 2–15-1956–57 (October 11, 1956).

50. Mapai, "Foreign Affairs Committee Meeting Protocol," LPA, 2–7-1956–64 (December 19, 1956).

51. See Lavon's analysis and Argov's depiction of Ben-Gurion's stance in Mapai Secretariat, meeting protocol, LPA, 2–24-1952–34 (October 24, 1952). See also Mapai Secretariat, meeting protocol, LPA, 2–24-1952–30 (March 28, 1952). Shalev, "Jewish Organized Labor and the Palestinians," 111.

52. See the arguments in Mapai Secretariat, meeting protocol, LPA, 2–24-1952-31 (May 15, 1952); Mapai Secretariat, protocol, LPA, 2–11-1950-8 (June 18, 1950); Mapai Secretariat, protocol, LPA, 2–24-1952-30 (March 28, 1952); Mapai Center, meeting protocol, LPA, 2–23-1952-60 (October 28, 1952); Mapai Secretariat, protocol, LPA, 2–24-1952-34 (October 24, 1952); Mapai Secretariat, meeting protocol, LPA, 2–24-1953-38 (December 25, 1953); Yaacov Cohen, "Letter to the ILP Center Regarding the Labor Party and the Arab Voter," LPA, 2–932-1968-456 (November 15, 1968); ILP Center, meeting protocol, LPA, 2–23-1968-95 (October 23, 1968); Mapai, "Announcement to the Newspapers," LPA, 2–937-1958-3 (1959); Mapai, press announcement, LPA, 2–937-1958-3 (February, 1959); Mapai, "Protocol of the Committee for Foreign Affairs," LPA, 2–7-1958-67 (January 1, 1959); ILP Center, meeting protocol, LPA, 2–23-1970–100 (June 25, 1970).

53. Mapai Youth Department, "Questions to Shimon Peres," LPA, 2–921-1960-39 (September 16, 1960).

54. Mapai, *Report of a Meeting of Youth Committee,* LPA, 2–932-1962-226 (October 11, 1962); Mapai, "Press Release: 'Mapai Discusses Activity among the Arab Youth,'" LPA, 2–932-1962-226 (1962); Mapai, *Report of a Meeting of Youth Committee and Arab Affairs Committee,* LPA, 2–932-1962-226 (November 28, 1962).

55. Mapai Secretariat, meeting protocol, LPA, 2–24-1968-92 (January 2, 1968).

56. ILP, *Questions and Answers: The Palestinian Issue: Leaflet for the Israeli Explainer abroad, no. 2,* LPA, 2–921-1974-375 (1974). See also Eban, "New Look at Partition."

57. For example, Allon, *Communicating Vessels;* Dani Rozolin in ILP Third Convention, protocols, LPA, 2–21-1980-136 (December 18, 1980); Yehuda Gottlehf in ILP Center, protocol, LPA, 2–23-1979-120 (December 30, 1979); Shimon Peres in ILP Center, protocol, LPA, 2–23-1981-124 (April 29, 1982); Oz, *Kol ha-tikvot* [All Our Hopes], 87, originally in *Yediot Ahronot,* March 31, 1996; Alignment, "Platform for the 12th Knesset, 1988."

58. For instances of the continued integrationist trend, see, for example, Central Ideational Circle, "Protocol of the Meeting of Committee for Arab Affairs," LPA, 2–14-1970-49 (June 24, 1970); ILP Center, "The Preparatory Committee: Subcommittee for Political Matters: Meeting Protocol," LPA, 2–921-1976-341 (November 19, 1976).

59. Mapai and Rafi Committee for the Formulation of the Covenant between Ahdut Haavoda, meeting protocol, LPA, 2–21-1967-82 (January 4, 1968).

60. ILP Center, "The Preparatory Committee: Subcommittee for Political Matters: Meeting Protocol," LPA, 2–21-1977-133 (December 10, 1976); ILP Subcommittee for Political Affairs, meeting protocol, LPA (December 12, 1976).

61. Labor Party Committee for Religion and State, meeting protocol, LPA, 2–21-1985-142 (December 26, 1985).

62. ILP Center, meeting protocol, LPA, 2–23-1987-132 (November 26, 1987).

63. ILP Center, "Decision from September 12, 1989, Regarding the Development of the Galilee, the Golan, and the North," LPA, 2–23-1989-140 (September 17, 1989); ILP Center, "Decision," LPA, 2–23-1990-142 (February 1, 1990). For earlier statements of this sentiment, see Mapai Center, "Letter to Representatives," LPA, 2–002-1948-41 (March 3, 1948); Mapai Center, "Divrei Haverim," LPA, 2–932-1948-24 (February 20, 1948).

64. Lustick, "Political Road to Binationalism"; Ian Lustick, "Creeping Binationalism within the Green Line," *New Outlook,* July 1988."

65. Quoted in Lustick, "Political Road to Binationalism," 110.

66. ILP Center, "meeting protocol, LPA, 2–23-1990-142 (April 10, 1990); ILP Center, "Proposed Guidelines for Peres' Government," LPA, 2–23-1990-142 (April 10, 1990).

67. See, for example, Gur in ILP Third Convention, protocols, LPA, 2–21-1980-136 (December 18, 1980). Raanan Cohen made a similar argument. ILP Third Convention, protocols, LPA, 2–21-1981-138 (February 2, 1981).

68. Shalev, "Jewish Organized Labor and the Palestinians," 113.

69. Lustick, "Creeping Binationalism within the Green Line."

70. Rouhana and Ghanem, "Crisis of Minorities in Ethnic States."

6. Ongoing Transformations of Israeli Nationalism

1. Lochery, "Netanyahu Era," 237 n. 17.

2. David Makovsky, "Bar-Ilan: We May Be Able to Accept a Limited Palestinian State," *The Jerusalem Post,* December 20, 1996.

3. Shindler, "View from the Right."

4. Makovsky, "Bar-Ilan."

5. Makovsky notes that Yitzhak Shamir was virtually the only one to complain about this statement. David Makovsky, "Netanyahu's Road to Oslo," *The Jerusalem Post,* December 27, 1996.

6. Liat Collins and Jay Bushinsky, "PM Warns Arafat: If PA Declares State, I'll Annex Territories," *The Jerusalem Post,* December 2, 1997; Rynhold and Steinberg, "Peace Process and the Israeli Elections."

7. Peretz, Kook, and Doron, "Knesset Election 2003."

8. Herut Movement, "Protocol of the National Council," JI, H1/11/17 (September 1974). See also the debate in Herut Central Committee, protocol, JI, H1/2/21/2 (December 16, 1973); Herut Central Committee, protocol, JI, H1/2/32/1 (January 8, 1978); Begin, speech, JI, P20/11/4 (January 2, 1977).

9. Naor, "Hawks' Beaks, Doves' Feathers." Shamir was an exception to this trend, since he defined the Land of Israel within which there would be no foreign sovereignty as the land to the west of the Jordan along with the Golan Heights.

10. Of course, security hawks continued to make the argument that had more settlements been established, the war might have been avoided. Naor, "Security Argument in the Territorial Debate."

11. Naor, "Hawks' Beaks, Doves' Feathers," 179. See, for example, Benjamin Netanyahu, "Peace In Our Time?" *The New York Times,* September 5, 1993; see also Shindler, *Israel, Likud, and the Zionist Dream.*

12. Mendilow, "Likud's Double Campaign," 190, 172.

13. Ibid.; Naor, "Security Argument in the Territorial Debate."

14. Mendilow, *Ideology, Party Change, and Electoral Campaigns,* 172–73.

15. Mendilow, "Likud's Double Campaign," 200.

16. Makovsky, "Netanyahu's Road to Oslo."

17. Sprinzak, "Politics of Paralysis I."

18. Pedahzur, Hirsch, and Canetti-Nisim, "Whose Victory?" 32.

19. Shindler, *Israel, Likud, and the Zionist Dream;* Aronoff, "When and Why Do Hard-Liners Become Soft?"; Mendilow, "Likud's Double Campaign."

20. Arian, "A People Apart," 606 n. 3.

21. Sheffer, "Individualism vs. National Coherence"; Yishai, "Bringing Society Back In," 673; Shafir and Peled, *New Israel;* Aronoff, "'Americanization' of Israeli Politics"; First and Avraham, "Globalization/Americanization and Negotiating National Dreams."

22. In fact, for many people in Israel, the Oslo Accords became associated with a lack of personal safety. Yoram Schweitzer at the 2000 conference on suicide terror in Herzelia. See also Rabinovitch, *Hevlei Shalom* [Waging Peace], 68.

23. Lochery, "Politics and Economics of Israeli Disengagement."

24. Steinberg, "Peace, Security, and Terror."

25. Torgovnik, "Strategies under a New Electoral System."

26. Naor, "Hawks' Beaks, Doves' Feathers," 176. See also Shindler, "View from the Right."

27. *Congressional Record,* vol. 142 (July 10, 1996), H7160–H7162 (from the Congressional Record Online via GPO Access, wais.access.gpo.gov [DOCID:cr10jy96–25]) (accessed December 7, 2009).

28. *Divrei Haknesset,* May 1, 1996. Special session, the 435th session of the 13th Knesset, "The Government's Failed Performance in Operation Grapes of Wrath," www.knesset.gov.il (accessed December 7, 2009, in Hebrew).

29. Lochery, "Politics and Economics of Israeli Disengagement."

30. Ibid.

31. Rynhold and Steinberg, "Peace Process and the Israeli Elections."

32. Makovsky, "Netanyahu's Road to Oslo."

33. Naor, "Security Argument in the Territorial Debate"; Naor, "Hawks' Beaks, Doves' Feathers"; Rynhold and Waxman, "Ideological Change and Israel's Disengagement from Gaza."

34. Brom, *From Rejection to Acceptance,* 10.

35. Quoted in Brom, *From Rejection to Acceptance,* 10.

36. Begin, speech, JI, P20/11/2 (October 23, 1967); Gahal Knesset Faction, protocol, JI, H2/2/11 (November 1, 1968); Aridor, "Talking Points," JI, H1/10/30 (October, 1968); MK Binyamin Avniel in Herut Movement, "Protocols of the 9th Herut National Convention, May 1968," JI, H1/13/9/16.

37. For example, Begin, "Our Right to Eretz Israel"; Menachem Begin, "Minister without Portfolio Mr. Menachem Begin at the Opening Rally of the 9th Herut Convention," JI, P20/11/2 (May 26, 1968); Menachem Begin, "Demographic Forecasts and Reality," *Maariv,* November 5, 1971; Menachem Begin, "Eretz Israel, Peace and Citizenship," *Maariv,* November 17, 1972; Menachem Begin, "Facts against Illusion and Misdirection," *Maariv,* June 18, 1976; Herut Central Committee, protocol, JI, H1/2/38 (October 28, 1982); see also Shamir in Naor, "Hawks' Beaks, Doves' Feathers," 171.

38. Rynhold and Waxman, "Ideological Change and Israel's Disengagement from Gaza."

39. Aronoff, "When and Why Do Hard-Liners Become Soft?"

40. Netanyahu, *Place among the Nations,* chap. 8.

41. See, for example, Rynhold and Waxman, "Ideological Change and Israel's Disengagement from Gaza."

42. Benjamin Netanyahu, "The Alternative Is Autonomy," *The Jerusalem Post,* April 8, 1994. See also his argument in Netanyahu, *A Durable Peace,* chap. 8.

43. http://www.netanyahu.org/binnetspeeca.html (accessed March 4, 2009).

44. Dowty, "Despair Is Not Enough"; Pedahzur, "Downfall of the National Camp?" See also the findings of the Tami Steinmetz Peace and War Index, March 1999 and October 2000.

45. In 1999, Netanyahu's stance famously oscillated with the demands of the campaign. Collins and Bushinsky, "PM Warns Arafat."

46. Ben-Aharon, *Temple Mount Zionism;* David Haneshke, "To Start from the Beginning," *Nekuda* 177 (1994); Karpel, *Emunit Revolution.*

47. Ben-Nun, "State of Israel against the Land of Israel?"

48. Segal, *Dear Brothers,* 207.

49. Sheleg, *New Religious Jews.*

50. Shochteman, *Ve-ya'amidea le-Yaacov le-hok* [And Jacob Shall Have It for a Law], 75; Fried, "Interview: Gush Emunim's Settlement Struggle," 137; Yaacov Ariel, "Every Flying Rock Is a Declaration of War," *Nekuda* 129 (1989). For calls to rebellion by others, see Baruch Lior, "To Prepare for Freedom, Prayer, and War," *Nekuda* 85 (1985); Yehuda Etzion, "Not in Our Name," *Nekuda* 131 (1989); Ben-Aharon, *Temple Mount Zionism,* 191–92; Feiglin, *Bemakom she-en anashim* [Where There Are No Men].

51. Feiglin, *Where There Are No Men;* Karpel, *Emunit Revolution.* The Yesha Council represents the Jewish municipalities in the West Bank (and, formerly, in the Gaza Strip) and is the primary political lobby representing the settlers.

52. Yehuda Etzion, "From 'Degel Yerushalayim' to the 'Movement of Redemption,'" *Nekuda* 94 (1985). See also Segal, *Dear Brothers,* 279.

53. Motti Karpel, "The Meaning of the Paralysis in Gush Emunim, the Yesha Council, and in the Ideological Religious Right," *Nekuda* 185 (1995).

54. Yehuda Etzion, "From a Pointed Paper...to a National Paper," *Nekuda* 101 (1986); Etzion, "Not in Our Name"; Etzion, "From 'Degel Yerushalayim' to the 'Movement of Redemption'"; Karpel, *Emunit Revolution,* 251, 261.

55. Noam Livant, "To the Glory of the State of Judea," *Nekuda* 129 (1989). See also Michael Ben-Horin, "Only Fascists See Everything in Ruling," *Nekuda* 150 (1991).

56. Quoted in Segal, *Dear Brothers*, 207–8. See also Ben-Aharon, *Temple Mount Zionism*; Karpel, *Emunit Revolution*.

57. Etzion, cited in Karpel, *Emunit Revolution*, 286–87, 333.

58. See Feiglin in interview by Arye Perlman, August 2002, http://www.yesha.org.il/feiglin1.asp. Also Livant, "To the Glory of the State of Judea"; Chaim Israel Sheffler, "A State of Judea Will Save the State of Israel," *Nekuda* 131 (1989); Ben-Horin, "Only Fascists See Everything"; Karpel, *Emunit Revolution*.

59. Achitov, "Halachic Considerations of Chief Rabbi Isaac Halevi Herzog"; Ravitzky, *Messianism, Zionism, and Jewish Religious Radicalism*, 139.

60. Liebman, "Neotraditional Developments among Orthodox Jews"; Ben-Simon, "Foreign Fire."

61. See, for example, the Yesha Council manifesto from February 6, 1980, in Aviezer, *Sefer Hagai* [The Book of Hagai], 71. See also Shapira, "Under the Rule of the Mandate."

62. For an example, Moshe Feiglin at the conference of Bayit Haleumi, http://www.baitle.org/frames/videos.htm.

63. Sheleg, *New Religious Jews*.

64. Cited in Sheleg, *New Religious Jews*. See also http://he.manhigut.org.

65. *Nekuda* 163 (1992). See also Rachel Gini, "Motti Karpel Tore the Fabric," *Nekuda* 171 (1993).

66. See Yoel Lerner, letter to the editor, *Nekuda* 163 (1992); Sheleg, *New Religious Jews*.

67. The phrase was used by Yitzhak Shilot in *Nekuda* 132 (1989).

68. Ben-Horin, "Only Fascists See Everything"; Feiglin, *Where There Are No Men*.

69. See, for example, Dan Bari, "Kookist Revolutionaries Are Needed," *Nekuda* 129 (1989); Dan Bari, "The Zionist Revolution Has Yet to Take Place," *Nekuda* 181 (1994). See also Rabbis Shlomo Aviner and Yaacov Ariel in Gorni, *Quest for Collective Identity*, 219–22.

70. Yoel Ben-Nun, "When the Land of Israel Expropriates the State of Israel," *Nekuda* 141 (1990).

71. See, for example, Uri Elitzur, "Live Broadcast," *Nekuda* 186 (1995).

72. Sprinzak, *Ascendance of Israel's Radical Right*; Roni Sofer, "Head of GSS: The Extremists among the Settlers Are No Longer Fringe Elements," *YNET*, February 5, 2005.

73. Yaacov Ariel, "The Father of Gush Emunim," *Nekuda* 147 (1991). See also Meir Gross in *Nekuda* 140 (1990); Matti Erlichman, "The Real 'and Only' Alliance Is with Our Haredi Brothers," *Nekuda* 140 (1990).

74. Yitzhak Shilot, "A Nationalist Agudist," *Nekuda* 135 (1989). See also David Haneshke, "The Dead End," *Nekuda* 134 (1989).

75. For example, Moshe Shamir in *Nekuda* 161 (1992); Haggai Ben-Artzi, "To Go with the Haredim," *Nekuda* 161 (1992).

76. See, for example, David Haneshke, "No One Rose Up," *Nekuda* 140 (1990), and the responses to it in *Nekuda*, 141 (June 1990).

77. Ilan Shachar, "The NRP's Platform Political Committee Supports the Annexation of the Territories and Opposes the Autonomy," *Haaretz*, April 10, 1992.

78. Azriel Ariel, "Was the Agudist Path the Correct One?" *Nekuda* 175 (1994). While Bari disagrees with this assessment, he notes its pervasiveness in "our camp." Bari, "The Zionist Revolution Has Yet to Take Place."

79. See, for example, Michael Zvi Nehorai, "Religious Zionism Is Retreating from Haredi Redemptionism," *Nekuda* 91 (1985).

80. Krausz and Bar-Lev, "Varieties of Orthodox Religious Behavior"; Liebman, "Neotraditional Developments among Orthodox Jews"; Nili Mendler, "Haredization in the State-Religious Education," *Haaretz*, April 4, 1986; Yael Fishbein, "There Is No State of Israel, There Is the Land of Israel," *Davar*, May 26, 1988.

81. See, for example, Hillel Wise, "Arise and Let Us Go up to Zion," *Nekuda* 186 (1995).

82. Hayerushalmi, *ha-Kipah ha-shaletet* [The Domineering Skullcap]; Galnoor, *Partition of Palestine*.

83. Achitov, "Metachim u-temurut be-manhigut datit" [Tensions and Changes in Religious Leadership]. Also Sagi, "Halacha, shikul da'at, ahrayut ve-zionut datit" [Halacha, Discretion, Responsibility, and Religious Zionism].

84. For expressions of concern about the Haredization of Gush Emunim and Religious Zionism more broadly, see Bnei Akiva, "Symposium on the Topic of 'Bnei Akiva in the Israeli society,'" RZA, Bnei Akiva unit, 202/3 (June 20, 1979); Rosen, "Nation of Israel to the Land of Israel"; Golan, "Conversation with Zerach Warhaftig"; Azrieli, *Knit Kippa Generation;* Israel Harel in Galili, *Rift among the Religious;* Avruch, "Political Judaism and the Post Zionist Era"; Michael Zvi Nehorai, "The Shattering of the Religious Zionist Movement," *Nekuda* 83 (1985); Uri Orbach, "Bnei-Akiva: To Enjoy All the Worlds," *Nekuda* 99 (1986); Moshe Shapira, "Gush Emunim Needs to Return to Religion," *Nekuda* 100 (1986); Avraham Nuriel, "The Haredization of Religious Zionism," *Nekuda* 105 (1986); Haneshke, "No One Rose Up"; Rosen, "The Haredim (with the Help of the Likud and the Alignment) Have Begun to Take Over the Chief Rabbinate"; Daniel Shiloh, "Is Dan Meridor More Loyal Than Zvulun Hammer?" *Nekuda* 159 (1992); Yoel Ben-Nun, "A National-Haredi State in the Exile of Judea," *Nekuda* 149 (1991); Yossi Artzicli, "A Leftist-Haredi Position," *Nekuda* 141 (1990).

85. Quoted in Liebman, "Neotraditional Developments among Orthodox Jews," 238.

86. Ben-Nun, "When the Land of Israel Expropriates the State of Israel."

87. Liebman, "Neotraditional Developments among Orthodox Jews," 240.

88. Friedman, "National Religious Party in Crisis"; Liebman, "Neotraditional Developments among Orthodox Jews."

89. Sagi, "Zionut datit" [Religious Zionism], Galili, *Rift among the Religious,* 20.

90. Raanan, *Gush Emunim;* Aran, *Eretz Yisrael ben dat u-politikah* [The Land of Israel between Politics and Religion].

91. See, for example, the letter to the editor in *Nekuda* 99 (1986). For other complaints about the failure to live up to the claims of welcoming secular settlers, see *Nekuda* 172 (1993); *Nekuda* 67 (1983); "Another Year of Growth and Strengthening," editorial, *Nekuda* 143 (1990); Meir Rabinowitz, "The Half Empty glass," *Nekuda* 149 (1991); *Nekuda* 150 (1991); Zvi Salonim, "Thinking Out Loud," *Nekuda* 157 (1992).

92. Bnei Akiva, "Symposium on the topic of 'Bnei Akiva in the Israeli society,'" RZA, Bnei Akiva unit, 202/3 (1979). See also Eliezer Shavid, "Between Religious and Secular: In the Thicket of the Break, the Polarization, and the Fear," *Nekuda* 71 (1984); Dan Bari, "Zionism, More than Ever," *Nekuda* 95 (1986); Friedman, "National Religious Party in Crisis"; Liebman, "Neotraditional Developments among Orthodox Jews."

93. See, for example, Bnei Akiva, "Symposium on the topic of 'Bnei Akiva in the Israeli society,'" 1979, RZA, Bnei Akiva unit, 202/3; Naomi Golan, "Interview with Zvulun Hammer," *Hatzofe,* December 16, 1994. See also Israel Harel in Oz, *In the Land of Israel,* 115–17; "Kav Vadis," *Nekuda* 71 (1984); Haggai Segal, "Interview with Hanan Porat," *Nekuda* 71 (1984).

94. *Nekuda* 99 (1986). See also Shavid, "Between Religious and Secular"; Bari, "Zionism, More than Ever."

95. See, for examples, Yehuda Zolden, "Fewer Confrontations, More Meetings," *Nekuda* 99 (1986); lead editorial, *Nekuda* 141 (1990); Gafni, "Right-Left, Right-Left, In-Place, March!"; *Nekuda* 172 (1993); Daniel Shalit, "Internal Conversation," *Nekuda* 177 (1994). See also the criticism of this view in Nehorai, "Religious Zionism Is Retreating from Haredi Redemptionism."

96. See, for example, Yehuda Ben-Meir's Knesset speeches on February 15 and 27, 1984, www.knesset.gov.il (accessed December 7, 2009). See also Bnei Akiva, *A Light unto the Nations or like All the Nations: Booklet on the Topic of Our Dealing with "Western Culture,"* RZA, Bnei Akiva instructional materials, 269; Goldberg and Ben-Zadok, "Gush Emunim in the West Bank," 59. For examples of this in *Nekuda,* see Karpel, "Meaning of the Paralysis," as well as many of the columns by Daniel Shalit. See also Feiglin, *Where There Are No Men.*

97. Livant, "To the Glory of the State of Judea"; Sheffler, "A State of Judea Will Save the State of Israel"; Ben-Horin, "Only Fascists See Everything"; Karpel, *Emunit Revolution,*

158, 314. Karpel even calls the defense element in the Israeli *Defense* Forces a fundamentally Christian value.

98. Liebman, "Neotraditional Developments among Orthodox Jews."

99. Erev Rav—literally "a multitude of people"—is the biblical term used to refer to the Egyptians who left Egypt with the Jews and who tried to convince them to return there. Hayerushalmi, *Domineering Skullcap*, 12. See also Greenfield, *Cosmic Fear.*

100. Schwartz, *Land of Reality and Imagination*, 16–17.

101. Karpel, *Emunit Revolution*, 49.

Nationalism and the Question of Change

1. Brubaker and Cooper, "Beyond 'Identity,'" 1.

2. See, for example, Rogers, *Diffusion of Innovations;* Kuran, "Now out of Never"; Kuran, "The Unthinkable and the Unthought"; Laitin, "National Revivals and Violence"; Kuran, "Ethnic Norms and Their Transformation."

3. Tooby and Cosmides, "Psychological Foundations of Culture," 63.

4. Seliger himself allowed for this possibility in his contention that the fundamental ideology itself may change to meet the needs of the political movement articulating it. Seliger, *Ideology and Politics*, 248–51, 263.

5. See, for example, Khalidi, *Iron Cage*, 169, 194. See also the Palestinian participants in "Operation Charlie." Alpher, *Ve-gar ze'ev 'im ze'ev* [And the Wolf Shall Dwell with the Wolf].

6. Khalidi, *Iron Cage*, 178–79.

7. Thomas L. Friedman, "The Arafat Voids," *The New York Times*, November 14, 2004.

8. Khalidi, *Iron Cage*, 178.

9. Palestinian National Council, "Political Programme for the Present Stage of the Palestine Liberation Organization Drawn Up by the Palestinian National Council, Cairo, June 9, 1974," *Journal of Palestine Studies* 3, no. 4 (1974), my emphasis.

10. Muslih, "Towards Coexistence," 18.

11. Ibid., 18–20.

12. For some examples, see Gülalp, "A Postmodern Reaction to Dependent Modernization: The Social and Historical Roots of Islamic Radicalism"; Keyman, "On the Relation between Global Modernity and Nationalism"; Sakallioğlu, "Parameters and Strategies of Islam-State Interaction"; Sakallioğlu, "Liberalism, Democracy, and the Turkish Centre-Right"; Gülalp, "Modernization Policies and Islamist Politics"; Önis, "Political Economy of Islamic Resurgence."

13. Suggestive evidence for this mixture is found in the use of loyalty to the state as the standard against which religious allegiance is judged, and the expression of the "Islamisized protest" of the "subdued masses" in a national, constitutional, idiom. Tapper and Tapper, "Religion, Education, and Continuity"; Olson, "Muslim Identity and Secularism."

14. Sakallioğlu, "Kemalism, Hyper-Nationalism, and Islam"; Ahmad, *Making of Modern Turkey*, 219–22.

15. Olson, "Use of Religious Symbol Systems and Ritual"; General Secretariat of the National Security Council, *12 September in Turkey;* Önis, "Political economy of Islamic Resurgence"; Tünay, "Turkish New Right's Attempt at Hegemony"; Yavuz, "Political Islam and the Welfare (Refah) Party."

16. Young, *Politics of Cultural Pluralism*, 121.

17. Savir, *Process*, ix. A similar suggestion was made by Holsti, "Belief System and National Images."

Bibliography

References to archival sources, short research reports, newspaper and magazine articles, and many primary documents are included in the notes, not in the bibliography.

Abdelal, Rawi, Yoshiko M. Herrera, Alastair Iain Johnston, and Rose McDermott. *Measuring Identity: A Guide for Social Scientists.* Cambridge: Cambridge University Press, 2009.

Achituv, Yosef. "Metachim u-temurut be-manhigut datit" [Tensions and Changes in Religious Leadership]. In *Ben samkhut le-otonomyah be-masoret Yisrael* [Between Authority and Autonomy in Jewish Tradition], edited by Avi Sagi and Zeev Safrai. Tel Aviv: Hakibbutz Hameuchad, 1997.

———. "Lebetav ha-halachtiyim shel harav harashi Yitzhak Halevi Herzog be-'asor ha-rishon la-medinah" [The Halachic Considerations of Chief Rabbi Isaac Halevi Herzog in the First Decade of the State of Israel]. In *Etgar ha-ribonut: Yetsirah ve-hagut be-'asor ha-rishon la-medinah* [The Challenge of Independence: Ideological and Cultural Aspects of Israel's First Decade], edited by Mordechai Bar-On. Jerusalem: Yad Yitzhak Ben-Zvi, 1999.

Adler, Emanuel. "Cognitive Evolution: A Dynamic Approach for the Study of International Relations and Their Progress." In *Progress in Postwar International Relations,* edited by Emanuel Adler and Beverly Crawford. New York: Columbia University Press, 1991.

Aharoni, Yair. "The Changing Political Economy of Israel." *Annals of the American Association of Political and Social Science* 555 (1998): 127–46.

Ahimeir, Abba. *ha-Tsiyonut ha-mahpkhanit* [Revolutionary Zionism]. Tel Aviv: The Committee for the Publication of Ahimeir's Writings, 1966.

Ahmad, Feroz. *The Making of Modern Turkey.* New York: Routledge, 1993.

Allon, Yigal. "Israel: The Case for Defensible Borders." *Foreign Affairs* 55, no. 1 (1976): 38–53.

——. "Israel and the Palestinians." *The Jerusalem Quarterly* 6 (1978): 20–40.

——. *Kelim shluvim* [Communicating Vessels: Essays]. Tel Aviv: Hakibbutz Hameuchad, 1980.

Alpher, Joseph. *Ve-gar ze'ev 'im ze'ev: ha-mitnahalim veha-Palestinim* [And the Wolf Shall Dwell with the Wolf: The Settlers and the Palestinians]. Tel Aviv: Hakibbutz Hameuchad, 2001.

Alter, Peter. *Nationalism.* London: Arnold, 1994.

Alterman, Natan. "Shalom ke-tahlit ve-lo ke-tahlif" [Peace as the Substance and Not as an Alternative]. In *Hakol: Gevulot ha-shalom shel Eretz Yisrael* [All of It: The Peace Frontiers of Eretz Israel], edited by Aharon Ben-Ami. Tel Aviv: Madaf, 1967.

Amital, Yehuda. *ha-Ma'alot min ha-ma'amakim* [Upwards from the Depths]. Jerusalem—Alon Shevut: Daf Chen, 1974.

Anderson, Benedict. *Imagined Communities: Reflections on the Origin and Spread of Nationalism.* New York: Verso, 1991.

Anno, Tadashi. "Collective Identity as an 'Emotional Investment Portfolio.'" In *Beyond Boundaries? Disciplines, Paradigms, and Theoretical Integration in International Studies,* edited by Rudra Sil and Eileen M. Doherty. Albany: State University of New York Press, 2000.

Ansky, Alex. *Mekhirat ha-Likud* [The Marketing of the Likud]. Tel Aviv: Zmora, Bitan, Modan Publishers, 1978.

Aran, Gideon. *Eretz Yisrael ben dat u-politikah: ha-tenu'ah la-'atsirat ha-nesigah be-Sinai u-lekaheha* [The Land of Israel between Politics and Religion: The Movement to Stop the Withdrawal in Sinai]. Jerusalem: Jerusalem Institute for Israel Studies, 1985.

——. "From Religious Zionism to Zionist Religion: The Roots of Gush Emunim." In *Studies in Contemporary Jewry,* edited by Peter Y. Medding. Bloomington: Indiana University Press, 1986.

——. "The Father, the Son, and the Holy Land: The Spiritual Authorities of Jewish-Zionist Fundamentalism in Israel." In *Spokesmen for the Despised: Fundamentalist Leaders of the Middle East,* edited by R. Scott Appleby. Chicago: University of Chicago Press, 1997.

Arian, Alan. *Ideological Change in Israel.* Cleveland: The Press of Case Western Reserve University, 1968.

Arian, Asher. "A People Apart: Coping with National Security Problems in Israel." *Journal of Conflict Resolution* 33, no. 4 (1989): 605–31.

Ariel, Israel. *Atlas Eretz Yisrael li-gevuloteha: 'al-pi ha-mekorot: yesodot ve-heker* [Atlas of the Land of Israel: Its Boundaries according to the Sources]. Jerusalem: Cana Publishing House, 1988.

Ariel, Yigal. *Eretz yarden ve-hermonim: ha-golan ve-ever ha-yarden ba-mikra ubehalacha* [The Land of Jordan and Hermon: The Golan and Transjordan in Scripture and the Halacha]. Hisfin: Midreshat HaGolan, 1996.

Aronoff, Myron J. "Political Polarization: Contradictory Interpretations of Israeli Reality." In *The Begin Era: Issues in Contemporary Israel,* edited by Steven Heydemann. Boulder: Westview Press, 1984.

——. *Israeli Visions and Divisions: Cultural Change and Political Conflict.* New Brunswick, NJ: Transaction Publishers, 1989.

——. *Power and Ritual in the Israeli Labor Party: A Study in Political Anthropology.* London: M. E. Sharpe, 1993.

——. "The 'Americanization' of Israeli Politics: Political and Cultural Change." *Israel Studies* 5, no. 1 (2000): 92–127.

Aronoff, Yael S. "When and Why Do Hard-Liners Become Soft? An Examination of Israeli Prime Ministers Shamir, Rabin, Peres, and Netanyahu." In *Profiling Political Leaders: Cross-Cultural Studies of Personality and Behavior,* edited by Ofer Feldman and Linda O. Valenty. Westport, CT: Praeger, 2001.

Association for Religious Councils in Israel. *Nes ve-ma'use be-shlavei ha-geula* [Miracles and Actions in the Steps of the Redemption]. Tel Aviv: Association for Religious Councils in Israel, 1968.

Attias, Moshe. *Sefer HaTeudot shel haVa'ad Haleumi leKnesset Yisrael B'eretz Yisrael: 1918–1948* [The Book of Documents of the National Assembly in Israel: 1918–1948]. Jerusalem: Rephael Haim HaCohen Press, 1963.

Auerbach, Yehudit, and Hemda Ben-Yehuda. "Attitudes Towards an Existence Conflict: Begin and Dayan on the Palestinian Issue." *International Interactions* 13, no. 4 (1987): 323–51.

Aviezer, Yishai, ed. *Sefer Hagai: zikaron le-'arba'ah mi-talmide Yeshivat Nir Kiryat Arba she-nirtsehu be-Hevron biyedi bnei ola beshnat tasham* [The Book of Hagai: In Memory of the Four Students from the Nir Kiryat Arab Seminary Who Were Murdered in 1979]. Kiryat Arba: Keren Hagai and the Nir Kiryat Arba Yeshiva, 1985.

Avineri, Shlomo. *The Making of Modern Zionism: The Intellectual Origins of the Jewish State.* London: Weidenfeld and Nicolson, 1981.

Avizohar, Meir. "Tochnit ha-medina etzel Ben-Gurion beshlav 'hazionut halochemet'" [Ben-Gurion's Militant Strategy for the Creation of a Jewish State]. In *Iyunim be-tokhniyot ha-halukah, 1937–1947* [Studies in the Palestine Partition Plans, 1937–1947], edited by Meir Avizohar and Isaiah Friedman. Sde Boker: Ben Gurion Research Center, 1984.

———. *Be-re'i saduk: idealim hevratiyim u-le'umiyim ve-hishtakfutam be-olamuh shel Mapai* [Broken Mirror: National and Social Ideals as Reflected in Mapai—The Israeli Labor Party, 1930–1942]. Tel Aviv: Am Oved, 1990.

Avizohar, Meir, and Avi Bareli, eds. *Akhshav o le-olam lo: diyune Mapai ba-shanah ha-aharonah la-Mandat ha-Briti: mevo'ot u-te'udot* [Now or Never: Proceedings of Mapai in the Closing Year of the British Mandate, Excerpts and Documents]. Beit Berl: Ayanot, 1989.

Avizohar, Meir, and Isaiah Friedman, eds. *Iyunim be-tokhniyot ha-halukah, 1937–1947* [Studies in the Palestine Partition Plans, 1937–1947]. Sde Boker: Ben Gurion Research Center, 1984.

Avruch, Kevin. "Political Judaism and the Post-Zionist Era." *Judaism* 47, no. 2 (1998): 146–59.

Azrieli, Yehuda. *Dor ha-kipot ha-serugot: ha-mahpekhah ha-politit shel ha-tse'irim be-mafdal* [The Knit Kippa Generation: The Political Revolution of the Youth in the NRP]. Israel: Avivim, 1990.

Baldwin, David A. "Power Analysis and World Politics: New Trends versus Old Tendencies." *World Politics* 31, no. 2 (1979): 161–94.

Banton, Michael. *Racial and Ethnic Competition.* Cambridge: Cambridge University Press, 1983.

———. "Modeling Ethnic and National Relations." *Ethnic and Racial Studies* 17, no. 1 (1994): 1–19.

Bar-Eyal, Avi. "Eretz Hermonim ve-negev, yam u-midbar: Gevulot Eretz Yisrael betfisato shel David Ben-Gurion" [Land of Hermons and Negev, Sea, and Desert: The Borders of the Land of Israel in the Conception of David Ben-Gurion]. *Kivunim* 21 (1983): 5–15.

Bar-Gal, Yoram. *Moledet ve-ge'ografyah be-me'ah shenot hinukh tsiyoni* [Homeland and Geography in a Hundred Years of Zionist Education]. Tel Aviv: Am Oved, 1993.

Bar-On, Mordechai. "Status-quo lifnei o achrei? hearot prashanut le-mediniyut habitachon shel Yisrael, 1949–1958" [Status Quo Before—or After? Commentary on Israel's Security Policy, 1949–1958]. *Iyunim Be'Tekumat Israel* 5 (1995): 65–111.

——. "Ha-bitchonism ve-mevakrav, 1949–1967" [Bitchonism and Its Critics, 1949–1967]. In *Etgar ha-ribonut: yetsirah ve-hagut be-'asor ha-rishon la-medinah* [The Challenge of Independence: Ideological and Cultural Aspects of Israel's First Decade], edited by Mordechai Bar-On. Jerusalem: Yad Yitzhak Ben-Zvi, 1999.

——. "Small Wars, Big Wars: Security Debates during Israel's First Decade." *Israel Studies* 5, no. 2 (2000): 107–27.

Barzilai, Gad. "A Jewish Democracy at War: Attitudes of Secular Jewish Political Parties in Israel toward the Question of War (1949–1988)." *Comparative Strategy* 9 (1990): 179–94.

Basson, Lauren L. *White Enough to Be American? Race Mixing, Indigenous People, and the Boundaries of State and Nation*. Chapel Hill: University of North Carolina Press, 2008.

Bates, Robert H. "Modernization, Ethnic Competition, and the Rationality of Politics in Contemporary Africa." In *State versus Ethnic Claims: African Policy Dilemmas*, edited by Donald Rothchild and Victor Olorunsola. Boulder, CO: Westview Press, 1983.

Bat-Yehuda, Geula. "Torat Eretz Yisrael shel ha-Ramban be-machshevet ha-techiya" [The Ideology of the Ramban in the Thought of the Revival]. *Sinai* 61, nos. 5–6 (1967): 226–39.

——. *ha-Rav Maimon be-dorotav* [The Times of Rabbi Maimon]. Jerusalem: Mosad Harav Kook, 1979.

Baumel, Judith Tydor. "Bridging Myth and Reality: The Absorption of She'erit Hapletah in Eretz Yisrael, 1945–48." *Middle Eastern Studies* 33, no. 2 (1997): 362–82.

Begin, Binyamin Ze'ev. *Kave imut* [Confrontations]. Tel Aviv: Miskal (Yedioth Ahronot Books and Chemed Books), 1993.

Begin, Menachem. "Russia and Zionism." *Hamadrich* 2, no. 3 (1943).

——. *ha-Mered: zikhronotav shel mefaked ha-Irgun ha-tseva'i ha- le'umi be-Eretz Yisrael* [The Revolt: Memoirs of the Commander of the Irgun in the Land of Israel]. Jerusalem: Ahi'asaf, 1950.

——. *Hashkafat hayim ve-hashkafah le'umit: kave yesod* [Life View and National View: Basic Lines]. Israel: 'BeSa'ar,' The Betar Commission in Israel, 1952.

——. *The Revolt*. New York: Nash Publishing, 1972.

——. "Realistic Foundations for a National Policy." *HaUma* 42 (1974).

Beilin, Yossi. *Mehiro shel ihud: mifleget ha-avodah ad milhemet Yom ha-Kipurim* [The Price of Unity: The Labor Party until the Yom Kippur War]. Tel Aviv: Revivim Press, 1985.

Beinin, Joel. "Political Economy and Public Culture in a State of Constant Conflict: 50 years of Jewish Statehood." *Jewish Social Studies* 4, no. 3 (1998): 96–141.

Ben-Aharon, Naaman. *Tsiyonut har ha-bayit: shalav 2 ba-tsiyonut* [Temple Mount Zionism: Zionism, Stage II]. Bet-El: Bet El Library, 1991.

Ben-Avram, Baruch. *Miflagot u-zeramim politiyim bitkufat ha-bayit ha-le'ummi, 1918–1948* [Political Parties and Organizations during the British Mandate for

Palestine, 1918–1948]. Jerusalem: The Historical Society of Israel, The Zalman Shazar Centre for the Study of Jewish History, 1978.

Ben-Gurion, David. "Zionist Policy." In *Ahdut haavodah: kovets Mifleget Po'ale Erets-Yisra'el; le-zekher Chayim Arlozorov: be'ayotenu ha-mediniyot* [Ahdut Haavoda—Our Political Problems: A Collection of Mapai in the Memory of Chaim Arlozorov], edited by I. Lofben. Tel Aviv, 1943.

——. *Ba-ma'arakhah* [In the Struggle]. Vol. 4. Tel Aviv: Am Oved, 1957.

——. *Medinat Yisrael Ha-mechudeshet* [The Restored State of Israel]. Tel Aviv: Am Oved, 1969.

——, ed. *Anachnu u-shcheneinu* [Us and Our Neighbors]. Tel Aviv: Davar, 1931.

Ben-Gurion, David, and Yitzhak Ben Zvi. *Eretz Yisrael ba-'avar uva-hoveh* [The Land of Israel in the Past and in the Present]. Jerusalem: Yad Ben-Zvi, 1980.

Ben-Haim, Efraim. "Temura ve-sikui" [Change and Possibility]. In *Hakol: Gevulot ha-shalom shel Eretz Israel* [All of It: The Peace Frontiers of Eretz Israel], edited by Aharon Ben-Ami. Tel Aviv: Madaf, 1967.

Ben-Horin, Meir. *The Land of Israel.* New York: Brith Trumpeldor Organization, 1941.

Ben-Hur, Rephaela Bilski. *Kol yachid hu melech: ha-machshava ha-hevratit vehu-medinit shel Ze'ev Jabotinsky* [Every Individual a King: The Social and Political Thought of Ze'ev Jabotinsky], Tel Aviv: Dvir, 1988.

Benziman, Uzi *Rosh memshala be-mazor* [Prime Minister under Siege]. Jerusalem: Adam Publishers, 1981.

Bercovici, Konrad, and Irving Wolfson, eds. *Packet about the Irgun.* New York: Information Department of the American League for a Free Palestine, 1947.

Berger, Peter L., and Thomas Luckmann. *The Social Construction of Reality: A Treatise in the Sociology of Knowledge.* New York. Doubleday, 1966.

Berlin, Meir, ed. *Kol Haaretz: kovetz be'she'elat halukat ha'aretz, mukdash letzirei hakongress hazioni ha-22* [The Entire Land: A Collection on the Question of the Partition of the Land; Dedicated to the Delegates of the 22nd Zionist Congress]. Jerusalem: "Group Opposing Partition," 1947.

Bernstein, Debora. "From Split Labor Market Strategy to Political Co-optation: The Palestine Labor League." *Middle Eastern Studies* 31, no. 4 (1995): 755–71.

——. "Challenges to Separatism: Joint Action by Jewish and Arab Workers in Jewish-Owned Industry in Mandatory Palestine." In *The New Israel: Peacemaking and Liberalization,* edited by Gershon Shafir and Yoav Peled. Boulder, CO: Westview Press, 2000.

Bernstein, Yishayahu. "Yesodot ve-maskanot" [Foundations and Conclusions]. In *Hazon ve-hagshamah* [Vision and Fulfillment], edited by S. Z. Shraggai. London: Tnuat Torah veAvodah, 1945.

——. "Achrit ke-resheet baspekleria shel zionut datit" [Last as First through the Prism of Religious Zionism]. In *Shai li-Yesha'yahu: sefer yovel le-R. Yesha'yahu Volfsberg ben ha-shishim* [A Gift for Yeshayahu: An Anniversary Book for R. Yehayahu Volfsberg on His Sixtieth], edited by Y. Tirosh. Tel Aviv: Hapoel Hamizrachi Cultural Center, 1955.

——. "Min ha-yesod" [From the Foundation]. In *Sefer ha-Tsiyonut ha-datit: iyunim, ma'amarim, reshimot, te'udot* [The Book of Religious Zionism: Articles, Notes, and Documents], edited by S.Z. Shraggai and Yitzhak Refael Jerusalem: Mosad Harav Kook, 1977.

Berry, Yedidia. *Hashivuto shel shem* [What's in a Name? (or Who Owns the State?)]. Tel Aviv: Yaron Golan, 1992.

Betar. *The Left of the Jordan: A One-Time Publication Dedicated to the Jewish Left of the Jordan.* Israel: Betar Leadership, 1946.

Bialer, Uri. "David Ben-Gurion veMoshe Sharett: Hitgabshut shtei orientatziot mediniyot-bitchoniyot bahevra hayisraelit" [David Ben-Gurion and Moshe Sharett: The Crystallization of Two Political-Security Orientations in the Israeli Society]. *Medina, mimshal veiyhasim benle'umiyim* 1, no. 2 (1971): 71–84.

Billig, Michael. *Banal Nationalism.* London: Sage Publications, 1995.

Brecher, Michael. *Decisions in Israel's Foreign Policy.* New Haven, CT: Yale University Press, 1975.

Brenner, Lenni. *The Iron Wall: Zionist Revisionism from Jabotinsky to Shamir.* London: Zed Books, 1984.

Breuilly, John. *Nationalism and the State.* Chicago: University of Chicago Press, 1994.

Brubaker, Rogers. *Citizenship and Nationhood in France and Germany.* Cambridge, MA: Harvard University Press, 1992.

——. *Nationalism Reframed: Nationhood and the National Question in the New Europe.* Cambridge: Cambridge University Press, 1996.

Brubaker, Rogers, and Fredrick Cooper, "Beyond 'Identity.'" *Theory and Society* 29 (2000): 1–47.

Burian, Richard M. "Adaptation: Historical Perspectives." In *Keywords in Evolutionary Biology,* edited by Evelyn Fox Keller and Elisabeth A. Lloyd. Cambridge, MA: Harvard University Press, 1992.

Calhoun, Craig. "Nationalism and Ethnicity." *Annual Review of Sociology* 19 (1993): 211–39.

Canaani, David. *Ha-aliya hashniya haovedet ve-yahasa le-dat u-le-masoret* [The Second Aliya and Its Relation to Religion and Tradition]. Tel Aviv: Sifriyat Poalim, 1976.

Canovan, Margaret. *Nationhood and Political Theory.* Cheltenham, UK: Edward Elgar, 1996.

Chatterjee, Partha. *The Nation and Its Fragments: Colonial and Postcolonial Histories.* Princeton, NJ: Princeton University Press, 1993.

Citrin, Jack, Ernst B. Haas, Christopher Muste, and Beth Reingold. "Is American Nationalism Changing? Implications for Foreign Policy." *International Studies Quarterly* 38, no. 1 (1994): 1–31.

Cohen, Asher. *ha-Talit veha-degel: ha-tsiyonut ha-datit ve-hazon medinat ha-torah bi-yeme reshit ha-medinah, 1947–1953* [The Talit and the Flag: Religious Zionism and the Concept of a Torah State, 1947–1953]. Jerusalem: Yad Yitzhak Ben-Zvi, 1998.

Cohen, Mitchell. *Zion and State: Nation, Class, and the Shaping of Modern Israel.* New York: Columbia University Press, 1992.

Cohen, Yonah. *Perakim be-toldot ha-tenu'ah ha-datit le'umit* [Chapters in the History of the Religious National Movement]. Tel Aviv: National Religious Party Department for Written Propaganda, 1972.

——. *Ha-Mafdal: emda, amida ve-ma'amad* [The NRP—Position, Stance, and Stature]. Tel Aviv: NRP, Hapoel Hamizrachi Organization Cultural and Propaganda Wing, 1980.

Connor, Walker. "A Nation Is a Nation, Is a State, Is an Ethnic Group Is a..." *Ethnic and Racial Studies* 1, no. 4 (1978): 377–400.

Daniel, S. *ha-Sar Hayim-Mosheh Shapira: deyokno shel medinai dati* [Minister Haim Moshe Shapira: Portrait of a Religious Statesman]. Tel Aviv: Yad Shapira, 1980.

Dawkins, Richard. *The Selfish Gene*. Oxford: Oxford University Press, 1976.

Dayan, Moshe. *Story of My Life*. New York: De Capo Press, 1992.

Dennett, Daniel C. *Darwin's Dangerous Idea: Evolution and the Meanings of Life*. New York: Simon & Schuster, 1995.

Denzau, Arthur T., and Douglass C. North. "Shared Mental Models: Ideologies and Institutions." *Kyklos* 47, no. 1 (1994): 3–31.

Derech, Shlomo. "Zionism as Ideology and Program." *Forum* 28–29 (1978): 21–26.

Deutsch, Karl W. *Nationalism and Social Communication: An Inquiry into the Foundations of Nationality*. Cambridge, MA: M.I.T Press, 1966.

Doak, Kevin M. "What Is a Nation and Who Belongs? National Narratives and the Ethnic Imagination in Twentieth-Century Japan." *American Historical Review* 102, no. 2 (1997): 283–309.

Don-Yehiya, Eliezer. "Yetzivut u-termurot be-mifleget mahane: ha-mafdal u-mahapechat ha-tzeirim" [Stability and Change in a Camp-Party: The NRP and the Revolution of the Young Guard]. *Medina, mimshal veiyhasim benle'umiyim* 14 (1980): 25–52.

——. "Hanukkah and the Myth of the Maccabees in Zionist Ideology and in Israeli Society." *Jewish Journal of Sociology* 34, no. 1 (1992): 5–23.

Don Yehiya, Eliezer, and Charles Liebman. "Hafrada ben dat u-medina" [Separation between Religion and State: Slogan and Content]. In *Ha-ma'arehet ha-politit ha-Yisraelit: mikra'ah* [The Israeli Political System: A Reader], edited by Moshe Lissak and Emanuel Gutmann. Tel Aviv: Am Oved, 1977.

Dowty, Alan. *The Jewish State: A Century Later*. Berkeley: University of California Press, 1998.

——. "Despair Is Not Enough: Violence, Attitudinal Change, and 'Ripeness' in the Israeli-Palestinian Conflict." *Cooperation and Conflict* 41, no. 1 (2006): 5–29.

Eagleton, Terry. *Ideology: An Introduction*. New York: Verso Press, 1991.

Eban, Abba. *Personal Witness: Israel through My Eyes*. New York: G. P. Putnam's Sons, 1992.

Eckstein, Harry. "A Culturalist Theory of Political Change." In *Regarding Politics: Essays on Political Theory, Stability, and Change*, edited by Harry Eckstein. Berkeley: University of California Press, 1992.

Eisenstadt, Shmuel Noah, and Berhard Geise. "The Construction of Collective Identity." *Archives Européennes de Sociologie* 36 (1995): 72–102.

Elitzur, Yehuda. "Gvulot ha-aretz be-masoret Yisrael" [The Borders of the Land in the Tradition of Israel]. In *Sefer Eretz Yisrael ha-shelemah* [The Book of the Whole Land of Israel], edited by Aharon Ben-Ami. Tel Aviv: The Movement for the Whole Land of Israel, 1977.

Elon, Amos. *The Israelis: Founders and Sons*. New York: Penguin Books, 1983.

Feiglin, Moshe. *Be-makom she-en anashim* [Where There Are No Men...: The Struggle of the "Zo Artzeinu" Movement against the Post-Zionist Collapse]. Jerusalem: Metzuda, 1997.

Feldestein, Ariel L. *Kesher gordi: David Ben-Gurion, ha-histadrut ha-tsiyonit ve-yahadut artsot ha-brit, 1948–1963* [Gordian Knot: David Ben-Gurion, the Zionist Organization, and American Jewry, 1948–1963]. Beersheva: Ben-Gurion University of the Negev Press, 2003.

Finbron, Moshe, ed. *Devar anshe-shem 'al tokhnit ha-halukah: kovets ma'amarim* [Words of Notable People about Partition]. Tel Aviv, 1937.

First, Anat, and Eli Avraham. "Globalization/Americanization and Negotiating National Dreams." *Israel Studies Forum* 22, no. 1 (2007): 54–74.

Fishman, Aryei. "'Torah and Labor': The Radicalization of Religion within a National Framework." *Studies in Zionism* 6 (1982): 255–71.

Frenkel, Michal, Yehuda Shenhav, and Hanna Herzog. "The Ideological Wellspring of Zionist Capitalism: The Impact of Private Capital and Industry on the Shaping of the Dominant Zionist Ideology." In *The New Israel: Peacemaking and Liberalization,* edited by Gershon Shafir and Yoav Peled. Boulder, CO: Westview Press, 2000.

Fried, Yochanan. "Ma'avak hitnachalut shel Gush Emunim" [Interview: Gush Emunim's Settlement Struggle]. In *Sefer Eretz Yisrael ha-shelemah* [The Book of the Whole Land of Israel], edited by Aharon Ben-Ami. Tel Aviv: The Movement for the Whole Land of Israel, 1977.

Friedman, Menachem. "ha-Mafdal be'tmura- ha-reka le-yeridata ha-electoralit" [The National Religious Party in Crisis]. *Medina, mimshal veiyhasim benle'umiyim* 19–20 (1982): 105–22.

——. "The State of Israel as a Theological Dilemma." In *The Israeli State and Society: Boundaries and Frontiers,* edited by Baruch Kimmerling. Albany: State University of New York Press, 1989.

Friedman, Robert I. *Zealots for Zion: Inside Israel's West Bank Settlement Movement.* New York: Random House, 1992.

Gagnon, V. P., Jr. "Ethnic Nationalism and International Conflict: The Case of Serbia." *International Security* 19, no. 3 (1994/1995): 132–68.

Gal, Allon. *David Ben-Gurion and the American Alignment for a Jewish State.* Bloomington: Indiana University Press, 1991.

Galanti, S. Ben-Rafael, W. E. Aaronson, and I. Schnell. "Power and Changes in the Balance between Ideology and Pragmatism in the Right Wing Likud Party." *GeoJournal* 53, no. 3 (2001): 263–72.

Galili, Zeev, ed. *Kera' ben ha-kipot: heshbon ha-nefesh shel dor ha-kipot ha-serugot* [A Rift among the Religious: Soul Searching of the Knit Kippa Generation]. Jerusalem: Sapir Center, 1993.

Galnoor, Itzhak. *The Partition of Palestine: Decision Crossroads in the Zionist Movement.* Albany: State University of New York Press, 1995.

Gellner, Ernest. *Nationalism.* New York: NYU Press, 1997.

——. *Nations and Nationalism.* Ithaca, NY: Cornell University Press, 1983.

Gelvin, James. *Divided Loyalties: Nationalism and Mass Politics in Syria at the Close of Empire.* Berkeley: University of California Press, 1998.

General Secretariat of the National Security Council. *12 September in Turkey: Before and After.* Ankara: Ongun Kardesler Printing House, 1982.

Genizi, Haim. "Nisyonot leshitoof peula be-mahane hayamin bein shtei milhamot ha-olam" [Attempts at Cooperation within the Right between the Two World Wars]. In *Dat u-mahteret be-Erets Yisrael bi-tkufat ha-mandat* [Religion and Resistance in Mandatory Palestine], edited by Haim Genizi. Tel Aviv: Menachem Begin Center for the Study of the Resistance, 1996.

Giuliano, Elise. "Who Determines the Self in the Politics of Self-Determination? Identity and Preference Formation in Tatarstan's Nationalist Mobilization." *Comparative Politics* 32, no. 3 (2000): 295–316.

Golan, Motti. *Shimon Peres: Biographia* [Shimon Peres: A Biography]. Tel Aviv: Schoken Publishing, 1982.

Goldberg, Giora, and Efraim Ben-Zadok. "Gush Emunim in the West Bank." *Middle Eastern Studies* 22, no. 1 (1986): 52–73.

Goldsheleg, Yitzhak. "Two Letters of Rabbi Meir Bar-Ilan." *Shraggai: A Journal for the Study of Religious Zionism and Immigration to Eretz Israel* 4 (1993): 68–72.

Goldstein, Yaacov. *Mifleget po'ale Eretz Yisrael: gormim le-hakamatah* [The Workers Party of the Land of Israel: Factors in Its Establishment]. Tel Aviv: Am Oved, 1975.

———. "Were the Arabs Overlooked by the Zionists?" *Forum* 39 (1980): 15–30.

———. "David Ben-Gurion and the Bi-National Idea in Palestine." *Middle Eastern Studies* 24, no. 4 (1988): 460–72.

Gorni, Yosef. *Ahdut-ha-avodah 1919–1930 ha-yesodot ha-ra'ayoniyim veha-shitah ha-medinit* [Ahdut Haavoda, 1919–1930: Ideological Foundations and the Political System]. Tel Aviv: Hakibbutz Hameuchad, 1973.

———. *ha-She'elah ha-'Arvit veha-be'ayah ha-Yehudit: zeramim mediniyim-ide'ologiyim ba-Tsiyonut be-yahasam el ha-yeshut ha-'Arvit be-Eretz-Yisrael ba-shanim 1882–1948* [The Arab Question and the Jewish Problem: The Treatment of the Arab Entity by Political-Ideological Streams in Zionism from 1882 to 1948]. Tel Aviv: Am Oved, 1985.

———. "Al 'nimoos' hevrati ve inteies leumi le-she'elat ha-du-kium bein hilonim le-datiyim ba-tenuah ha-zionit" [Social Manners, National Interest, and the Question of Coexistence between Religious and Secular in the Zionist Movement]. In *Kehunah u-melukhah: yahase dat u-medinah be-Yisrael uva-'amim: kovets ma'amarim* [Priesthood and Monarchy: Studies in the Historical Relationship of Religion and State], edited by Gafni Isaiah and Gabriel Motzkin. Jerusalem: Zalman Shazar Center, 1987.

———. *ha-Hipus ahar ha-zehut ha-le'umit: mekomah shel medinat Yisrael ba-mahshavah ha-Yehudit ha-tsiburit ba-shanim, 1945–1987* [The Quest for Collective Identity: The Place of the State of Israel in Public Jewish Thought, 1945–1987]. Tel Aviv: Am Oved, 1990.

Gould, Stephen Jay. "Tempo and Mode in the Macroevolutionary Reconstruction of Darwinism." *Proceedings of the National Academy of Sciences* 91 (1994): 6764–71.

Greenberg, Uri Zvi. "Shir tfelia le-meshichat ami" [A Song of Prayer for the Anointment of My Nation]. In *Sefer Eretz Yisrael ha-shelemah* [The Book of the Whole Land of Israel], edited by Aharon Ben-Ami. Tel Aviv: The Movement for the Whole Land of Israel, 1977.

Greenfeld, Liah. *Nationalism: Five Roads to Modernity*. Cambridge, MA: Harvard University Press, 1992.

Greenfield, Tzvia. *Cosmic Fear: The Rise of the Religious Right in Israel*. Tel Aviv: Miskal—Yediot Ahronot Books and Chemed Books, 2001.

Grinberg, Lev. *Split Corporatism in Israel*. Albany: State University of New York Press, 1991.

Grossman, David. *The Yellow Wind*. New York: Farrar, Straus and Giroux, 2002.

Guha, Ranajit. *Dominance without Hegemony: History and Power in Colonial India*. Cambridge, MA: Harvard University Press, 1997.

Gülalp, Haldun. "A Postmodern Reaction to Dependent Modernization: The Social and Historical Roots of Islamic Radicalism." *New Perspectives on Turkey* 8 (1992): 15–26.

———. "Modernization Policies and Islamist Politics in Turkey." In *Rethinking Modernity and National Identity in Turkey*, edited by S. Bozdoğan and R. Kasaba. Seattle: University of Washington Press, 1997.

Haas, Ernst B. "Reason and Change in International Life: Justifying a Hypothesis." *Journal of International Affairs* 44, no. 1 (1990): 209–40.

——. *Nationalism, Liberalism, and Progress.* Vol. 1, *The Rise and Decline of Nationalism.* Ithaca, NY: Cornell University Press, 1997.

Haffner, Y., and O. Schremer, eds. *ha-'Am veha-arets* [The People and the Land]. Mazkirut Olamit of Bnei Akiva, 1966.

Hall, Peter A. "Policy Paradigms, Social Learning, and the State: The Case of Economic Policymaking in Britain." *Comparative Politics* 25, no. 3 (1993): 275–96.

Halperin, Samuel. "Ideology or Philanthropy? The Politics of Zionist Fund-Raising." *The Western Political Quarterly* 13, no. 4 (1960): 950–73.

Hardin, Russell. *One for All: The Logic of Group Conflict.* Princeton, NJ: Princeton University Press, 1995.

Hattis, Susan Lee. *The Bi-National Idea in Palestine during Mandatory Times.* Tel-Aviv: Shikmona Publishing Co., 1970.

Hawkins, Alun. "The Discovery of Rural England." In *Englishness: Politics and Culture, 1880–1920,* edited by Robert Colls and Philip Dodd. London: Croom Helm, 1986.

Hayerushalmi, Levy Yitzhak. *ha-Kipah ha-shaletet* [The Domineering Skullcap]. Tel Aviv: Hakibbutz Hameuchad, 1997.

Hechter, Michael. *Internal Colonialism: The Celtic Fringe in British National Development.* New Brunswick, NJ: Transaction Publishers, 1999.

Heilman, Samuel C. "Guides of The Faithful: Contemporary Religious Zionist Rabbis." In *Spokesmen for the Despised: Fundamentalist Leaders of the Middle East,* edited by R. Scott Appleby. Chicago: University of Chicago Press, 1997.

Heller, Joseph. "Ha-mediniyut ha-tzionit ve-tochniyot ha-haluka shel E"I be-shnot ha-40" [Zionist Policy and the Partition Plans in the 1940s]. In *Iyunim be-tokhniyot ha-halukah, 1937–1947* [Studies in the Palestine Partition Plans, 1937–1947], edited by Meir Avizohar and Isaiah Friedman. Sde Boker: Ben Gurion Research Center, 1984.

——. *The Birth of Israel, 1945–1949: Ben-Gurion and His Critics.* Gainesville: University Press of Florida, 2000.

Hobsbawm, Eric. "Mass-Producing Traditions: Europe, 1870–1914." In *The Invention of Tradition,* edited by Eric Hobsbawm and Terence Ranger. Cambridge: Cambridge University Press, 1983.

——. *Nations and Nationalism since 1780: Programme, Myth, Reality.* Cambridge: Cambridge University Press, 1990.

Hobsbawm, Eric, and Terence Ranger, eds. *The Invention of Tradition.* Cambridge: Cambridge University Press, 1983.

Holsti, Ole. R. "The Belief System and National Images: A Case Study." *Journal of Conflict Resolution* 6, no. 3 (1962): 244–52.

Hroch, Miroslav. "From Ethnic Group toward the Modern Nation: The Czech Case." *Nations and Nationalism* 10, no. 1/2 (2004): 95–107.

Hutchinson, John. *Nations As Zones of Conflict.* London: Sage Publishers, 2005.

Ilan, Zvi. *ha-Nisyonot li-rekhishat adamah ule-hityashvut Yehudit be-ever ha-Yarden ha-mizrahi, 1871–1947* [Attempts at Jewish Settlement in Trans-Jordan, 1871–1947]. Jerusalem: Daf-Hen Press, 1984.

Jabotinsky, Ze'ev. *Shirim* [Songs]. Jerusalem: Eri Jabotinsky Ltd., 1947.

——. *Ba-derekh la-medinah* [On the Way to the State]. Edited by Eri Jabotinsky. Jerusalem: Eri Jabotinsky Press, 1953.

———. "Letter to Eri Jabotinsky." In *Ekronot manhim li-ve'ayot ha-sha'ah* [Guiding Principles for the Problems of the Day], edited by Yosef Nedava. Tel Aviv: Jabotinsky Institute, 1981.

Kafkafi, Eyal. "Ha-peshet ha-dati: ha-sikui she-avad" [The Religious "Peshet": The Chance That Was Lost]. *Medina, mimshal veiyhasim benle'umiyim* 31 (1990): 77–100.

Karpel, Motti. *Ha-mahapekhah ha-emunit* [The Emunit Revolution: The Waning of Zionism and the Rise of the Emunit Alternative]. Alon Shevut: Lechatchila, 2002.

Katz, Shmuel. *Jabo—biyografyah shel Ze'ev Jabotinsky* [Jabo—A Biography]. Tel Aviv: Dvir Publishing House, 1993.

Kedourie, Elie. *Nationalism*. New York: Praeger, 1961.

Keyman, E. Fuat. "On the Relation between Global Modernity and Nationalism: The Crisis of Hegemony and the Rise of (Islamic) Identity in Turkey." *New Perspectives on Turkey* 13 (1995): 93–120.

Khalidi, Rashid. *Palestinian Identity: The Construction of Modern National Consciousness*. New York: Columbia University Press, 1997

——— *The Iron Cage: The Story of the Palestinian Struggle for Statehood*. Beacon Press: Boston, 2006.

Khenin, Dov. "From 'Eretz Yisrael Haovedet' to 'Yisrael Hashniah': The Social Discourse and Social Policy of Mapai in the 1950s." In *The New Israel: Peacemaking and Liberalization*, edited by Gershon Shafir and Yoav Peled. Boulder, CO: Westview Press, 2000.

Kiernan, Victor. "State and Nation in Western Europe." *Past and Present* 31, no. 1 (1965): 20–38.

Kimmerling, Baruch. "Sociology, Ideology, and Nation Building: The Palestinians and Their Meaning in Israeli Society." *American Sociological Review* 57 (1992): 446–60.

———. *The Invention and Decline of Israeliness: State, Society, and the Military*. Berkeley: University of California Press, 2001.

King, Gary, Robert O. Keohane, and Sidney Verba. *Designing Social Inquiry: Scientific Inference in Qualitative Research*. Princeton, NJ: Princeton University Press, 1994.

Kohn, Hans. "The Nature of Nationalism." *The American Political Science Review* 33, no. 6 (1939): 1001–21.

Kolatt, Israel. "Ha-tenuah ha-tsiyonit veha-aravim" [The Zionist Movement and the Arabs] *Studies in Zionism* 5 (1982): 129–57.

———. "Pulmus ha-haluka be-tnuat ha-avoda" [The Debate on Partition within the Labor Movement]. In *Iyunim be-tokhniyot ha-halukah, 1937–1947* [Studies in the Palestine Partition Plans, 1937–1947], edited by Meir Avizohar and Isaiah Friedman. Sde Boker: Ben Gurion Research Center, 1984.

Kook, Zvi Yehuda. "Mizmor yud'tet shel medinat Yisrael" [Psalm 19 of the State of Israel]. In *Hakol: Gevulot ha-shalom shel Eretz Israel* [All of It: The Peace Frontiers of Eretz Israel], edited by Aharon Ben-Ami. Tel Aviv: Madaf, 1967.

———. "Between a Nation and Its Land." *Artzi: A Collection of Essays, Thoughts, and Studies for the Clarification of the Living Link between the Nation of Israel and Its Land in Our Generation* 2 (1982).

Krasner, Stephen D. "Approaches to the State: Alternative Conceptions and Historical Dynamics." *Comparative Politics* 16, no. 2 (1984): 223–46.

Krausz, Ernest, and Mordechai Bar-Lev. "Varieties of Orthodox Religious Behavior: A Case Study of Yeshiva High School Graduates in Israel." *Jewish Journal of Sociology* 20, no. 1 (1978): 59–74.

Kuran, Timur, "Now out of Never: The Element of Surprise in the East European Revolution of 1989." *World Politics* 44, no. 1 (1991): 7–48.

——. "The Unthinkable and the Unthought." *Rationality and Society* 5, no. 4 (1993): 473–505.

——. "Ethnic Norms and Their Transformation through Reputational Cascades." *Journal of Legal Studies* 27, no. 2 (1998): 623–59.

Laclau, Ernesto, ed. *The Making of Political Identities*. London: Verso, 1994.

Laclau, Ernesto, and Chantal Mouffe. *Hegemony and Socialist Strategy: Towards a Radical Democratic Politics*. New York: Verso, 1985.

Laitin, David D. "Hegemony and Religious Conflict: British Imperial Control and Political Cleavages in Yorubaland." In *Bringing the State Back*, edited by Peter Evans, Dietrich Rueschemeyer, and Theda Skocpol. Cambridge: Cambridge University Press, 1985.

——. "National Revivals and Violence." *European Journal of Sociology* 36 (1995): 3–43.

——. *Identity in Formation: The Russian-Speaking Populations in the Near Abroad*. Ithaca, NY: Cornell University Press, 1998.

Lamont, Michele, and Virag Molnar. "The Study of Boundaries in the Social Sciences." *Annual Review of Sociology* 28 (2002): 167–95.

Lang, David Marshall. *Armenia: Cradle of Civilization*. London: George Allen & Unwin, 1978.

Lavon, Pinchas. *Al 'arakhim u-nekhasim* [On Values and Assets]. Tel Aviv: Hakibbutz Hameuchad and Yad Tabenkin, 1986.

Lewontin, Richard C., Steven Rose, and Leon J. Kamin. *Not in Our Genes: Biology, Ideology, and Human Nature*. New York: Pantheon Books, 1984.

Liebman, Charles. "Diaspora Influence of Israel: The Ben-Gurion-Blaustein 'Exchange' and Its Aftermath." *Jewish Social Studies* 36, nos. 3–4 (1974): 271–80.

——. "Religion and Political Integration in Israel." *Jewish Journal of Sociology* 17, no. 1 (1975): 17–27.

——. "Hitpathut ha-neo-masortiyut bekerev yehudim ortodoxim be-Yisrael" [Neotraditional Developments among Orthodox Jews in Israel]. *Megamot* 27, no. 3 (1982): 231–50.

——. "Yesodot mosariyim ve-smalim be-techum ha-politika shel hayechasim bein Yisrael ve-ha-tfutzot" [Moral and Symbolic Foundations in the Political Realm of the Relations between Israel and the Dispersions]. In *Am ve-'edah: ha-masoret ha-medinit ha-Yehudit ve-hashlakhotehah le-yamenu* [Kinship and Consent: The Jewish Political Tradition and Its Contemporary Uses], edited by Daniel J. Elazar. Jerusalem: Jerusalem Center for Public Affairs, 1991.

Liebman, Charles S., and Eliezer Don-Yehiya. *Civil Religion in Israel: Traditional Judaism and Political Culture in the Jewish State*. Berkeley: University of California Press, 1983.

Llobera, Josep R. *The God of Modernity: The Development of Nationalism in Western Europe*. Providence: Berg, 1994.

Lochery, Neill. "The Netanyahu Era: From Crisis to Crisis, 1996–99." In *Israel: The First Hundred Years; from War to Peace?* edited by Efraim Karsh. New York: Frank Cass, 2000.

——. "The Politics and Economics of Israeli Disengagement, 1994–2006." *Middle Eastern Studies* 43, no. 1 (2007): 1–19.

Lustick, Ian S. *Arabs in the Jewish State: Israel's Control of a National Minority.* Austin: University of Texas Press, 1980.

——. "The Political Road to Binationalism: Arabs in Jewish Politics." In *The Emergence of a Binational Israel: The Second Republic in the Making,* edited by Ilan Peleg and Ofira Seliktar. Boulder, CO: Westview Press, 1989.

——. *Unsettled States, Disputed Lands: Britain and Ireland, France and Algeria, Israel and the West Bank-Gaza.* Ithaca, NY: Cornell University Press, 1993.

——. *For the Land and the Lord: Jewish Fundamentalism in Israel.* New York: Council on Foreign Relations Press, 1994.

Manor, Reudor. "Dimuyim kabalat hachlatot ve-hizun hozer be-mediniyut ha-huts ha-Yisraelit: Itzuv mapat ha-gvulot ha-Yisraelit be-mahalach milchemet ha-atzmaut" [Comparisons of Decision-Making and Feedback of Israeli Foreign Policy: The Shaping of the Map of Israeli Borders during the War of Independence]. *Medina, mimshal veiyhasim benle'umiyim* 13 (1979): 17–51.

——. "Dimuyim ve-kabalat hachlatot be-nose ha-gevulot bi-mediniyut ha-huts ha-Yisraelit, 1948–1973" [Images and Decision-Making on the Boundaries Issue in Israeli Foreign Policy in the Years 1948–1973]. PhD diss., Hebrew University, 1980.

Margalit, Elkana. *Anatomyah shel smol: poale-tsiyon smol be-eretz Yisrael (1919–1946)* [Anatomy of the Left: Poalei Zion Smol in Eretz Israel (1919–1946)]. Jerusalem: The Hebrew University, 1976.

Marx, Anthony. *Faith in Nation: Exclusionary Origins of Nationalism.* New York: Oxford University Press, 2003.

McKeown, Timothy J. "Case Studies and the Limits of the Quantitative Worldview." In *Rethinking Social Inquiry: Diverse Tools, Shared Standards,* edited by Henry E. Brady and David Collier. Lanham, MD: Rowman & Littlefield, 2004.

Meadwell, Hudson. "Breaking the Mould? Quebec Independence and Secession in the Developed West." In *Notions of Nationalism,* edited by Sukumar Periwal. Budapest: Central European University Press, 1995.

Medding, Peter Y. *Mapai in Israel: Political Organization and Government in a New Society.* Cambridge: Cambridge University Press, 1972.

Mendilow, Jonathan. "The Likud's Double Campaign: Between the Devil and the Deep Blue Sea." In *The Elections in Israel—1996,* edited by Asher Arian and Michal Shamir. Albany: SUNY Press, 1999.

——. *Ideology, Party Change, and Electoral Campaigns in Israel, 1965–2001.* Albany: SUNY Press, 2003.

Meyer, John W., John Boli, George M. Thomas, and Francisco O. Ramirez. "World Society and the Nation-State." *The American Journal of Sociology* 103, no. 1 (1997): 144–81.

Miron, Dan. "Teuda be-Yisrael" [A Document in Israel]. *Politika* 14–15 (1987): 37–45.

Misgav, Haim. *Sihot eem Yitzhak Shamir* [Conversations with Yitzhak Shamir]. Tel Aviv: Sifriyat Poalim, 1997.

Morris, Benny. "He'arot al ha-histografya ha-Tsionit ve-ra'ayon ha-transfer ba-shanim 1937–1947" [Comments on Zionist Historiography and the Idea of Transfer in the Years 1937–1944]. In *Ben hazon le-revizyah: meah shenot historyografyah Tsiyonit: kovets ma'amarim* [From Vision to Revision: A Hundred

Years of Historiography of Zionism], edited by Yechiam Weitz. Jerusalem: Zalman Shazar Center, 1997.

Muslih, Muhammad. "Towards Coexistence: An Analysis of the Resolutions of the Palestine National Council." *Journal of Palestine Studies* 19, no. 4 (1990): 3–29.

Nanda, B. R. "Nehru, the Indian National Congress, and the Partition of India, 1935–1947." In *The Partition of India: Policies and Perspectives, 1935–1947,* edited by C. H. Philips and Mary Doreen Wainwright. London: George Allen & Unwin, 1970.

Naor, Arye. "Ribonut medinat Yisrael ba-mahshava ha-Yehudit-ortodoxit" [The Sovereignty of the State of Israel in Orthodox-Jewish Thought]. *Politika* 2 (1998): 71–96.

——. "The Security Argument in the Territorial Debate in Israel: Rhetoric and Policy." *Israel Studies* 4, no. 2 (1999): 150–77.

——. *Eretz Yisrael ha-shelemah: emunah u-mediniyut* [Greater Israel: Theology and Policy]. Haifa: University of Haifa Press, 2001.

——. "Hawks' Beaks, Doves' Feathers: Likud Prime Ministers between Ideology and Reality." *Israel Studies* 10, no. 3 (2005): 154–91.

Nativ, David. "Kiddush ha-shem leinei ha-amim" [The Sanctification of God before the Eyes of the [Foreign] Nations]. In *Sefer Hagai: zikaron le-'arba'ah mi-talmide Yeshivat Nir Kiryat Arba she-nirtsehu be-Hevron biyedi bnei olu beshnat tasham* [The Book of Hagai: In Memory of the Four Students from the Nir Kiryat Arab Seminary Who Were Murdered in 1979], edited by Yishai Aviezer. Kiryat Arba: Keren Hagai and the Nir Kiryat Arba Yeshiva, 1985.

Neamanei Torah ve Avoda. *le-nohah ha-haslama ba-yahas la-aravim: ideologia ve-hinuch* [Given the Escalation Regarding the Arabs]. Jerusalem: Hakibbutz Hadati, 1985.

Nedva, Yosef. "Churchill and the Borders of the Land of Israel." *Kivunim* 27 (1985): 89–103.

Ne'eman, Yuval. *Mediniyut ha-reiya ha-mefukahat* [A Shrewd Policy]. Ramat Gan: Revivim, 1984.

Neria, Moshe Zvi. *Konters ha-vikuah: hilhot shabat behalihot hamedina* [Booklet of the Argument: Sabbath Rules and the Rules of the State]. Jerusalem: Or Olam, 1952.

——. "Ha-mafridim bein torat Yisrael ve-medinat Yisrael" [Those Who Distinguish between the Torah of Israel and the State of Israel]. In *Sefer ha-Tsiyonut ha-datit: iyunim, ma'amarim, reshimot, te'udot* [The Book of Religious Zionism: Articles, Notes, and Documents], edited by S. Z. Shraggai and Yitzhak Refael. Jerusalem: Mosad Harav Kook, 1977.

Netanyahu, Benjamin. *A Place among the Nations: Israel and the World.* New York: Bantam Press, 1993.

——. *Makom tachat hashemesh* [A Place under the Sun]. Israel: Yediot Ahronot, 1995.

——. *A Durable Peace: Israel and Its Place Among the Nations.* New York: Warner Books, 2000.

Nitzan, Jonathan, and Shimshon Bichler. "From War Profits to Peace Dividends: The New Political Economy of Israel." *Capital and Class* 60 (1996): 61–94.

North, Douglass C. "A Transaction Cost Theory of Politics." *Journal of Theoretical Politics* 2, no. 4 (1990): 355–67.

Norval, Aletta J. "Social Ambiguity and the Crisis of Apartheid." In *The Making of Political Identities,* edited by Ernesto Laclau. New York: Verso, 1994.

NRP Information Department. *The Sinai Episode: Discussions, Thoughts, Conclusions.* Tel Aviv: NRP, 1957.

O'Dea, Janet. "Gush Emunim: Roots and Ambiguities." *Forum* 25, no. 2 (1976): 39 50.

———. "Religious Zionism Today." *Forum* 28–29 (1978): 111–17.

Olson, Emelie A. "Muslim Identity and Secularism in Contemporary Turkey: 'The Headscarf Dispute.'" *Anthropological Quarterly* 58, no. 4 (1985).

———. "The Use of Religious Symbol Systems and Ritual in Turkey: Women's Activities at Muslim Saint's Shrines." *The Muslim World* 134, nos. 2–3 (1994).

Ona, Moshe. "Medinat Yisrael ve-golat Yisrael" [The State of Israel and the Diaspora of Israel]. In *Shai li-Yesha'yahu: sefer yovel le-R. Yesha'yahu Volfsberg ben ha-shishim* [A Gift for Yeshayahu: An Anniversary Book for R. Yehayahu Volfsberg on His Sixtieth], edited by Y. Tirosh. Tel Aviv: Hapoel Hamizrachi Cultural Center, 1955.

———. *Bi-derakhim nifradot: ha-miflagot ha-datiyot be-Yisrael* [In Separate Ways: The Religious Parties in Israel]. Alon Shavot, Gush Etzion: Yad Shapira, 1983.

Öniş, Ziya. "The Political Economy of Islamic Resurgence in Turkey: The Rise of the Welfare Party in Perspective." *Third World Quarterly* 18, no. 4 (1997): 743–66.

Oren, Michael B. *Six Days of War: June 1967 and the Making of the Modern Middle East.* New York: Ballantine Books, 2003.

Oz, Amos. *In the Land of Israel.* New York: Harcourt Brace Jovanovich, 1982.

———. *Kol ha-tikvot: mahshavot 'al zehut Yisraelit* [All Our Hopes: Essays on the Israeli Condition]. Jerusalem: Keter Publishing, 1998.

Pappe, Ilan. "Moshe Sharett, David Ben Gurion, ve-'ha-optzia ha-falastinit,' 1948–1956" [Moshe Sharett, David Ben-Gurion, and the "Palestinian Option," 1948–1956.] *ha-tzionut* 7, no. 1 (1986): 77–96.

Pedahzur, Ami. "The Downfall of the National Camp?" In *Israel at the Polls, 1999,* edited by Daniel J. Elazar and M. Ben Mollov. London: Frank Cass, 2001.

Pedahzur, Ami, Sivan Hirsch, and Daphna Canetti-Nisim. "Whose Victory? An Empirical Analysis of the Popular Votes for the Right-Wing Camp in the 2003 Elections." *Israel Affairs* 10, no. 4 (2004): 20–35.

Peled, Yoav, and Gershon Shafir. "The Roots of Peacemaking: The Dynamics of Citizenship in Israel." *International Journal of Middle East Studies* 28, no. 3 (1996): 391–413.

Peleg, Ilan. *Begin's Foreign Policy, 1977–1983: Israel's Move to the Right.* New York: Greenwood Press, 1987.

Peretz, Don, Rebecca Kook, and Gideon Doron. "Knesset Election 2003: Why Likud Regained Its Political Domination and Labor Continued to Fade Out." *Middle East Journal* 57, no. 4 (2003): 588–603.

Peri, Yoram. *Between Battles and Ballots: Israeli Military in Politics.* Cambridge: Cambridge University Press, 1983.

Pierson, Paul. "Increasing Returns, Path Dependence, and the Study of Politics." *American Political Science Review* 94, no. 2 (2000): 251–67.

Posner, Daniel N. *Institutions and Ethnic Politics in Africa.* Cambridge: Cambridge University Press, 2006.

Preuss, Teddy. *Begin ba-shilton* [Begin: His Regime]. Jerusalem: Keter, 1984.

Price, Robert. "Race and Reconciliation in the New South Africa." *Politics & Society* 25, no. 2 (1997): 149–78.

Raanan, Tzvi. *Gush Emunim* [Gush Emunim]. Tel Aviv: Sifriyat Poalim, 1980.

Raanan, Uri. *The Frontiers of a Nation: A Re-examination of the Forces Which Created the Palestine Mandate and Determined Its Territorial Shape.* Westport, CT: Hyperion Press, 1976.

Rabinovitch, Itamar. *Hevlei Shalom: Yisrael ve-haAravim, 1948–2003* [Waging Peace: Israel and the Arabs, 1948–2003]. Or Yehuda, Israel: Dvir Press, 2004.

Ragin, Charles C. "Turning the Tables: How Case-Oriented Research Challenges Variable-Oriented Research." In *Rethinking Social Inquiry: Diverse Tools, Shared Standards,* edited by Henry E. Brady and David Collier. Lanham, MD: Rowman & Littlefield, 2004.

Ram, Uri. "Postnationalist Pasts: The Case of Israel." *Social Science History* 22, no. 4 (1998): 513–45.

——. "National, Ethnic, or Civic? Contesting Paradigms of Memory, Identity, and Culture in Israel." *Studies in Philosophy and Education* 19, nos. 5–6 (2000): 405–22.

Ravitzky, Aviezer. *Messianism, Zionism, and Jewish Religious Radicalism.* Chicago: University of Chicago Press, 1996.

Remba, A. "Dat u-masoret be-hayav u-be-mishnato," [Religion and Tradition in His Life and Thought]. *HaUma* 9 (1964): 145–66.

Renan, Ernest. "What Is a Nation?" In *Nation and Narration,* edited by Homi K. Bhabha. New York: Routledge, 1991.

Rogers, Everett M. *The Diffusion of Innovations.* New York: The Free Press, 1983.

Rogowski, Ronald. "Causes and Varieties of Nationalism: A Rationalist Account." In *New Nationalism of the Developed World,* edited by Edward Tiryakian and Ronald Rogowski. Boston: Allen & Unwin, 1985.

Rosen, Dov. "Am Yisrael, le-eretz Yisrael al pi torat Yisrael" [The Nation of Israel to the Land of Israel according to the Torah of Israel]. In *Sefer ha-Tsiyonut ha-datit: iyunim, ma'amarim, reshimot, te'udot* [The Book of Religious Zionism: Articles, Notes, and Documents], edited by S. Z. Shraggai and Yitzhak Refael. Jerusalem: Mosad Harav Kook, 1977.

Rouhana, Nadim, and As'ad Ghanem. "The Crisis of Minorities in Ethnic States: The Case of Palestinian Citizens in Israel." *International Journal of Middle East Studies* 30, no. 3 (1998): 321–46.

Rynhold, Jonathan, and Gerald Steinberg. "The Peace Process and the Israeli Elections." *Israel Affairs* 10, no. 4 (2004): 181–204.

Rynhold, Jonathan, and Dov Waxman. "Ideological Change and Israel's Disengagement from Gaza." *Political Science Quarterly* 123, no. 1 (2008): 11–38.

Sagi, Avi. "Halacha, shikul da'at, ahrayut ve-zionut datit" [Halacha, Discretion, Responsibility, and Religious Zionism]. In *Ben samkhut le-otonomyah be-masoret Yisrael* [Between Authority and Autonomy in Jewish Tradition], edited by Avi Sagi and Zeev Safrai. Tel Aviv: Hakibbutz Hameuchad, 1997.

——. "Zionut datit: bein petihut le-sgirut" [Religious Zionism: Between Openness and Closeness]. In *Yahadut penim va-huts: dialog ben 'olamot* [Judaism: A Dialogue between Cultures], edited by Avi Sagi, Dudi Schwartz, and Yedidia Z. Stern. Jerusalem: The Hebrew University Magnes Press, 1999.

Sakallioğlu, Ümit Cizre. "Kemalism, Hyper-Nationalism, and Islam in Turkey." *History of European Ideas* 18, no. 2 (1994): 255–70.

——. "Liberalism, Democracy, and the Turkish Centre-Right: The Identity Crisis of the True Path Party." *Middle Eastern Studies* 32, no. 2 (1996).

——. "Parameters and Strategies of Islam-State Interaction in Republican Turkey." *International Journal of Middle East Studies* 28, no. 2 (1996): 231–51.

Salmon, Yosef. "Dat umedinah ba-leumiyut ha-Yehudit ha-modernit ve-ba-medina she-baderech: hazinonut hadatit" [Religion and State in the Modern Jewish Nationalism and in the State That is on the Way: Religious Zionism]. In *Kehunah u-melukhah: yahase dat u-medinah be-Yisra'el uva-'amim: kovets ma'amarim* [Priesthood and Monarchy: Studies in the Historical Relationship of Religion and State], edited by Isaiah Gafni and Gabriel Motzkin. Jerusalem: Zalman Shazar Center for Jewish History, 1987.

Savir, Uri. *The Process: 1,100 Days That Changed the Middle East.* New York: Vintage Books, 1998.

Sayyid, Bobby. "Sign O' Times: Kaffirs and Infidels Fighting the Ninth Crusade." In *The Making of Political Identities,* edited by Ernesto Laclau. New York: Verso, 1994.

Schechtman, Joseph B., and Yehuda Benari. *History of the Revisionist Movement.* Vol. 1, *1925–1930.* Tel Aviv: Hadar Publishing House, 1970.

Scholte, Jan Aart. "The Geography of Collective Identities in a Globalizing World." *Review of International Political Economy* 3, no. 4 (1996): 565–607.

Schuman, Howard, and Cheryl Rieger. "Historical Analogies, Generational Effects, and Attitudes toward War." *American Sociological Review* 57, no. 3 (1992): 315–26.

Schwartz, Dov. *Eretz ha-mamashut veha-dimyon: ma'amahda shel Eretz-Yisrael be-hagut ha-tsiyonit ha-datit* [Land of Reality and Imagination: The Land of Israel in Religious Zionist Thought]. Tel Aviv: Am Oved, 1997.

Seden, Eli. "The Aspiration to Peace and Our National Morality." *Artzi: A Collection of Essays, Thoughts, and Studies for the Clarification of the Living Link between the Nation of Israel and Its Land in Our Generation* 2 (1982).

Segal, Haggai. *Ahim Yekarim: korot ha-mahteret ha-Yehudit* [Dear Brothers: A History of the Jewish Underground]. Jerusalem: Keter Press, 1987.

Segev, Tom. *One Palestine, Complete: Jews and Arabs under the British Mandate.* New York: Metropolitan Books, 2000.

Seliger, Martin. *Ideology and Politics.* London: George Allen & Unwin, 1976.

Sella, Amnon. "Custodians and Redeemers: Israeli Leaders' Perceptions of the Peace, 1967–1976." *Middle Eastern Studies* 22, no. 2 (1986): 236–51.

Selushtz, Nahum. *Ever ha-yarden* [Transjordan]. Tel Aviv: Omanut Co., Sifriyat Eretz Israel of the Keren Kayemet LeYisrael, 1933.

Sewell, William H., Jr. "Ideologies and Social Revolutions: Reflections on the French Case." *The Journal of Modern History* 57, no. 1 (1985): 57–85.

Shafir, Gershon, and Yoav Peled. *Being Israeli: The Dynamics of Multiple Citizenship.* Cambridge: Cambridge University Press, 2002.

——, eds. *The New Israel: Peacemaking and Liberalization.* Boulder, CO: Westview Press, 2000.

Shaked, Yosef. "Eretz moledet—Eretz Yisrael" [Land of Birth—Land of Israel]. In *Sefer Eretz Yisrael ha-shelemah* [The Book of the Whole Land of Israel], edited by Aharon Ben-Ami. Tel Aviv: The Movement for the Whole Land of Israel, 1977.

Shalev, Michael. "Jewish Organized Labor and the Palestinians: A Study of State/Society Relations in Israel." In *The Israeli State and Society: Boundaries and Frontiers,* edited by Baruch Kimmerling. Albany: State University of New York Press, 1989.

Shalom, Zaki. "Emdot be-hanhagat ha-medina be-sugiyat ha-status-quo ha-territoriali be-shanim ha-rishonot she-leachar milhemet ha-atzmaut: bechina mechudeshet" [Positions of the Leadership of the State on the Issue of the Territorial Status Quo in the First Years after the War of Independence—A Renewed Examination]. *Iyunim B'tkumat Israel* 8 (1998): 110–49.

Shapira, Anita. "Parashat ha-optzia al admot ha-emir Abdalla be-Ghur-el-Kabd: reshit ha-kesher ben ha-hanhala haziyonit ve-ha-emir Abdallah" [The Option on the Emir's Land at Ghur-el-Kabd: The First Contacts between Emir Abdullah and the Zionist Executive]. *ha-Tsiyonut* 3 (1973): 295–345.

——. *Berl: The Biography of a Socialist Zionist.* Cambridge: Cambridge University Press, 1984.

——. *Yehudim hadashim, yehudim yeshanim* [New Jews, Old Jews]. Tel Aviv: Am Oved Publishers, 1997.

Shapiro, Yonatan. *The Formative Years of the Israeli Labor Party: The Organization of Power, 1919–1930.* London: Sage Publications, 1976.

——. *The Road to Power: Herut Party in Israel.* Albany: SUNY Press, 1991.

Sharett, Moshe. *Besha'ar ha-ummot: 1946–1949* [At the Gate of Nations: 1946–1949]. Tel Aviv: Am Oved Publishers, 1958.

——. "Israel and the Arab World—War and Peace: Reflections on the Years 1947–1957." *Ot* 1, no. 6 (1966): 5–10.

Shavit, Yaacov. *ha-Mitologyot shel ha-yamin* [The Mythologies of the Zionist Right Wing]. Kfar Saba, Israel: Beit Berl and the Moshe Sharett Institute, 1986.

Shaviv, Yehuda, ed. *Eretz nahalah: ma'amarim be-'inyanah shel Eretz Yisrael, ze-khutenu 'aleha, zikatenu eleha, hovotenu kelapeha* [A Land of Settlement: Articles about the Land of Israel, Our Rights to It, Our Bonds to It, and Our Obligations to It]. Jerusalem: The Young Mizrachi Generation, 1977.

Sheffer, Gabriel. "Individualism vs. National Coherence: The Current Discourse on Sovereignty, Citizenship, and Loyalty." *Israel Studies* 2, no. 2 (1997).

Sheleg, Yair. *ha-Datiyim ha-hadashim: mabat 'akhshavi 'al ha-hevrah ha-datit be-Yisrael* [The New Religious Jews: Recent Development among Observant Jews in Israel]. Jerusalem: Keter Publishing House, 2000.

Shimoni, Gideon. "Reformulations of Zionist Ideology since the Establishment of the State of Israel." In *Values, Interests, and Identity: Jews and Politics in a Changing World,* Studies in Contemporary Jewry 11, edited by Peter Y. Medding. New York: Oxford University Press, 1995.

——. *The Zionist Ideology.* Hanover, NH: Brandeis University Press, 1995.

Shindler, Colin. *Israel, Likud, and the Zionist Dream: Power, Politics, and Ideology from Begin to Netanyahu.* London: I. B. Tauris, 1995.

——. "The View from the Right: From Jabotinsky to Netanyahu." In *A Land Flowing With Milk and Honey: Visions of Israel from Biblical to Modern Times,* edited by Leonard J. Greenspoon and Ronald A. Simkins. Omaha, NE: Creighton University Press, 2001.

Shlaim, Avi. *Collusion across the Jordan: King Abdullah, the Zionist Movement, and the Partition of Palestine.* New York: Columbia University Press, 1988.

Shochteman, Eliav. *Va-ya'amidah le-Ya'akov le-hok: le-tokef ribonuto shel am Yisrael al Erets Yisrael veli-she'elat hezkatenu be-Erets Yisrael bi-mekom pikuah nefesh veshe-lo bi-mekom pikuah nefesh: she'elat ha-hovah le-tsayet li-pekudah le-pinui Yehudim vi-yishuvim Yehudiyim be-Erets Yisrael* [And Jacob Shall Have It for a Law: On the Sovereignty of the Nation of Israel in the Land of Israel and the Issue of Saving a Life: The Question of the Obligation to Follow Orders to Evacuate Jews and Jewish Settlements in the Land of Israel]. Jerusalem: Mahad, 1995.

Shraggai, S. Z. "Hazon ve-hagshama" [Vision and Fulfillment]. In *Hazon ve-hagshama* [Vision and Fulfillment], edited by S. Z. Shraggai. London: Tnuat Torah veAvodah, 1945.

———. *Al ha-tsiyonut ha-datit* [On Religious Zionism]. Printed in Eretz-Israel (Palestine): Pinchas Even Press, 1946.

———. "le-Heshbona shel haziyonut ha-datit ve-tnuat torah ve-avoda" [The Balance Sheet of Religious Zionism and the Torah and Labor Movement]. In *Sefer ha-Tsiyonut ha-datit: iyunim, ma'amarim, reshimot, te'udot* [The Book of Religious Zionism: Articles, Notes, and Documents], edited by S. Z. Shraggai and Yitzhak Refael. Jerusalem: Mosad Harav Kook, 1977.

Smith, Anthony D. *Theories of Nationalism.* London: Duckworth & Co., 1971.

———. "Gastronomy or Geology? The Role of Nationalism in the Reconstruction of Nations," *Nations and Nationalism* 1, no. 1 (1995): 3–23.

———. "Culture, Community, and Territory: The Politics of Ethnicity and Nationalism." *International Affairs* 72, no. 3 (1996): 445–58.

Smith, Rogers. *Stories of Peoplehood: The Politics and Morals of Political Membership.* Cambridge: Cambridge University Press, 2003.

Smooha, Sammy. "The Implications of the Transition to Peace for Israeli Society." *Annals of the American Association of Political and Social Science* 555 (1998): 26–45.

Snyder, Jack. *From Voting to Violence: Democratization and Nationalist Conflict.* New York: W. W. Norton & Co., 2000.

Snyder, Jack, and Karen Ballentine. "Nationalism and the Marketplace of Ideas." *International Security* 21, no. 2 (1996): 5–40.

Sofer, Sasson. *Begin: An Anatomy of Leadership.* New York: Basil Blackwell, 1988.

Sollors, Werner, ed. *The Invention of Ethnicity.* Oxford: Oxford University Press, 1989.

Sprinzak, Ehud. "Gush Emunim: The Tip of the Iceberg." *The Jerusalem Quarterly* 21 (1981): 28–47.

———. *The Ascendance of Israel's Radical Right.* New York: Oxford University Press, 1991.

———. "The Politics of Paralysis I: Netanyahu's Safety Belt." *Foreign Affairs* 77, no. 4 (1998): 18–28.

Stein-Ashkenazi, Esther. *Betar be-Eretz Yisrael, 1925–1947* [Betar in the Land of Israel, 1925–1947]. Jerusalem: Hasifria Hazionit, 1997.

Steinberg, Gerald M. "Peace, Security, and Terror in the 1996 Elections." *Israel Affairs* 4, no. 1 (1997): 209–34.

Sternhell, Zeev. *The Founding Myths of Israel: Nationalism, Socialism, and the Making of the Jewish State.* Princeton, NJ: Princeton University Press, 1998.

Swidler, Ann. "Culture in Action: Symbols and Strategies." *American Sociological Review* 51, no. 2 (1986): 273–86.

Tabenkin, Yitzhak. *Lekah sheshet ha-yamim: yeshuvah shel eretz bilti-mehuleket* [The Lesson of the Six-Day War: Settlement of an Undivided Land]. Tel Aviv: Hakibbutz Hameuchad, 1970.

Tal, Uriel. "The Nationalism of Gush Emunim in Historical Perspective." *Forum* 36 (1979): 11–14.

Tapper, Richard, and Nancy Tapper. "Religion, Education, and Continuity in a Provincial Town." In *Islam in Modern Turkey: Religion, Politics, and Literature in a Secular State,* edited by Richard Tapper. New York: I. B. Tauris, 1991.

Teveth, Shabtai. *Ben-Gurion and the Palestinian Arabs: From Peace to War.* Oxford: Oxford University Press, 1985.

Thompson, Andrew. "Nations, National Identities, and Human Agency: Putting People back into Nations." *The Sociological Review* 49, no. 1 (2001): 18–32.

Tilly, Charles. "Social Boundary Mechanisms." *Philosophy of the Social Sciences* 34, no. 2 (2004): 211–36.

Tooby, John, and Leda Cosmides. "The Psychological Foundations of Culture." In *The Adapted Mind: Evolutionary Psychology and the Generation of Culture,* edited by Jerome H. Barkow, Leda Cosmides, and John Tooby. Oxford: Oxford University Press, 1992.

Torah and Labor Leadership. *Igeret le-birur shealot hatzionut ve-ha-yishuv* [Letter for the Clarification of Questions of Zionism and the Yishuv]. Tel Aviv: Alexander Moses Press, 1933.

Torgovnik, Efraim. "Strategies under a New Electoral System: The Labor Party in the 1996 Israeli Elections." *Party Politics* 6, no. 1 (2000): 95–106.

Trevor-Roper, Hugh. "The Invention of Tradition: The Highland Tradition of Scotland." In *The Invention of Tradition,* edited by Eric Hobsbawm and Terence Ranger. Cambridge: Cambridge University Press, 1983.

Troen, S. Ilan. "Frontier Myths and Their Applications in America and Israel: A Transnational Perspective." *The Journal of American History* 86, no. 3 (1999): 1209–30.

Tünay, Muharrem. "The Turkish New Right's Attempt at Hegemony." In *The Political and Socioeconomic Transformation of Turkey,* edited by Etial Eralp, Muharrem Tünay, and Birol Yesilada. Westport, CT: Praeger Publishers, 1993.

Ulman, Hava. "Derech ha-mizrachi likrat hamedina (1945–1946)" [The Way of Mizrachi towards the State (1945–46)]. *Shraggai: A Journal for the Study of Religious Zionism and Immigration to Eretz Israel* 4 (1993): 82–109.

Van Evera, Stephen. "Hypotheses on Nationalism and War." *International Security* 18, no. 4 (1994): 5–39.

Varshney, Ashutosh. "Contested Meanings: India's National Identity, Hindu Nationalism, and the Politics of Anxiety." *Daedalus* 122, no. 3 (1993): 227–61.

Vital, David. "Hagdarat ye'adim be-mediniyut hutz" [The Definition of Goals in Foreign Policy]. *Medina, mimshal veiyhasim benle'umiyim* 13 (1979): 5–16.

Wallerstein, Immanuel. "The Construction of Peoplehood: Racism, Nationalism, Ethnicity." In *Race, Nation, Class: Ambiguous Identities,* edited by Etienne Balibar and Immanuel Wallerstein. London: Verso Press, 1991.

Warhaftig, Zerach. *Hamishim shanah ve-shanah: pirke zikhronot* [Fifty Years, from Year to Year: Memories]. Jerusalem: Yad Shapira, 1998.

Weissbrod, Lilly. "From Labour Zionism to New Zionism: Ideological Change in Israel." *Theory and Society* 10, no. 6 (1981): 777–803.

——. "Gush Emunim Ideology—From Religious Doctrine to Political Action." *Middle Eastern Studies* 18, no. 3 (1982): 265–75.

Weitz, Yechiam. "The Road to the 'Upheaval': A Capsule History of the Herut Movement, 1948–1977." *Israel Studies* 10, no. 3 (2005): 54–86.

Weizmann, Chaim. *Trial and Error: The Autobiography of Chaim Weizmann.* Philadelphia: The Jewish Publication Society of America, 1949.

Wodak, Ruth, Rudolf de Cillia, Martin Reisigl, and Karin Liebhart. *The Discursive Construction of National Identity.* Edinburgh: Edinburgh University Press, 1999.

Yavuz, M. Hakan. "Political Islam and the Welfare (Refah) Party in Turkey." *Comparative Politics* 30, no. 1 (1997): 63–82.

Yishai, Yael. *Si'atiyut bi-tenu'at ha-'avodah: si'ah bet be-Mapai* [Factionalism in the Labor Movement: Faction B in Mapai]. Tel Aviv: Am Oved—Tarbut VeChinuch, 1978.

—— . "Bringing Society Back In: Post-Cartel Parties in Israel." *Party Politics* 7, no. 6 (2001): 667–87.

Young, Crawford. *The Politics of Cultural Pluralism.* Madison: University of Wisconsin Press, 1976.

Zameret, Zvi. "Medina yehudit—ken; medina clericalit—lo: rashei Mapai ve-yahasm la-dat ve-la-datiyim" [Yes to a Jewish State, Not to a Clericalist State: The Mapai Leadership and Its Attitude to Religion and Religious Jews]. In *Shene 'evre hagesher: dat u-medinah be-reshit darkah shel Yisrael* [On Both Sides of the Bridge: Religion and State in the Early Years of Israel], edited by Mordechai Bar-On and Zvi Zameret. Jerusalem: Yad Yitzhak Ben-Zvi Press, 2002.

Zertal, Idith, and Akiva Eldar. *Lords of the Land: The War over Israel's Settlements in the Occupied Territories, 1967–2007.* New York: Nation Books, 2007.

Zerubavel, Yael. *Recovered Roots: Collective Memory and the Making of Israeli National Tradition.* Chicago: University of Chicago Press, 1995.

Index

Note: Page numbers in *italics* indicate figures; those with a *t* indicate tables.

Zionism, 4–7, 5t, 20–22, 28–31; Diaspora Jews and, 147–48, 152–53; as heretical project, 185; history of, 2–4; Labor (*See* Labor Zionism); neo-, 133; post-, 179–81; Religious (*See* Religious Zionism); Revisionist (*See* Revisionist Zionism); "socialist," 113

Zionist General Federation of Labor. *See* Histadrut
Zionist/Israeli nationalist movement, 14–15
Zionist Revisionist Organization, 83. *See also* New Zionist Organization
Zo Artzeneinu movement, 182